Business Valuation Update Yearbook 2018

BVR
What It's Worth
111 SW Columbia Street, Suite 750, Portland, OR 97201
(503) 479-8200 • www.bvresources.com

BVR

What It's Worth

Printed in the United States of America.

Editor: Andy Dzamba

Publisher: Sarah Andersen

Managing Editor: Monique Nijhout-Rowe

Senior Copy Editor: David Solomon

Chair and CEO: David Foster

President: Lucretia Lyons

Chief Revenue Officer: Lisa McInturff

Customer Service: Melissa Snow

Print/PDF ISBN: 978-1-62150-144-2

EPUB ISBN: 978-1-62150-145-9

Library of Congress Control Number: 2018932940

Table of Contents

Introduction

It was another eventful year for the business valuation profession in 2017, and *BVU* continues its tradition of 20-plus years by bringing you the latest thinking in methodologies as well as up-to-date news and analysis, changes in regulations and professional standards, publications of interest, and practice-building ideas. What follows is a wrap-up of the notable developments of 2017, which are covered in depth in the collection of articles you'll find in this *Yearbook*.

Regulatory. At an IRS public hearing in Washington, D.C., there were a record number of speakers, including from the AICPA, ASA, and NACVA, to oppose the controversial proposed IRC Section 2704 regulations designed to curb estate valuation discounts for minority interests. Almost all of the speakers agreed that the rules were so broad and convoluted that they should be withdrawn permanently or completely revised.[1] In October 2017, the Treasury officially withdrew the proposed regs.

The Public Company Accounting Oversight Board (PCAOB) solicited comments on two standard-setting proposals it issued in 2017: one on auditing accounting estimates including fair value measurements and the other on the auditor's use of the work of specialists (including valuation experts). One of the matters the new rules seek to reinforce is that of "professional skepticism" over information you get from management or other third parties.

An ongoing study of PCAOB inspection reports on auditing firms found that the number of audit deficiencies tied to fair value measurements (FVM) declined for the second year in a row, but they're still high. The valuation and litigation consultancy firm Acuitas Inc. conducted the analysis, the "2017 Survey of Fair Value Audit Deficiencies,"[2] which found that fair value deficiencies are increasingly attributable to a surge in business combination engagements.

A 2017 settlement between KPMG and the Securities and Exchange Commission (SEC) over alleged overvaluations of assets marked a shift in the agency's enforcement focus, observers said. The agency had primarily targeted policies, procedures, and internal controls, but, in this settlement, the SEC set its sights on the actual valuation of assets.[3]

1 "Strong Pushback of Sec. 2704 Regs at IRS Hearing" (*BVU*, January 2017).
2 www.acuitasinc.com/documents/2017_PCAOB_Fair_Value_Audit_Deficiencies_Survey-FINAL.pdf.
3 "SEC Settlement Over Fair Value Signals Shift of Focus" (*BVU*, October 2017).

The Department of Labor (DOL) continued its tough stance on ESOP valuations and prevailed in a number of cases.[4] Importantly, the DOL and First Bankers Trust Services Inc. (FBTS) entered into a settlement agreement[5] that essentially mirrors the DOL/GreatBanc Fiduciary Process Agreement that covers ESOP transactions and valuation issues. The two agreements should be required reading for ESOP trustees and their financial advisors.

Standards and guidance. In November 2017, the third working group at The Appraisal Foundation (TAF) issued Valuation for Financial Reporting (VFR) Valuation Advisory #3, The Measurement and Application of Market Participant Acquisition Premiums.[6] These guidelines are in the context of fair value for financial reporting and do not address premiums in other contexts, such as tax or disputes. The fundamental perspective of the working group is that a premium for control is not always warranted. Also, the group recognizes an ongoing need for benchmark data, but they should not be used as the sole input for the estimation of a premium. Auditors (who follow TAF advisories) will scrutinize comparables much more closely in the future. A fourth working group is developing guidelines on valuing contingent consideration.

TAF also issued the 2018-19 version of the Uniform Standards of Professional Appraisal Practice (USPAP) with enhanced features available in both print and electronic versions. The enhanced print version includes cross-references to applicable FAQs. Additionally, the electronic version includes hyperlinks to FAQs and other relevant references throughout the document, as well as a hyperlinked table of contents, footnotes, and an index.

The AICPA is working on several practice aids that valuation experts should watch out for. There will be a big impact on the valuation process for alternative investment funds with the coming of the AICPA's *Private Equity & Venture Capital Accounting and Valuation Guide.* A draft is expected to be released in April 2018 or May 2018. The guide is expected to be over 650 pages and contain examples of exercising valuation judgments and provide more in-depth industrywide guidance leading to greater global consistency. The AICPA also has a task force developing a practice aid on business combinations.

There has been some criticism in the past concerning the fragmentation of the business valuation profession and the multiple sets of BV standards that have been issued. The perception has been that the standards may be at odds with each other—but that is not the case, according to an analysis of the five sets of North American standards.[7] A side-by-side chart that compares the standards of NACVA, IBA, AICPA, ASA, and USPAP shows that the standards have some subtle differences, but these can be interpreted as being covered in one of the other standards but worded a little differently. The authors of the chart, Mark Hanson (Schenck SC), Mark Kucik (The Kucik Valuation Group LLC), and Carl Steffen (WSRP LLC), are finalizing a similar chart of the international standards (IVS, Canada, and RICS) that also demonstrates that they do not conflict with each other.

4 "2017's Top Business Valuation and Damages Cases" (*BVU*, January 2018).

5 *Acosta v. First Bankers Tr. Servs., Inc.*, S.D.N.Y., No. 1:12-cv-08648-GBD, consent order and judgment, Sept. 21, 2017.

6 appraisalfoundation.sharefile.com/d-sf6c518cbd8a41df9.

7 "Tale of the Tape: Different BV Standards Do Not Conflict" (*BVU*, August 2017).

On the accounting front, expect to see more asset acquisitions and fewer business combinations as a result of the new "Definition of Business" rules from the Financial Accounting Standards Board (FASB), which start to kick in during 2018. As a result, two areas will see heightened scrutiny: a company's workforce value, which must be recognized in an asset acquisition, and noncompete agreements. Also, new lease accounting rules are designed to more accurately reflect the financial picture of firms that lease assets. For example, a trucking company can show no trucks on the balance sheet if they are all leased. In addition, there are sweeping new rules for revenue recognition.[8] Of course, accounting changes of this sort generally would not impact the underlying economic value of a firm, but they do have impacts that valuation experts need to consider. For example, certain ratios will change when the new rules are implemented.

New credentials. A major accomplishment in 2017 was the launch of the new credential for fair value for financial reporting for U.S. publicly traded companies, Certified in Entity and Intangible Valuations (CEIV). The AICPA, ASA, and RICS have spearheaded this effort, and the credential is now being issued.[9] A Mandatory Performance Framework (MPF) requires professionals to better document their assumptions, which will help make auditors more comfortable with valuation estimates. While CEIV holders are required to comply with the MPF, it should be considered best practices for anyone doing this type of work. We quote this paragraph from the MPF:

> **Valuation professionals without the CEIV credential.** As noted previously, the framework and the Application of the MPF were designed for use by all valuation professionals. Although only those valuation professionals who have the CEIV credential are required to adhere to the MPF documents, the Performance Requirements Work Stream believes that adhering to the MPF documents should be considered best practice by valuation professionals who do not have the CEIV credential and who perform valuation of a business, business interest, intangible asset, certain liabilities, and inventory used to support management assertions made in financial statements issued for financial reporting purposes.

The AICPA also announced in 2017 that it is developing a second new credential on its own, Certified in Valuation of Financial Instruments (CVFI).[10] Public comments are being reviewed on an exposure draft of a "disclosure framework" similar to the CEIV's MPF.

Methodology. The standard boilerplate in many valuation reports that explain the estimation of a discount for lack of marketability (DLOM) may go by the wayside with the introduction of a new model, the Restricted Stock Study Quintile Calculator (RSQC).[11] Many valuation experts use restricted stock studies when developing a DLOM, but certain characteristics of the issuer of the restricted stock can impact the discounts in the studies. The RSQC model is designed to adjust for those characteristics in order to develop a relevant sample for the subject company. The source of the restricted stock discount data in the model is the Stout (FMV) Restricted Stock Study.

8 "What You Should Know About FASB Changes to Revenue Recognition and Lease Accounting" (*BVU*, July 2017).

9 "ASA BV Chair Discusses Recent Changes to New FV Rules and CEIV" (*BVU*, April 2017) and "AICPA BV Chair Nathan DiNatale Discusses the New CEIV Credential" (*BVU*, February 2017).

10 "AICPA Fields Questions About New CVFI Credential" (*BVU*, October 2017).

11 "Using a Restricted Stock Study Quintile Analysis for a DLOM" (*BVU*, November 2017).

The discussion of personal versus enterprise goodwill got kicked up a notch when a family law attorney and several top valuation experts provided interesting perspectives on the allocating of enterprise and personal goodwill.[12] Discussed were a twist on the excess earnings method, the strengths and weaknesses of the multiattribute utility model (MUM), and a new residual method based on the purchase price allocation concept. Also, the new concept of "pure" personal goodwill was discussed—a concept that broke new ground in divorce law when an appellate court in Wisconsin held that all the salable personal goodwill in a professional practice (as evidenced by a noncompete agreement) is a divisible marital asset.[13] This is an area that should be further discussed and brought to the courts' attention in every jurisdiction.

A methodology under increased pressure on a number of fronts is the use of prospective financial information (PFI). The perception is that too many valuation experts simply accept projections and forecasts they're given without applying enough scrutiny—or any scrutiny at all.[14] The matter has been an issue in court cases and has been the focus of rule makers and standard setters. Valuation experts should become familiar with the Mandatory Performance Framework (MPF) for the CEIV credential, which includes significant performance requirements related to PFI. The architects of the fair value quality initiative recognized the concern over PFI and included a section on professional skepticism in the MPF, which lays out the factors and common procedures to consider when preparing an assessment of a company's PFI. These include, but are not limited to: a comparison of prior forecasts to actual results, a comparison of PFI to industry expectations, checking PFI against other internally prepared financial information for consistency, a comparison of entity PFI to historical trends, an understanding of who prepares the PFI and how often is it prepared, and the performance of mathematical and logic checks.

Tax affecting the earnings of a PTE has been an issue of much debate in the valuation community, but we may be having a different conversation about it soon. The tax-affecting issue has been argued in a number of Tax Court cases in which the IRS and the court have refuted the notion that shareholder-level taxes affect a firm's value, so the valuation conclusions in these cases were based on earnings not being tax affected. The valuation community disagrees, so a number of models were developed that are designed to reflect the impact of shareholder taxes on value. At the time of this writing, two cases are pending in Tax Court, one in which both sides made very similar adjustments using the S corporation economic adjustment model (SEAM).[15] The other case is the *Estate of Michael Jackson*, in which the court denied the IRS's motion to exclude testimony concerning tax affecting, with the judge writing: "It is highly likely that the proper use of the discounted cash flow method will be an important issue in this case. Whether and how to take tax effects into account in that valuation will likely be crucial to the final numbers."

12 "Attorney's Slant on Three Methods to Estimate Personal Goodwill" (*BVU*, May 2017).

13 *McReath v. McReath*, 2011 WL 2706249 (July 12, 2011).

14 "Do You Share Business Valuation's 'Dirty Little Secret'?" (*BVU*, May 2017).

15 *Cecil et al. v. Commissioner of Internal Revenue.*

In the meantime, the debate continues. A new statistical analysis of data in the *Pratt's Stats* private-company transaction database explains how transaction size and the entity form of the buyer and seller support the existence (and the magnitude) of a PTE premium.[16] Also, there is a view that there is a "bright-line rule" that precludes tax affecting S corporations under the fair market value standard.[17]

In the healthcare arena, some groundbreaking research and data analytics have emerged to challenge commonly held beliefs about survey data, physician compensation, and fair market value. Most practitioners focus on survey data, especially data from the MGMA, in establishing reasonable or fair market compensation. But this method is said to be based on several false premises, including that the surveys have statistical significance for the 90% or so of physicians not included in the surveys.[18] The fair market value of physician compensation is an essential issue in the government's qui tam (whistleblower) cases it has been winning in False Claims Act (FCA) lawsuits against a number of hospitals, which have been hit with hundreds of millions of dollars in fines. These lawsuits—and there will be more coming—have been triggered by hospitals acquiring medical practices, which raises the bar for appraisers and employing physicians.

Data and publications. Private-company business transaction data in *Pratts Stats* increased to over 28,000 acquired private companies plus up to 150 data points that include six valuation multiples and 13 financial ratios. During 2017, one of the largest business brokerage firms in the United States and Canada, Murphy Business & Financial Corp., started to contribute its private-company transaction data to *Pratt's Stats.* BIZCOMPS, *Done Deals,* and the *IBA Market Database* also expanded their number of private-company transactions.

BVR launched a new data product in 2017: The Fairness Opinion Research Service (FORS) that enables professionals to easily know "what's market" and benchmark their work against hundreds of board books, proxies, and fairness opinion letters filed at the SEC over the last five years.

Two of the leading books on business valuation published revised editions in 2017: *Financial Valuation: Applications and Models (FVAM),* 4th edition, + Website, by James Hitchner, and *Understanding Business Valuation: A Practical Guide to Valuing Small- to Medium-Sized Businesses,* 5th edition, by Gary Trugman. *BVU* published reviews[19] of both books, which are available from BVR.

BVR added to its line of industry-specific special reports under the series title *What It's Worth.* New entries in the series are: law firms; HVAC companies; electrical contractors; and oil, gas, and alternative energy assets.

16 Eric J. Barr and Peter L. Lohrey, "Inside *Pratt's Stats:* Impact of Entity Form on Selling Price" (*BVU,* December 2017 (Part 1) and January 2018 (Part 2)).

17 Alan Zipp, "Tax Affecting S Corporations: It's Not a Matter of Whether. It's a Matter of When," (*BVU,* December 2017).

18 Mark Dietrich, "Revisiting the Meaning of Fair Market Value" (*BVU,* April 2017).

19 Ronald Seigneur, "Book Review: *Financial Valuation: Applications and Models,* 4th Edition + Website" (*BVU,* June 2017), and James W. Brockardt, "Book Review: *Understanding Business Valuation: A Practical Guide to Valuing Small to Medium Sized Businesses,* 5th Edition" (*BVU,* January 2018).

Some of the other books and guides of note published in 2017 include:

- *Narrative and Numbers: The Value of Stories in Business,* Dr. Aswath Damodaran;
- 2017 editions of the Duff & Phelps *Valuation Handbooks - Cost of Capital* series (two U.S. and two international editions);
- *BVR/AHLA Guide to Valuing Physician Compensation and Healthcare Service Arrangements,* 2nd Edition, Mark Dietrich and Timothy Smith;
- *The Business Valuation Bench Book,* Jay Fishman and William Morrison;
- *Discount for Lack of Marketability Guide and Toolkit,* James Hitchner, Jim Alerding, Josh Angell, and Kate Morris;
- *The BVR Private Company Value Benchmark Guide,* 2017-2018 edition;
- *BVR/ktMINE Royalty Rate Benchmarking Guide,* 2017/2018 global edition;
- *A Practical Guide to Bankruptcy Valuation,* 2nd edition, Dr. Israel Shaked and Robert F. Reilly; and
- *Business Valuations and the IRS: Five Books in One,* Michael Gregory.

All of these books are available from BVR.

Practice management. During 2017, BVR published the findings of a survey that examined BV firm performance, compensation, billing rates, marketing and practice development, and more.[20] Some of the issues that are keeping practitioners up at night include increased competition, fee pressures, hiring, and succession planning. Among the other findings were that about two-thirds of BV firms said they expect to do more business than the previous year. Also, traditional face-to-face techniques continue to be the best methods to bring in valuation business, such as one-on-one meetings with prospective clients, public speaking, and joining business organizations such as associations, committees, and boards.[21]

Another survey, this one done by a leading BV practitioner and report reviewer, discovered a declining trend in the quality of valuation reports—and not just in the style of writing, but in the framework (i.e., professional standards) and content as well. Some of the major issues include struggles with the section on discounts and premiums, as well as not tying sections of the report such as the company background, economic overview, and industry outlook back to the subject company.[22]

20 www.bvresources.com/products/the-bvr-business-valuation-firm-economics-best-practices-guide.

21 See "30 Field-Tested Ideas to Bring in More BV Business" (*BVU,* January 2017) and "How Do Your BV Firm's Billing Rates and Practices Stack Up?" (*BVU,* September 2017).

22 Rod Burkert, "Ongoing Survey Reveals Need to Improve Report Writing" (*BVU,* October 2017).

Global. The International Valuations Standards Council (IVSC) made some impressive advances over the past year, releasing a final version of IVS 2017 in its efforts to harmonize valuation standards for the global economy.[23] Also in 2017, the IVSC's new boards became operational—a Standards Review Board that will amend and approve international valuation standards. The new board has two focused subject matter expertise boards reporting to it: a Tangible Assets Standards Board (covering real estate, plant and machinery, and personal property) and a Business Valuation Standards Board. Another subject matter expertise board will also be formed: a Financial Instruments Board. This is all part of the IVSC's new infrastructure within which focused boards will continuously revise and improve IVS to help ensure that they add value and can be implemented by valuation professional organizations (VPOs) around the world.

During 2017, the IVSC also issued an Agenda Consultation Paper on future revisions to IVS, which is part of the IVSC's new efforts to continually evolve IVS instead of issuing completely revised standards every few years. Public comments are being reviewed, and the IVSC will release a document giving the rationale for how it prioritizes areas of future focus.

Work toward a global valuation credential moved forward as the International Association of Consultants, Valuators and Analysts (IACVA) and the International Institute of Business Valuers (iiBV) joined forces to boost IACVA's International Certified Valuation Specialist (ICVS) designation. The two groups will develop in-class and online certification training and testing that will reflect IVS and will be translated into other languages as well as allow for the addition of nation-specific modules. This is designed to bring consistency to valuation practices around the world, which can diverge quite significantly.

A discussion about offshoring some of the components of a valuation engagement triggered some lively debate. Many valuation experts rule out this practice, but there are those who do indeed use it. For those who consider it, there are certain things to think about.[24]

That's a look at some of what happened in 2017, and *BVU* looks forward to keeping you fully informed of important developments during 2018.

Sincerely,

Andrew Dzamba
Executive Editor
Business Valuation Update

23 "Final IVS 2017 Seeks to Standardize Conduct and Approach to Global Valuation" (*BVU*, March 2017).

24 Bharat Kanodia, "Look Before You Leap Into Offshoring Some Valuation Components" (*BVU*, May 2017).

Section I.
Business Valuation Approaches, Methods, and Entity-Specific Issues

How to Better Validate the Reasons for Private-Company Discounts

By Anthony Carlton,
Macquarie Applied Finance Centre (Sydney, Australia)

Editor's note: In the June 2016 issue of Business Valuation Update, *Gilbert Matthews wrote an article*[1] *about whether private companies are valued for less than public companies solely on the basis of being private or whether other factors are involved. Tony Carlton (Macquarie University's Applied Finance Centre), who shares his viewpoint, wrote the following article.*

Gilbert Matthews refers to research by Micah Officer (2007), which found that, compared to acquired public companies, private companies sold at average discounts of 17% but that subsidiaries (of listed parents) sold at average discounts of 28%. Matthews suggests this result should be subjected to further empirical research.

Like Matthews, I was uneasy about this result, particularly the fact that unlisted subsidiaries had reported discounts much higher than private companies. The research to which Matthews refers attributed the discounts to parent companies being under financial pressure and thus selling at a discount—effectively the fire sale argument. There is good evidence (and logic) that, most commonly, public companies are likely to exit underperforming or noncore assets. Assets with high profitability and/or growth potential have the potential to be exited by spinoffs or IPOs. Assets sold by trade sale are therefore more likely to have lower underlying valuations than public-market comparables. Consequently, any reported discounts will simply reflect differences in underlying values rather than any form of private-company discount.

Using U.S. data for the period 1997 to 2009, I compared transaction multiples for the sale of unlisted subsidiaries by public companies with those for the acquisition of comparable publicly listed companies. Comparable acquisitions were selected on the basis of time period, industry, and size. I found a small subset of fire sale-type transactions for which there was a material discount to comparable transactions. However, the number of such transactions did not explain the presence of pervasive discounts.

1 Gilbert E. Matthews, "DLOMs in N.Y. Fair Value Cases: Private Company Discounts Are Not Caused by Lack of Marketability," *Business Valuation Update,* June 2016. (See also a follow-up article, "Adjustment Mapping and the Public-vs.-Private-Company Discount Debate," Mike Smith, *Business Valuation Update,* August 2016.)

More importantly, I found that the discounts Officer reported were largely attributable to the measurement methods used. In measuring these discounts, three key decisions are made:

1. How you calculate the *average* of the comparables (arithmetic, geometric, harmonic means, or median);

2. How you calculate the *discount* (percentage or logarithmic); and

3. How you select the *sample* (particularly outliers).

Officer used the arithmetic mean, percentage discount, and eliminated a number of outlier transactions. This combination explains the high reported discount and also makes the results very sensitive to the treatment of outliers. Using alternative averaging methods and calculating the discount using the logarithmic method resulted in a significant reduction in reported discounts. In fact, the samplewide discount was lower than that for private-company sales, more in line with intuition (*Note: In some cases, the discounts were eliminated*). Furthermore, the results were much more stable to different treatments of outliers.

I then tested whether asset-specific characteristics help explain the discount differences. As an alternative to using multiples, I constructed a regression model to calculate the "warranted value" of a deal, based on size, profitability, and industry type of each target. This approach allows a target-specific estimate of fair value using each target's own profitability. Using this method, reported discounts averaged zero for the sample. This implies that asset-specific characteristics largely explain reported discounts, in line with Matthews' suspicions. Other analyses further confirmed the role that asset characteristics, particularly profitability, play in explaining variations in transaction values. These results were further confirmed by analyzing share market reactions to asset sales, where I found no evidence that the market reacted as if unlisted subsidiaries were sold at discount to underlying value.

My conclusions from this research are threefold. First, discount calculations are sensitive to the measurement procedures used. The combination of arithmetic mean and percentage discounts generates results that are sensitive to the sample and the treatment of outliers. At a minimum, analysts should test the robustness of their results with sensitivity analysis to alternative methods. Second, it is important to allow for asset-specific characteristics, particularly size and profitability. This can be achieved by appropriate selection of comparable transactions or the use of regression-type approaches as an alternative to the simple multiples approach. Finally, this research highlights the need for the reporting of appropriate financial data on private transactions. Financial data on private trade sales are not as available as they are for public companies, and much of the multiples analysis ends up based largely around revenue multiples. If we are really going to decide whether a transaction is at fair value, we need to be able to use target-specific financials to form such a view.

The Use of Historical Information to Project But-For Profits

By Stacey Udell,
Gold Gerstein Group LLC (Moorestown, NJ, U.S.A.)

Editor's note: This is an excerpt from Chapter 11 in the recently released book, Calculating Economic Damages in Intellectual Property Infringement Cases.[1] *The entire chapter, titled "Projecting But-For Profits," includes a full discussion on the topic, including the methods used in determining lost revenue, the use of management projections, methods to forecast revenue and expenses, growth considerations, and other topics.*

Analysts should begin a lost profits engagement by performing a detailed review of historical profit-and-loss statements, cash-flow reports, income tax returns, and any relevant business plans for changes or trends over time in revenue, costs, assets, or liabilities. Ratio analysis and depositions or interviews with key members of the management team should be performed to fully understand the subject company's historical financial results. This type of analysis may provide insight into management's reactions to external developments and events, help pinpoint unusual items, and indicate possible changes in the business.

The most common techniques consist of comparing:

- Current financial information with that of previous periods;
- Actual past results with comparable budgets or forecasts;
- Amounts or ratios with expectations developed by management; and
- Projected ratios with industry averages or those of similar, publicly traded companies.

It may be helpful to analyze the following financial ratios for the complete period for which information is available:

- Current ratio;

1 Nancy Fannon and Jonathan Dunitz, *Calculating Economic Damages in Intellectual Property Infringement Cases,* 2016, Business Valuation Resources (www.bvresources.com).

- Days sales outstanding;
- EBITDA margin;
- Effective tax rate;
- Depreciation of each asset class to carrying amounts;
- Quick ratio;
- Inventory turnover;
- Pretax margin;
- Net margin; and
- Debt to equity.

These ratios may help the expert identify any patterns or trends that might affect the analyst's projection of revenues or profits.

When the past indicates the future. The most common method of forecasting revenue is to apply a projected growth rate to an appropriate revenue base. However, the analyst should assess and determine whether the past is a reasonable indicator of the future. While past operations are not always a good indicator of the future, they may convey useful information.

In analyzing the past, the analyst should consider growth in terms of both dollars and percentages. When there is no apparent trend in revenue, analysts sometimes use an average of the prior years' revenue, often somewhat blindly using a three-to-five-year historical period. Further, there are many examples of experts "cherry-picking" years and growth rates during a selected historical period that serves to support their client's objectives. The historical period should encompass a relevant time horizon that can be used to reliably estimate the future. When possible, it is helpful to include periods of both growth and decline.

Where a trend emerges in the historical results, some experts utilize a weighted average of some prior number of years, often the same blind selection of the prior three-to-five years discussed above. In computing a weighted average, many experts will apply the most weight to the most recent years and decreasingly less weight to each prior year. However, this can lead to misleading results. As an example, consider Exhibit 1.

Simple application of an average or weighted average, without an understanding of what caused the company's results to decline, could lead to a revenue projection that is unreasonable or not credible. Suppose, for example, the company lost its largest client in the third quarter of 20X4 and has little hope of recovering that revenue. Alternatively, suppose the company's revenue is highly dependent

Exhibit 1. Misleading Results

	20X1	20X2	20X3	20X4	20X5	Projected Revenue for 20X6
Revenue	$1,200,000	$1,800,000	$1,800,000	$1,500,000	$900,000	
Using un-weighed (or straight) averages						
Most recent 5 years						$1,440,000
Most recent 3 years						$1,400,000
Using weighted averages						
Most recent 5 years	1	2	3	4	5	$1,380,000
Most recent 3 years			1	2	3	$1,250,000

Weightings

Exhibit 2. Annual Revenue Growth

	Revenue Growth
20X0	30%
20X1	10%
20X2	50%
20X3	-30%
20X4	25%

on government contracts and it was just awarded the largest contract in its history at the end of 20X5. What if the company had a large nonrecurring job that spanned the course of 20X2 and 20X3 and into 20X4? None of these exercises in averaging would result in a reasonable conclusion. Therefore, when using averages or weighted averages, the analyst should understand not just the financial results, but also the reasons for them.

Analyzing growth rates. Growth rates may be analyzed based on a median, arithmetic average, or geometric average. The median is the amount that is the half-way point of the data set. The arithmetic average is the simple average of past growth rates, while the geometric average takes into account compounding that occurs from year to year. Compound annual growth rate represents the growth over time, had it grown at a steady rate.

To illustrate, assume the annual revenue growth shown in Exhibit 2.

In this example, the median growth rate is 25% because, when you order the growth rates from high to low, 25% is the middle number.

An arithmetic average growth rate would be calculated by adding each year's growth and divide by the number of years:

$$0.3 + 0.1 + 0.5 - 0.3 + 0.25 = 0.85/5 = 0.17, \text{ or } 17\% \text{ arithmetic average}$$

The calculation of the geometric average or compound annual growth rate (CAGR) is a little more complicated and has the following steps:

1. Add 1 to each year's growth and multiply;

2. Take the product in Step 1 and multiply it by the power of 1/(number of items in series); and
3. Subtract 1 from Step 2.

For example:

Step 1: 1.3 × 1.1 × 1.5 × 0.7 × 1.25 = 1.877

Step 2: 1.877 ^ (1/5) = 1.134

Step 3: 1.134 - 1 = 0.134, or 13.4%

When calculating the CAGR based on values, rather than growth rates, the following formula can be used:

$$\left(\frac{\text{Ending value}}{\text{Beginning value}}\right)^{1/n} - 1$$

where "n" represents the years of growth in the group.

$$\left(\frac{188}{100}\right)^{1/5} = 1.88^{1/5} = 1.134 - 1 = 0.134, \text{ or } 13.4\%$$

The compound annual growth rate (CAGR) represents the average growth over time and is illustrated in Exhibit 3.

Clearly, there can be significant differences, depending on the measure of growth the analyst used. The greater the volatility in the growth rates, the larger the difference will be between the arithmetic and geometric averages. It is up to the analyst to decide which method is the most reliable under the circumstances.

Exhibit 3. CAGR

	Actual Revenue Growth	Annual Growth	Revenue Growth Using CAGR	Annual Growth
20X0	$100	–	$100	–
20X1	$130	30%	$113	13.4%
20X2	$143	10%	$129	13.4%
20X3	$215	50%	$146	13.4%
20X4	$150	-30%	$165	13.4%
20x5	$188	25%	$188	13.4%

According to Dr. Aswath Damodaran, professor of finance at New York University's Stern School of Business:

> In a study of the relationship between past growth rates and future growth rates, Little (1960) coined the term "Higgledy Piggledy Growth" because he found little evidence that firms that grew fast in one period continued to grow fast in the next period.[2]
>
> If past growth in earnings is not a reliable indicator of future growth at many firms, it becomes even less so at smaller firms. The growth rates at smaller firms tend to be even more volatile than growth rates at other firms in the market.[3]
>
> You should be more cautious about using past growth, especially in earnings, for forecasting future growth at [smaller] firms.[4]
>
> In general, revenue growth tends to be more persistent and predictable than earnings growth. This is because accounting choices have a far smaller effect on revenues than they do on earnings.[5]

Alternatives. When a trend does not appear to exist or the future is not expected to follow historical trends, the use of an average or weighted average is likely inappropriate. To identify whether a trend exists, one suggestion is to look back at least twice as far as you plan to project.[6] For example, you are projecting five years; go back 10 years to look for a pattern. However, this may not always be possible (for example, the company may not have been in business that long) or practical (for example, the company may have changed so dramatically that the past is not an indicator of the future).

In some cases, econometric modeling and regression analysis may be used to project into the future. Analysts who are sufficiently familiar with statistical methods may use regression analysis, Monte Carlo simulations, or other statistical methods to forecast revenues or profits.

These models are beyond the scope of this chapter. A discussion of regression analysis can be found in Chapter 37 of the *Comprehensive Guide to Economic Damages, Calculating Economic Damages in Intellectual Property Infringement Cases.*

Stacey Udell, *CPA/ABV/CFF, CVA, is a partner at Gold Gerstein Group LLC where she specializes in valuation and litigation support services but also provides accounting, tax, and consulting services for closely held and family businesses. She is a contributing author to the* Comprehensive Guide to Economic Damages, Calculating Economic Damages in Intellectual Property Infringement Cases, BVR/AHLA Guide to Healthcare Valuation, *and other publications.*

2 Aswath Damodaran, *Damodaran on Valuation: Security Analysis for Investment and Corporate Finance,* 2nd ed. (Somerset, N.J.: John Wiley & Sons, 2006) (hereinafter, "Damodaran"), 7-8. Used with permission.

3 Damodaran 8.

4 Ibid.

5 Damodaran 9.

6 Paul Saffo, "Six Rules for Effective Forecasting," *Harvard Business Review,* July-August 2007, hbr.org/2007/07/six-rules-for-effective-forecasting.

How ESOP Trustees Size Up a Potential Valuation Analyst

When you land an engagement to value an ESOP, it can lead to a rewarding and long-term assignment. But it's not easy to break into it. The ESOP market is saturated to a certain degree, so you will have to jump through a lot of hoops to get in the door.

Plus, ESOP trustees are fiduciaries, so they will be careful who they hire to do the valuation, says Brian Bornino (GBQ Consulting). "I want to stress the point that ultimately the trustee has a lot of responsibility and they are not going to take chances when they are hiring their independent valuation firm. They want to make sure that they are hiring a qualified firm and someone with experience. They are going to make a safe pick."

Bornino provides the accompanying 43-point checklist of potential questions and information requests a valuation expert could face from an ESOP trustee. Tracy Woolsey, an ESOP trustee with Horizon Trust & Investment Management, comments on some of the aspects of the checklist she feels are particularly important.

ESOP experience. Section II of the checklist focuses on specific experience with ESOPs. Note that you may also be asked about articles or any presentations you have done. "If you have not done any of that, then that is likely going to mean that we are going to be uncomfortable working with you," says Woolsey. The ESOP trustee will want to see that your firm is working on a "good number" of annual updates, including experience with startups. If your firm has not had a history of experience but has hired someone who does, the trustee will want to know that person's prior experience.

Industry-specific experience. Typically, the ESOP trustee has a specific client in mind when it has a valuation firm do a questionnaire. Woolsey points out that different industries can have different valuation expectations, so experience in a particular industry is a factor. However, lack of industry experience doesn't mean you're out for good. "We may add someone to our approval list, but we exclude them on a specific valuation because of lack of experience in that industry," she says.

Due diligence process. The due diligence process for both annual update and transaction valuations is important. One important aspect of this is site visits. "One of the things that we require is that our valuation firm visit the company at least every other year, and every year would be best," she says. An internal peer review process is also important—the ESOP trustee does not want to find errors in a report that an internal review should have caught.

Research sources. The ESOP trustee will expect that you subscribe to different research data sites. "We are going to question what your databases are and how you are using them," she says. These questions will continue during the valuation process itself.

E&O insurance. "We will not work with a valuation firm that has no errors and omissions insurance coverage," Woolsey says, who points out that this matter will frequently get a valuation firm bumped out of contention.

Knowledge of *GreatBanc*. "This actually got quite a few firms bumped off of our approved list after the *GreatBanc* settlement," says Woolsey. Also known as the DOL/GreatBanc Fiduciary Process Agreement,[1] this is a settlement agreement that covers ESOP transactions and valuation issues. After it was issued, valuation analysts began to incorporate relevant parts of it into their reports, such as additional boilerplate language and more explanation and documentation. The ESOP trustee will make sure you know about it and that your process is consistent with what the agreement covers.

Sample report. "We always look for a sample report, which is typically 60 to 250 pages," she says. If you are already engaged on an ESOP and a new trustee takes over, make sure you provide an actual report. "We have had valuation firms before try and sneak in a 'sample report' of better quality than their actual existing report," she recalls. Those firms were bumped.

Once you complete the questionnaire, the ESOP trustee and/or committee will review it as well as your sample valuation report. You will then be called in to an interview, and you will be asked questions about your responses. You can expect that this could last about an hour or so, but it will depend on the nature of your responses.

For more information. Bornino and Woolsey conducted a webinar, Sell-Side Advisory Services: A Savvy Way to Excel in the ESOP Market, on Nov. 30, 2016. You can access a recording at sub.bvresources.com/pastevents.asp.

1 A free copy of the agreement is at www.dol.gov/ebsa/pdf/esopagreement.pdf. You can purchase a version with commentary from the attorneys who negotiated the agreement at www.nceo.org/.

Checklist for the Evaluation of a Valuation Firm for an ESOP Engagement

This checklist is an example of the questions and requests for information a valuation firm or analyst would receive from an ESOP trustee when being considered for an ESOP valuation engagement. The same or similar questions would be asked or requests would be made by a law firm representing the client or by an internal trustee.

I. Background and Qualifications

- ☐ Describe your firm and your valuation practice.
- ☐ What percentage of your firm's total revenue comes from valuation-related services?
- ☐ How many valuation analysts does your firm employ on staff?
- ☐ Please give details of the ESOP-related valuation experience of the individual valuation analyst(s) who would work on this engagement. Please include the individuals' experience, credentials, memberships, and number of years in doing valuations of ESOP companies.
- ☐ Provide the name of the primary contact(s) for this engagement. Please include their resumes.
- ☐ Please list all valuation-related and ESOP-related speaking engagements and/or articles on which the primary contacts have written or spoken (include title, type of presentation, venue or publication, and date).

II. Experience With ESOP Valuations

- ☐ Describe your firm's valuation experience with respect to ESOP companies in this or a related industry.
- ☐ How many years has your firm been performing ESOP valuations?
- ☐ What percentage of your firm's total revenue comes from ESOP valuation services?
- ☐ How many preliminary ESOP valuations has your firm completed, and how many are completed on an average annual basis?
- ☐ How many fairness opinions in connection with ESOP transactions has your firm prepared, and how many are rendered on an average annual basis?
- ☐ What is your firms' experience rendering fairness and solvency opinions for leveraged ESOP transactions?
- ☐ How many ESOP annual update valuations does your firm prepare?
- ☐ How many ESOP feasibility studies has your firm completed, and how many are prepared on an average annual basis?

☐ Describe your firm's non-ESOP valuation experience.

☐ Describe your firm's overall experience with valuing synthetic equity including warrants, SAR plans, and phantom stock plans and their impact on a transaction and existing ESOPs.

☐ Describe the firm's experience in analyzing equity-based compensation programs in the context of ESOP transactions.

☐ Will the work be performed in conformity with appraisal standards such as ASA or USPAP?

III. Valuation Process

☐ Describe your due diligence process for both annual update and transaction valuations.

☐ How does your firm interact with company management throughout the valuation process?

☐ What company documents will your firm rely upon to perform the valuation analysis?

☐ What internal resources does your firm utilize to conduct research?

☐ Describe any research databases or external resources to which your firm subscribes.

☐ Explain your firm's internal methodology for reviewing analyses, reports, and opinion letters before releasing them to the client.

☐ Describe the timing and process, including deliverables such as draft and final valuation reports, after your firm has received the necessary information.

☐ Please give a description of your valuation process (valuation methodologies commonly employed, weighting approaches, etc.).

☐ Does your firm use the market, the income, and/or the asset valuation methodologies?

☐ Please provide a brief description as to how and when you utilize the various methodologies.

☐ Does your firm consider tax-affected earnings in the valuation of 100% owned S-corp ESOP companies?

☐ Discuss the marketability discount as it relates to non-publicly traded stock taking into account the ESOP put option right.

☐ Describe the circumstances when your firm applies a discount for lack of control.

☐ Describe the circumstances when your firm applies an ownership control premium.

☐ What is your firm's practice in utilizing tax shields to value the company?

☐ How does your firm handle repurchase obligation in the valuation process, and how is it documented in the valuation report?

- ☐ Discuss any other relationship or work that has been performed for the company.
- ☐ To your knowledge, have any of your firm's current staff members previously performed advisory work at another financial or professional advisory services firm that may be currently advising the company?
- ☐ Will the financial advisor and your firm be independent of all parties to the proposed transaction? If so, will the financial advisor provide a representation to that effect in the engagement letter and the valuation report?

IV. Regulatory, Litigation, and Risk Management

- ☐ Who is the person at your firm who is responsible for handling DOL, IRS, and company auditor reviews and questions?
- ☐ Have any members of your firm been called on to testify as an expert witness in litigation matters involving the IRS, the DOL, or ESOP participants? If so, on whose behalf did they testify and what was the outcome of the litigation?
- ☐ Have any of the firm's ESOP valuations or fairness opinions been challenged? If so, by whom and what was the outcome?
- ☐ What level of errors and omissions insurance coverage does your firm carry?
- ☐ Does any single referral source comprise 20% of your revenue or more? If so, please explain.
- ☐ Please provide a detailed explanation of changes you made to your valuation policies and procedures with regard to the *GreatBanc* settlement.
- ☐ Please provide a sample ESOP report.

(Source: Sell-Side Advisory Services: A Savvy Way to Excel in the ESOP Market, Brian Bornino (GBQ Consulting) and Tracy Woolsey (Horizon Trust & Investment Management), BVR webinar, Nov. 30, 2016)

The Residual Contribution Method for Valuing a Corporate Brand

By René Hlousek, Beacon Valuation Group LLC
(San Francisco, Calif., USA)

Editor's note: In 2004, the author published a paper that introduced a new school of thought to the valuation of a corporate brand. This has since evolved into a method he refers to as the residual contribution method (RCM), which he explains in this article. We welcome feedback on this method, so please send your comments to the editor at andyd@bvrescources.com.

Despite the significant progress made within the accounting profession in recognizing intangibles, and the corresponding improvements exhibited within the appraisal community in measuring the value of these key assets, the business community continues to be concerned that traditional accounting fails to recognize a company's total asset base—thus making it difficult for investors, management, and financiers to recognize a realistic company value. Analysts often bypass the balance sheet as a means of assessing value, particularly when vital assets, such as corporate brands, go either unrecognized or recognized in a manner that is less than convincing.

While Wall Street analysts focus their efforts on translating business performance into expected stock price for the investor's consumption, too little (reliable) pricing analysis is placed at corporate management's disposal for the purpose of making an informed decision as to the quantitative effect a particular course will have on the corporation's brand value.

Traditional benchmarks and methods used to value brands, whether they are for financial reporting, strategic, or other purposes, are losing relevance, especially in relation to companies whose value is often based upon intangibles such as brands.

One of the primary objectives of this article is to show that the valuation of a corporate brand, which can be viewed in many cases as one of the most valuable assets a corporation holds, is a function of thoroughly identifying, isolating, and quantifying the economic value of that complex array of intangible asset forces that make up a business enterprise. Very often, the intangible assets the entity employing it holds may dominate and lead the valuation drivers surrounding a corporate brand. In all cases, it must be recognized that a corporate brand would not exist were it not for the presence of the elaborate combination of elements embodied in the intangible assets unique to, and held by, the enterprise being examined.

From a purely unbiased point of view, current and popular methods to value a corporate brand, although traditionally deemed as being adequate or "passable" for financial reporting purposes, are far less than sufficient when it comes to measuring the full or realistic value of this intangible asset.

In response, and in an effort to fill the solution gap above, the "residual contribution method" (RCM) for valuing corporate brands, as presented here, is designed to minimize the high level of irrelevance, subjectivity, as well as lack of practicality that are inherent in much of the existing population of models by systematically exploring the relation between a business enterprise, its underlying key intangible assets, goodwill, and, ultimately, corporate brand value.

The roots of RCM can be traced back to 2001, when I first began to formulate, as a personal hobby, the ingredients and formulae required to tame this elusive intangible called brand. The fruit of this effort was first formally introduced in an article[1] I wrote in 2004. Much has evolved in the arena of intangible asset valuation since then. During the course of the development of this methodology, and ultimately leading up to what is now known as the RCM, I knew all along that, to successfully develop a working and adoptable model to value corporate brands, we must be both willing and able to think outside of the box—this means navigating through vast uncharted analytical territory, unencumbered by counterproductive agendas or affiliations, while being (at least) cognizant of the less-than-reliable paths that have already been mapped through the valiant efforts made by others who have, likewise, explored the valuation metrics of this very well-recognized but highly elusive corporate asset. This reminds me of a quote I once came across that characterized the world of brand valuation and all of its participants: "It's a jungle out there."

To expose the audience to the most efficient sequence of information necessary to grasp and apply the concepts behind this corporate brand valuation model, and ultimately be able to develop user-friendly valuation schemata, we will cover the most relevant and core bodies of knowledge with the following agenda as our overriding premise:

1. *Identify* and *isolate* key components of overall company value attributable to brand;

2. *Extract* brand value elements through the lens of other intangibles, including goodwill;

3. *Quantify* the most esoteric components of brand value; and

4. *Leverage* a wide spectrum of intangible asset valuation techniques commonly used in financial reporting engagements.

1 "Unlocking the Corporate Brand," *Valuation Strategies*, March/April 2004.

Corporate brand definitional framework. Within the context of the valuation methodology presented here, it's important to note that the reference to "brand" relates solely to a company's umbrella corporate brand inclusive of its underlying portfolio of related brands, as opposed to any single product brand or single brand families that the owner entity may house or the company's umbrella corporate brand may envelop.

Corporate brand, as opposed to product brands, is a single umbrella image that groups together the experiences, values, and images of a corporation's panoply of activities. It can be depicted as a network of knowledge about a company stored in the mind of the target communities such as customers, employees, shareholders, investors, journalists, analysts, business partners, and competitors.

Companies under U.S. GAAP will often have the term "trademarks" or "trade names" when listing their acquired intangibles, which implies an intellectual property-centric view of these marketing assets. Although a corporate brand is defined partly by identifiable intangible assets, such as a company trade name, trademark, or logo, all of which represent intellectual property (IP) that can be legally protected, the greatest value of a corporate brand is even more intangible than these assets. This should leave the user of a company's financial statements wondering whether the reported book value of an entity's marketing intangibles is based on a value that is both fully encapsulating and realistic.

Unlike product brands, or other intangible assets a company holds, corporate brands cannot be separated from the rest of the assets, without substantially diminishing the value of the majority of the company's intangible assets or the overall business enterprise housing them. Conversely, it is not uncommon for companies to be able to increase revenue and profitability, and realize a commensurate increase in value, by virtue of disposing of their nonperforming product brands.

In researching brand valuation methodologies, we are often exposed to the term "brand equity," which is merely a phrase used primarily in the marketing industry to describe the value of having a well-known brand name, based on the idea that the owner of a well-known brand name can generate more money from products with that brand name than from products with a less well-known name. The RCM notes and acknowledges this but moves far beyond this commonsense premise.

The common thread among most definitions of brand, whether they are in reference to a single product or a collection, is that the presence of a brand is most directly manifested through a company's customers—the consumers of products and services who are collectively the source of an entity's cash flows. The RCM builds upon this foundation.

The role of goodwill as the foundation. The definition of goodwill often depends on the context in which the term is being defined, and that is why various bodies define this intangible in ways that can differ significantly. For purposes of this content, we need only a sample to illustrate this definitional range.

From a stakeholder's point of view, the *IRS Glossary to Publication 551* touches upon some of the more common-sense aspects by defining goodwill as "the value of a trade or business based on expected continued customer patronage due to its name, reputation, or any other factors." And, similarly, the *International Glossary of Business Valuation Terms* defines goodwill as "that intangible asset arising as a result of name, reputation, customer loyalty, location, products, and similar factors not separately identified." Here, we should note the similarity of the above definitions, particularly through the keywords used, to those outlined earlier for brand.

From an accountant's point of view, tempered by a perhaps more technical approach compared to that of an average stakeholder, the term "goodwill," as derived from financial reporting (accounting) guidance, is "the premium that a buyer would be willing to pay for an entity over the net of the amounts assigned to assets and liabilities of the business. This premium amount recognized as goodwill includes acquired intangible assets that do not meet the economic criterion for recognition as assets apart from goodwill." To that end, the RCM directly examines the portion of goodwill value stemming from nonaccounting intangibles and intangible asset valuation impacts on goodwill that are not associated with brand.

Although the valuation of a corporate brand, as presented herein, is not performed strictly for acquisition-related financial reporting purposes, the "excess" element of the above concept becomes, to a certain degree, very much applicable and central to the development of the basis of corporate brand value. One could see the resemblance of the descriptors used in the preceding definitions to our perception of what constitutes a brand name of a company. The fact is that, frequently, the academic and business communities view many elements of both goodwill and corporate brand as one and the same. This seemingly obscure and often-overlooked observation quickly takes on a much more visible presence once we begin to explore the quantitative and qualitative interrelatedness among the various intangible assets the business enterprise holds and particularly through the employment of the RCM to value a corporate brand.

Shortcomings of existing schools of thought and applications. The success of the academic and business communities in identifying the various relations between market perception and consumer behavior must not go unrecognized, especially if the processing of this information by corporate brand managers results, from time to time, in increased sales, profit margins, and benefits to the company's stakeholders. The communities attempting to identify, define, isolate, or value corporate brands for marketing purposes would generally agree that a presence of a strong brand will allow the company to achieve one or more of the following: (1) capture more market share; (2) realize better profit margins; (3) maintain revenue growth while others do not; (4) become less vulnerable to price fluctuations than others; and (5) achieve a higher score on marketing surveys designed to rank against competitors the products and services of the company.

Although various marketing-driven brand valuation methods have successfully identified a quantitative relation between a specific brand element (such as brand recall) and a financial metric (such as revenue), these attempts have yet to clearly establish the magnitude of such relation. Moreover, without first establishing the magnitude of the above relation(s), one cannot ultimately translate these findings into a reliable and valid valuation algorithm or applicable metric. Although potentially useful to brand managers, the frequently referred to qualitative relations (i.e., awareness impacts loyalty) are more common sense than science and provide only little practical use for the valuation community.

The popular point systems, although providing valuable marketing data to brand managers, are highly dependent on the relevance of their surveys and target audiences to the key valuation drivers of a corporate brand and are usually more applicable to single product brands rather than the corporate umbrella brand housing them.

Several developers have valiantly attempted the collection of these observations and the conversion of the resulting relations into a "valuation model." While existing schools of thought catering to brand managers and end consumers of the brand have successfully identified the correlation between certain brand elements and the manifestation of their presence, they fall short of providing a transparent and analytically traceable translation to value.

As it relates to valuing brands for financial reporting purposes (in connection with acquisition-related compliance), the two methodologies most commonly used to value this strategic asset's trade name or trademark component are the relief-from-royalty method (RFR) and multiperiod excess earnings method (MPEEM). We will touch upon these methods later in this article but only to the extent that these methods provide employable features that can be leveraged as part of the overall RCM presented herein. Full immersion into the analytical components of the RFR and MPEEM is clearly outside of the scope of this article, under the reasonable assumption that the user of the RCM already possesses measurable experience in the area of intangible asset valuation where these methods are routinely used to value various intangibles, which may or may not include brand.

Brand valuations using the MPEEM can inadvertently include "goodwill" components, while the RFR fails to distinguish the strategic/financial component of brand value from the legal aspects of ownership due, in part, to the nature of the royalty data used as the key input. Additionally, the above methods do not recognize or examine the economic influence that a brand has on other financially permeable intangible assets the business enterprise holds. Within a financial reporting valuation context, the value a brand adds, particularly when it is a key asset of the business, is often embedded within other discretely identifiable intangibles or becomes an undistinguishable component of the goodwill residual by default.

One of the common threads among the above schools is the attempt each of them make to identify the sets of appropriate valuation parameters that act as the main drivers of a specific company brand value; any analysis stemming from this basis is highly subjective, given the vast universe of potential internal and external economic forces or brand elements that could have such impact.

In some ways, this can be likened to the medieval chemical science and speculative philosophy that has become known as alchemy.

In a sense, it appears that the various attempts to value brand creatively move the subjectivity of the task, rather than reducing it. This is most evident when examining the various "black box" valuation approaches, such as those certain ranking agencies, among others, use, which clearly offer either limited or no transparency for third-party assessment of the presumed brand value drivers. As alchemy has long ago become the predecessor to modern-day chemistry, I believe that one day soon less transmutational methods will cannibalize so much of the existing school of thought on brand valuation. Mark your calendars.

Defining corporate brand value limits and boundaries. Valuing an intangible asset as esoteric as a corporate brand, without first setting the upper and lower limits of value, could result in a limitless range of brand values, which is not the outcome desired in any valuation practice.

The RCM is designed specifically to assess that portion of the overall company value attributable solely to the entity's corporate brand (firm-level), inclusive of its umbrella of related product and service brands that the business enterprise may employ. The analytical flow of the RCM, also depicted in Exhibit 1, consists of the following seven distinct steps:

1. Business enterprise valuation;
2. Monetary and tangible asset isolation;
3. Identification and valuation of accounting intangibles (excluding brand);
4. Identification and valuation of nonaccounting intangibles (excluding brand);
5. Calculation of pure goodwill residual and implied royalty on brand;
6. Revaluation of primary intangibles with contributory asset charge to brand; and
7. Unification of corporate brand value elements.

Exhibit 1. Analytical Flow of the Residual Contribution Method

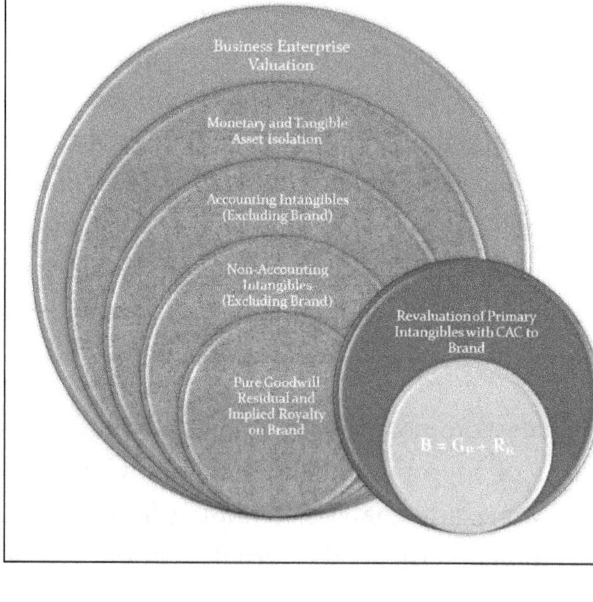

The first four of the above seven steps are focused on setting and resetting the maximum portion of the overall business enterprise value allocable to corporate brand by systematically isolating and extracting the values attributable to assets other than brand. The function of this conceptual framework can be analogized to the process of mining for precious metals, wherein the sought-after asset (such as gold) is extracted from its source by applying sequential filters. In that sense, the business enterprise value, as established in Step 1 of the RCM-based valuation system, represents the total volume of raw material from which gold is extracted, while the valuation and isolation of the company's monetary, tangible, and intangible assets (other than brand), through Steps 2 through 4, represent the process of filtering out of the total volume of raw material all of those elements that do not qualify as gold. Steps 5 through 7, involving the identification, isolation, and unification of additional brand elements, could be likened to the process of further gathering of gold particles and the cleansing of this precious material from undesirable and nonprecious impurities.

Business enterprise value foundation. In applying the RCM, we must be cognizant of the well-grounded view that a business enterprise, regardless of the industry in which it operates, is a portfolio of assets, with each asset group possessing different economic attributes (see Exhibit 2).

By default, the business enterprise value (BEV) represents the upper limit of value for any one, or all, of the asset (categories) the entity houses. Of the three approaches to value the enterprise (cost, market, and income), the multiperiod discounted cash flow (DCF) method within the income approach is most reliable when setting the basis (upper limit) for the valuation of a corporate brand, since it directly captures the expected risk-adjusted economic benefit stream (and its relevant components) generated by the entire portfolio of assets associated with this key intangible (see Exhibit 3).

At this juncture, it is important to note that the premise of value that is used to value the business enterprise sets the posture for the entity's underlying assets. For example, if the business is valued under the fair market value premise utilizing purely entity-specific inputs (this would be Step 1 of the RCM valuation process), we cannot abruptly switch to the use of market-participant inputs for the underlying intangibles (during Step 3 of the RCM), as would be done in fair value premise valuations performed for financial reporting purposes.

Intangible asset isolation. Subtracting monetary and tangible asset values from the BEV establishes the maximum value allocable to the corporate brand, consistent with: intangible assets including goodwill (IA) = BEV - (MA + TA), where MA refers to monetary assets and TA the tangible assets. The next step in applying the RCM is to "filter out" all elements included within the intangible asset group value that are not a component of, or driven by, the entity's corporate brand. Indeed this is where the analogy between the process of extracting (eliminating) nonbrand elements and the industrial process of mining for precious metals becomes most transparent.

Exhibit 2. Asset Groups of a Business Enterprise

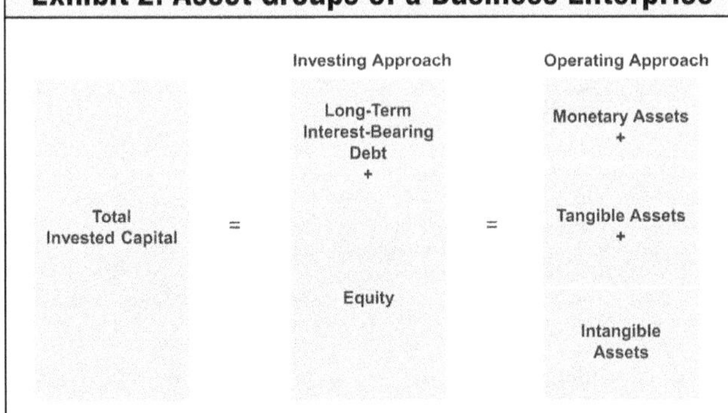

Since corporate brand does not exist in a vacuum, but rather in conjunction with other assets that it enhances, as well as assets by which it is impacted, including other intangible assets or impacts, it is important to have a keen understanding of the valuation metrics behind the intangibles with which corporate brand is associated. And to accomplish that, we must understand the different components of the total intangible asset value base, as depicted in Exhibit 4.

Exhibit 3. Multiperiod Discounted Cash Flow Method

ACME Group Inc.
Business Enterprise Value Model
Multiple Period Discounting Method—Discounted Cash Flow Analysis

($000's)			12/31/2016	12/31/2017	12/31/2018	12/31/2019	12/31/2020	12/31/2021	12/31/2022	Terminal Value
Revenues			$1,360,000	$1,468,800	$1,571,616	$1,665,913	$1,749,209	$1,819,177	$1,873,752	
% Growth				*8.0%*	*7.0%*	*6.0%*	*5.0%*	*4.0%*	*3.0%*	
EBIT			$136,000	$146,880	$157,162	$166,591	$174,921	$181,918	$187,375	
% of Revenue			*10.0%*	*10.0%*	*10.0%*	*10.0%*	*10.0%*	*10.0%*	*10.0%*	
Provision for Income Taxes	40.0%		$54,400	$58,752	$62,865	$66,637	$69,968	$72,767	$74,950	
Net Income			$81,600	$88,128	$94,297	$99,955	$104,953	$109,151	$112,425	
Plus: Depreciation & Amortization			$13,600	$29,376	$31,432	$33,318	$34,984	$36,384	$37,475	
Less: Increase in Working Capital @	10.0%		$4,080	$10,880	$10,282	$9,430	$8,330	$6,997	$5,458	
Less: Capital Expenditures			$13,600	$29,376	$31,432	$33,318	$34,984	$36,384	$38,599	
Net Free Cash Flow			$77,520	$77,248	$84,015	$90,525	$96,623	$102,154	$105,843	$109,019
Discount Rate		12.0%								
Long-Term Growth Rate		3.0%								
Valuation Date		12/31/2015								
Terminal Value		$1,211,318								
PV of Interim Cash Flows			$73,250	$65,172	$63,287	$60,884	$58,023	$54,772	$50,669	
Sum of the PV Interim Cash Flows		$426,057								
PV of the Terminal Value		$579,884								
Business Enterprise Value (rounded)		$1,000,000								

Exhibit 4. Components of the Total Intangible Asset Value Base

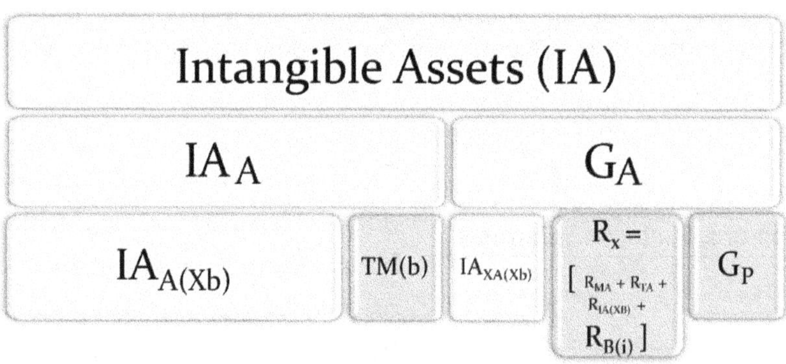

IA = Intangible Asset Value
IA_A = Discretely Identifiable Accounting Intangible Assets
$IA_{A(Xb)}$ = IA_A excluding Brand Value Elements
TM(b) = Trademark Value as Measured for Financial Reporting (Accounting) Purposes
G_A = Accounting Goodwill Value
IA_{XA} = Intangible Assets Not Measured for Financial Reporting (Accounting) Purposes
$IA_{XA(Xb)}$ = IA_{XA} excluding Brand Value Elements
G_P = Pure Goodwill Value
R_X = Returns on Assets Not Allocated to Any Specific Asset Group
R_{MA} = Return on Monetary Contributory Assets
R_{TA} = Return on Tangible Contributory Assets
R_{IA} = Return on Intangible Contributory Assets
$R_{IA(Xb)}$ = Return on Intangible Contributory Assets Other than Corporate Brand
$R_{B(i)}$ = Return on Corporate Brand's Intrinsic Component

Location of Corporate Brand Value Elements

Setting boundaries: discrete accounting intangibles (IAA). For a discrete intangible asset to exist from a valuation or economic perspective, typically it should possess certain attributes. The more common attributes include that the asset may:

- Be subject to specific identification and recognizable description;
- Be subject to legal existence and protection;
- Be subject to the right of private ownership, and this private ownership may be legally transferable;
- Include some tangible evidence or manifestation of the existence of the intangible asset (for example, a contract, a license, or a set of financial statements); and
- Have been created or have come into existence as an identifiable item or as the result of an identifiable event.

For a discrete intangible asset to have a quantifiable value in terms of an economic analysis or appraisal, it should possess certain additional attributes. Some of the additional attributes include the following:

- It should generate some measurable amount of economic benefit to its owner; this economic benefit could be in the form of an income increment or of a cost decrement; this economic benefit is sometimes measured by comparison to the amount of income otherwise available to the intangible asset owner (for example, the business) if the subject intangible asset did not exist; and
- It should be able to enhance the value of the other assets with which it is associated; the other assets may encompass all other business assets including tangible personal property, tangible real estate, or other intangible assets.

Discrete (accounting) intangible asset categories. Marketing-related intangibles are typically assets used in the marketing or promotion of products or services and may include trademarks, domain names, and newspaper mastheads. Customer-related intangibles are related to existing customer relationships and may include customer lists and order backlogs. Artistic-related intangibles usually arise from legal rights such as those copyright provides and may include plays, operas, literary works, and musical works. Contract-based intangibles arise from contractual agreements and may include value-added reseller channels, OEM agreements, and favorable supply agreements. Finally, technology-based intangibles relate to innovations or technological advances and may include patented or nonpatented technology, in-process research and development (IPR&D), databases, and trade secrets.

Concept of successor key intangibles. Engraved within the DNA of the RCM is the concept of "successor key intangibles" (SKI). Here, we recognize that for every "key" (not necessarily primary income-generating) intangible asset that is normally categorized as a separately identifiable intangible for financial reporting purposes, such as existing customers or existing technology, a corresponding successor intangible asset exists, such as future customers or future technology, which often, by virtue of specific reporting requirements, becomes part of accounting goodwill. The RCM, possibly appearing as a gesture of noncompliance but not designed as such, reopens this black box classified as goodwill and breathes new life into the value of all of those assets and valuation impacts that have been systemically suspended in their accounting slumber. By doing so, the RCM is able to extract brand value through the lens of a company's existing as well as successor intangibles. Such extraction is most complete when an entity's primary income-generating asset(s) is used as the lens. Exhibit 5 illustrates this concept, in a simplified form, by reference to a company's customer-based intangible assets (existing versus future customer relationships).

A primary asset is generally considered to be the asset most responsible for the revenue and profit-making potential for a business. The primary asset often varies depending on the nature of a company and its industry. For example, the primary asset for many consumer products companies is their brands/trade names portfolio, while the primary asset of most service businesses is their customer relationships.

Primary income-generating assets—link to corporate brand. Corporate brand value is often directly manifested through the entity's primary income-generating asset(s) (PIGA), such as customer

Exhibit 5. Existing vs. Future Customer Relationships

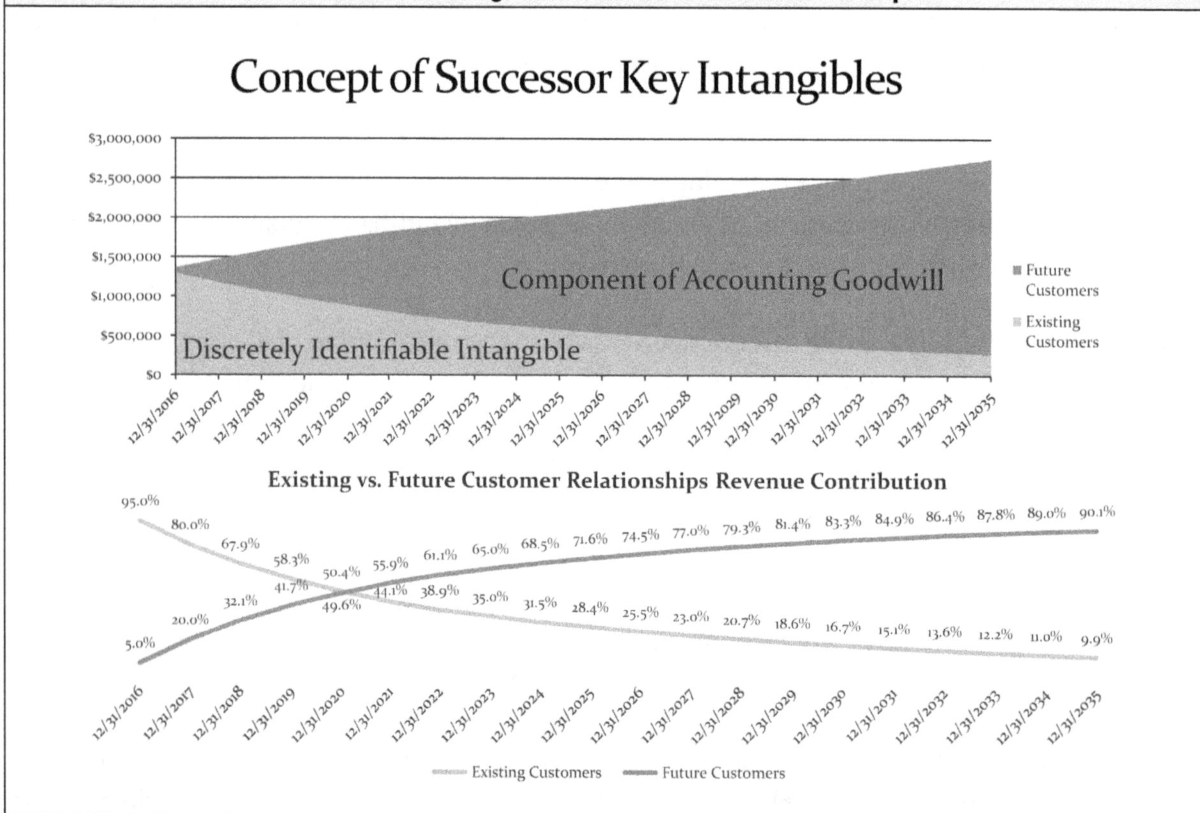

relationships, and the revenue and associated cash flows this intangible generates. When customer relationships represent the entity's primary income-generating asset, the future economic benefit stream associated with a corporate brand can be quantified through (extracted from) a systematic examination of the value components embedded within the entity's existing customer relationships (discretely identifiable accounting intangible) and future customer relationships (generally a component of accounting goodwill).

The key is to focus on the corporate brand value components embedded within (manifested through) the entity's primary income-generating asset—this could also be the company's technology-based intangibles (existing and future technology) as opposed to customer-related intangibles. The example we will use assumes that customer relationships (existing and future) are the entity's PIGA, representing 100% of the company's future revenue/income stream.

To capture the entire future economic benefit stream associated with a corporate brand, we must therefore value both existing customer relationships (limited economic life—IA_A) and future customer relationships (indefinite economic life assuming a going-concern business—IA_{XA}).

Gateway to brand value: multiperiod excess earnings method (MPEEM). MPEEM is an income-based valuation approach (that is, it estimates value based on expected future economic earnings attributable to an asset). It is most commonly used to value the primary or most important asset responsible for the income-generating ability of a business enterprise or a key segment of a business enterprise. Typical intangible assets deemed to be primary income-generating assets and valued using MPEEM include customer-related intangible assets or enabling ("key") technology (generally sold to third parties). For those who enjoy history, the excess earnings method was first used in the 1920s to estimate the value of intangibles lost when Prohibition shut down liquor manufacturers. Some of the main attributes of this earnings-based valuation model include the following:

- Projection of earnings typically spans over a finite life (economic life of technology);
- A return on contributory assets is subtracted from operating or net income, unlike in traditional DCF-based models;
- The amount in excess of net income is the basis of the asset value; and
- The earnings stream can therefore be broken down into two components: (1) normal return on tangible and intangible assets; and (2) an "excess" amount.

By separating the valuation problem into two parts, MPEEM focuses attention on the factors that create value for a firm. The MPEEM is most appropriate for primary income-generating or -enabling intangible assets (such as customer relationships).

Setting boundaries: nonaccounting intangibles. While descriptive conditions, such as high market share, high relative profitability, monopoly position, above-normal market potential, or other

Exhibit 6. Valuation of Existing Customer Relationships (MPEEM)

ACME Group Inc.
Valuation of Existing Customer Relationships—IA_A
Multiperiod Excess Earnings Method

($000's)		12/31/2016	12/31/2017	12/31/2018	12/31/2019	12/31/2035
	year	*1*	*2*	*3*	*4*	*20*
Total Customer Revenue (Existing & Future)		$1,360,000	$1,468,800	$1,571,616	$1,665,913	$2,751,668
Revenue Growth			*8.0%*	*7.0%*	*6.0%*	*3.0%*
Existing Customer Relationship Revenue		$1,292,000	$1,174,428	$1,067,555	$970,408	$272,071
EBIT Margin		10.0%	10.0%	10.0%	10.0%	10.0%
Add: Sales & Marketing Expense on New Accounts	1.0%	1.0%	1.0%	1.0%	1.0%	1.0%
Adjusted EBIT Margin		11.0%	11.0%	11.0%	11.0%	11.0%
EBIT		$142,120	$129,187	$117,431	$106,745	$29,928
Less: Return on Brand Component @	*0.00%*	*$0*	*$0*	*$0*	*$0*	*$0*
Pretax Income		$142,120	$129,187	$117,431	$106,745	$29,928
Provision for Income Taxes	40.0%	$56,848	$51,675	$46,972	$42,698	$11,971
Net Income		$85,272	$77,512	$70,459	$64,047	$17,957
Less: Return on Working Capital		*$6,202*	*$5,637*	*$5,124*	*$4,658*	*$1,306*
Less: Return on Fixed Assets		*$5,103*	*$4,639*	*$4,217*	*$3,833*	*$1,075*
Less: Return on Assembled Workforce		*$6,202*	*$5,637*	*$5,124*	*$4,658*	*$1,306*
Total Return on Contributory Assets		*$17,507*	*$15,913*	*$14,465*	*$13,149*	*$3,687*
CAC as a % of Existing Customer Revenue		*1.36%*	*1.36%*	*1.36%*	*1.36%*	*1.36%*
Cash Flow Attributable to Customer Relationships		$67,765	$61,599	$55,993	$50,898	$14,270
Discount Rate	14.0%					
Valuation Date	12/31/2015					
Present Value of Cash Flows		$63,468	$50,607	$40,353	$32,176	$1,109
Sum of PV Cash Flows		$315,197				
Value of Existing Customer Relationships (rounded)		**$320,000**				

economic phenomena, do not qualify as identifiable (accounting) intangible assets themselves, they may indicate the existence of identifiable nonaccounting intangible assets or forces that do have substantial economic value. Moving beyond the visible spectrum of discretely identifiable accounting intangibles, and assuming a going-concern entity construct, we must also recognize that a continuum of value exists that is inevitably fueled by the intangible assets and intangible elements included (by default) in accounting goodwill, which can be tied to the following (non-exhaustive) list:

- Assembled workforce;
- Future customers;
- Future technology-based intangibles:
  - Future patents;

- Next-generation technology;
- Know-how; and
- Internal technology.

- Future strategic contractual intangibles or noncontractual relationships; and
- Other future intangibles:
  - Marketing-based that are unrelated to the company's corporate brand;
  - Future noncompete agreements; and
  - Artistic and other less likely intangible assets.

Typically, the projected net income of the intangible asset being valued using the MPEEM is reduced by the return on the underlying assets whose employment predicated the operation of the business to determine the cash flows attributable to the intangible asset. Almost by default, this recognition and treatment of contributory assets often result in the present value of the underlying collective charge not being allocated to any other discretely identifiable asset group, other than goodwill. Therefore, the other intangible elements included in accounting goodwill will also include:

- Returns on assets not allocated to any specific asset group (R_X):
  - Returns on monetary contributory assets (R_{MA});
  - Returns on tangible contributory assets (R_{TA});
  - Returns on intangible contributory assets (R_{IA}):
    - Returns on intangible contributory assets other than corporate brand ($R_{IA(Xb)}$); and
    - Returns on corporate brand's intrinsic component ($R_{B(i)}$).

Since the MPEEM is utilized primarily to value assets with a defined or limited economic life, the amount of incremental value not captured initially, through the valuation of discretely identifiable intangible assets, can often be tied to future successor intangibles, which represent that portion of a company's going-concern value residing outside of the economic life of the intangibles separately valued.

If a combination of the mutually exclusive cash flows of the primary income-generating assets of the business enterprise already fully captures the entire economic benefit stream the entity will generate into perpetuity, then it can be assumed that all of the going-concern value of the business is already captured within the value of those primary assets.

As an example, valuing both existing customer relationships (assuming a finite life) and future customers (assuming indefinite/infinite life), representing the residual from the overall business after deduction for existing customers, fully allocates the going-concern value of the business enterprise to these two assets. (This, of course, assumes that the company's customers drive 100% of the business.)

Although the above underscores the importance of identifying the value of successor intangibles, the central concept here is that, in order to completely isolate corporate brand value, we must account for 100% of the business entity's revenues and cash flows through an orderly valuation of all of the intangibles that generate (or otherwise contribute to) those cash flows (see Exhibit 7).

Exhibit 7. Valuation of Future Customer Relationships (MPEEM)

ACME Group Inc.
Valuation of Future Customer Relationships—IA $_{XA}$
Multiperiod Excess Earnings Method

($000's)		12/31/2016	12/31/2017	12/31/2018	12/31/2019	12/31/2035
	year	*1*	*2*	*3*	*4*	*20*
Total Customer Revenue (Existing & Future)		$1,360,000	$1,468,800	$1,571,616	$1,665,913	$2,751,668
Revenue Growth			*8.0%*	*7.0%*	*6.0%*	*3.0%*
Existing Customer Relationships Revenue		$1,292,000	$1,174,428	$1,067,555	$970,408	$272,071
Percentage of Total		*95.0%*	*80.0%*	*67.9%*	*58.3%*	*9.9%*
Future Customer Relationships Revenue		$68,000	$294,372	$504,061	$695,505	$2,479,597
Percentage of Total		*5.0%*	*20.0%*	*32.1%*	*41.7%*	*90.1%*
EBIT Margin [3]		10.0%	10.0%	10.0%	10.0%	10.0%
Add: Sales & Marketing Expense on Existing Accounts	0.50%	0.5%	0.5%	0.5%	0.5%	0.5%
Adjusted EBIT Margin		10.5%	10.5%	10.5%	10.5%	10.5%
EBIT		$7,140	$30,909	$52,926	$73,028	$260,358
Less: Return on Brand Component @	*0.00%*	*$0*	*$0*	*$0*	*$0*	*$0*
Pretax Income		$7,140	$30,909	$52,926	$73,028	$260,358
Provision for Income Taxes	40.0%	$2,856	$12,364	$21,171	$29,211	$104,143
Net Income		$4,284	$18,545	$31,756	$43,817	$156,215
Less: Return on Working Capital		*$326*	*$1,413*	*$2,419*	*$3,338*	*$11,902*
Less: Return on Fixed Assets		*$269*	*$1,163*	*$1,991*	*$2,747*	*$9,794*
Less: Return on Assembled Workforce		*$326*	*$1,413*	*$2,419*	*$3,338*	*$11,902*
Total Return on Contributory Assets		*$921*	*$3,989*	*$6,830*	*$9,424*	*$33,599*
CAC as a % of Future Customer Revenue		*1.36%*	*1.36%*	*1.36%*	*1.36%*	*1.36%*
Cash Flow Attributable to Customer Relationships		$3,363	$14,557	$24,926	$34,393	$122,616
Discount Rate [6]	17.0%					
Valuation Date	12/31/2015					
Present Value of Cash Flows		$3,109	$11,502	$16,834	$19,853	$5,740
Sum of PV Cash Flows		$265,739				
Value of Future Customer Relationships (rounded)		**$270,000**				

Pure goodwill residual—bridge to corporate brand. From a prudent business perspective, goodwill is the favor or prestige that a business has acquired beyond the mere value of what it sells. The accounting-based technical interpretation is that the goodwill amount represents the premium that a buyer would be willing to pay for a company, in excess of the total value of its underlying monetary, intangible, and identifiable intangible assets. The fact that a buyer would be willing to pay this premium suggests that the company has developed an identifiable corporate brand, and, hence, goodwill with its stakeholders. In essence, "pure" goodwill—pure in a sense of not including any other accounting or nonaccounting intangible asset value—is a fundamental component of the corporate brand.

By this juncture, we have valued the business enterprise, isolated monetary and tangible asset values, and separately valued all of the company's accounting and nonaccounting intangibles, except brand. We have also identified and extracted components of the company value traditionally included in goodwill. This allows us to estimate the value residual, which we can refer to as the "intrinsic component of brand value," or *pure goodwill* (see Exhibit 8).

I am not suggesting that traditional methods of valuing intangibles result in the inadvertent inclusion of certain asset values within goodwill or that somehow a portion of goodwill value should be added to the value of certain contributory assets. Instead, we are recognizing that certain inputs and dependent calculations resulting in a value decrement at the intangible asset level often results in a commensurate increment in goodwill value, given the inherent mathematical relations. As a means of filtering out all nonbrand value components, the above impacts must be identified, quantified, and removed.

To that end, the technical aspects of contributory asset charges can be complex. Since the discussion of the full spectrum of analytical considerations related to these charges is not specifically the subject or scope of this article, I strongly encourage the readers to refer to The Appraisal Foundation's "The Identification of Contributory Assets and Calculation of Economic Rents."

The next set of calculations presented focus on the isolation and quantification of that portion of the overall company value, or economic rent, attributable to the intrinsic components of brand value, as derived through our pure goodwill calculation, as defined and presented earlier. This group of calculations is comprised of the following two actions:

1. Derivation of implied royalty rate for intrinsic component of corporate brand (Exhibit 9); and

2. Revaluation of primary intangibles with contributory asset charge to brand (Exhibits 10 and 11).

Consolidation of corporate brand value elements: $B = G_P + R_B$. From the previous steps of the RCM analysis (Steps 1 through 5), and as depicted in Exhibit 8, we have determined the value of pure

Exhibit 8. Pure Goodwill (Intrinsic Component of Corporate Brand)

Pure Goodwill = BEV - All Intangibles ($IA_A + IA_{XA}$) - Unallocated Returns on Assets

	Fair Value	% of BEV
BEV	$1,000,000	100.0%
Less: Working Capital	$70,000	7.0%
Less: Return on NWC (Existing Customers)	$28,846	2.9%
Less: Return on NWC (Future Customers)	$25,795	2.6%
Less: Fixed Assets	$30,000	3.0%
Less: Return on NFA (Existing Customers)	$23,737	2.4%
Less: Return on NFA (Future Customers)	$21,227	2.1%
Less: Existing Customer Relationships	$320,000	32.0%
Less: Future Customer Relationships	$270,000	27.0%
Less: Trade Names—RFR Method (Excluded)	$0	0.0%
Less: Assembled Workforce (AWF)	$55,000	5.5%
Less: Return on AWF (Existing Customers)	$28,846	2.9%
Less: Return on AWF (Future Customers)	$25,795	2.6%
Less: Return on Brand (Existing Customers)	$0	0.0%
Less: Return on Brand (Future Customers)	$0	0.0%
Equals: G_P (Intrinsic Component of Corporate Brand)	**$100,755**	10.1%

Exhibit 9. Implied Royalty Rate for Intrinsic Component of a Corporate Brand

ACME Group Inc.
Corporate Brand Valuation
Calculation of Implied Royalty Rate for Intrinsic Component of Corporate Brand
Relief From Royalty Method

($000's)		Forecasted period 2016	2017	2018	2019	2020	2021	2022	Terminal Year
Calculation of Royalty Savings:									
Total Revenues		$1,360,000	$1,468,800	$1,571,616	$1,665,913	$1,749,209	$1,819,177	$1,873,752	
Royalty Rate		Iterate 0.94%	0.94%	0.94%	0.94%	0.94%	0.94%	0.94%	
Royalty Savings		$12,784	$13,807	$14,773	$15,660	$16,443	$17,100	$17,613	
Provision for Income Taxes		$5,114	$5,523	$5,909	$6,264	$6,577	$6,840	$7,045	
Net Royalty Savings		$7,670	$8,284	$8,864	$9,396	$9,866	$10,260	$10,568	$10,779
Capitalized Value for Residual Year (CVRY)									$119,768
Discount Rate	12.0%								
Valuation Date	12/31/15								
Present Value of Net Royalty Savings		$7,248	$6,989	$6,677	$6,319	$5,924	$5,501	$5,059	$57,336
Sum of PV of Net Royalty Savings		$43,718							
Present Value of CVRY		$57,336							
After Tax Value		$101,054							
Value of Brand Component (rounded)		**$101,000**	**Solve for: 100,755**						

goodwill (G_p), which represents the intrinsic component of corporate brand value. The derivation of pure goodwill can be displayed in the following simplified version:

Business enterprise value

Less: monetary and tangible asset value

Less: accounting intangibles (excluding brand) value

Less: nonaccounting intangibles (excluding brand) value

Equals: pure goodwill residual (G_p) = intrinsic component of corporate brand value.

In valuing a corporate brand, we capture the totality of this asset's economic value by consolidating the above pure goodwill (intrinsic) component of brand with the present value of all of the expected unallocated returns that have been taken on this contributory asset (R_b) during the course

Exhibit 10. Revaluation of Existing Customer Relationships (MPEEM)

ACME Group Inc.
Valuation of Existing Customer Relationships—IA $_A$
Multiperiod Excess Earnings Method

($000's)		12/31/2016	12/31/2017	12/31/2018	12/31/2019	12/31/2035
	year	*1*	*2*	*3*	*4*	*20*
Total Customer Revenue (Existing & Future)		$1,360,000	$1,468,800	$1,571,616	$1,665,913	$2,751,668
Revenue Growth			*8.0%*	*7.0%*	*6.0%*	*3.0%*
Existing Customer Relationship Revenue		$1,292,000	$1,174,428	$1,067,555	$970,408	$272,071
EBIT Margin		10.0%	10.0%	10.0%	10.0%	10.0%
Add: Sales & Marketing Expense on New Accounts	1.0%	1.0%	1.0%	1.0%	1.0%	1.0%
Adjusted EBIT Margin		11.0%	11.0%	11.0%	11.0%	11.0%
EBIT		$142,120	$129,187	$117,431	$106,745	$29,928
Less: Return on Brand Component @	*0.94%*	*$12,145*	*$11,040*	*$10,035*	*$9,122*	*$2,557*
Pretax Income		$129,975	$118,147	$107,396	$97,623	$27,370
Provision for Income Taxes	40.0%	$51,990	$47,259	$42,958	$39,049	$10,948
Net Income		$77,985	$70,888	$64,438	$58,574	$16,422
Less: Return on Working Capital		*$6,202*	*$5,637*	*$5,124*	*$4,658*	*$1,306*
Less: Return on Fixed Assets		*$5,103*	*$4,639*	*$4,217*	*$3,833*	*$1,075*
Less: Return on Assembled Workforce		*$6,202*	*$5,637*	*$5,124*	*$4,658*	*$1,306*
Total Return on Contributory Assets		*$17,507*	*$15,913*	*$14,465*	*$13,149*	*$3,687*
CAC as a % of Existing Customer Revenue		*1.36%*	*1.36%*	*1.36%*	*1.36%*	*1.36%*
Cash Flow Attributable to Customer Relationships		$60,479	$54,975	$49,972	$45,425	$12,736
Discount Rate	14.0%					
Valuation Date	12/31/2015					
Present Value of Cash Flows		$56,643	$45,166	$36,014	$28,716	$989
Sum of PV Cash Flows		$281,304				
Value of Existing Customer Relationships (rounded)		**$280,000**				

of valuing both the existing (accounting) and future (nonaccounting) income-producing intangibles that depend on the brand's employment by the business enterprise, as depicted quantitatively in Exhibit 12, with the visual depiction of the end result presented in Exhibit 13.

RCM brand value—financial reporting context. On one side, you have expert groups who believe that brands, as assets, should be recognized within companies' financial statements. And, on the other side, you have various groups who believe brand values are "too uncertain" and based on a series of highly subjective judgments, which make them inappropriate for the balance sheet. It could be said that both of these sides, to a certain degree, have been right up to now. The RCM is designed to remedy this apparent dilemma.

Exhibit 11. Revaluation of Future Customer Relationships (MPEEM)

ACME Group Inc.
Valuation of Future Customer Relationships—IA $_{XA}$
Multiperiod Excess Earnings Method

($000's)		12/31/2016	12/31/2017	12/31/2018	12/31/2019	12/31/2035
	year	*1*	*2*	*3*	*4*	*20*
Total Customer Revenue (Existing & Future)		$1,360,000	$1,468,800	$1,571,616	$1,665,913	$2,751,668
Revenue Growth			*8.0%*	*7.0%*	*6.0%*	*3.0%*
Existing Customer Relationships Revenue		$1,292,000	$1,174,428	$1,067,555	$970,408	$272,071
Percentage of Total		*95.0%*	*80.0%*	*67.9%*	*58.3%*	*9.9%*
Future Customer Relationships Revenue		$68,000	$294,372	$504,061	$695,505	$2,479,597
Percentage of Total		*5.0%*	*20.0%*	*32.1%*	*41.7%*	*90.1%*
EBIT Margin [3]		10.0%	10.0%	10.0%	10.0%	10.0%
Add: Sales & Marketing Expense on Existing Accounts	0.50%	0.5%	0.5%	0.5%	0.5%	0.5%
Adjusted EBIT Margin		10.5%	10.5%	10.5%	10.5%	10.5%
EBIT		$7,140	$30,909	$52,926	$73,028	$260,358
Less: Return on Brand Component @	*0.94%*	*$639*	*$2,767*	*$4,738*	*$6,538*	*$23,308*
Pretax Income		$6,501	$28,142	$48,188	$66,490	$237,050
Provision for Income Taxes	40.0%	$2,600	$11,257	$19,275	$26,596	$94,820
Net Income		$3,900	$16,885	$28,913	$39,894	$142,230
Less: Return on Working Capital		*$326*	*$1,413*	*$2,419*	*$3,338*	*$11,902*
Less: Return on Fixed Assets		*$269*	*$1,163*	*$1,991*	*$2,747*	*$9,794*
Less: Return on Assembled Workforce		*$326*	*$1,413*	*$2,419*	*$3,338*	*$11,902*
Total Return on Contributory Assets		*$921*	*$3,989*	*$6,830*	*$9,424*	*$33,599*
CAC as a % of Future Customer Revenue		*1.36%*	*1.36%*	*1.36%*	*1.36%*	*1.36%*
Cash Flow Attributable to Customer Relationships		$2,979	$12,896	$22,083	$30,470	$108,631
Discount Rate [6]	17.0%					
Valuation Date	12/31/2015					
Present Value of Cash Flows		$2,754	$10,190	$14,914	$17,588	$5,085
Sum of PV Cash Flows		$235,431				
Value of Future Customer Relationships (rounded)		**$240,000**				

If we are to use the RCM-derived brand value, as presented herein, for financial reporting purposes, we must perform the following two conversion steps:

- Calculate the implied royalty rate for the total brand—this royalty rate is for both the intrinsic component of brand value and the portion attributable to the returns on this component from the primary income-generating assets (see Exhibit 14); and
- Revalue the discretely identifiable PIGA (in our example, existing customer relationships) using the above implied royalty rate for total brand as the total contributory asset charge on this intangible (see Exhibit 15).

Method matching. Technically, the RCM does not fall solely under the income approach. Although primarily an income-based approach, the RCM can possess attributes of income, market, and

Exhibit 12. Total Economic Value of Corporate Brand (Quantitative Depiction)

($000's)

Intrinsic Component of Corporate Brand (G_P)	$100,755
Add: Value of Returns on Corporate Brand From Primary Intangibles (R_B)	
Existing Customers	$40,000
Future Customers	$30,000
Other Intangibles	$0
	$170,755
Equals: Corporate Brand Value	**$170,000**

Exhibit 13. Total Economic Value of Corporate Brand (Visual Depiction)

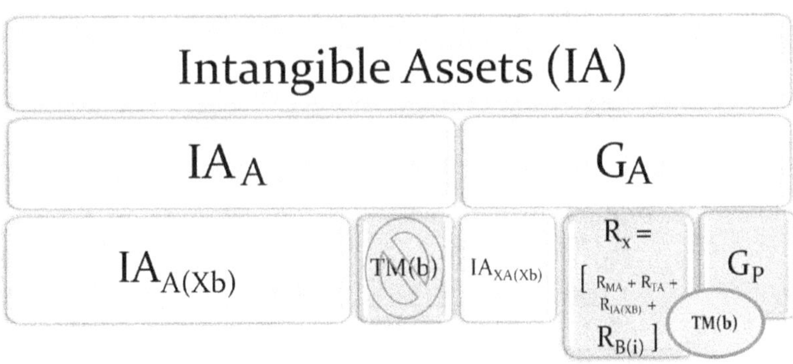

IA = Intangible Asset Value
IA_A = Discretely Identifiable Accounting Intangible Assets
$IA_{A(Xb)}$ = IA_A excluding Brand Value Elements
TM(b) = Trademark Value as Measured for Financial Reporting (Accounting) Purposes
G_A = Accounting Goodwill Value
IA_{XA} = Intangible Assets Not Measured for Financial Reporting (Accounting) Purposes
$IA_{XA(Xb)}$ = IA_{XA} excluding Brand Value Elements
G_P = Pure Goodwill Value
R_X = Returns on Assets Not Allocated to Any Specific Asset Group
R_{MA} = Return on Monetary Contributory Assets
R_{TA} = Return on Tangible Contributory Assets
R_{IA} = Return on Intangible Contributory Assets
$R_{IA(Xb)}$ = Return on Intangible Contributory Assets Other than Corporate Brand
$R_{B(i)}$ = Return on Corporate Brand's Intrinsic Component

Location of Corporate Brand Value Elements

asset-based valuation approaches, since this technique requires the valuation of the full spectrum of intangible assets the enterprise employs. As such, the RCM uses the:

- Income approach to value customer-relationships, different forms of technology, or non-competes;
- Market approach to value certain licenses and market approach concepts that are employed when assessing royalty rates for certain intangibles (technology/patents); and
- Asset (cost) approach to value an assembled workforce or internally developed technology.

In this article, we are valuing the brand through the lens of a company's existing and future customer relationships, as the primary income-generating asset. In practice, the PIGA through which the brand is valued could be any other asset for which the MPEEM is selected as the valuation methodology (such as existing and future technology).

If the corporate brand is the only primary income-generating asset of the company and the MPEEM is not applicable to any other asset, then the RCM can be fully applied, as presented herein, by extracting the brand value through the use of the distributor method (DM) to value customers (existing and future). When combined with the RCM, the DM is equally well-suited, as the MPEEM, as the gateway to brand value, given its recognition and treatment of contributory assets. In this instance, the DM results in a pure goodwill residual (intrinsic component of brand value) that is more consistent with the relative importance of the brand being valued. Therefore, when the

Exhibit 14. Calculation of Implied Royalty Rate for Total Corporate Brand

ACME Group Inc.
Corporate Brand Valuation
Calculation of Implied Royalty Rate for Total Corporate Brand
Relief From Royalty Method

($000's)		Forecasted period							Terminal
Calculation of Royalty Savings:		2016	2017	2018	2019	2020	2021	2022	Year
Total Revenues		$1,360,000	$1,468,800	$1,571,616	$1,665,913	$1,749,209	$1,819,177	$1,873,752	
Royalty Rate		Iterate 1.58%	1.58%	1.58%	1.58%	1.58%	1.58%	1.58%	
Royalty Savings		$21,488	$23,207	$24,832	$26,321	$27,637	$28,743	$29,605	
Provision for Income Taxes		$8,595	$9,283	$9,933	$10,528	$11,055	$11,497	$11,842	
Net Royalty Savings		$12,893	$13,924	$14,899	$15,793	$16,582	$17,246	$17,763	$18,118
Capitalized Value for Residual Year (CVRY)									$201,314
Discount Rate	12.0%								
Valuation Date	12/31/15								
Present Value of Net Royalty Savings		$12,183	$11,747	$11,223	$10,622	$9,958	$9,247	$8,504	$96,373
Sum of PV of Net Royalty Savings		$73,483							
Present Value of CVRY		$96,373							
After Tax Value		$169,856							
Total Value of Corporate Brand (rounded)		**$170,000**							

brand is the PIGA, we are no longer looking to the MPEEM as the only available option to value the secondary primary or nonprimary intangibles of the business.

To illustrate the expanded valuation options the introduction of the RCM enables, Exhibit 16 identifies the prescribed valuation methodology as a function of three commonly identified intangible asset types and their relative rankings as either primary or nonprimary assets.

The application of the RCM to value corporate brand portfolios for financial reporting purposes may initially appear to be more time-consuming, and correspondingly less economically feasible to the client, than the more commonly used valuation techniques (such as the RFR or MPEEM). However, the time saved by not having to perform a thorough query for, and analysis of, market and transactional data on royalty rates potentially fully mitigates the additional time required to

Exhibit 15. Revaluation of Existing Customer Relationships Using the Implied Royalty Rate for Total Brand as the Total Contributory Asset Charge

ACME Group Inc.
Valuation of Existing Customer Relationships—IA $_A$
Multiperiod Excess Earnings Method

($000's)		12/31/2016	12/31/2017	12/31/2018	12/31/2019	12/31/2035
	year	*1*	*2*	*3*	*4*	*20*
Total Customer Revenue (Existing & Future)		$1,360,000	$1,468,800	$1,571,616	$1,665,913	$2,751,668
Revenue Growth			*8.0%*	*7.0%*	*6.0%*	*3.0%*
Existing Customer Relationship Revenue		$1,292,000	$1,174,428	$1,067,555	$970,408	$272,071
EBIT Margin		10.0%	10.0%	10.0%	10.0%	10.0%
Add: Sales & Marketing Expense on New Accounts	1.0%	1.0%	1.0%	1.0%	1.0%	1.0%
Adjusted EBIT Margin		11.0%	11.0%	11.0%	11.0%	11.0%
EBIT		$142,120	$129,187	$117,431	$106,745	$29,928
Less: Return on Total Brand @	*1.58%*	*$20,414*	*$18,556*	*$16,867*	*$15,332*	*$4,299*
Pretax Income		$121,706	$110,631	$100,564	$91,412	$25,629
Provision for Income Taxes	40.0%	$48,683	$44,252	$40,225	$36,565	$10,252
Net Income		$73,024	$66,379	$60,338	$54,847	$15,377
Less: Return on Working Capital		*$6,202*	*$5,637*	*$5,124*	*$4,658*	*$1,306*
Less: Return on Fixed Assets		*$5,103*	*$4,639*	*$4,217*	*$3,833*	*$1,075*
Less: Return on Assembled Workforce		*$6,202*	*$5,637*	*$5,124*	*$4,658*	*$1,306*
Total Return on Contributory Assets		*$17,507*	*$15,913*	*$14,465*	*$13,149*	*$3,687*
CAC as a % of Existing Customer Revenue		*1.36%*	*1.36%*	*1.36%*	*1.36%*	*1.36%*
Cash Flow Attributable to Customer Relationships		$55,517	$50,465	$45,873	$41,698	$11,691
Discount Rate	14.0%					
Valuation Date	12/31/2015					
Present Value of Cash Flows		$51,997	$41,460	$33,059	$26,360	$908
Sum of PV Cash Flows		$258,227				
Value of Existing Customer Relationships (rounded)		**$260,000**				

Exhibit 16. Prescribed Valuation Methodologies

	MPEEM	RCM	DM	RFR
PIGA I - Brand (TM/TN)		X		X_c
PIGA II - Customers	X		X_c	
PIGA I - Brand (TM/TN)		X		X_c
PIGA II - Technology	X			X_c
PIGA I - Customers			X	
PIGA II - Technology	X			X_c
PIGA I - Customers	X			
Secondary I - Brand (TM/TN)		X		X_c
Secondary II - Technology				X
PIGA I - Brand (TM/TN)	X	X_c		X_c
Secondary I - Customers			X	
Secondary II - Technology				X
PIGA I - Technology	X			X_c
Secondary I - Customers			X	
Secondary II - Brand (TM/TN)		X		X_c

'X_c' denotes method to be used as an <u>optional</u> check to value derived from primary approach, indicated by 'X'.

value the collection of nonaccounting/successor intangibles (such as future customer relationships or technology). Additionally, the derivation of pure goodwill (intrinsic component of brand value) is a relatively simple calculation, which is based on the accounting intangibles whose value has to already be determined regardless of the use of the RCM to value the brand.

And, for those who prefer to visualize analytical flows, remembering the analogy of mining for precious metals, and, more specifically, the seven-step diagram in Exhibit 1, will help to keep the RCM analysis on the right track.

Design for active use. The fact is that traditional benchmarks and methods used to value brands, whether they are for financial reporting, strategic, or other purposes, are losing relevance, especially in relation to companies whose value is often based upon intangibles such as brands.

The tracking of corporate brand values with the residual contribution method on an ongoing or regular basis can benefit management internally and be used as a strategic planning and evaluation tool aimed at maximizing value for the company's stakeholders. RCM-based brand tracking systems can also be used as a means of better monitoring marketing efficiency, improving marketing budget allocation, and highlighting marketing's contribution to the bottom line in financial and valuation terms.

I strongly believe that a full adoption of the RCM, as applied and presented in this article, will provide a direct path to brand values that is more realistic and therefore more useful to the wide range of stakeholders and end users who depend on them.

René Hlousek, *ASA-BV/IA, MRICS, is the president and founder of Beacon Valuation Group LLC, a business valuation firm based in San Francisco. He has been a guest speaker at numerous venues nationwide on the subject of intangible asset valuation. René is a co-developer of the ASA's BV301 and BV302 intangible asset courses, which are requirements to obtain the designation in the intangible asset valuation specialty. For more information on the residual contribution method for corporate brand valuation, contact Hlousek at 415-357-1227 or by email at rh@beaconval.com.*

Do Your Valuations Weigh Up?[1]

By Chris Thorne (Bristol, U.K.)

"In a competition of experts to see which can generate the greatest judicial skepticism regarding valuation, this case, so far, takes the prize." These were the words of the vice chancellor of the Court of Chancery of the State of Delaware in a recent judgement that should resonate with all valuers, whether they are providing evidence in court or not.

Analyzing or estimating the benefits that will accrue to an owner of an asset are at the heart of most valuation methods for a good reason. Actual or imputed revenues provide an empirical basis for estimating the value of those benefits and can explain or justify that estimate. Two recent judicial decisions concerning very different assets situated in different jurisdictions illustrate that the courts prefer methods that provide the most detailed analysis of current or projected cash flow.

The Delaware case *In re ISN Software Corp* arose from a disagreement as to the fair value of two minority shareholders' interests following a merger of the company. The experts for the two plaintiffs put forward similar valuations of (in round figures) $230,000 and $222,000 per share. The contrast between these valuations and the $29,000 the expert for the respondent put forward was the reason for the judge's pithy observation at the top of this article. The experts used multiple methods to arrive at their opinions. All three had used a discounted cash flow (DCF) model and a guideline public company (GPC) method. Two also used the evidence of other transactions and one a direct capitalization of cash flow (DCCF) method. However, each expert put a different weight on the results obtained from each method.

The vice chancellor ignored the experts' weightings and relied solely on the DCF method, rejecting the other methods put forward. The reasons he gave were that, on the facts of this case:

- The prior transactions of the company's shares were not open-market transactions and also included noncash consideration;

1 This article is republished with permission from www.valuology.org.

- The prior transactions in other companies' shares were not considered to be sufficiently similar;
- Company cash flows had not stabilized, so the current income could not reasonably be assumed to continue into the future; and
- The company had no publicly quoted competitors, and it was difficult to identify any quoted company with similar characteristics.

The judge adopted the DCF model of one of the experts and then adjusted the various inputs after considering the rationale each expert provided as to whether an item should be included and, if so, what figure was the most appropriate. He concluded that fair value per share should be, in round terms, $99,000 and awarded accordingly.

At much the same time, on the other side of the Atlantic, the High Court of Justice in London also had to consider the most appropriate method in a valuation involving estimated cash flows. *Barclays v Christie Owen & Davies* concerned alleged negligence against a valuation firm by the claimant bank. The defendant valuers had valued adjoining seaside family amusement arcades in 2007 at a combined value of £4.2 million. Following a default by the borrower in 2010, the arcades were sold for a significantly lower figure, resulting in a loss to the bank. The bank contended that the correct value at the time of the 2007 valuations was £3.1 million. This was a case that really has something for everybody with the issues in contention including the experience and impartiality of one of the experts, the efficacy of conditions in the report, the way in which the loss was calculated, and the extent to which the bank contributed to that loss. In this article, I just summarize the valuation arguments.

There were opposing arguments as to whether the court should agree with one or other of the experts rather than attempt its own valuation or whether it should decide the weight to be placed on the different aspects of the experts' evidence and then reach its own conclusion as to the true value. The court agreed with the second argument and set about analyzing the experts' evidence with enthusiasm.

In preparing the disputed valuation, the defendants had adopted a method of applying a multiplier to the turnover of each arcade. It was common ground between the expert valuers appointed for the trial that the preferred method would be to estimate earnings before interest, tax, depreciation, and amortization (EBITDA) and then apply an appropriate multiplier (capitalization rate) to estimate the value. However, the expert for the defendant valuers defended the use of a multiplier of turnover on the grounds that there was little reliable evidence to support the analysis required to calculate EBITDA but that turnover information was more freely available for comparable businesses.

The court was not persuaded that there was any established authority for the use of a turnover multiplier or that, armed with knowledge of the turnover, a buyer in the market would assume a percentage of this figure as representing the profit that could be expected. The judge considered that this "rule of thumb" approach was of doubtful reliability because common sense suggests that net profit margins will vary, perhaps significantly, from case to case. He considered that the correct approach was to adopt a method that involved estimating the EBITDA for each arcade.

Having made this decision, the judge then examined the estimates of the experts for the various heads of income and expenditure before deciding on the most realistic, together with evidence of the ratio of actual or estimated EBITDA figures for similar transactions in order to determine the appropriate multiplier. He found that true combined value in 2007 should have been £3.5 million instead of £4.2 million and that the defendant had acted as no reasonably competent valuer would have done by not attempting to estimate EBITDA. It was therefore negligent.

While it is easy to assume that these cases have little in common given the differences in subject matter and some of the valuation terminology and methods used, a closer study indicates that the approach of the judges was remarkably similar. In each case, the court preferred the method that analyzed and considered the variable inputs in greater detail. In *In re ISN Software Corp,* this was DCF over DCCF; in *Barclays v Christie Owen & Davies,* it was EBITDA over headline turnover. And, having identified the preferred method, in both cases, the judges showed no hesitation in using the evidence to apply them and reach a valuation that was very different to those the experts advocated.

The overriding lesson for valuers is that courts in countries that apply the principles of common law will take a dim view of valuations arrived at using short cut or "rule of thumb" methods unless there is irrefutable evidence that these are the predominant methods used in a particular market. They will put more weight on methods that examine variables and that allow these to be adjusted on a case-by-case basis, even if those inputs are based on reasonable estimates rather than hard data. And last, but not least, they are not afraid to step in and make a decision as to what those inputs should be.

***Chris Thorne** is a director at Valuology. He spent over 35 years as a valuer in the private sector, primarily involved with commercial real estate. He is a former chairman of the International Valuation Standards Board and, between 2010 and 2015, was the IVSC's technical director.*

Using Monte Carlo to Value Warrants With Down-Round Protection

By Oksana Westerbeke and Jared Hannon, Grant Thornton, LLP (Boston, Mass., USA)

Warrants with down-round protection (also referred to as a price protection feature) have been a hot topic lately, from the perspective of both auditors and the U.S. Securities and Exchange Commission (SEC). Because of this increased scrutiny, valuation specialists and issuers have had to expend significant time and resources to properly understand and value these instruments for financial reporting purposes. In this article,[1] we will illustrate the application of Monte Carlo simulation to value a warrant with down-round provisions issued by a public or private company with a simple capital structure.[2]

Plain vanilla warrants are typically valued using a Black-Scholes model. Warrants on publicly traded common stock can be valued using a Black-Scholes model and inputs based on: (1) the publicly traded common stock price as the fair value of the underlying stock; (2) the contractual strike price as the strike price of the warrant; (3) a term to expiration commensurate with the remaining contractual term of the warrant; (4) a common stock volatility based on the expected volatility of the common stock; (5) a risk-free rate of return based on market indications; and (6) the expected dividend yield on the common stock over the remaining contractual term of the warrant. Implicit in these inputs is the assumption that the warrant's strike price is fixed—which is not the case when the instrument in question has down-round protection. Additionally, many down-round protection features will also adjust the number of shares issuable upon exercise of the warrant. Thus, the Black-Scholes model is not an appropriate methodology for valuing such warrants. In these situations, we require a more granular model that allows us to factor in the potential down-round adjustment to the warrant's strike price and number of shares issuable. One such methodology is the Monte Carlo simulation that we will illustrate below.

1 This article is an excerpt from *Monte Carlo Simulations, Advanced Techniques,* a BVR special report to which the authors have contributed. It is available at www.bvresources.com/publications.

2 The material by the authors in the special report also examines the valuation of a warrant a private company issued with a more complex capital structure.

The two main reasons for the use of Monte Carlo simulation to value warrants with down-round provisions are: (1) a Black-Scholes model does not appropriately capture the features of the instrument; and (2) the SEC's requirements. In many SEC comment letters to S-1 filers, the SEC questioned the Black-Scholes methodology management used to value warrants with price protection features. In fact, the SEC actually states that Black-Scholes is not an appropriate methodology and that management needs to use a binomial model or a Monte Carlo simulation to value the warrants. In addition, the SEC has indicated that not having a down-round financing in the past was not sufficient justification for reliance on a Black-Scholes model instead of a lattice or Monte Carlo simulation-based model.

In this article, we will illustrate the valuation of a warrant with two different types of common ratchet provisions (full and half) in a company with a simple capital structure. The methodology and application apply equally to public and private companies with simple capital structures consisting only of common stock and common stock-based derivatives (i.e., no preferred stock, no convertible debt).

Full-ratchet example. First, we will illustrate a hypothetical public company, but, as mentioned earlier, *our analysis applies to either a public company or a private company with a simple capital structure.* Focusing on a public company allows us to perform our analysis at the per-share value level, rather than requiring consideration of the total equity value and how the value of different components of the company's capital structure changes with fluctuations in value.

In this example, we will simulate the per-share value of common stock. Most of the inputs into the model are very similar to those used with the Black-Scholes model: (1) stock price; (2) initial strike price; (3) term; (4) volatility; (5) risk-free rate; and (6) dividend yield. There may be additional inputs depending on the nature of the price protection feature. You will need to know the expected time to next equity round (or rounds), typically provided by management. In certain cases, you will also need the amount expected to be raised at the time of the next equity financing. Once you have developed your inputs, you can model the evolution of the stock price in a Monte Carlo simulation with a risk-neutral framework assuming geometric Brownian motion.

The key objective in this example is to see how the presence of the down-round provision impacts the fair value of the warrants and how sensitive the value of the warrant is to time to the next round. The primary drivers of warrant value, and also of the value of the down-round provision, are the starting stock price and "moneyness," which is the ratio of stock price to strike price. For a hypothetical warrant where the stock price is $1.00 and the strike price is $2.00, indicating a moneyness ratio of 0.5x, there is a greater chance that the next round is going to be a down round from the $2.00 strike price. Therefore, the strike price is more likely to be adjusted. For a hypothetical warrant where the stock price is $5.00 and the strike price is $3.00, the probability that the next financing is going to be a down round is significantly smaller, and the warrant value will not be as sensitive to valuation using a Black-Scholes model versus a Monte Carlo simulation model.

Time to the next equity round, remaining time to expiration after the next equity round, and volatility generally have a positive correlation with the value of the warrants and with the value of the down-round provision. This is due to the manner in which expected term and volatility impact the expected future stock prices—the expected term and the volatility are multiplicative in estimating cumulative volatility of returns on the underlying stock. The longer the time before the expected financing, the greater the chance the stock price will decrease and the greater the chance there might be a down round. Additionally, the longer the remaining term of the warrants after the expected financing event and the greater the volatility, the greater probability that the stock price will increase above the down-round-adjusted strike price.

The risk-free rate and dividend yield generally do not have a significant impact on value of a warrant with a down-round protection feature versus the same warrant without the down-round protection feature.

Below are the key facts in our hypothetical example:

- Public company issued five-year common stock warrants to its investors;
- The warrants were issued at the money (moneyness ratio of 1.0x) with a strike price of $1.00; and
- The warrants have a down-round provision that is triggered if the company raises equity or issues convertible instruments that imply a common stock price of less than the strike price of the warrants then in effect ($1.00 as of the issuance date).

We ran sensitivities assuming that there was no price protection feature and a partial ratchet instead of a full ratchet. We also ran sensitivities to time to the next round: 0.5 year, 1.0 year, 1.5 years, and 2.0 years. The summary of the sensitivity analysis for the full ratchet is provided in Exhibit 1. In this case, we assumed a 65% volatility and a 0% dividend yield. As mentioned above, we also assumed a market price of the common shares of $1.00.

Full ratchet is a most direct but relatively aggressive price protection feature. When the company chooses a down round, the full ratchet implies that the strike price is reset to the issue price of the dilutive round. The number of shares is adjusted upward in a similar manner. It is the easiest type of ratchet provision to model because the warrant strike price resets to the price of the dilutive round and the number of shares is adjusted accordingly at the same ratio.

Here is an example of just one path from a simulation (see Exhibit 2). In this case, we have the new round price at $0.50 per share. As of the next financing date, the warrant was in the money with an initial strike price of $1 per share; therefore, the down-round provision adjusted the new warrant strike price to $0.50 per share. The warrant was exercisable for 500,000 shares

Exhibit 1. Public Company, Full Ratchet (US$ in Actuals)		
ABC Company, Inc. assumptions		
Common shares outstanding	150,000,000	
Market price per common share	$1.00	
Common market capitalization	$150,000	*For illustrative purposes only*
Preferred shares outstanding	0	*For illustrative purposes only*
Price per preferred share	n/a	*For illustrative purposes only*
Value of preferred shares	$0	*For illustrative purposes only*
Selected expected 5-year equity volatility	65.0%	
Selected expected 5-year dividend yield	0.00%	
Warrant terms (pre-financing)		
Issuance date	12/31/2013	
Expiration date	12/31/2018	
Warrant term	5.0 years	
Valuation date	12/31/2013	
Time to expiration	5.0 years	
Underlying security	Common stock	
Shares issuable	500,000	
Strike price per share	$1.00	
Down-round protection	Full ratchet	

before adjustment, and it is exercisable for one million shares after the adjustment. Typically, full ratchet has the most significant impact on the value of the warrant and provides the best anti-dilution protection.

Exhibit 2 shows the example of a Monte Carlo simulation. The Monte Carlo simulation is driven by the random variables (normal distribution with a mean of 0, standard deviation of 1) estimated by the simulation software, which determines where on the distribution of potential future stock prices a specific trial of the simulation ends up. We simulate in one step from the valuation date to the financing date, which is one year from the valuation date (also illustrated in Exhibit 2). In this particular sample path, the random variable was -1 for the period between the valuation date and the next financing date, and 2 for the period between the next financing date and the expiration date. Based on our other inputs, these random variables indicate that this trial path resulted in a common stock price of $0.42 per share at the time of the financing and of $2.67 per share at the warrant's expiration date. To arrive at a concluded value for the warrant from the Monte Carlo simulation, we would typically run a significant number of trials and take the mean result as the concluded value. In this case, the stock price declined from $1.00 at the issuance date to $0.42 at

Exhibit 2. Down-Round and Warrant Calculations (US$ in Actuals)

Down-round protection sample calculation

New round price	$0.50

Step 1: Determine warrant notional value

Strike price pre-financing	$1.00
Shares issuable pre-financing	500,000
Warrant notional	$500,000

Step 2: Determine new strike price

Strike price pre-financing	$1.00
Price of new securities	$0.50
Strike price post-financing	$0.50

Step 3: Determine new number of shares

Warrant notional	$500,000
Strike price post-financing	$0.50
Shares issuable post-financing	1,000,000

Warrant terms (post-financing)

Issuance date	12/31/2013
Expiration date	12/31/2018
Warrant term	5.0 years
Valuation date	12/31/2013
Time to expiration	5.0 years
Underlying security	Common stock
Shares issuable	1,000,000
Strike price per share	$0.50
Down-round protection	Full ratchet

Monte Carlo simulation (sample path)

Description	Time	Term of simulation	Risk-free rate (a)	Dividend rate (b)	Volatility	Random variable	Stock price
Valuation date	0.0 years	n/a	n/a	n/a	n/a	n/a	$1.00
Financing date	1.0 years	1.0 years	0.13%	0.00%	65.00%	-1.0000	$0.42
Expiration date	5.0 years	4.0 years	2.15%	0.00%	65.00%	2.0000	$2.67

Exhibit 3. Warrant Down-Round Protection Calculation (US$ in Actuals)

Warrant down-round protection calculations (single path within a Monte Carlo simulation)

Down-round protection sample calculation

Time of financing	0.5 years	1.0 years	1.5 years	2.0 years
New round price	$0.65	$0.42	$0.38	$0.34

Step 1: Determine warrant notional value

Time of financing	0.5 years	1.0 years	1.5 years	2.0 years
Strike price pre-financing	$1.00	$1.00	$1.00	$1.00
Shares issuable pre-financing	500,000	500,000	500,000	500,000
Warrant notional	$500,000	$500,000	$500,000	$500,000

Step 2: Determine new strike price

Time of financing	0.5 years	1.0 years	1.5 years	2.0 years
Strike price pre-financing	$1.00	$1.00	$1.00	$1.00
Price of new securities	$0.65	$0.42	$0.38	$0.34
Strike price post-financing	$0.65	$0.42	$0.38	$0.34

Step 3: Determine new number of shares

Time of financing	0.5 years	1.0 years	1.5 years	2.0 years
Warrant notional	$500,000	$500,000	$500,000	$500,000
Strike price post-financing	$0.65	$0.42	$0.38	$0.34
Shares issuable post-financing	773,294	1,195,608	1,325,458	1,467,576

0.5 year financing warrant terms (post-financing)

Shares issuable	773,294
Strike price per share	$0.65

1.0 year financing warrant terms (post-financing)

Shares issuable	1,195,608
Strike price per share	$0.42

1.5 year financing warrant terms (post-financing)

Shares issuable	1,325,458
Strike price per share	$0.38

2.0 year financing warrant terms (post-financing)

Shares issuable	1,467,576
Strike price per share	$0.34

the financing date. Because the stock declined to $0.42 at the financing date, the full ratchet took effect and the strike price of the warrant will reset to $0.42.

In this example, by expiration, this sample path's stock price actually increased to $2.67 per share. This implies that, in this sample path, the down-round provision had significant value, increasing the value of each share issuable by $0.58 per share (the impact of the reduction in the strike price).

An alternative to continuing the Monte Carlo simulation from the financing date to the expiration date is to use a Black-Scholes model as of the financing date to capture the remaining life of the warrant, once the assumptions (including strike price) are known and fixed (see Exhibit 3). If this route is pursued, the Monte Carlo simulation covers the term from the valuation date to the financing date, and the Black-Scholes model covers the term from the financing date to the expiration date.

In this sample path of the simulation, you have the new round price at 0.5 year of $0.65; at one year, it was $0.42; 1.5 years, it was $0.38; and then, at two years, it was $0.34 (see Exhibit 3). You can see that, in Step 2, we determined the new strike price, which was reset to the issue price of the new securities from the dilutive round. The number of shares was then multiplied by the same prefinancing number of shares-to-strike-price ratio, so the number of shares increased dramatically as the strike price declined.

In Exhibit 4, you can see the resulting value of the warrants for the same stock price path, varying only the date on which the financing occurs: payoff per share was $1.67 in the no-price-protection feature scenario; $2.02 if the equity round was issued at 0.5 year from the valuation date; $2.25 at one year from the valuation date; $2.29 at 1.5 years from the valuation; and $2.33 at two years from the valuation date. Since this warrant value is a future value, we discount it back to the valuation date. Since we performed the Monte Carlo simulation in a risk-neutral framework, we discount the payoff back at the risk-free rate.

Exhibit 4. Warrant Payoff Calculation (US$ in Actuals)

Warrant payoff calculation (single path within a Monte Carlo simulation)

Time of financing	n/a	0.5 years	1.0 years	1.5 years	2.0 years
Stock value at warrant expiration	$2.67	$2.67	$2.67	$2.67	$2.67
Strike price per share	$1.00	$0.65	$0.42	$0.38	$0.34
Payoff per share	$1.67	$2.02	$2.25	$2.29	$2.33

Time of financing	n/a	0.5 years	1.0 years	1.5 years	2.0 years
Time from financing to expiration	5.0 years	4.5 years	4.0 years	3.5 years	3.0 years
Timing of future value	5.0 years	5.0 years	5.0 years	5.0 years	5.0 years
Risk-free rate (continuous)	1.74%	1.74%	1.74%	1.74%	1.74%
Discount factor	0.9166	0.9166	0.9166	0.9166	0.9166
PV of warrant, per share	$1.53	$1.85	$2.06	$2.10	$2.13

The present values (PV) per share are shown at the bottom of Exhibit 4. The difference is, if you don't consider the price protection feature, the present value per share is $1.53, and, at the two-year term, the present value per share is $2.13. Since this is only one sample path within a Monte Carlo simulation, the final result will not have such extreme differences in value as there will also be paths where the strike price is not reset. The assumptions we chose, including a one-year term to the financing event and the warrant life of five years, are not too aggressive when compared to a typical warrant. When you have a scenario with much higher volatility, and if the warrant begins out of the money as of the valuation date, then the impact of incorporating the price protection feature will be more pronounced.

If you were to value this warrant using Black-Scholes, you would get $0.55 (see Exhibit 5). If you were to consider the down-round protection, the value would be approximately $0.59 per share assuming a 1.0-year time to the financing event. Depending on how many warrants the company issued, the overall value of the warrants may materially impact the company's financial statements.

Partial-ratchet example. In our second example in the context of a public company, the partial ratchet, we have the same scenario, only now we need to know the size of the expected financing and the number of common shares outstanding as of the valuation date since they are used in the calculation. We wanted to show you that everything else is the same with the exception of the partial ratchet.

Assumptions for the partial ratchet:

- Common shares outstanding: 150,000,000;
- Market price per common share: $1.00;
- Common market capitalization: $150,000,000;

Exhibit 5. Black-Scholes Value of Warrant (US$ in Actuals)

Black-Scholes value of warrant (no anti-dilution)

	Stock	Strike	Term	Risk-free	Dividend	Volatility	Call value
Black-Scholes value	$1.00	$1.00	5.0 years	1.74%	0.00%	65.00%	$0.55

Monte Carlo simulation conclusions

Sample statistics from simulation

Time of financing	Mean warrant value (per share)	Std. Deviation	Low 95%	High 95%
n/a	$0.55	$0.00	$0.54	$0.55
0.5 years	$0.58	$0.00	$0.57	$0.59
1.0 years	$0.59	$0.00	$0.58	$0.59
1.5 years	$0.59	$0.00	$0.59	$0.60
2.0 years	$0.59	$0.00	$0.59	$0.60

- Preferred shares outstanding: 0;
- Value per preferred share: n/a;
- Preferred market capitalization: $0;
- Selected expected five-year equity volatility: 65.0%;
- Selected expected five-year dividend yield: 0.00%; and
- Size of expected financing: $50,000,000.

The most common definition of a partial ratchet is where the weighted average dilution determines the strike price. This is done by multiplying the original number of warrants by a fraction, where: (a) the numerator is the sum of the number of shares outstanding immediately prior to the issuance of the additional shares and the number of additional shares issued; and (b) the denominator is the sum of the number of shares immediately prior to the additional issuance and the number of additional shares that the aggregate consideration for the total number of additional shares would have purchased at the original per-share price.

In this case, we assumed that the dilutive round was at $0.50 per share and that the warrant strike price at issuance was $1.00 per share.

Warrant terms (prefinancing):

- Issuance date: Dec. 31, 2013;
- Expiration date: Dec. 31, 2018;
- Warrant term: 5.0 years;
- Valuation date: Dec. 31, 2013;
- Time to expiration: 5.0 years;
- Underlying security: common stock;
- Shares issuable: 500,000;
- Strike price per share: $1.00; and
- Down-round protection: partial ratchet.

We have 150 million shares outstanding immediately prior to the issuance of additional shares due to this equity round. The adjustment factor is the number of shares outstanding prior to the financing, 150 million (indicated as "A" in Exhibit 6), plus the additional shares issued during the prefinancing based on initial strike price ("B" in Exhibit 6), divided by the sum of "A" and the shares issued in the financing based on the size of the financing of $50 million at the adjusted strike price of $0.50. The resulting ratio equals 0.8.

The resulting strike price is $0.80, compared to $0.50 for a full ratchet. In this case, because the ratio was 0.8, the number of shares issuable for financing is not one million as in the full ratchet. Instead, the number of shares issuable is 625,000 and is calculated by dividing the warrant notional of $500,000 by the $0.80 post-financing strike price.

We also performed the same stepwise simulation of the stock price as of the 0.5-year term, the 1.0-year term, the 1.5-year term, and the 2.0-year term (see Exhibit 7).

The new round price ranged from $0.65 at the 0.5-year term to $0.34 at the two-year term, and the adjusted strike price of the warrant ranged from $0.88 at the 0.5-year term to $0.67 at the two-year term. Thus, the difference in strike price is not as extreme when compared to the same calculation performed with a full ratchet. Once we calculated the adjusted strike price in Step 2, we calculated the new number of shares issuable post-financing in Step 3. You can see the number of shares increased again but not as rapidly as in the full-ratchet scenario.

Exhibit 6. Partial-Ratchet Price Calculation (US$ in Actuals)

Partial ratchet price calculations

Step 1: Determine new strike price

Shares outstanding pre-financing	150,000,000 [A]
Size of financing	$50,000
Strike price pre-financing	$1.00
Shares issuable pre-financing	50,000,000 [B]
Size of financing	$50,000
New round price	$0.50
Shares issued in the financing	100,000,000 [C]
Adjustment factor ([A] + [B]) / ([A] + [C])	0.80
Original strike price of the warrant	$1.00
Calculated strike price of the warrant	$0.80
Adjusted strike price of the warrant	$0.80

Down-round protection sample calculation

Step 2: Determine warrant notional value

Strike price pre-financing	$1.00
Shares issuable pre-financing	500,000
Warrant notional	$500,000

Step 3: Determine new number of shares

Warrant notional	$500,000
Strike price post-financing	$0.80
Shares issuable post-financing	625,000

Monte Carlo simulation

Description	Time	Term of simulation	Risk-free rate	Dividend rate	Volatility	Random variable	Stock price
Valuation date	0.0 years	n/a	n/a	n/a	n/a	n/a	$1.00
Financing date	1.0 years	1.0 years	0.13%	0.00%	65.00%	-1.0000	$0.42
Expiration date	5.0 years	4.0 years	2.15%	0.00%	65.00%	2.0000	$2.67

Exhibit 7. Down-Round Protection Sample Calculation (US$ in Actuals)

Down-round protection sample calculation

Time of financing	0.5 years	1.0 years	1.5 years	2.0 years	
New round price	$0.65	$0.42	$0.38	$0.34	

Step 1: Determine new strike price

Time of financing	0.5 years	1.0 years	1.5 years	2.0 years	
Shares outstanding pre-financing	150,000,000	150,000,000	150,000,000	150,000,000	[A]
Size of financing	$50,000	$50,000	$50,000	$50,000	
Strike price pre-financing	$1.00	$1.00	$1.00	$1.00	
Shares issuable pre-financing	50,000,000	50,000,000	50,000,000	50,000,000	[B]
Size of financing	$50,000	$50,000	$50,000	$50,000	
New round price	$0.65	$0.42	$0.38	$0.34	
Shares issued in the financing	77,329,391	119,560,841	132,545,764	146,757,588	[C]
Adjustment factor ([A] + [B]) / ([A] + [C])	0.88	0.74	0.71	0.67	
Original strike price of the warrant	$1.00	$1.00	$1.00	$1.00	
Calculated strike price of the warrant	$0.88	$0.74	$0.71	$0.67	
Adjusted strike price of the warrant	$0.88	$0.74	$0.71	$0.67	

Step 2: Determine warrant notional value

Time of financing	0.5 years	1.0 years	1.5 years	2.0 years
Strike price pre-financing	$1.00	$1.00	$1.00	$1.00
Number of shares issuable pre-financing	500,000	500,000	500,000	500,000
Warrant notional	$500,000	$500,000	$500,000	$500,000

Step 3: Determine new number of shares

Time of financing	0.5 years	1.0 years	1.5 years	2.0 years
Warrant notional	$500,000	$500,000	$500,000	$500,000
Strike price post-financing	$0.88	$0.74	$0.71	$0.67
Shares issuable post-financing	568,323	673,902	706,364	741,894

0.5 year financing warrant terms (post-financing)

Shares issuable	568,323
Strike price per share	$0.88

1.0 year financing warrant terms (post-financing)

Shares issuable	673,902
Strike price per share	$0.74

1.5 year financing warrant terms (post-financing)

Shares issuable	706,364
Strike price per share	$0.71

2.0 year financing warrant terms (post-financing)

Shares issuable	741,894
Strike price per share	$0.67

When comparing the value of a Black-Scholes warrant calculation to a Monte Carlo simulation for a down-round warrant, you should compare the total value of the warrants rather than the per-share value because there is a variable number of warrants and a variable strike price for those warrants. This is where a mistake can find its way into the analyses that we review. Once you have estimated what the payoff will be for all warrants issued (i.e., the aggregate value based on per-warrant value times number of shares), you can recalculate the value per share issuable based on the initial number of warrants. The concluded value should be based on the initial number of warrants.

Next, we illustrate the calculation of payoff per share as of the valuation date, just as we did for the full-ratchet example (see Exhibit 8). In this case, you can see again that the change in the value of the warrant is not as dramatic for each financing date assumption and does not increase as dramatically as it does under the full-ratchet provision.

To put it all together, in Exhibit 9, we have the Black-Scholes model where we assume no ratchet and no down-round provision, and we calculate the value of the warrant on a per-share basis assuming no financing, as well as for each financing scenario discussed above.

Exhibit 8. Warrant Payoff Calculation (US$ in Actuals)

Warrant payoff calculation (single path within a Monte Carlo simulation)

Time of financing	n/a	0.5 years	1.0 years	1.5 years	2.0 years
Stock value at warrant expiration	$2.67	$2.67	$2.67	$2.67	$2.67
Strike price per share	$1.00	$0.88	$0.74	$0.71	$0.67
Payoff per share	$1.67	$1.79	$1.93	$1.96	$1.99

Time of financing	n/a	0.5 years	1.0 years	1.5 years	2.0 years
Time from financing to expiration	5.0 years	4.5 years	4.0 years	3.5 years	3.0 years
Timing of future value	5.0 years	5.0 years	5.0 years	5.0 years	5.0 years
Risk-free rate (continuous)	1.74%	1.74%	1.74%	1.74%	1.74%
Discount factor	0.9166	0.9166	0.9166	0.9166	0.9166
PV of warrant	$1.53	$1.64	$1.76	$1.80	$1.83

Exhibit 9. Black-Scholes Value of Warrant (US$ in Actuals)

Black-Scholes value of warrant (no anti-dilution)

	Stock	Strike	Term	Risk-free	Dividend	Volatility	Call value
Black-Scholes value	$1.00	$1.00	5.0 years	1.74%	0.00%	65.00%	$0.55

Monte Carlo simulation conclusions

	Sample statistics from simulation			
Time of financing	Mean warrant value (per share)	Std. Deviation	Low 95%	High 95%
n/a	$0.56	$0.00	$0.55	$0.56
0.5 years	$0.57	$0.00	$0.56	$0.57
1.0 years	$0.57	$0.00	$0.56	$0.58
1.5 years	$0.57	$0.00	$0.56	$0.58
2.0 years	$0.57	$0.00	$0.56	$0.58

Exhibit 10. Summary of Fair Values (US$ in Actuals)

Summary of fair values

Time to financing	Fair value of the warrants No ratchet	Full ratchet	Partial ratchet
0.5 years	$0.55	$0.58	$0.57
1.0 years	$0.55	$0.59	$0.57
1.5 years	$0.55	$0.59	$0.57
2.0 years	$0.55	$0.59	$0.57

There is variation in the per-warrant share value, but the variation occurs in the decimals beyond the two you see in Exhibit 9. However, the impact of time to next round is very minimal in the partial ratchet down-round protection (see Exhibit 10). The base case scenario accounts for the majority of the value.

What we have presented here is just one form, the most common, of partial ratchets. There are other forms, and some of them have complex triggering conditions.

Oksana Westerbeke *is a principal in Grant Thornton's Financial and Valuation Services practice in the New England Cluster, specializing in the valuation of debt and embedded derivatives, contingent assets and liabilities, warrants with anti-dilution provisions and other contingencies, privately held securities, performance and market condition options, and other complex securities.* ***Jared Hannon*** *is a manager at Grant Thornton LLP in Boston specializing in the valuation of businesses, privately held equity securities, and complex financial instruments.*

Revisiting the Meaning of Fair Market Value

By Mark O. Dietrich (Framingham, Mass., USA)

We all know the classic definitions of fair market value from Revenue Ruling 59-60 and the *International Glossary,* which I'll repeat here for sake of clarity (see sidebar). At its core, fair market value (FMV) asks the appraiser to answer the question of what a hypothetical buyer and seller would agree to as the appropriate price for a given asset, equity interest, etc. In healthcare valuation, we are routinely called upon to determine the fair market value of specific transactions reflected in actual documents; if one believes the anecdotal evidence, transaction valuation in general is not a common engagement for most appraisers.

My goal here is to stimulate a rethinking of how FMV is determined in a real-world transaction setting *in general across all industries.* Market data from such actual transactions—as reflected in purported databases—are utilized in *nontransaction* settings (divorce, litigation, estate) to determine FMV. When using such data, it is critical to understand how the terms of the transaction influence the price while at the same time not to confuse transaction-oriented investment value with FMV.

Fair market value in a transaction. In a transaction setting (and any setting, for that matter), FMV is the price the hypothetical buyer and seller would agree to for the actual thing being transacted.

Definitions of Fair Market Value

The common meaning of fair market value as derived from Revenue Ruling 59-60 is "the price at which the property would change hands between a willing buyer and a willing seller when the former is not under any compulsion to buy and the latter is not under any compulsion to sell, both parties having reasonable knowledge of relevant facts."

The *International Glossary of Business Valuation Terms* provides that fair market value is defined as "the price, expressed in terms of cash equivalents, at which property would change hands between a hypothetical willing and able buyer and a hypothetical willing and able seller, acting at arm's length in an open and unrestricted market, when neither is under compulsion to buy or sell and when both have reasonable knowledge of the relevant facts."

It is not a hypothetical thing or a hypothetical transaction structure; it is an actual thing and the actual transaction documents that determine fair market value. That said, outside a regulated healthcare transaction, the *actual* buyer and seller may agree to a price that is other than the fair market value of the *hypothetical* buyer and seller, which would be denoted investment value or strategic value (the value to a specific buyer) or something other than FMV. There is no way to discern from the usual sources of market data for small business whether the price paid was FMV or something else. We'll look at an example later herein.

Real-world transactions are a very different setting than FMV for estate tax purposes, marital dissolution, or litigation where FMV is the standard, or other engagements. This is because the appraiser is compelled to assume or create some hypothetical transaction structure and assumed terms of the hypothetical sale. Importantly, when the market approach is utilized in the determination of fair market value in these *non*transaction settings, it is incumbent upon the appraiser to be familiar with typical transaction structures in the industry—if any. This highlights a critical source of error in the use of market data: lack of knowledge of actual transaction terms that influence the price reported in the market databases.

A good example of misuse of market data. As the first example of using market data, consider the purchase of a control interest in an ambulatory surgery center (ASC) by a public company or a private equity firm.[1] Even if you have never done such an appraisal and don't contemplate doing so, this is an excellent case study of misuse of the market approach. Appraisers commonly look to the annual survey by Healthcare Appraisers (HAI, a healthcare valuation firm) of large public and private companies that purchase ASCs in order to obtain or benchmark the EBITDA multiples being paid for both control interests and minority interests. For the example below, we'll use a control EBITDA multiple of 8.0 and a minority multiple of 4.5 and EBITDA of $1 million.

Back in 2001, at the AICPA BV Conference (when I had hair), I did a session with the late Jim Rigby and Butch Williams on the circumstances where strategic value equates with FMV due to the actions of consolidators. That session is relevant in the ASC example because there is a very active market for ASC purchases that is influenced by high valuation multiples for such entities in the stock market, enabling them to pay high prices for acquisitions to sustain revenue and earnings growth. Thus, if an appraiser is valuing a control interest, one of the first questions should be is the valuation subject in an area where such buyers (consolidators) are present, a threshold question for the relevance of consolidator-driven value. The cost of capital and valuation multiples available to the purchasers included in the HAI survey are not available to the vast universe of other potential buyers who lack access to the public equity and debt markets or to the private equity markets. This is especially true of single-location ASCs when looking to buy back a noncontrol interest.

1 *Editor's note: The newly released 4th edition of the* BVR/AHLA Guide to Healthcare Industry Finance and Valuation *contains extensive discussions of these transactions. It is available a www.bvresources.com/publications.*

Typical transaction structure. The next thing the appraiser needs to understand is typical transaction structure as it is not possible to understand value without understanding the terms that generated that value. Most importantly, the typical control transaction for an ASC involves a 51%[2] interest—not 100%. That is due to the fact that the key to a successful ASC is surgeon-owners who have a financial motivation through an equity share to do their surgical cases in the facility. As such, there is typically significant financial risk for the acquirers in the HAI survey of ASC purchasers to leave the minority owners without a significant stake in the entity. Thus, to value a 100% interest in an ASC using the market approach requires two valuations: one of the 51% interest and the other of the remaining 49% as it would appear post-transaction, i.e., *assuming the 51% transaction actually took place.* Thus, the value of 100% of an ASC based upon HAI market data consists of a 51% control share and a 49% noncontrol share.

Management fees. Another key aspect of such a control transaction is whether or not the acquirer is charging a management fee to the acquired ASC post-transaction; many acquirers charge such fees, while others do not. Such management fees range from 2% to as much as 7% of revenue and *are part of the cash flow the acquirer is buying.* The problem for the appraiser in using market data is that such management fees are generally not disclosed and they affect the reported EBITDA multiple in the HAI survey and other databases.[3] The value paid for the management fee as well as the EBITDA is the numerator in the multiple, but the denominator only includes the EBITDA. As an example, $1.0 million of EBITDA times a 51% interest equals $510,000. Multiplying $510,000 by an 8.0 multiple apparently gives a control value of $4.080 million. However, if the acquirer purchased a management fee revenue/profit stream[4] of $200,000, then the actual cash flow purchased was not $510,000 but rather $710,000. As such, the actual multiple is $4,080,000/$710,000, or 5.75.[5]

The post-transaction noncontrol interests. Now one needs to ask: What does the aggregate of the 49% noncontrol interests look like post-transaction? Here, one cannot make any generic or hypothetical assumptions about that aggregate interest. The buyers in the HAI survey reporting to the SEC or hoping someday to do so need to have a fairly uniform transaction structure to allow consistent financial statement reporting, e.g., consolidating a control interest. One would imagine the 49% interest will be well spread out among the various surgeon owners and thus be very small units. If a management fee is charged pursuant to the transaction, the post-transaction share of EBITDA will be consequentially less than 49% of pretransaction EBITDA. For example, if revenue is $4.0 million and the management fee is 5%, that results in a $200,000 reduction in EBITDA. Our example assumed EBITDA was $1.0 million at the time of the transaction; post-transaction, it is $800,000.

2 It may be as high as 60%—yet another complication.

3 In fact, in the course of a valuation for an actual transaction, the management fee is often subject to a separate valuation, separate from the EBITDA; since that fee is based on top-line revenue rather than bottom-line operating income, it is less risky.

4 Another nuance of the management fee analysis is assessing what portion of it represents cash flow "profit" versus what represents actual costs incurred. Again, reading the actual transaction documents is required to seeing what costs of the managed ASC the acquirer is entitled to be directly reimbursed for outside the management fee.

5 Yet another nuance is that actual pricing multiples could be based upon post-transaction EBITDA, reflecting the reduction caused by the management fee.

Transaction documents. The purchaser will have a detailed management agreement granting it control over day-to-day activities and many financial transactions not exceeding a threshold agreed to as part of the deal. The operating agreement (one should expect an LLC structure) will have a variety of provisions that will impact the fair market value of the holders of the noncontrol shares, including a buyout provision. Such provisions are key to the control owner's ability to bring in new noncontrol surgeon-owners to keep the facility operating at capacity and generating profits and justify the EBITDA used to calculate the purchase price. That provision may specify a formula, such as 3.0 times EBITDA less outstanding debt for both buy-ins and buyouts. Three times EBITDA may well be less than the fair market value of the interest *absent* the contractual buyout provision. This, then, highlights the next issue to address, the impact on FMV of the rights, obligations, benefits, and restrictions that contracts provide/impose on a given ownership interest. Of course, one cannot value such an interest—or use purported market data to value such an interest—when the contracts are not understood or not available.

The control owner often wants to sell new noncontrol interests as well, and the transaction documents may permit dilution of the existing noncontrol members to accomplish same. Another variation is where a control purchase involves 60% of the equity in order to provide the control owner with up to 9% to sell off to new noncontrol owners.

Regulatory matters. This article is not intended to get side-tracked with regulatory matters, but they abound. In addition, knowing whether a transaction took place in a state with a certificate of need (CON) requirement from a state authority to open an ASC, the terms of transferability of that CON, and the difficulty of obtaining a CON to open a de novo center are critical to evaluating market data.

Summary. Returning to this particular example, if post-transaction EBITDA is $800,000, 49% of that is $392,000, and the valuation formula is 3.0 times EBITDA, the 49% noncontrol share has an enterprise value of $1.176 million.[6] If we combine that with the control value of $4.080 million, we get an enterprise value of $5.256 million. Dividing that amount by the original EBITDA of $1.0 million results in an EBITDA multiple of 5.26.

It is safe to say that, for an appraiser with extensive transaction experience in a given industry or industries, there will be deal terms that the parties negotiate that impact the price being paid for the asset(s). Accounting firms often sell on the basis of revenue, for example, with payments made over a period of years. Dental practices sell as a percentage of revenue or a multiple of discretionary earnings. Accounts receivable are typically excluded from the assets of a professional practice that are sold, so an appraiser has to take that into account when using market data. As the ASC example demonstrates, such an entity is considerably more complex in terms of analyzing market data.

6 This is the aggregate noncontrol value to the existing owners assuming that 51% of the entity was sold and the remaining 49% retained subject to the transaction documents.

Impact on FMV of features in a contract of security. The rights, obligations, benefits, and restrictions in a contract or security have an impact on FMV, and numerous examples could be presented, but we'll look at a few of the more common ones.

Noncompetes, a generic transaction term. A relatively common provision in just about any small-business transaction is a noncompete agreement. The aforementioned ASC transactions typically include a noncompete, for example, precluding noncontrol owners from owning an interest in a competing facility. It is possible, of course, that in a real transaction this provision may be negotiated to grandfather noncontrol owners who already have an interest in a competing facility—but the appraiser has no way to know when looking at reported or purported EBITDA multiples what the impact of grandfathering on these multiples might have been.

We can explore noncompetes in more detail. First off, one would hope that most readers would agree that the presence or lack of a noncompete would influence the fair market value of a business being sold, unless perhaps the owner was dead, or permanently disabled, or leaving town—there is always an exception. The geographic area and length of time a noncompete applies should also impact the value. The extent of enforceability of a noncompete under state law might affect the value as well. Provisions similar to a noncompete, such as a nondisclosure of trade secrets provision or a nonsolicitation provision, would also be expected to have some influence on the fair market value of the actual interest being transacted that is subject to the various contractual provisions.

Contractual rights and benefits of a security. Contracts can also convey special rights and benefits to a noncontrol ownership interest that run counter to the generic expectation of DLOCs and DLOMs.[7] For example, it is not unusual for a noncontrol interest to be entitled to be redeemed at a pro rata share of the fair market value of the entity without regard to discounts.[8] Why would an appraiser ignore the contractual right of the noncontrol interest to a pro rata share of the control value of the entity? Certainly, such an entitlement would suggest a smaller, if any, DLOC than for a noncontrol interest without such a contractual right. Further, the hypothetical buyer of such an interest would pay more for such an entitlement, and the seller would expect more for the entitlement. Personally, I would think a smaller, if any, DLOM would be appropriate. If you are using control transactions of single-owner businesses to value minority interests in the same type of business, how can you possibly assume or calculate a DLOC without knowing whether the noncontrol interest you are valuing has contractual rights analogous to that of a control owner? Such conundrums are why many experienced transaction appraisers will use a discount rate reflecting the actual noncontrol, nonmarketable interest's value, rather than DLOCs and DLOMs.

Assessing such contracts is no different than valuing preferred stock or a class of common stock that has a dividend priority, a liquidation preference, a nondilution right, attached warrants, or

7 Discounts for lack of control and lack of marketability.

8 See, e.g., Shannon Pratt and Alina Niculita, *Valuing a Business, The Analysis and Appraisal of Closely Held Companies*, 5th edition, page 402.

any of a virtually infinite number of possible rights. Another example is the value of nonvoting stock versus voting stock where each class has rights other than solely whether it votes or not. Any security or ownership interest can have a fair market value, and the actual characteristics of the security determines that value. The standard of fair market value does not change or cease to exist because a noncontrol interest has the contractual characteristics of a control interest.

In contrast, a contractual provision that provides that the noncontrol interest is to be redeemed at fair market value taking into account "normal" or "appropriate" discounts clearly implicates more generic DLOCs and DLOMs, permitting the appraiser to invoke the standard approach to such discounts. If no mention is made beyond fair market value, then that also implicates more generic DLOCs and DLOMs.

A contractual provision that requires the entity to redeem the noncontrol interest at a price based upon fair market value (a put right)—whether at a pro rata share of control value or at fair market value with discounts—provides liquidity to the interest, assuming that the entity has the wherewithal to fund the purchase. Such a provision typically requires the holder to sell at the fair market value price. If there is a history of successful redemptions of such interests, that would likewise contribute to the extent of any DLOM. Practically, this is a contractual compulsion situation for buyer and seller where it is incumbent upon the appraiser to remove that compulsion from the fair market value analysis of the property's value. Alternatively stated, if the contract specifies that the interest must be bought/sold at a fair market value price, that contract precludes consideration of compulsion.

Aside from the value of the interest when it is sold under such a provision, another significant characteristic of its fair market value is access to cash distributions. Thus, a key contractual element of fair market value is the presence of any contractual clause that determines the timing and amount of cash distributions. Periodic, e.g., quarterly, distributions are more valuable than annual distributions, of course, and distributions that approximate taxable income are more valuable than simply income tax cost distributions. Returning to our ASC example, a common clause would provide for annual distributions equal to 40% (or some similar number) of taxable income, such that the owners can pay their taxes. Another common example would be all cash in excess of a normal working capital reserve as determined by the managers. The history of distributions and their consistency with the contract language are critical to the DLOC analysis and fair market value.

The 'market' for professional practice noncontrol interests. Of course, there is a difference between taking a noncontrol interest in a privately held business to "the market" and attempting to sell it to a third party and having the entity itself being required/compelled to have it redeemed based on an appraisal. And one appraiser's opinion of fair market value may be very much at odds with another appraiser's opinion of same.

However, given that most small businesses—and virtually all professional practices—with multiple owners preclude a noncontrol owner from trying to sell his or her interest to a third party without the agreement of all the other owners, it is highly unlikely that many third-party buyers would exist for an interest subject to a basket of contractual rights and restrictions that the third party would be violating if the purchase actually occurred. Why buy trouble, as the saying goes? As such, the idea that the "fair market value" of a noncontrol interest cannot exist due to a lack of "hypothetical" buyers and sellers is inconsistent with the market that such interests are transacted in; the nature of the interest simply constrains the market universe.

Conclusion. To determine the fair market value in a transaction of any ownership interest in a business entity, the appraiser has to take into account the actual characteristics of that interest as reflected in actual contracts and transaction documents and be certain not to use assumptions that represent investment or strategic value—unless a consolidator market exists in the subject's market area. When the engagement precedes the actual transaction as is often the case, the appraiser needs to be familiar with the expected terms and to reserve the ability to modify his or her opinion in the event that the actual terms differ from those assumed in the valuation.

When using market data to determine fair market value in a transaction or nontransaction setting, the appraiser has to be familiar with the actual transaction documents and terms behind the market data. Lacking that familiarity, there is limited utility to the market approach. Claiming that fair market value is indifferent to actual transaction terms in the subject interest—or in purported market data—fails the test of real-world experience and common sense.

Acknowledgement. It is a privilege to have thoughtful, critical prepublication analysis from one's colleagues, whatever their view of the end product. The author would like to thank Mike Crain (Florida Atlantic University), Don DeGrazia (Gold Gerstein Group), Robert Levis (Levis Consulting), Jim Lloyd (Pershing Yoakley & Associates PC), Harold Martin (Keiter), Todd Sorensen (VMG Health), and Jeff Urbach (Urbach & Avraham, CPAs LLP) for their commentary and critique of this article.

***Mark O. Dietrich**, CPA/ABV, MBA, MST, is a nationally recognized author, speaker, and expert in the field of healthcare valuation. He serves as Of Counsel to Meyers, Harrison & Pia. Mark's career experience includes serving as partner-in-charge of the annual audit of an 80-physician tax-exempt faculty group practice, representation of tax-exempt and taxable entities in Internal Revenue Service field audits, participation in the development of a 250-physician independent network and negotiation of its managed care and Medicare Advantage contracts, and more than 400 valuation engagements in the healthcare industry.*

Five Action Steps to Verify the Financials of a Cash Business

By Pasquale Rafanelli,
Grassi & Co. (Jericho, N.Y., USA)

When performing a business valuation, there are areas that are always ripe for manipulation—especially if you're dealing with a cash business. In some cases, the manipulation is to avoid paying taxes, while others are more deliberate and intended to hurt a particular person. We see this all the time in matrimonial actions and shareholder disputes. When working on an engagement, it's not uncommon to find that an action came as a surprise to one party and then we discover that the other party was planning this for months or even years. In cases such as this, we as professionals need to be more skeptical of the information and data received.

While it is important to properly apply the valuation methodology and to arrive at an appropriate market multiple, capitalization rate, and discounts (if applicable), it is equally as important to verify the accuracy of the data. Even if you arrive at the appropriate valuation metrics, if the data you are applying them to are inaccurate, then the concluded value for the business would be inaccurate as well.

Case in point. This brings to mind a particular matrimonial engagement that I worked on a while ago. We needed to address many issues with this engagement, but the one that I believe was the most crucial issue in settling this case was our creative approach to determine a realistic revenue stream. For purposes of this case study, all names, dates, locations, and values have been redacted.

During this engagement, we were working for the nonproperty spouse Jane Doe, the wife of John Doe. John and Jane were married on July 15, 1994, and filed for divorce on Sept. 17, 2012. During their marriage, they had three children: two sons, 14 and eight years old, and a daughter, 11 years old. Jane worked as a cashier at a department store, and John owned a pizzeria restaurant on Long Island, N.Y. The pizzeria was strictly a take-out restaurant (no tables), and it had the typical menu for a place such as this (pizza, sandwiches, salads, hot entrées). The restaurant did not have a liquor license. The business had reported revenues of $2.4 million on net income of $40,000, or 1.7%.

Of course, a business such as this does a lot of cash transactions, which immediately raises a red flag. Our investigation and subsequent valuation entailed a five-step process.

1. Check benchmarks. At first glance, the net income of 1.7% seemed low, so we checked a few reference sources. The *Business Reference Guide* indicated a net income of approximately 6%, and RMA showed a net income of approximately 5.1% in the current year with a 10-year net income to sales ranging from a low of 3.1% to a high of 5.1%. It is important to note that the above metrics are estimates and are not meant to indicate where a particular business should fall as some businesses naturally are better than the industry, while some are worse.

2. Analyze lifestyle. After we performed our preliminary analysis and before we met with Mr. Doe, we had an interview with our client, Mrs. Doe, to get a better understanding of their lifestyle. During our interview, we obtained the following key information:

- Mrs. Doe worked as a cashier in a department store where she has a salary of $40,000 a year before taxes, medical etc.;
- Mr. Doe brought home a salary of $1,000 a week from the restaurant, which is equal to $52,000 a year before taxes;
- The couple had three children who each went to private school, costing approximately $1,200 a month per child;
- Both Mr. and Mrs. Doe drove BMWs;
- The family took one vacation a year usually during the summer months;
- The children were involved in sports, music lessons, and dance lessons; and
- Mrs. Doe indicated that she handled the expenses and that on average the family spends $8,000 to $10,000 a month on expenses.

A simple calculation right there indicated that the family on average spent anywhere from $96,000 to $120,000 per year. Mr. and Mrs. Doe have a combined salary of $92,000 before taxes and other deductions. Using the clients' combined effective tax rate of 28%, medical insurance payments of approximately $10,000 for the year and Mrs. Doe's 401(k) contribution of $7,500 per year, their after-tax annual take-home pay is $53,600. Even if we were to assume Mr. Doe took all business profits at year-end, the after-tax amount of these would be $28,800 ($40,000 minus taxes of $11,200). This would bring their combined annual income after taxes, medical, and retirement contributions to $82,400, which is still below the low end of their lifestyle of $96,000.

So here's what we have at this point: a business with an extremely low net profit margin and a lifestyle that is above the couple's means. Before leaping to the ultimate conclusion of unreported cash, I wanted to close one more loop: their debt situation and any inheritances. It is possible that the couple is living this lavish lifestyle purely on debt or an inheritance. Mrs. Doe indicated that their only sources of income are from her job and her husband's business. There is no inheritance that they received, and they have very little to no debt, as her husband insisted on paying all debts before the due date to avoid late fees or additional interest charges.

The conclusion at this point was that something fishy was definitely going on and potentially something to which Mrs. Doe was unaware.

3. Ask more probing questions. My next line of questions pertained to Mrs. Doe's involvement in preparing the business and personal tax returns. She indicated that, while she handled the expenses, she had no access to the business activities or returns and that her husband handled their personal tax return. Mr. Doe would bring the return to Mrs. Doe each year, asking her to sign the return so he could file it with the IRS. I then proceeded to ask her whether her husband brought home cash at any time during the marriage. According to Mrs. Doe, every week her husband would come home with an envelope full of cash. Mrs. Doe recalled that, when times were good and she was privy to this information, the weekly amount would range from anywhere between $2,000 and $3,000. That's an annual average of $104,000 to $156,000. One can see that, even on the low end, this would cover their lifestyle gap.

4. Do a sanity check. Just as a sanity check to see whether this could be in the realm of reasonableness, we looked to see what the impact would be on the profit margin of the business if the above potential revenues were added back and then tax affected at the corporate level (Exhibit 1).

This helps to show that it is possible that Mr. Doe is pocketing cash without reporting it because, had he reported it, his profit margin would fall right in line with his peers. Right or wrong, it is a fact that cannot be ignored at this point.

Exhibit 1. Impact of Potential Missing Revenue

Revenues	$2,400,000	$2,400,000	$2,400,000
Net income before tax	$60,600	$144,000	$196,000
Tax rate	34%	34%	34%
Net income after tax	$40,000	$95,000	$129,400
Net income before tax (%)	2.53%	6.00%	8.17%
Net income after tax (%)	1.67%	3.96%	5.39%

5. Get the proof. The only question is how we would prove this to the courts. The courts can't rely on Mrs. Doe's word that cash would come in weekly, especially when it was obvious that Mr. Doe would not admit to it because it represents income that he concealed from the IRS. In addition, if he admitted that it existed, it would cause a potential increase in the alimony that he would potentially be paying out to his soon-to-be ex-wife.

We've hit a road block and now need to come up with a way to proving this income existed and helped sustain their lifestyle.

Exhibit 2. Surveillance of Restaurant Customer Count					
June 9, 2012 Saturday		June 11, 2012 Monday		June 13, 2012 Wednesday	
Time	Take Out	Time	Take Out	Time	Take Out
1 p.m.	35	3 p.m.	25	11 a.m.	6
2 p.m.	32	4 p.m.	17	12 p.m.	49
7 p.m.	31	5 p.m.	30	1 p.m.	50
8 p.m.	24	6 p.m.	26	2 p.m.	27

After some careful consideration, I approached our attorney and came up with a potential solution. It is important to note that the below analysis was time-consuming and costly, which is why I had approached the attorney first with not only the potential solution, but also the estimated costs and a cost-benefit ratio so the attorney could make a well-informed decision on whether or not it was worth proceeding. The solution was a two-pronged test that would help to quantify any potential unreported income: (1) surveillance of the restaurant; and (2) examination of the books and records and contact with vendors.

For the first test, we wanted to see how many customers would come and go over a period. We selected a two-week period as our test period. This test period, while after the valuation date, was done to give us a comfort level of whether or not it was worthwhile to proceed with this line of thinking, as well as to demonstrate to the court why we needed not only full access to the books and records, but also permission to contact key vendors. During this phase of the test, either I or one of my associates would sit outside of the pizzeria (without the owner knowing) and physically count the people that came and went on any given day in one-hour intervals. Exhibit 2 has a sample of this analysis.

For those who took out, we counted the number of pizza boxes that left the store and the number of paper bags. To the extent that we could determine the approximate number of meals in each bag, we would made note of that. Please note that sometimes a pizzeria will put the meals in a box and not a bag. So, to that extent, we felt our estimate was conservative because a typical meal cost more than a typical pizza. Exhibit 3 contains a sample of this analysis.

By doing this surveillance over a two-week period, we were able to get a sample of the type of business that the pizzeria has in order to try and extrapolate that over a one-year time span. We

Exhibit 3. Estimation of Take-Out Food											
June 9, 2012 Saturday				June 11, 2012 Monday				June 13, 2012 Wednesday			
Time	Boxes*	Slices**	Meals**	Time	Boxes*	Slices**	Meals**	Time	Boxes*	Slices**	Meals**
1 p.m.	18	28	20	3 p.m.	3	8	15	11 a.m.	8	6	2
2 p.m.	8	37	27	4 p.m.	6	21	32	12 p.m.	6	41	37
7 p.m.	10	27	24	5 p.m.	12	31	19	1 p.m.	12	37	29
8 p.m.	6	21	16	6 p.m.	8	27	22	2 p.m.	2	22	17

* Boxes were assumed to be a full pie
** Estimated based on the shape of the bag

Exhibit 4. Estimated Revenues

	Observed 2 weeks	Estimated 1 year	Average Price	Estimated Revenues
Meal	3,640	94,640	$20.00	$1,892,800
Pizza slice	4,284	111,384	$3.25	$361,998
Pizza pie	1,386	36,036	$15.00	$540,540
Estimated revenues				$2,795,338

felt that the two-week time span was enough to help account for anomalies and determine a more accurate base level. The next step in this analysis was to determine the average price per meal, the average price per pizza slice, and the average price per whole pizza pie. These prices were then applied to the number of customers that we observed. Based on the review of the menu, the average meal price was around $20, the average price per pizza slice was $3.25, and the average price per whole pie was around $15. Using these amounts and the data we collected and analyzed, we were able to estimate the revenues for our subject business (see Exhibit 4).

Based on this limited test, we were able to demonstrate the possibility of unreported sales, especially given the fact that we did a two-week period in June, which does not include the peak season of Lent, nor did it account for times when the restaurant is slower such as a bad storm. Our attorney went to the courts and requested an extended discovery period, which included all pertinent invoices and permission to contact all pertinent vendors.

The court approved our request, so we could continue our investigation.

We asked Mr. Doe for all invoices for the period that covered Jan. 1, 2009, through Sept. 30, 2012. We informed him that we wanted to see every expense related to the vendors that supplied: (i) the boxes for take-out; (ii) the aluminum tins for meals; and (iii) paper plates. It turned out that the vendor that supplied the pizza boxes also supplied the aluminum tins, so we only had to focus on two vendors. You might ask why these vendors were an area of focus. The answer is that these vendors will allow us to determine the estimated sales of the restaurant from the angles of whole pizza pie sales, meal sales, and individual slice sales.

Once we had the invoices, we created three databases, each listing the invoice date, the quantity purchased, and the price per purchase. Our major concern at this point was

Exhibit 5. Analysis of Supplies Inventory

Pizza Boxes				
	2009	2010	2011	Sept. 30, 2012
Starting inventory	-	1,500	1,500	1,500
Purchases	36,200	37,200	38,500	29,700
Sales	34,700	35,700	37,000	28,200
Ending Inventory	1,500	1,500	1,500	1,500
Plates				
	2009	2010	2011	Sept. 30, 2012
Starting inventory	-	10,000	10,000	10,000
Purchases	114,700	117,900	122,000	94,200
Sales	104,700	107,900	112,000	84,200
Ending Inventory	10,000	10,000	10,000	10,000
Aluminum Tins				
	2009	2010	2011	Sept. 30, 2012
Starting inventory	-	2,500	2,500	2,500
Purchases	94,200	96,800	100,200	77,400
Sales	91,700	94,300	97,700	74,900
Ending Inventory	2,500	2,500	2,500	2,500

that Mr. Doe withheld invoices from us to indicate that his restaurant was not doing the level of business we thought. So, with the assistance of our attorney, we contacted the vendors directly. Once we received the copies of the invoices from the vendor, we compared them to the database we previously created from Mr. Doe's records, and any invoices that were missing were added to the database. We now had a comfort level; we had all sales made to Doe Pizzeria during this three-year period (unless the vendor was in cahoots with Mr. Doe).

The next step was to perform an inventory count of the pizza boxes, aluminum tins, and paper plates as of the current date, which was July 15, 2013. I assumed that any purchases made between the valuation date of Sept. 30, 2012, to the current date were sold. This would mean that in essence the current ending inventory would approximate the ending inventory at the valuation date. I then assumed that the inventory at the start of our analysis, Jan. 1, 2009, was zero. This was done as we did not have the records going back to properly determine the actual inventory at our starting point. We did an analysis of the physical purchases made each year and an estimated inventory that approximated what we counted as of Sept. 30, 2012 (see Exhibit 5).

The next step was to determine the estimated revenues for the years 2009 through 2011 and the nine months ending Sept. 30, 2012. To do this, we did three simple calculations: (1) average price per pizza pie multiplied by the estimated boxes sold; (2) average price per meal multiplied by the estimated number of aluminum tins sold; and (3) average price per slice multiplied by the number of plates sold.

The final step was to account for waste, which consisted of lost items, items in which staff took extra food home at the end of the night, and damaged items. We assumed 15% was a reasonable amount to estimate as waste. Exhibit 6 is our reconstruction of estimated revenues.

Upon the completion of the above test, we were able to quantify the potential unreported

Exhibit 6. Reconstruction of Estimated Revenues

	Sales	Average Price	Estimated Revenues
2009			
Meal	91,700	$20.00	$1,834,000
Pizza slice	104,700	$3.25	$340,300
Pizza pie	34,700	$15.00	$520,500
Estimated revenues			$2,694,800
2010			
Meal	94,300	$20.00	$1,886,000
Pizza slice	107,900	$3.25	$350,700
Pizza pie	35,700	$15.00	$535,500
Estimated revenues			$2,772,200
2011			
Meal	97,700	$20.00	$1,954,000
Pizza slice	112,000	$3.25	$364,000
Pizza pie	37,000	$15.00	$555,000
Estimated revenues			$2,873,000
Sept. 30, 2012			
Meal	74,900	$20.00	$1,498,000
Pizza slice	84,200	$3.25	$273,700
Pizza pie	28,200	$15.00	$423,000
Estimated revenues			$2,194,700

Exhibit 7. Estimate of Potential Unreported Revenue				
	2009	2010	2011	Sept. 30, 2012
Reported revenues	$2,450,000	$2,523,500	$2,599,205	$2,007,900
Estimated revenues	$2,694,800	$2,772,200	$2,873,000	$2,194,700
(Underreported)/Overreported revenues	($244,800)	($248,700)	($273,795)	($186,800)

revenues, which equaled our calculated revenues less the revenues reported on the tax return. For the years at issue, this is close to $1 million (Exhibit 7).

We presented our findings to our attorney who felt it best to schedule a meeting with all parties.

Just desserts. At the meeting, we presented the facts and we were initially given a lot of push back from our opponent. First, there was total denial, and then the allegation that our calculations and analysis must be flawed. That was the end of the meeting, and we felt we hit a dead end. But then, about a week later, I received a call from our attorney, who said that the other side wanted another meeting. It was at this meeting that the other side conceded to the unreported income and did not want to go to trial. After settling on terms, we walked away with a very favorable outcome for our client.

In this case, questioning the veracity of the financials made all the difference. A good dose of skepticism can usually cure a case of bias in information you receive from management or other third parties.

***Pasquale Rafanelli,** CPA/ABV, ASA, CVA, CBA, CFE, MAFF, is valuation manager at Grassi & Co., a firm with offices in the New York City metropolitan area that specializes in accounting, auditing, tax, technology, and business consulting services. He has over 10 years of valuation experience and focuses on appraisals of interests in privately held companies for marital dissolutions, estate and gift purposes, shareholder dissolutions, buy/sell transactions, M&A, and litigation support. He can be reached at PRafanelli@grassicpas.com.*

Do You Share Business Valuation's 'Dirty Little Secret'?

Recent developments have put the spotlight squarely on projected financial information (PFI). The perception is that too many valuation experts simply accept projections and forecasts they're given without applying enough scrutiny—or any scrutiny at all. Fortunately, there is some new guidance on how to examine and substantiate PFI you get from management or other third parties.

Watch out. "Projections are valuation's dirty little secret," says Jim Hitchner (Financial Valuation Advisors Inc.). Hitchner and Harold Martin (Keiter) conducted one of the most popular sessions at the last AICPA FVS conference titled "How to Detect a Rigged Valuation." They stressed that appraisers must not simply accept the projections the client provides, plug them into a discounted cash flow analysis, slap on a discount rate, and be done with the analysis.

While there are other ways to manipulate a valuation (e.g., through the discount rate or growth rate), the PFI can be particularly troublesome. Hitchner warns that clients, knowing that the appraiser applies a discount rate, may manipulate their projections accordingly. Similarly, clients may change projections in anticipation of litigation. A "good appraiser" performs an independent review and keeps a record of his or her questions to management and the resulting changes, the speakers advise.

New spotlight. The architects of the Fair Value Quality Initiative (FVQI) have recognized the concern over PFI in their development of the new credential for fair value for financial reporting.[1] During a recent BVR webinar,[2] Anthony Aaron, chair of the Performance Requirements Work Stream of the FVQI, pointed out that there is a section on "professional skepticism" in the new set of best practices for appraisers doing fair value work. These best practices, known as the Mandatory Performance Framework[3] (MPF), lay out the requirements for documenting the extent of the work done during a fair value engagement.

During the webinar, an attendee asked: "Is there any area addressed in the MPF where valuation specialists may have been particularly lax?" The questioner suggested that one area is possibly the

1 Certified in Entity and Intangibles Valuation, or CEIV (www.ceiv-credential.org).

2 Promoting Quality in Providing Fair Value Measurements for Financial Reporting, BVR webinar, Feb. 22, 2017 (www.bvresources.com/pastevents).

3 Available at www.ceiv-credential.org.

scrutiny of management projections and noted that the MPF has a section on professional skepticism. Aaron confirmed that there is a perception that too many projections have been accepted without applying an appropriate level of skepticism. He made it clear that he is not suggesting that everyone just accept projections mindlessly or that anyone does so, but the perception is there.

"I think personally, the emphasis on skepticism is not just in the valuation field but more broadly in the audit area," said Aaron, who had a long career in business valuation at Ernst & Young and is now an adjunct professor with the Leventhal School of Accounting at the University of Southern California. "And it's an area that regulators are concerned about. I think that the potential for bias to creep into our analysis is something that we always have to be on guard for and concerned about."

He also noted that some valuation professionals may say, "Well, I don't have to do it because the auditors are going to do it." But he points out that the auditor's role is not to examine the PFI, but rather to review the work that the third-party specialist has done to make sure that it's appropriate. The valuation expert's job is to analyze the PFI and make sure that it's appropriate. But it is not enough to simply think about and apply your judgment and say: "This is how I'm going to apply a particular valuation method." You need to write it down to memorialize it. Aaron recalls an axiom in auditing standards that says: "If you didn't write it down, you didn't do it."

PFI assessment. There are several general considerations when evaluating PFI, which can be boiled down to four questions you should be asking:[4]

- Does the forecast correspond to internal budgets or external forecasts by stock analysts?
- Is the current forecast consistent with previous forecasts?
- Do the assumptions in the forecast appear reasonable in relation to historical performance?
- Do the assumptions in the forecast appear reasonable in relation to performance of guideline companies or assets?

The recently finalized MPF takes these general considerations and crafts a series of best practices that get more into the specifics. While this is designed specifically for fair value engagements, the concepts are applicable in other situations where PFI comes into play. We summarize here the factors and common procedures to consider, but note that the MPF says that this list is not necessarily all inclusive.

1. *Compare the PFI for an underlying asset of the subject entity to expected values of the cash flows.* The evaluation of any differences between PFI and expected cash flows should be thoroughly documented in the work file.

4 AICPA Fair Value Measurements Workshop, March 2017 (New York, N.Y.) conducted by Mark Zyla (Acuitas).

2. *Examine the frequency of preparation.* Does management regularly prepare forecasts? If so, they are likely to be consistent and meaningful.

3. *Measure prior forecasts against actual results.* This will help assess whether management's forecasts tend to be optimistic, conservative, or just generally inaccurate.

4. *Do a mathematical and logic check.* Common errors include inaccurate cell references, simple summation errors, use of improper functions, and many others.

5. *Compare to historical trends.* The PFI should be compared to historical information and trends focusing on items such as revenue growth, decline, or variability; various levels of profitability; and levels of specific items (such as sales and marketing expense).

6. *Match up to industry expectations.* Analyze the PFI relative to the economy, industry, and other external data.

7. *Check for internal consistency.* Evaluate whether all of the metrics used in the analysis are collectively consistent with each other. For example, if a PFI has an aggressive growth rate and improving margins but also shows significant reduction in sales and marketing expenses, this would not be consistent.

Work file checklist. To demonstrate that an appropriate assessment of PFI was done, the MPF requires, at a minimum, that certain items be documented *in writing* within the work file. The accompanying sidebar presents a checklist of what the work file must contain with regard to PFI.

Work File Checklist: MPF Requirements for Documenting the Assessment of Prospective Financial Information

The valuation professional, at a minimum, must document the following in writing within the work file, if applicable:

☑ Identification of who was responsible for preparation of the PFI;

☑ A description of the process used to develop the PFI from the perspective of market participants;

☑ The explanation of key underlying assumptions used in the PFI such as revenue forecasts, percentage of market share captured by the entity, or how the projected profit margins compare to those of other market participants;

☑ The steps used in testing the PFI for reasonableness and the results of the testing, including, but not limited to:

- A comparison of the PFI to expected cash flows;

Continued on next page

- A comparison of the PFI to historical performance;
- A comparison and evaluation of prior year's PFI against actual historical results (when prior PFIs are available); and
- An analysis of the forecast relative to economic and industry expectations.

☑ An analysis of any evidence that contradicts management's assumptions or conclusions used in its PFI;

☑ The rationale for any adjustments made to management's PFI;

☑ Evidence that a mathematical and logic check was performed; and

☑ The components of the prospective balance sheet and cash flow statements, if available

(Source: Summarized from the Application of the Mandatory Performance Framework for the CEIV; www.ceiv-credential.org).

It's important to note that CEIV credential holders must submit a work file periodically for a quality control review to the organization that issued the credential. The work file will be reviewed for compliance with the MPF. Auditors or an outside agency may also hold practitioners without the credential to these standards. Therefore, the MPF is relevant for everyone doing fair value work.

Attorney's Slant on Three Methods to Estimate Personal Goodwill

A family law attorney as well as several top valuation experts recently provided interesting perspectives on the allocating of enterprise and personal goodwill.[1] Discussed were a twist on the excess earnings method, the new concept of "pure" personal goodwill, the strengths and weaknesses of the multiattribute utility model (MUM), and a new residual method based on the purchase price allocation concept.

Modified excess earnings. Jim Alerding (Alerding Consulting LLC) discussed a modified version of the excess earnings method that he used as the expert in an Indiana divorce case, *Burnett v. Burnett*[2] (unpublished). Alerding successfully applied an "excess compensation" method to value the husband's interest in an anesthesiology practice's enterprise goodwill.

The husband was one of nearly 70 partners in an anesthesiology practice who owned an equal number of shares and executed a covenant not to compete. The firm billed its services according to rates published by a trade association (the American Society of Anesthesiologists) and paid its practitioners based on their comparative units of productivity. For the two years prior to divorce, the husband's productivity ranked between the 75th and 90th percentiles of the association's rates. At the same time, his earnings exceeded the 90th percentile of anesthesiologists in a national survey of medical compensation (MGMA).

At trial, Alerding (the expert for the wife) used the excess earnings method, but he did not calculate the husband's excess earnings by comparing them to the median or average earnings of an anesthesiologist because it would have yielded the husband's total goodwill, both personal and enterprise. Instead, Alerding calculated the husband's excess earnings by using the difference between his actual earnings and an anesthesiologist earning at the 90th percentile in MGMA statistics. From this analysis, he concluded that all of the goodwill was enterprise, rather than personal, and was therefore subject to division.

1 Enterprise vs. Personal Goodwill: Case Studies With Legal Insights, BVR webinar, March 2017 (www.bvresources.com/pastevents).

2 *Burnett v. Burnett*, 2012 Ind. App. Unpub. LEXIS 1477 (Nov. 13, 2012).

The trial court adopted Alerding's value, and the husband appealed, arguing that the analysis failed to exclude personal goodwill as required by Indiana law. The appellate court disagreed, stating:

> We are clearly able to determine from the [evidence] what portion of the aggregate value given by [the expert] was attributable to the husband's personal goodwill, that is, none. [The expert's] method of calculating the value of the husband's interest in [the practice] excluded the husband's personal goodwill, and left only … enterprise goodwill.

Even though the *Burnett* case is unpublished, it still serves as good instruction on what courts will accept as reliable evidence of valuing the goodwill of professional practices in divorce, particularly in the application of the excess earnings method by the expert.

Attorney comments. Michael Berger (Berger Schatz) is a family law attorney who represents professionals and high net worth individuals in divorce actions involving complex issues including the segregation of personal and enterprise goodwill interests. "I believe from my experience that this methodology seems like a reasonable approach," he says. While there is not much specific support for it, the excess compensation method "does fall from or result from an excess earnings type of methodology, which is generally accepted in many states."

However, he points out a problem with this as well as all of the methods: They are all "incredibly subjective." Taking the present value of expected earnings in excess of average earnings for a comparable individual within the same industry and then adjusting for risk is an art, not a science. "But it requires a similarly situated professional, the value of the ownership interest, in a similar value of interest in the tangible and intangible assets."

Plus, the "devil is in the detail," he says. "Anytime a business valuator is going to rely on a survey, the survey is only as good as the information requested assuming the answers are truthful and the data collected." A lawyer would review the MGMA survey data and see that the pool of doctors who responded was approximately one-tenth of 1% to 3% of all anesthesiologists in the U.S. without regard to being board certified or whether they had a single or multiple specialty as part of their practice. "In dealing with this technique, it seems to me that a lawyer could create serious doubt as it relates to the survey," he says. Questions the expert could be asked are:

- Did you as the expert have access to the actual responses?
- Were the questions that were contained in the survey complete enough for you to come to a meaningful conclusion?
- Do you even know who completed the questionnaire? Many professionals don't do this work themselves, so they will have an assistant do it. So who really did the response?

Berger suggests that getting the actual names of the responding doctors if possible and then explain and receive redacted copies as you go through this methodology would result in a court being more inclined to accept it.

Three Parts of Goodwill

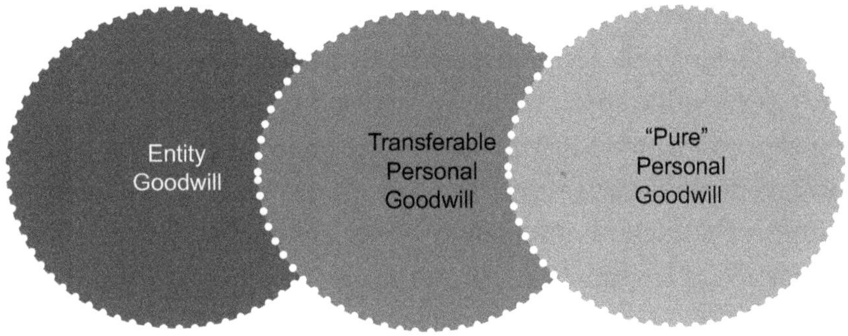

Source: Copyright R. James Alerding (used with permission)

Pure goodwill. Of course, unlike the *Burnett* case, there will be cases where personal goodwill does indeed exist. But Alerding points out that it's not enough to simply allocate goodwill between enterprise and personal—you need to split out the personal goodwill into two components: (1) transferrable personal goodwill; and (2) "pure" personal goodwill. Therefore, overall goodwill consists of three parts, not two, as per the traditional definition (see the exhibit).

The concept of transferrable goodwill reared its head in a litigation setting when the Wisconsin Court of Appeals broke new ground in divorce law when it held that all the *salable* personal goodwill in a professional practice (as evidenced by a noncompete agreement) is a divisible marital asset. The husband appealed, and, in *McReath,*[3] the state Supreme Court affirmed, ruling that a trial court "shall" include salable professional goodwill in the divisible marital estate. It specifically rejected the then-current majority rule, reasoning that "some courts" follow that rule, but the "premise on which the distinction is grounded—that enterprise goodwill is salable and personal goodwill is not salable—is mistaken."

Attorney comments. The concept of transferrable or salable goodwill is an "incredibly important and interesting topic," says Berger. But he is not familiar with this concept being addressed where he practices (Illinois) or in any other divorce situation other than the *McReath* case. What's more, it has never been cited by any other case, not only in Wisconsin, but in any other case in the United States, he points out. And it is the only case to acknowledge that some personal goodwill is salable and transferable.

"Notwithstanding the Wisconsin opinion, I truly believe that it is an area that should be further discussed and brought to the courts' attention in every jurisdiction," he says. "I would say that the *McReath* case is very unique not only from my perspective as to the set of facts, but it is a strict interpretation of Wisconsin statute regarding to what is includable and what is not includable in the marital estate."

3 *McReath v. McReath*, 2011 WL 2706249 (July 12, 2011).

MUM approach. During his section of the workshop, Ron Seigneur (Seigneur Gustafson LLP CPAs) described the multiattribute utility model (MUM),[4] which has been accepted in court.[5] MUM is an analytical framework under which various attributes of the individual and enterprise are examined, scored, and weighted. Seigneur notes, importantly, that MUM has been used for many years in other contexts, such as scientific applications, so it wasn't something totally new. David Wood, a business valuation expert, adapted MUM for use in a goodwill context. In the 2006 *Alexander* case, the appellate court accepted Wood's testimony as acceptable under *Frye* but did its own math and came up with a different allocation of personal versus enterprise goodwill that it felt was more appropriate in the particular circumstance.

In the *Alexander* case, Wood described his approach as scientific but acknowledged that the whole process is subjective. MUM is used simply to try to make a precise decision from imprecise and subjective criteria. "I can't overemphasize that because it seems like folks are always looking for the Holy Grail of how we calculate unsystematic risk or how we make the subjective determinations that we make," says Seigneur. "I don't think we will ever get there, but having a framework that helps you to tee up and explain and articulate your thought process can be very useful to a trier of fact. I think that is what we are talking about in the application of MUM in this type of application."

Attorney comments. "While I respect the hard work that Mr. Wood did in connection with MUM, I see it very much the same as Ron, which is as a framework," says Berger. "To me, it is not a methodology but rather it is something that is useful for business valuators to concern themselves with insofar as each and every attribute as well as others that are captured in this particular model."

Any reasonably good lawyer could "rip this methodology into shreds," he says, predicating his statement on Wood's own testimony in the *Alexander* case. Wood acknowledged that the attributes could be described as opposite sides of the same coin and that one valuator could attribute the same category to personal and another valuator could attribute the same category to enterprise goodwill. Still, it is a "great framework to make sure that you have done due diligence and to be able to explain how you arrived at your ultimate opinion after reviewing each and every one of these types of attributes of an asset."

While the workshop's speakers and the attorney praised the method, they felt that, in some cases, it may be better to use the MUM framework in a more simplified way. For example, instead of using a 1-to-5 scoring scale for each attribute of goodwill, a plus-or-minus indicator could be used. Then you wouldn't get a pointed question such as: "Why did you choose a '3' and not a '4'?"

Residual method. During the workshop, a new methodology was described by Harold G. Martin Jr. (Keiter, Stephens, Hurst, Gary & Shreaves PC), who said his firm has used this method in divorce cases. The residual method is analogous to a purchase price allocation for tax purposes or

4 See "'MUM's the Word'™: A Formal Method to Allocate Blue Sky Value in Divorce," *Business Valuation Update*, March 2007.

5 For example, in *Lieberman v Lieberman*, Case No. FD-2008-956 (Tulsa, Okla.), Judge Funderburk presiding, the expert witness relied on the Illinois case *In re Marriage of Alexander* (2006 Ill. App. Lexis 836) to defend against a *Daubert*-like challenge.

the acquisition method for financial reporting purposes. After determining the business enterprise value, you allocate value to the tangible assets and then to the specifically identifiable intangibles such as trade names, customer lists, employment contracts, trade secrets, etc. While the assembled work force is not separately reportable as an intangible, value must also be allocated to this asset for purposes of determining contributory charges. After making the allocations to the tangible and specifically identifiable intangible assets, the resulting residual value equals the value of total goodwill. You then allocate value to personal goodwill based on analysis of the facts and circumstances. For example, one of the key characteristics in determining the existence of personal goodwill is whether or not a professional's customers would follow him or her if the professional were to leave the business. Another key consideration is whether or not a noncompete agreement exists. If such an agreement exists, it would effectively result in the transfer of transferable personal goodwill to the entity. After allocating value to personal goodwill, any remaining value equals the value of entity goodwill.

Although Martin's firm has used this method, he notes that there has not yet been a case where there is a published court opinion. He also points out that it may be a costly process, depending on the number and complexity of the intangible assets to be valued. Also, there could potentially be overlap in certain of the specifically identifiable intangibles and personal goodwill, especially customer relationships. Therefore, if you are going to apply this approach, make sure you have considered this issue.

Attorney comments. "I think from my perspective that there are many things about this method that are supportable," says Berger, speaking from a lawyer's vantage point. For example, he observes that some of the process is rooted in the accounting and financial reporting rules. "Going to the fundamental concept that all business valuation is an art and not a science, this method probably has a little more science than some of the others."

The valuation methodologies required to perform purchase price allocations for tax purposes and the acquisition method for financial reporting are extremely complex, so there's an issue with explaining and communicating this in an understandable way. Martin acknowledged that you need to present it at a level that is understandable to the trier of fact, but you also have to be able to have the supporting detail in order to demonstrate that you have done the appropriate analysis and haven't simply made assumptions or relied totally on management. You must show that you have done enough homework to be able to support the positions that you have taken.

Berger also pointed out that this method could be incredibly expensive to develop. Alerding agreed and said that this is probably a methodology that would require a larger case in most situations. Small businesses often wouldn't have a lot of these identifiable intangible assets, he points out, and the cost of doing the analysis will be fairly high. "That is not to say that it is not a good method—it is just saying to take into account that you will need to do a lot of work to support this. It may or may not be possible in the case you are doing." Martin agreed and also pointed out that, since there has yet to be a published case on this, his firm also uses alternative methods, such as the excess earnings approach.

Berger urged Martin to try to get this method out into the valuation world for interpretation and feedback. In future issues of *Business Valuation Update,* we will bring you details of this method as well as further analyses of the other approaches.

Recent Developments Trigger a Fresh Look at DLOM

In the field of business valuation, there is no consensus as to an overall approach in reaching a conclusion as to a discount for lack of marketability (DLOM). Practitioners focus on a lot of individual procedures, and there is debate over these methods. For example, some argue that using restricted stock data is the only valid method, but others disagree and opt for a specific computational method.

Recent news. The latest BVR survey on DLOM does not signal any tidal shift in the specific methods used in practice. Restricted stock studies and pre-IPO studies remain the most cited methodologies for quantifying a DLOM. Three-quarters (76%) of respondents say they use restricted stock studies, and 43% say they rely on pre-IPO studies. The use of option price models has gained steam. The Finnerty model is used by 20% of respondents, which is up 9% from the last survey (2013). The Longstaff model saw similar gains (13% versus 6% in 2013), and the Chaffee model saw a slight increase (10% versus 9% in 2013).

There is also a new resource: *The Discount for Lack of Marketability Guide* and Toolkit by Jim Hitchner, Jim Alerding, Josh Angell, and Kate Morris (reviewed on page 389). The DLOM Guide is a very detailed and well-documented text that includes a comprehensive discussion of the current theory, empirical studies, databases, and methods (qualitative and quantitative) used to determine a DLOM.

Michael Gregory (Michael Gregory Consulting LLC; www.mikegreg.com) is also reviewing the DLOM Toolkit for NACVA's *QuickRead* publication. Gregory is a former territory manager with the IRS and was one of the authors of the IRS document "Discount for Lack of Marketability Job Aid for IRS Professionals." Although the document is from 2009, Gregory says it is still relevant today.[1]

We agree and point out that the need to determine a DLOM often arises in a federal tax situation. The IRS reviews these valuations, and it is useful to understand its thinking on DLOMs. However, we are not aware that the IRS has ever published an official position regarding its stance toward DLOM. Rev. Rul. 59-60 is silent on this issue. Rev. Rul. 77-287 discusses restricted stock transactions but provides no general guidance on the subject of DLOMs. The DLOM Job Aid is not an official

1 The IRS DLOM Job Aid is available in BVR's Free Resources section at www.bvresources.com.

IRS pronouncement. At the bottom of each page, it contains the following disclaimer: "This Job Aid is not Official IRS position and was prepared for reference purposes only; it may not be used or cited as authority for setting any legal position." However, this is a document the IRS prepared for use by its professionals, and it is useful in gaining an understanding of the IRS view regarding some issues relevant to DLOM.

Gregory has stated that the purpose of the DLOM Job Aid was to provide a consistent set of initial commentary and not to assist practitioners in preparing analyses of DLOMs. In addition, he stated that there was an IRS position for which the authors of the Job Aid could not contact the sources of the various methods discussed. The methods that were discussed were those that were elevated by request to IRS business valuators in the engineering function at the time.

Key point. The Job Aid is a 112-page document, and it did not break any new ground in the area of DLOM, but it does provide a good reference work on the IRS view of certain aspects of the DLOM. There is, however, one item that clearly stands out and is worth pointing out. On page 74 of the Job Aid, the following quote appears: "If you are approaching the question of DLOM fresh, either as a reviewer confronted with an unreasonable taxpayer position based on invalid approaches or as a valuator charged with making your own valuation discount decisions, it is often helpful to start with a basic question as relates to DLOM. That question is: 'Under the prevailing facts and circumstances and considering the nature of the interest to be valued, why is the DLOM not zero?' By enumerating the factors that would lead to a conclusion that some DLOM at all is appropriate, you will be building a framework as to how substantial a discount for lack of marketability might be reasonable. This process will give you a reality check on DLOM amounts that you might ultimately derive using some of the approaches discussed in this job aid." This quote seems to indicate a philosophy of no DLOM, which is not a neutral position. It seems that a better philosophy would be to determine what the best DLOM is in the particular situation.

The bulk of the Job Aid presents items relevant to the DLOM, which it calls approaches, and discusses background information. It also presents, from the IRS point of view, areas of focus, strengths, weaknesses, prevalence in the profession, and what the courts say.

If you are considering using an approach or article that is discussed in the Job Aid, it is useful to read what the IRS has to say about it. Another resource that describes most of the methods is *BVR's Guide to Discounts for Lack of Marketability*, by John Stockdale Sr.

The Job Aid spends a good bit of time on restricted stock analysis and pre-IPO analysis. Restricted stock studies quantify the DLOM by comparing trading prices of public company stocks with prices paid in private transactions involving restricted stock of the same company. Restricted shares are generally identical to their publicly traded counterparts, except that they're subject to a minimum holding period. Because the restriction will eventually be lifted, restricted stocks tend to be more marketable than comparable closely held stocks. Average discounts from restricted stock studies generally range from 20% to 45%.

Pre-IPO studies compare IPO prices with prices of the same stock in private transactions before the IPO. The increase in stock price before an IPO and at the time of the IPO represents the stock's relative lack of marketability. These studies may be adjusted to exclude non-arm's-length transactions, such as sales to insiders or exercises of stock options. Average discounts from IPO studies generally range from 30% to 60%.

The IRS Job Aid makes some criticisms about restricted stock and pre-IPO studies. Valuators should be particularly aware of these criticisms so that they are properly considered in developing an analysis. BVR presented several articles and webinars that address these criticisms.[2]

Another good feature in the Job Aid is a suggested Initial Information Document Request (on pages 9-11). You should be aware of the details of this and consider them relevant in performing an analysis.

Suggested procedure. In light of the debate and controversy concerning the applicability of computational methods, it is premature to suggest any best practice in the determination of DLOMs. However, we can glean from all of this discussion the following suggested overall procedure for the determination of DLOMs:

1. Determine whether a buy/sell, shareholder, or other agreement fixes the price and provides a certain market for the security.

2. A base value for the security will have been determined using standard approaches, methods, and procedures as if it were readily salable in its relevant market. The relevant market in which the base value lies and the inherent liquidity should be understood to insure determination of a consistent discount.

3. Determine a discount consistent with the base value by applying one or more computational methods. Consistency between the base and the discount would be indicated by factors, such as rate of return and volatility, that indicate consistent liquidity and are based on consistent evidence or evidence adjusted to make it consistent.

4. If available, use evidence studies in conjunction with a factor analysis as a reasonableness test. If possible, the evidence can be adjusted using the relative liquidity as indicated by the volatility.

5. Compute the value resulting from the use of the discount and also the resulting rate of return. The rate of return would be determined through use of an income approach, if conducted, or reasonable returns on the assets a private investment company holds. Compare this rate to rates on securities with a reasonable basis for comparison. Several of the

2 See, for example: FMV Responds to the IRS DLOM Job Aid, BVR webinar, Oct. 12, 2011; "Restricted Stock Studies That Back Up the DLOM" (*Business Valuation Update*, November 2013); "Is the Lingering Criticism of Using Pre-IPO Studies for DLOM Justified?" (*Business Valuation Update*, February 2014).

computational methods use the rate of return directly in determining the discount, and this step would not be relevant to these methods. This procedure is more easily performed when an income approach has been used to value the security. For holding companies, a convincing determination of a rate of return is more difficult because a unique determination of the future outlook is more difficult.

6. Adjust this value for current economic and market conditions and the expected salability of the security relative to other securities of this type.

7. Apply judgment to consider any other factors as necessary to reach a reasonable conclusion relevant to the specific situation.

Needless to say, this is an exciting time for the profession as it sees how future theoretical developments and emerging evidence and tools shed new light on the determination of the discount for lack of marketability.

Probing the Values of Professional Service Firm Brands

By Christof Binder, Capstone Branding GmbH (Germany), and Stefan Rüssli, Assessa GmbH (Switzerland)

Although marketing has become more important for accounting and advisory firms, branding is usually not a big issue. The corporate brand typically carries the name of the founders, a combination of the former names of now merged entities, or an abbreviation of the first letters of the founders. The logotype will be updated every now and then, but that's about it. However, things can sometimes change dramatically. This article discusses if, when, and why the brand names of advisory firms are valuable.

Recent skirmish. Recently, a hitherto unknown firm based in Paris appeared from nowhere in the accounting community, boldly claiming to be the legal successor of the defunct Arthur Andersen, which went out of business after the Enron scandal in 2002. By doing so, the French firm, Arthur Andersen & Co. SAS (AAC), challenged the rights to the Andersen trademark of San Francisco-based Andersen Tax LLC, which had emerged as a spin-off of the tax business of defunct Arthur Andersen under the name Wealth and Tax Advisory Services USA Inc. (WTAS). This entity adopted the Andersen name in 2014 after acquiring the rights from the inactive but still existing Arthur Andersen LLP. Andersen Tax did not intend to enter the audit business again, which was at the core of the Enron scandal.

The bizarre fight over the trademark rights became public in March 2017. A French company, Quatre Juillet Maison Blanche SAS (QJMB), domiciled somewhere in rural Brittany, had filed various trademark registrations in September 2014 for the names "Andersen" and "Arthur Andersen." These registrations were accepted, except in the U.S. where Andersen Tax opposed them. Outside the U.S., there seems to be a race to see which organization first occupies territories under the mark by acquisition, association, or licensing. AAC (which has the same president as QJMB) now operates as a franchisor of a network of accounting firms all using the Arthur Andersen name.

Certainly, lawyers and the courts will have their work cut out for them to resolve the case. Apart from this, some rather commercial details became known. Apparently, the French side had offered to sell its trademark rights to Andersen Tax for $87 million—which Andersen Tax firmly rejected. The royalty fee the French firm charged to its independent network affiliates for the use of the Arthur Andersen name is said to be 2% on revenues. These figures exemplify the dichotomy inherent in the value of brand names, in particular with professional service firms. Sometimes, there is a fight over brand names, but, sometimes, brand names are replaced and phased out. It is a question of the perspective and the options.

In relation to Andersen's former size, reputation, and revenues of $15 billion, an amount of $87 million comes close to nothing. For Andersen Tax, with revenues of $197 million, an amount of $87 million would be hard to finance for an asset that does not generate additional cash. The royalty rate of 2% would be high for Andersen Tax, considering that it would be paid on revenues that it is already generating. Faced with the choice, Andersen Tax would likely return to its former brand name, WTAS. For Andersen network franchisees somewhere in the Middle East or Asia, paying a 2% royalty for the name may be justified because the Andersen name helps to attract new clients locally, at least more than their current name does.

Two key issues. Two major issues determine the importance and value of the names of professional service firms. One is about the nature of customer relationships. If the business is recurring—such as major parts of audit, accounting, tax, and outsourced services—the name of the service firm is of minor importance. If, however, the business is rather one-time and project-based, the attractiveness of a firm's name is of major importance to secure future business. The other issue is about the specific know-how required to fulfill client mandates. If this know-how is scalable (manuals, instructions), any person can fulfill client mandates. If, however, the know-how is based more on individual skill and experience, a client will look to engage the individual expert or specialist rather than the firm.

Back in 2000, the IT consulting business of Arthur Andersen (Andersen Consulting) sought independence from the audit business, after having successfully operated since 1989 and establishing a leading global business under the Andersen Consulting brand name with annual revenues close to $10 billion. The price for the independence was to give up the Andersen name, so Andersen Consulting was rebranded Accenture in January 2001. How much was the Andersen brand name worth to Andersen Consulting? Nobody knows, but obviously not very much. The company simply dropped and replaced it. The one-time cost for the rebranding was in the area of $100 million and certainly increased marketing expenses during the years thereafter. The benefit was that it saved the firm from paying 15% of annual profits to Arthur Andersen.[1] The new branding had no negative effect whatsoever on the business; the new Accenture continued to grow steadily, even during the dot-com crisis. Apparently, the existing customer relations were strong enough to easily "survive" the new brand name.

1 US$300 million in 1999, and equaling a proxy royalty rate of 3.5% on revenues from 1997 to 1999.

Ever since its rebranding, Accenture's success story continued. Sixteen years later, in 2016, Accenture was listed on all of the four major 100 Top Global Brand rankings. Its brand value was estimated in a range from $12 billion to $23 billion and had a mean value of $15 billion.[2] It must be noted that these are noncommissioned outside-in valuations, without access to relevant internal data. Typically, these brand value rankings serve as a marketing tool to promote brand-related consulting services. We are left to wonder whether these brand value estimates for Accenture are realistic.

High interest. There seems to be a high level of public interest in the brand values of the Big Four in particular. *Economia,* the member publication of British chartered accountants, ran an article last February titled "PwC Has Most Powerful Brand of Big Four"[3] and another one in April, "EY Has UK's Fifth Most Powerful Brand."[4] Brand Finance, a specialized brand valuation consultancy, published its 2017 ranking on the world's most valuable commercial services brands in April.[5] *Australian Financial Review* commented last February under the headline "Rapid Growth of Deloitte, EY, KPMG and PwC Puts Brands at Risk."[6] The article discusses brand value of global professional service firms, including the Big Four, Accenture, and McKinsey, and the risk of brand dilution resulting from ever-increasing revenues and service range extensions.

According to Brand Finance, the brands of the Big Four plus McKinsey and Accenture enjoy the highest brand strength in their sector, resulting in brand ratings from AAA+ (PwC and McKinsey) to AA+ (Accenture) (see Exhibit 1). Considering revenues and profitability, PwC has the highest brand value, followed by Accenture. Back-solving the brand values estimated by Brand Finance under the relief-from-royalty method, we find implied royalty rates for the brand names between 4% and 5%.[7] Such royalty rates are typically found for consumer staples brands, so we have reason to doubt whether these royalty rates reasonably apply to high-end B2B services.

Reality check. Looking at real-world evidence, the Accenture case provides an insightful plausibility check. Accenture is ascribed a mean brand value of roughly $15 billion by the brand valuation firms, from revenues of $34.8 billion and a market cap of $62.8 billion in 2016. Assuming that Accenture would have to buy back its brand from somebody else because it would—hypothetically—not

2 Millward Brown/BrandZ: No. 38, $22.813 billion; Forbes: No. 42, $13 billion; Brand Finance: No. 95, $12.687 million; Interbrand: No. 37, $12.033 billion.

3 See Raymond Doherty, "PwC Has Most Powerful Brand of Big Four," *Economia,* Feb. 2, 2017. economia.icaew.com/en/news/february-2017/pwc-has-most-powerful-brand-of-big-four.

4 See Raymond Doherty, "EY Has UK's Fifth Most Valuable Brand," *Economia,* April 27, 2017. economia.icaew.com/en/news/april-2017/ey-has-uks-fifth-most-valuable-brand.

5 brandfinance.com/knowledge-centre/reports/brand-finance-commercial-services-50-2017/.

6 See Edmund Tadros, "Rapid Growth of Deloitte, EY, KPMG and PwC Puts Brands at Risk," *Australian Financial Review,* Feb. 7 2017, www.afr.com/business/accounting/rapid-growth-of-deloitte-ey-kpmg-and-pwc-puts-brands-at-risk-20170203-gu4ras#ixzz4djkVh8Yg.

7 The back-solving was performed with the MARKABLES royalty rate calculator. The main assumptions were a discount rate of 10%, a long-term growth rate of 2%, an average tax rate of 30%, and an indefinite (perpetual) useful life. No tax amortization benefit was applied, as these are value-in-use calculations of internally generated brands. www.markables.net.

Exhibit 1. Brand Finance—Top Global Professional Service Firms 2017

	Brand Rating	Revenues $ billion 2016	Brand Value $ billion 2017	Brand/ EV	Brand Royalty % on rev
PwC	AAA+	35.9	18.5	na	~5%
Accenture	AA+	34.8	17.5	30%	~4%
Deloitte	AAA	36.8	16.8	na	~4.5%
EY	AAA	29.6	13.4	na	~4.5%
KPMG	AAA-	25.4	11.0	na	~4%
McKinsey	AAA+	8.4	4.5	na	~5%

Source: Brand Finance Global 2017; royalty rates back-solved with MARKABLES royalty rate calculator.

own it, it would certainly not pay an amount of $15 billion (roughly one half of revenues). This is very reminiscent of Accenture's not wanting to continue paying for the Andersen brand when it sought its independence in 2000 and very much like Andersen Tax recently refusing to acquire the Andersen rights for $87 million.[8] Andersen Tax would rather rebrand again, pay the one-time replacement cost, and increase its advertising spending.

Using a cost-based approach, we find that Accenture reports annual advertising spending of $80 million, or 0.2% of revenues.[9] For a period of 10 years, and considering amortization effects and upcounting to the current date, the current brand value is not more than $1 billion. In contrast, Accenture spends roughly $3.5 billion annually, or 10% of revenues, on sales efforts (i.e., to acquire clients, business, and projects) and $1 billion on training. We must assume that Accenture's management understands where to invest and how to generate returns and create value. Advertising has a rather low priority. Investing 0.2% of revenues annually for advertising to obtain net returns from the brand of 3.5% on revenues (brand royalty earnings or savings) is not quite plausible.

This situation is not much different for the other firms listed in Exhibit 1. They do advertise, but their main investments go directly into customer relations and people. No doubt, these are great firms that enjoy superb reputations all over the world. They are among the best companies to work for, and their average revenues per consultant are the highest in their sectors. They certainly have strong brands. But they could easily live without them or rebrand. The brand values stated on these rankings seem to be overstated.

8 Again, roughly half of their revenues.

9 In the past, Accenture's advertising expenses oscillated between 0.2% and 0.4% of revenues.

The flexible, nonbinding approach to branding has been applied in the accounting sector for over a century. All of the top firms today were involved in mergers in the past. Each of the countless mergers resulted in one of the merged brands being dropped or a new combined brand being established. Coopers & Lybrand, Haskins & Sells, Touche Ross, Peat Marwick, Klynveld Main Goerdeler, Ernst & Whinney, or Arthur Young once were strong and established brand names. Dropping or rebranding these names certainly involved emotionally difficult discussions and decisions; commercially, keeping all of these established brand names was no alternative. Abandoning the former names proved to be more efficient and value creating, indicating that former brand names were substitutable and brand values rather insignificant.

Case evidence. There is some evidence in the business valuation field suggesting reasonable royalty rates for brand names in the professional services sector. In a marital dissolution case from 2002, the Ernst & Young brand name was valued with a 1.5% royalty rate and a useful life of five years.[10] The short useful life might be surprising, but it reflects the fact that Ernst & Young's IT consulting arm had been previously sold to Cap Gemini under a transitional brand name license for four years, the rebranding of many Arthur Andersen branches Ernst & Young took over at that time, and Ernst & Young's own rebranding history. Under these assumptions, the brand names account for 3% only of Ernst & Young's enterprise value.

Another illustrative case involves the MBO of Duff & Phelps from Webster in 2004.[11] In the purchase price allocation, the Duff & Phelps brand name was valued at less than a 1.0% royalty rate and an indefinite life assumption. During its long history, Duff & Phelps had never changed its branding nor did it merge among equals, which explains Duff & Phelps' different approach to RUL. Usually, Duff & Phelps rebranded all of its acquisitions, including S&P's valuation business, Chanin, Kinetic Partners, and American Appraisal, among others. Duff & Phelps' weak profitability and enterprise value back in 2004 explains the relatively low royalty rate of 1% for the trade name, still resulting in a brand value accounting for 25% of enterprise value.

Value driver structure. Both illustrative cases are rather specific—Ernst & Young for its limited life and Duff & Phelps for its low profitability. To develop a more profound view of brand value in the professional service sector, it helps to look at the overall business and value driver structure and at the interrelations between customer relationships and brand in particular. Accordingly, brand importance and value depends on the following characteristics:

- *Repeat business.* Some professional services are on an ongoing or recurring basis, i.e., audit, tax, accounting, outsourced services (i.e., payroll); management services (hosting, network); and monitoring services (i.e., IP management). Other services are rather one-time or project-based (advisory, corporate finance, consulting, and litigation). For the former categories, the brand name is rather unimportant. The latter involve the acquisition of new clients and

10 Valued in a marital dissolution, see *Bobrow v. Bobrow*, Hamilton County No. 29 DO1-0003-DR-166 (Indiana Superior Court).

11 Valued in a purchase price allocation, see report S-1 of Duff & Phelps Corp. filed with SEC on May 23 2007.

engagements at a much higher level and frequency; a strong reputation and brand awareness in the target audience must support such acquisition activity.

- *Degree of specialization.* Branding is typically involved to convey constant quality of the branded products or services. Some professional services are scalable, meaning they can be standardized in some way, replicated in other situations, or repeated for other clients (manuals, handbooks, and guidelines); new staff can be trained to perform such scalable services. Such scalable services include audit, tax, outsourcing, and management services. Other services are rather specialized and linked to individuals and their particular experience (experts and specialists), i.e., strategy consulting and litigation. The more scalable the services of a professional service firm, the more important is the brand.

- *Client size.* The larger an individual client and the higher its contribution to overall revenues, the more efficient the relationship with this client can be handled directly and personally. The more personal the relation, the less important is brand and brand value.

A good indicator of brand value is what happens if a key professional (a partner) leaves the firm. If the clients and the business go with him or her, it is rather a relationship business. If they stay, it is rather a firm and brand business. In any case, professional service firms rely to a much greater extent on strong customer relations than on brands.

Empirical data. Exhibit 2 provides the empirical interquartile ranges for different intangibles assets in professional service firms, depending on their business characteristics. The ratios are derived from a peer group of 18 different professional service firms valued in purchase price allocations. The sample includes audit, advisory, and law firms from three countries.

Accordingly, the average professional service firm has a price/revenue multiple of 1.7x. Its brand name is valued with a royalty rate of 1.5% over 20 years, resulting in brand value accounting for 5% of enterprise value. Customer relations with 32% of enterprise value and goodwill with 53% are considerably more important than brand. Goodwill relates to cost savings expected from the combination; to the cross-selling potential in combining territories, customer groups, and

Exhibit 2. Value Driver and Asset Structure of Professional Service Firms

	Brand Royalty Rate	Brand Useful Life	Brand/EV	Customer/EV	Goodwill/EV	Price/ Revenue
Low	0.75%	5y	2.5%	17%	42%	1.3x
High	2.50%	indef	9.0%	40%	68%	2.2x
Median	1.50%	20y	5.0%	32%	53%	1.7x

Source: Purchase price allocations 18 professional service firms; MARKABLES

service ranges; and to the ability of the acquired firm to master the future beyond the current planning horizon (in particular to create enough new business to keep the firm running at its current profit level). For professional service firms, retaining key individuals is vital for this. Any acquisition of a professional service firm must therefore include clear measures to retain key staff. In light of all this, its brand name is only "nice to have" and can be replaced rather easily, as history shows.

Although they may be highly admired firms, professional service providers are primarily acquired for their existing customer relations and goodwill and much less for their brand names.

Christof Binder, *Ph.D., MBA, is the managing director of Capstone Branding GmbH in Germany, an advisory firm specializing in trademark extensions and transactions. He is involved in the valuation of trademarks for transactional and licensing purposes.*

Stefan Rüssli, *MBA, is the managing director of Assessa GmbH in Switzerland, a boutique advisory specializing in brand asset management. His primary focus is as a brand finance advisor to the banking, investment, M&A, and accounting communities.*

Binder and Rüssli are co-founders and directors of MARKABLES, a Switzerland-based online database providing comparable data from over 9,000 published and audited trademark valuations.

Looking to Private Markets for Private Firm Cost of Capital

Some valuation experts are not comfortable with the theory that public-company data can be substituted for private value. They see some financial theory risks to the standard valuation process of applying a myriad of judgments and assumptions to convert measurable public market data into proxies for private-company valuation. The capital asset pricing model (CAPM) needs to be "modified" with a series of adjustments to the cost of capital figures derived from the public markets. Yet, this all has been implicitly sanctioned by valuation standards and by IRS Revenue Ruling 59-60, which justifies valuation methods based on data from actively traded stocks.

Equal debate. Those with the idea that private and public markets are not substitutes for one another point to a long list of reasons, such as public and private markets have different risks and returns, liquidity, access to capital, pricing mechanisms, holding periods, and transaction costs. This thinking has gained some steam over the past few years. For example, Pablo Fernandez (University of Navarra, IESE Business School) created a stir after the release of his 2014 paper, "CAPM: An Absurd Model,"[1] which generated so many comments that he issued a revised version and also published the comments as a separate paper.[2] Most of the commenters agreed with him. Also, over the past few years, an alternative to the buildup method (BUM) has been under development to value small private companies: the implied private-company pricing line (IPCPL) and its companion, the implied private-company pricing model (IPCPM). This method uses data points on private-company transactions from *Pratt's Stats* for companies with revenues from $2.5 million to $10 million.[3] IPCPL has received several favorable independent reviews.[4]

This thinking and the approaches developed are equally open to debate as the notion that private and public markets can be used as substitutes for each other. A testament to this is that the modified

1 papers.ssrn.com/sol3/papers.cfm?abstract_id=2505597.

2 papers.ssrn.com/sol3/papers.cfm?abstract_id=2523870.

3 Rod Burkert, Peter Butler, and Bob Dohmeyer, "The Implied Private Company Pricing Line," *Business Valuation Update*, September 2013, and "The Implied Private Company Pricing Model," *Business Valuation Update*, March 2014.

4 Igor Gorshunov, "IPCPL and Margin Reversion: Implications for the Valuation of Small Privately Held Companies," *Business Valuation Review*, Vol. 34, No. 2 (reprinted in *Business Valuation Update*, September 2015). See also David H. Goodman and Malcolm McLelland, "The Implied Private Company Pricing Line (IPCPL): On the Nature, Scope, and Assumptions of IPCPL Theory," SSRN (papers.ssrn.com/sol3/papers.cfm?abstract_id=2609159).

CAPM and BUM continue to be at the center of most income-based valuations. Some of the reasons could be simple inertia, a natural resistance to change, or the power of readily available, plentiful, public security market data.

Private capital markets. Business Valuation Resources has been a research sponsor of the work of the Pepperdine University Graziadio School of Business and Management and its Private Capital Markets Project. This ongoing research is designed to understand the true cost of private capital across market types and the investment expectations of privately held business owners. The project is celebrating its 10th year and represents the hard work of researchers in developing a private cost of capital method as a legitimate alternative to looking to the public markets. Their method is simply to ask private capital market players what returns they project.

The 2017 edition of their research (based on a survey deployed in January 2017) is now available.[5] The researchers divide the private capital markets into six segments aligned with the major institutional arms of the private investment world, each with different return, investment, and research characteristics:

1. Bank lending;
2. Asset-based lending;
3. Mezzanine;
4. Private equity;
5. Venture capital; and
6. Angel investors.

They are careful to stress some assumptions in their model to keep their resulting cost of capital conclusions "comparable" to the types of businesses that appraisers value. Specifically, the survey collects data on "rates of return *to the provider*" (which is different from the costs to the borrower, who has transaction and other costs). Also, "expected returns are used because capital providers offer credit and structure deals based on what they expect to receive."

It should also be noted that it is well established that the cost of capital to the borrower equals the expected returns of the provider. Cost of capital is an opportunity cost—the expected return required to tempt the provider away from alternative investments.[6]

5 Craig R. Everett,"2017 Private Capital Markets Report" (2017). Pepperdine University Graziadio School of Business and Management. http://digitalcommons.pepperdine.edu/gsbm_pcm_pcmr/10

6 Franco Modigliani and Merton H. Miller, "The Cost of Capital, Corporation Finance and the Theory of Investment," *The American Economic Review* 48, no. 3 (1958): 261-97, www.jstor.org/stable/1809766.

Of course, the cost of capital for privately held firms varies by capital type, size, and risk assumed. Pepperdine's findings in the 2017 report on the median cost of capital rates appear in the table. There is much more detail in the report itself, including first and third quartiles by different criteria such as amount of financing, EBITDA levels, and financing stage.

Type of Private Capital Funding	Pepperdine Median Rate of Return (Range)
Banks	4.0%-6.5%
Asset-based lenders	5.5%-14.0%
Mezzanine financers	10.0%-24.0%
Private equity groups	20.5%-27.5%
Venture capital investors	25.0%-35.0%
Angel investors	35.0%-60.0%

The survey also asks privately held business owners what they believe is their cost of equity. Over half (59%) of the 1,034 respondents believe their cost of equity is less than or equal to 12%. What's more, half (50%) of the respondents say it is no higher than 10% and almost a third (31%) say it is less than or equal to 8%.

We note that the majority of survey respondents had 20 employees or fewer, with 55% having no more than five employees. Also, approximately 58% of the respondent firms had annual revenues less than $1 million.

PCOC model. Pepperdine's model for identifying a specific private cost of capital (PCOC) requires adjustments, of course, just like any other cost of capital derivation. These adjustments are:

1. Determine which of the types of private capital match your subject company (all six may apply, or some subset).

2. Since a subject company is unlikely to meet the optimum requirements set by potential funders, the median expected returns above need to be subjected to a risk adjustment. For example, if a manufacturer has a lower EBITDA, its cost of capital from the private capital markets might be closer to the upper quartile rather than the median figures from the Pepperdine results.

3. Each source of capital for the subject company must be valued so that a percentage of the total capital structure for each source can be derived.

4. The PCOC is the sum of the individual percentages for each capital source.

For a full explanation of the PCOC model, the program's founders, John Paglia (Pepperdine University) and Robert Slee (Robertson & Foley), wrote several articles.[7] The program is now led by Dr. Craig Everett, who can be reached at craig.everett@pepperdine.edu.

It's not likely that CAPM and BUM will disappear anytime soon. But that doesn't mean that valuation professionals can't benefit from adding a private cost of capital analysis to their toolbox.

7 John Paglia and Robert Slee, "Private Cost of Capital Model," *Value Examiner*, March/April 2010 (businessappraisers.com/article/Slee-Paglia.pdf), and "Using the Private Cost of Capital Model," *Value Examiner*, May/June 2011 (www.robertsonfoley.com/pdf/using_the_private_cost_of_capital_model.pdf).

Tips on Handling 10 Key Issues in Bankruptcy Valuations

A number of issues have emerged that analysts will encounter when performing a valuation in a bankruptcy context. During a recent BVR webinar,[1] Robert Reilly (Willamette Management Associates) cautioned that valuation analysts who become involved in bankruptcy-related assignments should expect their work to come under a great deal of scrutiny because most of these engagements are done within a litigation or some other adversarial context. Based on his extensive experience in this area, Reilly offers his advice on how to handle the challenges valuation experts will face.

1. Limited guidance on definition of 'value.' The U.S. Bankruptcy Code doesn't define any standard of value. The closest you'll find is in Bankruptcy Code Section 506a, which states that "*value shall be determined in light of the purpose of the valuation* [emphasis added] and of the proposed disposition or use of such property, and in conjunction with any hearing on such disposition or use or on a plan affecting such creditor's interest." Analysts and legal counsel will need to look to judicial precedent to see what value definitions the courts have accepted. The trouble is, you'll still find limited guidance as to which standard of value is appropriate in which bankruptcy circumstances.

Tip. Be familiar with the relevant sections of the Bankruptcy Code and the Bankruptcy Rules, but you should not be making legal decisions. Do not hesitate to ask for legal instructions from counsel with regard to any bankruptcy-related legal issues.

2. Hindsight is discouraged. The use of hindsight is an issue with most all valuations, but it's particularly controversial in a bankruptcy context. This is because everybody knows what actually happened to the debtor company (it filed for bankruptcy protection), so the tendency to use hindsight is quite common. Most bankruptcy valuations use a retrospective valuation date because there's a specific historical event that triggered the distress, such as a dividend payment or a financing transaction. There is usually controversy over when the actual debtor company events would have been known or knowable.

Tip. The courts seem to adopt the known or knowable rule, Reilly says. You should consider only that information that was known or knowable as of the time of the valuation date.

1 Robert Reilly, Advanced Bankruptcy Valuation, BVR webinar, April 28, 2017; available at bvresources.com/pastevents.asp.

3. Reliance on management projections. In a bankruptcy context, it is not uncommon for debtor company management to prepare various financial projection versions. One version could be prepared for the debtor board, one for the debtor's bank, one for a potential acquirer, and maybe others. In this case, you should perform sufficient due diligence regarding these projections to conclude which version is most appropriate for the purpose and objective of the bankruptcy valuation. If possible, you should avoid relying on projections prepared after the bankruptcy litigation is filed. Even if such post-petition filing projections are perfectly reasonable, some party in interest may allege that the projections are biased and litigation-driven. Also, try to learn who prepared the projections and whether those individuals were qualified to do it.

Tip. If you say that you relied on management's projections, be prepared for this question from the judge: "So these projections were prepared by management. This is the same management team that led this company into bankruptcy today. Why are you relying on this management team again? Obviously, they didn't do a very good job of managing the company." Good point, and that's probably right, but that may be the most reliable data you have available. You need to take that into consideration and be ready to explain.

4. Choice of variables. You will get questions on your selection of individual valuation variables. A few examples: Do the individual variables really reflect the current state of the debtor company as of that valuation date, or do they reflect the reorganized state of the company? How do you consider the current financial condition of the company when coming up with a cost of debt, cost of equity, debt equity mix, and so forth? How do you consider the current condition of the debtor company when coming up with an expected long-term growth rate?

One question in particular to think about is this: Should the selected discount rate relate to the business risk of the debtor company or to the performance risk of the specific set of financial projections? There is performance risk associated with the debtor company's financial projections. If you do not adjust the discount rate for that performance risk, any projected increase in revenue or cash flow will increase the value conclusion. But that may not be reasonable. If greater risk is inherent in the enhanced cash flow projections, then there should be a correspondingly risk-adjusted discount rate. With more aggressive financial projections, it is often appropriate to apply a larger (risk-adjusted) discount rate. And, with less aggressive financial projections, it is often appropriate to apply a lower discount rate.

Tip. Make sure you carefully document how you selected your valuation variables to show that the process was unbiased, transparent, and replicable. Be prepared to justify the quantity and quality of data elements considered in the selection of the valuation.

5. Debt interest rates. The current commercial debt interest rates may be considered unreasonably low, Reilly points out. You need to determine whether the use of such interest rates is appropriate in determining the debtor company WACC.

Tip. An unreasonably low cost of debt can understate WACC, which may overstate the debtor company value. As yourself this question: If the debtor company went out to obtain new financing today, could it actually enjoy the benefit of current relatively low interest rates?

6. Due diligence. Rest assured that you will always be questioned on the reasonableness of your due diligence. That's because you typically have limited access to financial or operational documents (troubled firms are lax in filing documents) and company management has typically moved on, so you may not even be able to talk with certain key people.

Tip. Keep in mind that "hindsight is always 20/20" and it's easy for the opposition to point out that everyone knows what really happened. So be prepared to show that you did enough due diligence to be convinced that the valuation was correct as of the valuation date.

7. Income tax effects. Income tax effects on company value are probably more relevant in a bankruptcy valuation than other types of valuations, according to Reilly. The reason is that attributes such as a net operating loss (NOL) will have a different value to the debtor company than it would to a corporate acquirer. The acquirer has to spread out the use of that NOL over many years while the subject company can use it sooner.

Tip. A change in ownership affects how the acquirer can use the debtor company income tax attributes and will affect what the asset tax basis is of the debtor company assets. Those factors should be taken into consideration, and you want to make sure you are consistent in the assumptions you made in the valuation.

8. Rules of thumb. The bankruptcy court does not look very favorably on rules of thumb, notes Reilly. If they apply at all, they may apply to an average company in that industry, but your subject company is in financial distress, so it's probably not average.

Tip. Do not use industry rules of thumb as a primary valuation method. If rules of thumb are used at all, they should be supported by actual empirical data.

9. Cash flow test. When doing a cash flow test within a solvency analysis, you should document whether you assumed the inclusion of new debt or new equity during the discrete projection period. You should also document any considerations of the debtor's current credit availability, such as whether all of the credit is used up in the cash flow projection. Also document any assumptions of any asset sales in your discrete cash flow projection.

Tip. For the cash flow test, project out to the expiration of the longest term of debt outstanding. This is to show that the company can pay off all of its long-term debt.

10. The market approach. Be very careful if you use a market approach in an inactive market, Reilly advises. You may not be able to identify sufficiently comparative guideline public companies. It's not that they don't exist, but they are probably not in the same distressed financial condition as your subject. For the same reason, you may not be able to identify sufficiently comparative guideline M&A transactions. Very large normalization adjustments may be necessary, so you'll have to decide whether it's really appropriate to apply the market approach.

Tip. Be particularly careful if you are using the backsolve method when you are looking at actual sales transactions in the debtor company securities, he cautions. If those transactions occurred some time ago, do they really represent the financial condition of the company as of the valuation date?

Before relying on the backsolve method, you should assess two factors. First, consider whether the recent debtor company transactions are actually arm's-length transactions. For example, the distressed debtor company may be willing to exchange any amount of equity to be relieved from a maturing debt obligation. Second, consider whether the debtor company's financial condition has materially deteriorated between the backsolve transaction date and the current valuation date.

Of course, this has just hit the high points of one facet of valuations in a bankruptcy context. One interesting piece of advice he gave when summing up that your valuation report should be "your best friend," available at your fingertips to help you answer every question you will face. But, to fulfill this role, your report must be clear, convincing, and cogent. It also must be replicable, transparent, and well-supported with source documents. Then you can answer every question by starting with "As I said in my report," which will heighten your credibility.

For all of the above issues, one key caveat from Reilly: Document everything including the methods and variables you used—and didn't use. Be especially thorough in documenting your due diligence. And make sure you document the projections you used because there are usually many sets of projections. Be ready to answer this question: Why did you use the projection you did?

Dual Valuation/Forensic Experience Is Best for Litigation Engagements

By Pasquale Rafanelli,
Grassi & Co. (Jericho, N.Y., USA)

When performing services for a litigation action, valuation experts are often called upon to perform forensic analysis as well. While many valuation professionals will decline and require the attorney to hire a separate forensic expert, it begs the question of whether or not this is in the best interest of the client. Ideally a valuation expert should be a master not only in valuations, but also in forensic accounting to properly carry out the responsibilities of the job holistically. This article will explain the distinct roles of valuation experts and forensic experts and how they overlap, as well as what an attorney looks for and needs in an expert he or she engages.

Business valuation. Business valuation is a specialty practice area of accounting that uses a set of procedures to estimate the economic value of an owner's interest in a business. Valuations are used to determine the price that an individual is willing to pay or receive to conduct a sale of a business and may also be used by businesses to resolve conflicts related to shareholder disputes, matrimonial actions, estate and gift taxation, allocation of business purchase price among business assets, establishment of a formula for estimating the value of partners' ownership interest for buy-sell agreements, and many other business and legal purposes.

A business valuation can be further classified as one of two types: contested or noncontested. A noncontested valuation is one performed for estate and trust, such as a buy-sell, merger and acquisition, purchase price analysis, etc. These valuations typically do not require a forensic component, and lacking this skill does not preclude properly performing the valuation.

A contested valuation is one that is typically performed in a litigation setting, for example, a shareholder dispute, a matrimonial action, or a bankruptcy, etc. As this analysis typically requires a forensic component, it either requires the valuation expert to have this skill or to outsource this responsibility to a qualified third party. In some cases, the court appoints a joint expert to perform both the business valuation and the forensic examination.

Forensic accounting. Forensic accounting, also known as financial forensics, is a practice area of accounting that describes engagements resulting from actual or anticipated disputes or litigation. The work performed will typically provide answers regarding the who, what, where, why, and how of an event based on the underlying financial records. Ultimately, it is the jurisdiction of the court or trier of fact to decide the outcome of the case and not the forensic expert.

In its simplest form, forensic means suitable for use in a court of law, and it is that standard that forensic accountants follow during the course of their examination.

Financial forensic engagements may fall into several categories such as:

- Business valuation;
- Economic damages calculations, whether suffered through tort or breach of contract;
- Post-acquisition disputes such as earn-outs or breaches of warranties;
- Bankruptcy, insolvency, and reorganization;
- Securities fraud;
- Tax fraud;
- Money laundering; and
- Computer forensics/e-discovery.

Applicable standards. AICPA Statement on Standards for Valuation Services, paragraph 13, professional competency, states the following:

> A member shall "undertake only those professional services that the member or the member's firm can reasonably expect to be completed with professional competence. Performing a valuation engagement with professional competence involves special knowledge and skill. A valuation analyst should possess a level of knowledge of valuation principles and theory and a level of skill in the application of such principles that will enable him or her to identify, gather, and analyze data, consider and apply appropriate valuation approaches and methods, and use professional judgment in developing the estimate of value."

AICPA Statement on Standards for Consulting Services, paragraph 6, professional competency, states the following:

> A member shall "undertake only those professional services that the member or the member's firm can reasonably expect to be completed with professional competence."

Based on the above standards, if a valuation expert is hired to perform any engagement that requires a forensic component, he or she must have the required competency in order to do so. If lacking, he or she must either withdraw from the engagement or refer the attorney to a qualified professional. This could become very costly due to a potential overlap of work and lack of communication between the two parties.

Attorney expectations. Business valuation experts and forensic accountant experts are often referred new clients through relationships with attorneys, especially litigators. It is crucial for these referred individuals to understand what attorneys expect and what they are looking for when hiring an expert.

These sentiments are captured in the following dialogue, which is a composite of interviews I conducted with several attorneys.

Q: *At what point do you decide to bring in either a valuation or forensic expert?*

A: The decision to bring in a valuation expert or forensic accountant expert must mean that complicated financial issues are so crucial to a case that they justify the additional expense. In other words, the benefit must exceed the costs. This is a critical part—and one I love—as I get to choose the witness who will testify or present on a critical issue.

Q: *Do you require your experts to be certified?*

A: As a result of the complexity of litigation issues, I require that my valuation expert or forensic accountant expert possess a unique set of skills. He or she must have more than just a CPA, meaning all our valuation experts and forensic experts are required to have at least one recognized credential—in fact, the more the better. The expert must wear many hats in this process, functioning as part accountant, part investigator, part lawyer, and part professor.

Q: *What is the most important characteristic you look for in an expert?*

A: In my opinion, possessing the requisite financial competence is a given. The accountant must be qualified and willing to assist the lawyer with the required financial analysis, valuation, and investigation. This includes a thorough understanding of not only the financial principles at issue, but also an understanding of the industry context in which those principles are being applied. Recognized professional certifications as well as other objective evidence of professional expertise can assist a lawyer in selecting the right expert.

Q: *What are some of the other things you look for in an expert besides his or her credentials?*

A: Besides an expert's credentials, I look for articles that he or she has written and where they were published. An expert that is published in trade journals, newspapers, and magazines, as well as industry publications, goes a long way toward showing that he or she is an expert in his or her field. I also seek to understand the nature of the topics and through which organizations the expert has presented.

Has the expert testified and, if so, where? If the expert has not testified before, it is not a deal breaker as long as he or she possesses the knowledge and skills required for the engagement. But it is a deal breaker if the expert has been excluded to testify due to a *Daubert* challenge, especially if it pertains to the same subject matter as the case I am trying.

Access to quality valuation and forensic software, as well as programming skills, is also a strong plus as the amount of potentially relevant data available in these matters continues to grow.

Q: *Fees tend to always be an issue with clients. What do you do to help keep the fees down?*

A: As I evaluate a case, if a valuation expert or forensic accounting expert is needed, I will involve him or her as early as possible. I have found this helps to streamline the process, both in terms of time and dollars spent, and to maximize the quality of the analysis. Having an expert oversee the process from the start can allow us to better request documents during deposition to ensure we get what we need to support our case.

It is critical that the two experts communicate often with lawyers to make certain everyone knows what needs to be done and how much it will cost. This is where it is critical that if the engagement is a valuation engagement the expert has both skill sets required to perform the job. Otherwise, it could become very time-consuming and costly if the two experts do not communicate well. In my opinion, this tends to not be an issue if the engagement is solely a forensic engagement, in which case I need to make sure my expert possesses the required forensic skill set, with little to no concern for the valuation skill set.

Q: *How important is communication in an engagement?*

A: This needs to be addressed during the course of the engagement and at its completion. During the engagement, the expert cannot assume that he or she knows what is required of him or her in performing his or her work to support the attorneys' case or that the attorney who hires him or her would necessarily want a given task performed.

At the completion of the engagement, the valuation expert or forensic expert must be able to communicate his or her relevant findings in a well-written report, in the boardroom, or in a court that will likely include numerous adversarial challenges to those conclusions.

A valuation expert or forensic expert must understand that he or she operates under a microscope. Therefore, he or she must understand the various stages of the litigation and investigation process to make certain that the focus remains on the quality of the analysis and presentation.

The expert must recognize and be ready to clarify with counsel any potential issues as they arise so they can be rectified early on and not cause undo problems that would create additional unwarranted billings. Most critically, the financial expert must know how to clearly and persuasively present his or her conclusions to the necessary audience in a manner that will survive challenge or cross-examination. In essence, the expert must be able to tell a believable and more importantly supportable story.

As you can see, the need for effective communication, coordination, and cooperation cannot be overstated.

Q: *Any final comments or advice you would like to give?*

A: If the expert does a good job, the results often are reflected in both the outcome and the invoice. But, if the job is done poorly, the outside professional can become part of the problem and not the solution, often with negative cost and delays in the engagement that can quickly become a client concern.

A valuation expert or forensic expert can maximize his or her chance of getting an engagement in several ways:

- Obtain the required designations for his or her practice area;
- Work to establish and maintain an impeccable reputation as a testifying expert;
- Write articles and have them published in the right venues;
- Give presentations and seminars to not only show his or her expertise in the field, but also his or her effective communication skills; and
- Join professional organizations that involve lawyers.

Conclusions. As shown throughout this article, it is critical to ensure that the valuation expert or forensic expert has the required competency before taking on an engagement and representing himself or herself as an expert. Our analysis leads us to conclude that:

- For a valuation in a litigation setting, the expert should have both valuation and forensic experience to help the engagement run smoothly and at a reasonable cost, without requiring two separate experts;
- For a valuation in a nonlitigation setting, an expert with just valuation experience will suffice; and
- For a purely forensic engagement, an expert with just forensic experience will suffice.

Pasquale Rafanelli, *CPA/ABV, ASA, CVA, CBA, CFE, MAFF, is a valuation and forensics expert and is valuation manager at Grassi & Co., a firm with offices in the New York City metropolitan area that specializes in accounting, auditing, tax, technology, and business consulting services. He has over 10 years of valuation experience and focuses on appraisals of interests in privately held companies for marital dissolutions, estate and gift purposes, shareholder dissolutions, buy-sell transactions, M&A, and litigation support. He can be reached at PRafanelli@grassicpas.com.*

Economic Obsolescence: Determining Loss of Value Caused by External Factors

By Charles Sapnas and Joseph Mickle,
Valuation Research Corp. (Princeton, N.J., USA)

Editor's note: Economic obsolescence is a topic that deserves more attention than it has been given. While the phenomenon arises regularly, it is often overlooked in a valuation analysis. Also, there is scant information on it in the main business valuation textbooks. The September 2016 issue of Business Valuation Update *includes an article by Gary Trugman on it, and we have asked the experts from VRC for their perspective, which we present here.*

Economic obsolescence (EO) is the loss of value resulting from external economic factors to an asset or group of assets. EO is often encountered in valuation work performed for financial reporting purposes, bankruptcy emergence, and in other practice areas when dealing with companies in capital-intensive industries. Identifying, measuring, and applying the adjustment for EO can be a complex and iterative process, requiring expertise and interaction across multiple valuation disciplines, including real property, personal property, business valuation, and intangible asset valuation.

Many factors may cause EO, including but not limited to:

- The economics of an industry;
- Loss of resources (material and/or labor);
- New legislation and ordinances;
- Increased cost of inputs (or the inability to pass on those costs);
- Reduced demand, increased competition; and
- Reduced earnings or margins and other factors and operating restrictions.

EO is frequently outside the scope of the owner's influence or control, and it may occur anytime in an asset's life. EO manifests itself in the profit margin of business. If the operating margin of an asset or group of assets is below what provides a sufficient economic return to the supporting assets, and there is a difference between the existing operating level/capacity and a sufficient operating/level capacity, EO may be an issue.

Estimating the level of EO. The process of identifying and measuring EO requires input from specialists in fixed asset valuation and business valuation. At Valuation Research Corp. (VRC), we most often deal with EO related to fixed assets in the context of business combinations, where the assets will be valued for financial reporting purposes pursuant to ASC 805. Ideally, the sum of the fair value of assets that comprise the subject company (e.g., net working capital + fixed assets + intangible assets (excluding goodwill)) is less than the purchase price, where goodwill will be the residual. In some cases, the initial estimate of goodwill may be negative, although the cause of this may actually be EO rather than a bargain purchase. This is especially true in fixed asset-heavy industries, where the underlying economics of the assets drive the economics of the business.

Fixed asset valuation considerations. In the initial stages of the valuation process, fixed assets are valued under an in-use premise by applying all necessary forms of depreciation (e.g., physical deterioration and functional obsolescence). The actual utility of the asset or asset group is then compared to its rated utility or capacity, which is the physical productive capacity of the facility at full operation as it exists at the time of valuation. Full utilization, depending on the type of facility or process, is generally in the range of 85% to 95% of capacity, as most facilities have some normal amount of downtime for routine maintenance, equipment changeovers, etc. If an asset is less than fully utilized, the EO adjustment would be applied directly to the asset in the determination of fair value.

If the initial view of the transaction suggests potential EO, or other business, industry, or economic factors suggest a high likelihood of EO, it is also prudent to estimate the floor value of the fixed assets subject to the potential EO indication, which is typically based on the net orderly liquidation value (NOLV), or salvage value, of the assets. Determining the floor value provides assurance that the EO is not overestimated. Generally, post-EO fair values will fall somewhere between the value in use and NOLV. However, in cases where the EO is likely to be significant, forced liquidation value (FLV) can be used to support the floor values.

If the subject entity or asset group owns real property, the appraiser must determine whether or not EO is applicable and to what components. The application of EO to real property may differ in nature from that of personal property given that the approach to value for land is based on comparable sales (which assumes a sale or orderly liquidation).

Business valuation considerations. Once the fixed assets are valued under an in-use premise (as if no EO was present), the fair value of all identified net assets (including any other assets in scope) must be reconciled to business enterprise value. Within the context of a purchase price allocation under ASC 805 or asset impairment analyses under ASC 360, asset values are initially measured discretely, and EO is potentially indicated when a purchase price or allocated enterprise value does not support the sum of discretely measured tangible and intangible asset values. If the fair value of the fixed assets plus working capital and intangible assets (excluding goodwill) fit within the purchase price or enterprise value, further refinement may not be required as one may conclude that the value of the fixed assets is reasonable. However, if the purchase price or enterprise value remains lower than the sum of the fair value of the assets or thus the initial implied value of goodwill is negative, it may suggest that further review of the fixed assets (within the continuum of NOLV to in-use fair value) and the related returns is necessary to determine the level of EO.

In the case of a single-plant, single-reporting unit company, the purchase price or enterprise value of the total company will determine EO. Exhibit 1 illustrates this simple single-unit example in which initial valuation procedures indicate that the total fair value of the acquired assets exceeds the purchase price. In this case, it is assumed for simplicity that identifiable intangibles are de minimis.

The calculations, without further examination, would suggest a negative goodwill indication. However, if it is determined that this gap exists due to a loss of value in the fixed assets arising from external factors, as opposed to transaction-specific facts and circumstances (e.g., distressed sale), it is necessary to perform additional steps related to EO in the fixed assets.

Exhibit 1. Initial Valuation (Negative Goodwill)

($ in Millions)		Book Value at Closing	Valuation Adjustments (Iteration 1)	Initial Fair Value (Iteration 1)
Net working capital		200	0	200
Personal Property	[1]	200	25	225
Buildings	[1]	100	25	125
Land		50	5	55
PP&E, Net		350	55	405
Intangible Assets		0	0	0
Net Assets		550	55	**605**
Purchase Price/EV				**575**
Implied Goodwill	[2]			**-30**

[1] Reflects the Fair Value in Use
[2} Prior to tax or purchase accounting adjustments

Once the total EO is estimated, it is often spread across the appropriate fixed assets (typically personal property and buildings) taking into account the floor values of the individual assets (Exhibit 2). This may not be an even, or pro rata, allocation across all fixed assets. As noted, EO may not be applicable to land given the market-based approach utilized to determine the fair value of land.

In certain instances involving more complex or diversified operations, it may be necessary to disaggregate total company value, reporting unit value, or purchase price among groups of assets (e.g., on an individual location or plant basis). The number of units to be considered depends upon the structure of the business and the interrelated or disaggregated nature of plants, asset groups, and reporting units. When a company has multiple plants or asset groups, it is often necessary to determine whether EO is a function of the business as a whole (and therefore applicable ratably to all fixed assets), is applicable only to specific assets or groups of assets, or whether certain assets have a higher degree of EO than other assets. The relative allocation of enterprise value to the different components of the business can be derived via a series of discounted cash flow (DCF) models, which reconcile back to the aggregate value, in consideration of the asset-specific characteristics and floor value estimates prepared by fixed asset professionals. It can be determined that certain plants have no EO as their economics fully support the in-use fair values of the individual assets, while others may have low profitability and considerable EO.

Intangible asset considerations. The identification of intangible assets should be considered when EO is present in the fixed assets. Whether or not assets such as patents/technologies, brands, and customer relationships have positive fair value in a situation where fixed assets are penalized for

Exhibit 2. Allocation of Economic Obsolescence Adjustment

($ in Millions)	Initial Fair Value (Iteration 1)	NOLV	Economic Obsolescence Adjustment	Concluded Fair Value (Iteration 2)
Net working capital	200	200		200
Personal Property	225	100	(20) - (30)	195-205
Buildings	125	50	(10) - (20)	105-115
Land	55	55		55
PP&E, Net	405	205		355-375
Intangible Assets	0	0		0
Net Assets	**605**	405		**555-575**
Purchase Price/EV	**575**			**575**
Implied Goodwill	**-30**			**0-20**

not generating sufficient returns is a rather subjective assessment that requires careful consideration of business/industry, relevant reporting units, and operations and market participant factors. In practice, intangibles are frequently assigned no value or minimal value in components of the business where significant EO is present in the fixed assets. This reflects the grouping of assets and the lowest level for which there are identifiable cash flows, as well as attribution of cash flows to fixed assets and intangible assets and the floor value of fixed assets (as described above). In other cases, customer-related intangibles or IP-related assets that could have value to other market participants may be ascribed a positive fair value. However, this can be an area of diversity in practice, which should be addressed early, as it will affect the magnitude of the EO adjustment. A market participant perspective, both qualitatively and quantitatively, is critical to determining the fair value of the assets with appropriate attribution of EO.

Conclusion. Often it can be apparent from the onset of an engagement that there is some level of EO present. The expertise and interaction across multiple valuation disciplines, including real property, personal property, business valuation, and intangible asset valuation, is essential in identifying and determining the EO in fixed assets and can have a material impact on the conclusions of value. It is important to recognize this issue as early as possible and have the appropriate teams in place to execute the analysis expertly and thoroughly.

Charles Sapnas, *CFA, ASA, CEIV, is senior vice president of VRC and specializes in business enterprise valuations, purchase price allocations, and impairment analyses and intellectual property valuations for financial reporting and tax purposes. He can be reached at csapnas@valuationresearch.com.* ***Joseph Mickle,*** *ASA, is managing director of VRC and is a 35-year veteran of the valuation industry, specializing in both machinery and equipment and real estate. He can be reached at jmickle@valuationresearch.com.*

Lessons Learned in *Amazon v. IRS* on Valuing Marketing Intangibles

By John Wiora, ktMINE (Chicago, Ill., USA)

In a landmark decision, the Tax Court sided with Amazon.com Inc. when the IRS challenged the valuation of trademarks the company transferred to its overseas subsidiary.[1] The case involved tax deficiencies of over $200 million. As the provider of the data used to calculate the proper royalty rate for marketing intangibles in the opinion, our analysts at ktMINE have done a thorough review of the case in order to discern what this means, going forward, for analysts and tax professionals around the globe. Given this decision and the OECD's work on BEPS,[2] practitioners must be more vigilant than ever when analyzing royalty and licensing data.

Case facts. To set the stage for the valuable lessons practitioners can learn from the case, there are a few important facts to consider regarding marketing intangibles:

- *CUT method transfer pricing.* While both sides of the case came to different conclusions for what the proper buy-in payment was, both parties agreed that the comparable uncontrolled transaction (CUT) method was the best for determining arm's-length pricing.[3]

- *Intangible asset valuation dispute.* Ultimately, there were five points of disagreement with regard to the intangible asset valuation:

    - "(1) the proper royalty rate;

    - "(2) the useful life of the marketing intangibles;

    - "(3) the revenue base to which the royalty should be applied;

1 *Amazon.com, Inc. v. Commissioner,* 2017 U.S. Tax Ct. LEXIS 9 (March 23, 2017). (Hereafter *Amazon.com Inc.* (2017)). An in-depth discussion and the full court opinion are available at *BVLaw.*

2 The Organization for Economic Cooperation and Development (OECD)'s Base Erosion and Profit Shifting (BEPS) initiative targets tax avoidance by companies that move operations or shift intangibles to lower tax jurisdictions.

3 *Amazon.Com, Inc.* (2017), page 127.

- "(4) the appropriate discount rate; and
- "(5) the extent (if any) to which the buy-in payment must be adjusted to reflect the European Subsidiaries' prior ownership of certain marketing intangibles."[4]

Royalty rate calculation. The expert for Amazon, Robert Reilly (Willamette Management), selected a median royalty rate of 0.59% based on a comparable transaction analysis containing a final set of six agreements.[5] The expert for the IRS, David Haigh (Brand Finance), chose a rate of 2.0%, the highest rate of his set. After a review of each analyses, and subsequently choosing its own comparables, the court agreed with Haigh regarding choosing the highest rate. However, the court chose 1.0% as the final rate based on the strength of Amazon's brand in 2005.[6]

Lesson 1: The CUT method of transfer pricing is not dead. The *Amazon* case is not the only high-profile tax case involving intangible asset valuation in the last few years (think *Veritas* and *Medtronic*). One commonality between these cases is the use of the CUT method for transfer pricing as the court's preferred methodology. The lesson here? Pursuing comparable agreements and rates is worthwhile, even when not perfect, as long as they are defensible.

To properly apply the CUT method to their analyses, the petitioner, respondent, and court all used ktMINE royalty rate and data from a database that contains over 17,000 royalty rate agreements. When comparables exist, ktMINE's intuitive search filters give users quick access to agreement summaries. Plus, the full text is available to confirm comparability. In addition to finding intangible license agreements such as trademark license agreements, patent license agreements, and software license agreements, the ktMINE database includes nonstandard agreement types, including:

- Benchmark distribution;
- Sales agent;
- Buying agent;
- Financial services; and
- Contract manufacturing activities.

The first step in evaluating the CUT method of transfer pricing is confirming the existence of comparables not only covering the computation of arm's-length pricing of a transaction, but also providing proof that third parties would agree to similar contract terms. The OECD recently stated

4 Ibid.

5 An article with more detail on Reilly's method is available in the Free Resources section of www.bvresources.com. The article, "Three-Step Analysis to Manage the 'Noise' in IP Royalty Rate Data," first appeared in the May 2014 issue of *Business Valuation Update*.

6 *Amazon.com Inc.* (2017), page 129.

the importance of confirming the arm's-length nature of a transaction outside of the pricing of the transaction.

"In many instances, transfer pricing rules operate to consider whether a transaction has occurred at all, or has occurred in a way that is substantively different from that which is described in contracts or documentation."[7]

Lesson 2: Know your transfer pricing data. To make sure every one of your transfer pricing analyses are strong and defensible, there are a few takeaways from the court's critique of each party's analyses:

- *Pay attention to your search strategy.* Whether conducting transfer pricing research yourself or using a third-party provider, always pay attention to the source of information, as well as how the final set of agreements were chosen. Choose agreements based on:

    - Similar functions and risks;
    - Similar intellectual property; and
    - Between unrelated parties.

    If the data, at the very least, do not satisfy these criteria, you may need to reconsider your approach.

- *Always review the full text of the agreement.* As is evident in Judge Lauber's opinion, each one of the agreements was reviewed in its entirety. Based on this review, he dismissed a few of the agreements. For example, the agreement for the use of the trademark for MacGregor-branded products was rejected due to a settlement, which could have been found in the background section of the agreement.

    If you're using a license agreement database that does not include the full text of the agreement, it may be time to source your transfer pricing data elsewhere. By manually reviewing each agreement, you have all the details regarding the royalty structure and other important pieces of the contract. These data points can be hidden within the agreement and missed by search algorithms or human error. A full review of each document gives you the confidence your analyses are correct and allows you to confidently defend your decisions.

Ensure proper due diligence. In Judge Lauber's review of the party's agreements, he dismissed a few based on a review of additional sources of information, namely news surrounding the deals and licensors/licensees. This was seen in the rejection of the agreement for the FAO Schwarz trademark based on media describing the transaction as that of a "distress sale."

7 *OECD, IMF, UN, WBG, January 2017. A Toolkit for Addressing Difficulties in Accessing Comparables Data for Transfer Pricing Analyses,* page 6.

Always ensure proper due diligence by checking additional sources of information. This includes news sources and press releases that can provide any missing context from the agreement. As seen in the *Amazon* case, additional context can make the difference between the court accepting or rejecting an agreement from your final set. Ultimately, had either party sought information beyond the agreements, they could have avoided rejection.

Analysts who use ktMINE have direct access to the system that allows them to modify, expand, and narrow their searches as they see fit. This control gives users the ability to build the best searches to fit their transaction facts. There is also access to a full agreement summary tied directly to the source documents of full-text information. As seen in the *Amazon* case, the court can decide to review the agreements in the case and come to its own determination, based on a combination of full-text review and outside news and investor research. When users are unable to conduct unlimited searches, their analysis often suffers. Additionally, if they must pay extra to view the full text of the agreement, focus shifts from creating a thorough analysis to creating an analysis constrained by a budget. ktMINE allows users to create comprehensive and defensible analyses without the threat of added costs, eliminating budget worries from the equation.

Lesson 3: Conduct your royalty rate calculation wisely. The most important question you can ask yourself regarding the selection of the final agreement rate is: "Does it meet the facts of the tested transaction?" Many practitioners rely on their database providers to give them a single rate per agreement. However, depending on the facts of your transaction, the selection of the royalty rate is not always that simple.

In some respects, the *Amazon* case can be subtitled "A Tale of Two Rates." For example, we can evaluate the royalty rate selection for the Sports Authority license agreement. While the opposing experts chose the same agreement, the two sides derived different royalty rates. This particular agreement specified royalty rates declining from 1.2% in the initial year to 0.5% over the next 12 years (see exhibit). While one expert elected to use the highest rate, the court and the other expert elected to use a simple average of the rates in the agreement. It is also possible to use the lowest rate for an analysis, but no one opted for this choice. Additionally, we've seen customers elect to use a weighted average based on sales volumes or profits, depending again on the transaction.

As you can see, many of these royalty rate calculation methods would not be possible if only one rate was relied upon. It's important to understand the royalty rates of agreements in comparison to your transaction before selecting the final rate. This will allow you to better defend your choice and protect yourself during audit and litigation.

Final point. To perform an analysis as outlined in the *Amazon* case, analysts need access to a royalty rate database offering full-text documents and valuable summaries of all the disclosed royalty rates. Relying on a database that only provides a single rate per document can lead to incorrect assumptions that do not fit all transaction facts.

Sports Authority License Agreement

License Actuals	Value	Agreement Base	Modifier	Common Base
	1.2%	GROSS SALES	Beginning with the Effective Date, during the initial Term and any Renewal Term, and if applicable, after termination of the Agreement to the extent any amounts are accrued and unpaid, Licensee shall pay the Royalties to Licensor in the manner and at the times specified below. In Fiscal Year 2003 - ONE and TWO TENTHS of ONE PERCENT (1.2%) of any and all Gross Sales.	GROSS SALES
	1.1%	GROSS SALES	Beginning with the Effective Date, during the initial Term and any Renewal Term, and if applicable, after termination of the Agreement to the extent any amounts are accrued and unpaid, Licensee shall pay the Royalties to Licensor in the manner and at the times specified below. In Fiscal Year 2004 - ONE and ONE TENTH of ONE PERCENT (1.1%) of any and all Gross Sales.	GROSS SALES
	1%	GROSS SALES	Beginning with the Effective Date, during the initial Term and any Renewal Term, and if applicable, after termination of the Agreement to the extent any amounts are accrued and unpaid, Licensee shall pay the Royalties to Licensor in the manner and at the times specified below. In Fiscal Year 2005 - ONE PERCENT (1.0%) of any and all Gross Sales.	GROSS SALES
	0.9%	GROSS SALES	Beginning with the Effective Date, during the initial Term and any Renewal Term, and if applicable, after termination of the Agreement to the extent any amounts are accrued and unpaid, Licensee shall pay the Royalties to Licensor in the manner and at the times specified below. In Fiscal Year 2006 - NINE TENTHS of ONE PERCENT (0.9%) of any and all Gross Sales.	GROSS SALES
	0.8%	GROSS SALES	Beginning with the Effective Date, during the initial Term and any Renewal Term, and if applicable, after termination of the Agreement to the extent any amounts are accrued and unpaid, Licensee shall pay the Royalties to Licensor in the manner and at the times specified below. In Fiscal Year 2007 - EIGHT TENTHS of ONE PERCENT (0.8%) of any and all Gross Sales.	GROSS SALES
	0.8%	GROSS SALES	Beginning with the Effective Date, during the initial Term and any Renewal Term, and if applicable, after termination of the Agreement to the extent any amounts are accrued and unpaid, Licensee shall pay the Royalties to Licensor in the manner and at the times specified below. In Fiscal Year 2008 - EIGHT TENTHS of ONE PERCENT (0.8%) of any and all Gross Sales.	GROSS SALES
	0.8%	GROSS SALES	Beginning with the Effective Date, during the initial Term and any Renewal Term, and if applicable, after termination of the Agreement to the extent any amounts are accrued and unpaid, Licensee shall pay the Royalties to Licensor in the manner and at the times specified below. In Fiscal Year 2009 - EIGHT TENTHS of ONE PERCENT (0.8%) of any and all Gross Sales.	GROSS SALES
	0.8%	GROSS SALES	Beginning with the Effective Date, during the initial Term and any Renewal Term, and if applicable, after termination of the Agreement to the extent any amounts are accrued and unpaid, Licensee shall pay the Royalties to Licensor in the manner and at the times specified below. In Fiscal Year 2010 - EIGHT TENTHS of ONE PERCENT (0.8%) of any and all Gross Sales.	GROSS SALES
	0.8%	GROSS SALES	Beginning with the Effective Date, during the initial Term and any Renewal Term, and if applicable, after termination of the Agreement to the extent any amounts are accrued and unpaid, Licensee shall pay the Royalties to Licensor in the manner and at the times specified below. Fiscal Year 2011 - EIGHT TENTHS of ONE PERCENT (0.8%) of any and all Gross Sales.	GROSS SALES
	0.8%	GROSS SALES	Beginning with the Effective Date, during the initial Term and any Renewal Term, and if applicable, after termination of the Agreement to the extent any amounts are accrued and unpaid, Licensee shall pay the Royalties to Licensor in the manner and at the times specified below. Fiscal Year 2012 - EIGHT TENTHS of ONE PERCENT (0.8%) of any and all Gross Sales.	GROSS SALES
	0.8%	GROSS SALES	Beginning with the Effective Date, during the initial Term and any Renewal Term, and if applicable, after termination of the Agreement to the extent any amounts are accrued and unpaid, Licensee shall pay the Royalties to Licensor in the manner and at the times specified below. Fiscal Year 2013 - EIGHT TENTHS of ONE PERCENT (0.8%) of any and all Gross Sales.	GROSS SALES
	0.8%	GROSS SALES	Beginning with the Effective Date, during the initial Term and any Renewal Term, and if applicable, after termination of the Agreement to the extent any amounts are accrued and unpaid, Licensee shall pay the Royalties to Licensor in the manner and at the times specified below. Fiscal Year 2014 - EIGHT TENTHS of ONE PERCENT (0.8%) of any and all Gross Sales.	GROSS SALES
	0.5%	GROSS SALES	Beginning with the Effective Date, during the initial Term and any Renewal Term, and if applicable, after termination of the Agreement to the extent any amounts are accrued and unpaid, Licensee shall pay the Royalties to Licensor in the manner and at the times specified below. In each subsequent Fiscal Year during the Term and any Renewal Term To be negotiated; provided, however, that it shall not exceed FIVE TENTHS of ONE PERCENT (0.5%) of any and all Gross Sales.	GROSS SALES

License Statistics	Minimum	Mean	Maximum	# of Observations	Common Base
	0.5%	0.85384615385%	1.2%	13	GROSS SALES

(Source: ktMINE)

John Wiora *is a former transfer pricing professional who is now director of operations at ktMINE where he manages all sales, marketing, and research operations. He also heads up data acquisition, analysis, and implementation and has researched trends, patterns, and relationships surrounding specialized facets of IP intangibles transactions. He has personally analyzed thousands of IP license agreements. For more information on the ktMINE royalty rate database, go to www.bvresources.com/products/ktmine-royalty-rate-database.*

How to Estimate WACC for a Cross-Border Valuation

One of these days, you will be asked to value a company located in a foreign country. One of the first questions you will have is: How do I estimate the discount rate? Of course, the overall concept is the same as for a U.S. valuation, but you need to reflect foreign country risk into your valuation. Right off the bat, you'll want to ask a few questions.

1. In what country is the subject company? Yes, this is an obvious question, but it's the first thing you need to know.

2. Is the subject company exposed to country risk? Another basic question, but it must be asked. If the answer is "no," there's no need to deal with country risk. If there is exposure, country risk must be considered, and it can be reflected in one of two ways: (a) in the cash flows; or (b) layered into the WACC calculation as a country risk premium (CRP).

3. Are there good projected cash flows? If the answer is "yes," this is the ideal situation. Then there is no need to estimate a country risk premium at all because all of the country-specific risks are baked into the cash flows. This is known as the "scenario" approach, and it is akin to having good projections for a domestic firm, which eliminates the need to layer in a premium for company-specific risk. The trouble is, if you do not have good projections, you can't use a scenario approach—you must layer in a CRP, which, of course, is a lot more work and is not as optimal. Some people may find it hard to imagine that you can't get good projections somehow, so every effort should be made in this regard. However, if it's impossible to do so, you will have to deal with a CRP.

4. In what currency are the projected cash flows? If the projected cash flows are in the foreign currency, you could do the valuation in the foreign currency—but only if you have the necessary inputs from a foreign perspective (e.g., the risk-free rate for local government bonds, local ERPs, local betas). If you do have these inputs, you can use a single-country CAPM in developing the WACC. If you do not, you must calculate WACC in your home currency (e.g., USD). To do this, you must convert the currency.

To do the valuation in USD when the projected cash flows are in foreign currency, you must convert to USD. You do this by using a forecast exchange rate (from Bloomberg). Don't make the mistake of using a spot rate when you do this. A forecast exchange rate must be used because cash flow

Exhibit 1. Basic Cost of Equity Formula
$K_{e,\ foreign\ country} = R_{f,\ home\ country} + \beta_{,\ home\ country} \times ERP_{,\ home\ country} + CRP$
where:
$K_{e,\ foreign\ country}$ = *cost of equity capital in the foreign country (denominated in the home country currency)*
$R_{f,\ home\ country}$ = *risk-free rate on government-issued bonds in the home country currency*
$\beta_{,\ home\ country}$ = *beta appropriate for a company located in the home country in a similar industry as the foreign country's subject company (i.e., beta is measured using returns expressed in the home currency)*
$ERP_{,\ home\ country}$ = *equity risk premium of home country; and*
CRP = country risk premium

projections are looking into the future, so they need to reflect currency risks over the period of the projections.

With the projections converted into USD, you can calculate a cost of equity and apply a CRP. See the basic formula in Exhibit 1.

This basic formula is used with the number of international cost of capital models available, each with their own strengths and weaknesses.[1] You should consider using several models in your analysis because there is no consensus among academics and practitioners as to the "best" model to use. When choosing a model, the goal is to balance several objectives, such as acceptance and use, data availability, and simplicity.

Once you have estimated your cost of equity, you then calculate the cost of debt—also in USD with the application of a CRP. Now you are able to calculate the estimated WACC, and it will be in USD from the perspective of a U.S. investor looking to invest in the foreign country.

Example. Last year, a hypothetical U.S. institutional investor was planning to make an investment in a company in Brazil. The target company (also hypothetical) provides information technology services in South America. The U.S. investor needed to estimate an appropriate WACC to price the investment. Here's how it was done.

The majority of the target company's cash flows are generated in Brazil. So we know where the target is located and we know the purpose of the valuation. We also have determined that the company is definitely exposed to country risk, so it must be reflected. The projected cash flows are in Brazilian reals, so the question is: Do these cash flows reflect country risk? Do they embody the political, economic, and financial conditions of the locality? You hope the answer is "yes" because then country risk is already reflected and you can avoid using a CRP at all. Unfortunately, for some reason, the answer is "no," and the projections are totally devoid of any country risk.

1 Models are explained in the *2017 Valuation Handbook: International Guide to Cost of Capital* from Duff & Phelps, available from BVR's Cost of Capital Resource Center at www.bvresources.com.

The next thing to look at is whether there is any reliable information in the local currency, such as risk-free ERPs. If this information is available, you can do the valuation in Brazilian reals using a single-country CAPM. However, this information does not exist, so you must calculate WACC in USD. You use a forecast exchange rate to convert the foreign cash flows into USD.

Here are the assumptions for this example:

Valuation date: March 31, 2016

Investor perspective: United States (USD)

Investee county: Brazil (BRL)

Cash flow projections: Real (BRL)

Industry: Information technology

Subindustry: Software and services

Industry beta: 1.5

Capital structure: D/TC = 10%

Tax rate: 34% (Brazil)

Company credit rating: BB

U.S. normalized risk-free rate: 4.0% (D&P recommended guidance)

U.S. equity risk premium (ERP): 5.5% (D&P recommended guidance)

With these inputs, you now can calculate a cost of equity by plugging into the basic formula (same as above):

$$K_{e,\ Brazil} = R_{f,}\ US + \beta_{US} \times ERP_{US} + CRP$$

$$K_{e,\ Brazil} = 4.0\% + 1.5 \times 5.5 + CRP$$

As you can see, we need the CRP, so you have to look to one or more of the models available. It is often prudent to use several, so, for this example, three models are used: country yield spread model, relative volatility model, and the Erb-Harvey-Viskanta country credit rating (CCR) model.

Country yield spread model. In this model, the CRP is determined as the difference between the yield to maturity on a foreign country government bond (issued in the home country's currency) and the yield to maturity on a home country government bond with a similar maturity. If you go to Data Exhibit 2 in the *Handbook*, you will find CRP estimates derived using this model. There are CRP estimates for 188 countries from the perspective of investors based in the U.S. and Germany. We need the CRP estimate for a U.S.-based investor perspective in Brazil for March 2016, which is 4.7% (see Exhibit 2).

Exhibit 2. Brazil CRP (March 2016)—Country Yield Spread Model

Investor Perspective: United States
Currency: United States dollar (USD)

Country Yield Spread Model:
Country Risk Premia (CRPs)

The country risk premium (CRP) is not the cost of equity capital (COE). The CRP is to be added to base COE. See Chapter 4 for proper application.

	Data Updated Through December 2015		Data Updated Through March 2016			
Investee Country	December 2015 Country Risk Premium (CRP) (%)	Tier Method*	March 2016 Country Risk Premium (CRP) (%)	Tier Method*	S&P Sovereign Credit Rating §	MSCI Market Classification †
Afghanistan	11.9	4	11.1	4		
Albania	7.4	3	5.9	3	B+	
Algeria	5.5	4	5.3	4		
Angola	8.4	2	9.2	2	B	
Antigua & Barbuda	2.7	2	2.8	2		
Bhutan	15.8	4	15.0	4		
Bolivia	3.6	3	3.8	3	BB	
Bosnia & Herzegovina	7.4	3	7.4	3	B	
Botswana	1.1	3	1.2	3	A-	
Brazil	5.7	2	4.7	2	BB	Emerging

* Tier 1: S&P sovereign credit rating = AAA, CRP assumed to be 0.0%; Tier 2: Observed Yield Spread, Tier 3: S&P Regression Yiel d Spread, Tier 4: Euromoney (ECR) Regression Yield Spread. For purposes of this analysis, the U.S. is being treated as if it were rated AAA by S&P.
§ S&P Credit Rating based on long-term foreign currency issuer rating. See http://www.standardandpoors.com/. Moody's or Fitch sovereign credit rating was used for countries where S&P sovereign credit rating was not available.
† MSCI Market Classification based on MSCI Market Classification Framework. See http://www.msci.com/products/indexes/market_classification.html

Source: Duff & Phelps, *2016 International Valuation Handbook - Guide to Cost of Capital*, Data Exhibit 2

We plug that CRP into our formula from above and get:

$$K_{e,\,Brazil} = 4.0\% + 1.5 \times 5.5 + 4.7\%$$

$$K_{e,\,Brazil} = 17.0\%$$

Relative volatility model. For this model, the cost of equity formula changes a little bit to reflect a relative volatility factor, so it becomes:

$$K_{e,\,Brazil} = 4.0\% + 1.5 \times 5.5 \; x \; RV$$

The RV factor is determined as the ratio of the annualized monthly standard deviation of the foreign country equity returns (as denominated in home country currency) relative to the annualized monthly standard deviation of the home country equity returns (as denominated in home country currency). If you go to Data Exhibit 3 in the *Handbook,* you will find relative volatility (RV) factor estimates using this model for 75 countries from the perspective of investors based in the U.S. and Germany. The RV estimate we need (U.S.-based investor perspective in Brazil for March 2016) is 2.1 (see Exhibit 3). We plug that RV into our formula from above and get:

$$K_{e,\,Brazil} = 4.0\% + 1.5 \times 5.5 \; x \; 2.1$$

$$K_{e,\,Brazil} = 21.3\%$$

CCR model. The Erb-Harvey-Viskanta country credit rating (CCR) model is based on the notion of creditworthiness. The assumption is that countries with lower creditworthiness, which is translated into *lower* credit ratings, are associated with *higher* costs of equity capital, and vice versa. Data Exhibit 4 in the *Handbook* provides CRP estimates for 179 countries from the perspective of investors based in a 56 countries. The CRP estimate is then used in the same formula we used before:

$$K_{e,\ Brazil} = 4.0\% + 1.5 \times 5.5 + CRP$$

The CRP estimate for March 2016 from a U.S. perspective investing in Brazil is 6.4% (see Exhibit 4), so we plug that in:

$$K_{e,\ Brazil} = 4.0\% + 1.5 \times 5.5 + 6.4\%$$

$$K_{e,\ Brazil} = 18.7\%$$

Exhibit 3. Brazil RV (March 2016)—Relative Volatility Model

Investor Perspective: United States
Currency: United States dollar (USD)

Relative Volatility Model:
Relative Volatility RV Factors

The RV Factor is to be multiplied to the ERP. See Chapter 5 for proper application.

		Data Updated Through March 2016		
Investee Country	December 2015 Relative Volatility Factor (RV)*	March 2016 Relative Volatility Factor (RV)*	S&P Sovereign Credit Rating §	MSCI Market Classification †
Argentina	3.6	3.6	SD	Frontier
Australia	1.0	1.0	AAA	Developed
Austria	1.8	1.8	AA+	Developed
Bahrain	1.2	1.2	BB	Frontier
Bangladesh	2.1	1.8	BB-	Frontier
Belgium	1.4	1.4	AA	Developed
Botswana	1.5	1.4	A-	
Brazil	1.9	2.1	BB	Emerging
Bulgaria	2.2	1.9	BB+	Frontier
Canada	1.0	1.0	AAA	Developed

* S&P sovereign credit rating = AAA, RV assumed to be 1.0. For purposes of this analysis, the U.S. is being treated as if it were rated AAA by S&P.
§ S&P Credit Rating based on long-term foreign currency issuer rating. See http://www.standardandpoors.com/. Moody's or Fitch sovereign credit rating was used for countries where S&P sovereign credit rating was not available.
† MSCI Market Classification based on MSCI Market Classification Framework. See http://www.msci.com/products/indexes/market_classification.html

Source: Duff & Phelps, *2016 International Valuation Handbook - Guide to Cost of Capital,* Data Exhibit 3

Exhibit 4. Brazil CRP (March 2016)—Country Credit Rating Model

Investor Perspective: United States
Currency: United States Dollar (USD)

Erb-Harvey-Viskanta
Country Credit Rating (CCR) Model

The country risk premium (CRP) is not the cost of equity capital (COE). The CRP is to be added to base COE. See Chapter 6 for proper application.

		Data Updated Through March 2016					
Investee Country	December 2015 Country Risk Premium (CRP) (%)	March 2016 Country Risk Premium (CRP) (%)	S&P Sovereign Credit Rating §	World Rank Out of 179*	MSCI Market Classification †	Institutional Investor Region ‡	Regional Rank ‡
Afghanistan	24.6	25.2		170		Asia/Pacific (South & East)	23 out of 24
Albania	11.0	10.7	B+	82		Eastern Europe/Central Asia	18 out of 29
Algeria	8.0	8.3		72		North Africa/Middle East	9 out of 19
Angola	12.5	11.9	B	93		Africa (Sub-Saharan)	7 out of 49
Argentina	16.1	15.0	SD	129	Frontier	Latin America/Caribbean	24 out of 29
Bosnia & Herzegovina	14.4	14.4	B	118		Eastern Europe/Central Asia	23 out of 29
Botswana	5.0	4.6	A-	46		Africa (Sub-Saharan)	1 out of 49
Brazil	5.8	6.4	BB	61	Emerging	Latin America/Caribbean	10 out of 29
Bulgaria	6.9	6.3	BB+	60	Frontier	Eastern Europe/Central Asia	10 out of 29
Burkina Faso	18.2	17.1	B-	144		Africa (Sub-Saharan)	25 out of 49

§ S&P Credit Rating based on long-term foreign currency issuer rating. See http://www.standardandpoors.com/.
* World rank based on 179 countries covered by Institutional Investor. Ranking based on ascending order in which '1' equals the smallest country risk premium (CRP) and '179' equals the largest country risk premium (CRP).
† MSCI Market Classification based on MSCIMarket Classification Framework. See http://www.msci.com/products/indexes/market_classification.html
‡ Regional classification based on Institutional Investor. Regional rankings based on ascending order in which '1' equals the smallest country risk premium (CRP) for each region.

Source: Duff & Phelps, *2016 International Valuation Handbook - Guide to Cost of Capital,* Data Exhibit 4

We now have a range of cost of equity estimates using three different models. The next step in the WACC calculation is to figure the cost of debt.

Cost of debt. Using Bloomberg data for U.S. technology companies and the corporate yield curve (BB credit rating) for March 31, 2016, a 15-year yield to maturity (the longest term available) is 7.3%. This is the base pretax cost of debt (in USD), which then must reflect the Brazil CRP to estimate an implied pretax cost of debt, which reflects the incremental risk of the debt in Brazil. Adding in the CRP estimates from the three different models yields a range of estimates for implied pretax cost of debt:

Model	Implied Pretax Cost of Debt	Pretax+ CRP		Cost of Debt
Country yield spread	7.3%	4.7% (see Note 1)	=	12.0%
Relative volatility model	7.3%	6.1% (see Note 2)	=	13.4%
Country credit rating model	7.3%	4.7% (see Note 3)	=	12.0%

Note 1: The 4.7% is the CRP estimate from the model.

Note 2: Instead of the factor from the model, an implied CRP is developed and used to calculate implied cost of debt.

Note 3: The CCR model uses only equity indices, so the CRP estimate from that model is not used here. The CRP from the country yield spread model is used as a proxy.

WACC estimates. Using our assumptions (10% debt to total capital; 34% tax rate), the WACC can now be estimated using the three models.

Model	Implied Pretax Cost of Debt	Cost of Equity	WACC
Country yield spread	12.0%	17.0%	16.0%
Relative volatility model	13.4%	21.3%	20.1%
Country credit rating model	12.0%	18.7%	17.6%

This is the end result: a range of estimates for the WACC in USD for an investment in Brazil from the perspective of a U.S.-based investor.

If the client asks that the valuation be done in foreign currency, you can develop a local WACC and you don't have to convert the cash flows to USD. However, you may not have the local inputs to develop a local WACC. In that case, you need to use the above procedure and compute the discount rate in USD and then translate the discount rate into local currency using the International Fisher Effect (explained in the *Handbook*). This gives you a local WACC, and you can then do the valuation in foreign currency.

Learn more. International cost of capital is a complex topic, and BVR has a free webinar, International Case Studies Using the Duff & Phelps *Valuation Handbooks*, with James P. Harrington and Carla S. Nunes, both with Duff & Phelps. They go through much more detail than we can in this article, and they present current case studies with step-by-step guidance for developing cost of capital estimates. This webinar is part of a two-day session, on September 20 and 21, with Day 1 presenting U.S. case studies and Day 2 presenting the international case studies. To attend, go to the Training section of the BVR website (www.bvresources.com).

Valuation of Dual Class Shares

By Gilbert E. Matthews, CFA,
Sutter Securities Inc. (San Francisco, Calif., USA)

The high-profile class action lawsuit between minority shareholders and Hollywood icon Jeffrey Katzenberg over the additional consideration being paid to him in the sale of DreamWorks to Comcast[1] puts the spotlight on "dual class" companies. Dual class companies have classes of common shares with unequal voting rights but equal or similar economic interests (entitlement to earnings). For U.S. companies, high-vote shares commonly have 10 times the votes but the same economic interest as low-vote shares. In some cases, the superior class elects a majority of the board and the class sold to the public elects a minority of the board. In this article, "dual class" includes companies with two classes of common stock or more, and "low-vote" shares include nonvoting shares.

Companies that choose a dual class structure often posit that it enables the management to take a long-term view by insulating it from the pressures of meeting the market's quarterly expectations. This protects the control shareholders, usually the founders, who own the high-vote shares and retain voting control. The structure serves to protect management from the possibility of a hostile takeover (for better or worse). In recent years, numerous companies, particularly in the high-tech area, have elected to set up dual class structures and to issue low-vote shares when they go public in U.S. markets.

Listing dual class shares in the U.S. The New York Stock Exchange (NYSE) prohibited the listing of nonvoting common shares from 1926 to 1985, but it sometimes permitted low-vote shares, e.g., Ford Motor Co. In 1976, the American Stock Exchange (AMEX) permitted the listing of low-vote shares provided that they could elect at least 25% of the board and that the voting ratio was no worse than 10 to 1. In the mid-1980s, high-vote shares began being used as an anti-takeover device. The NYSE responded in 1985 by permitting the listing of low-vote shares with the AMEX limitations. Several listed companies took advantage of this rule change by creating a class of high-vote shares through exchange offers or recapitalizations.

1 *See* Stephen Davidoff Solomon, "Lawsuit Aims at Jeffrey Katzenberg and His Dual Class Shares," *New York Times*, July 8, 2016, available at www.nytimes.com/2016/07/09/business/dealbook/lawsuit-aims-at-jeffrey-katzenberg-and-his-dual-class-shares.html.

Since 1994, the NYSE has prohibited listed companies from creating dual class shares or reducing the voting rights of existing shares. Prior dual class listings are grandfathered. Importantly, companies that have dual class structures when they go public may be listed, and nonvoting shares are no longer banned. (Nasdaq now has the same standard.)

Opposition to high-vote shares. There is growing opposition to dual class structures from institutional investors. Major money managers in the U.S. have begun to campaign actively against high-vote shares. Sixteen firms managing over $17 trillion in assets (including BlackRock, Vanguard, State Street, and CalPers) recently formed the Investor Stewardship Group, which indicated that it would push for a ban on dual class shares and would seek to have existing dual class structures phased out.

On July 31, 2017, S&P Dow Jones Indices, which manages the eponymous indices, announced that companies with dual class structures would no longer be admitted to the S&P 500, the S&P MidCap 400, and the S&P SmallCap 600.[2] A few days earlier, FTSE Russell announced that it would exclude companies from its indices unless unrestricted shareholders held at least 5% of voting rights. This decision will adversely affect the market for companies with dual class structures because exchange-traded funds (ETFs) and mutual funds based on these indices are major participants in the market.

Market prices of high-vote shares are not informative. Several studies have attempted to determine the premium per share for high-vote shares by comparing market prices of high-vote and low-vote shares of the limited number of U.S. companies where both classes are publicly traded. These studies generally show that, on average, high-vote shares sell at slightly higher prices than low-vote shares of the same issuer. However, the aggregate publicly traded high-vote shares in the float rarely can impact control because the control party normally owns a majority of the vote. Therefore, these studies are of little value—if a company's publicly traded high-vote shares collectively cannot affect control, their market-price shares cannot measure the value of control.

Since the total number of publicly traded high-vote shares are almost always a substantial minority of the class, the market price of high-vote shares seldom, if ever, is a direct function of the value of their voting power. Without shares owned by insiders, purchasers of high-vote shares in the market cannot acquire voting control. It is not uncommon for high-vote shares to sell at a discount to low-vote shares, primarily due to the fact that, in most cases, the number of publicly traded high-vote shares is materially lower than the number of publicly traded low-vote shares, and, therefore, the high-vote shares are less liquid.

Premium in excess of economic interest. The premium for voting control should not be calculated on a per-share basis but instead should be determined as a percentage of the value of the entire company allocated to the class of high-vote shares. It is illogical to posit that the voting premium

2 Companies already in these indices were grandfathered. The Dow Jones indices do not include any dual class companies.

per share is the same regardless of the percentage of shares that are high-vote. The relevant factor is the relationship between the aggregate premium paid to the high-vote shares as a class as a percentage of the aggregate equity value of the company. We describe the aggregate premium for the high-vote class divided by the equity value of the company as the "premium in excess of economic interest." In the 1998 acquisition of Giant Food Inc. by Royal Ahold N.V., the voting shares, which were only 0.4% of the outstanding shares, received a premium of 870% per share but an aggregate premium in excess of economic interest of 3.5%.

The "premium in excess of economic interest" in a transaction is the difference between the consideration the high-vote class would have received with no premium and the consideration it received in the transaction.[3]

As an example of the calculation of premium in excess of economic interest, assume that a company has 25% high-vote shares and 75% low-vote shares and it exchanges high-vote shares for low-vote shares on a 1.2-to-1 basis.

1.2 × 25% =30%

30% (high-vote) + 75% (low-vote) = 105%

30%/105% = 28.6%

The voting shares as a class have a 25% economic interest before the transaction and 28.6% after the unification, i.e., a 3.6% premium over economic interest:

Data re: relative value of classes. To obtain data that can be useful in determining the relative value of high-vote and low-vote shares, we look at data available from corporate events in U.S. dual class companies. Some U.S. corporations with dual class structures have been acquired; others have combined high-vote and low-vote shares into a single class through recapitalizations or reclassifications. Acquisitions and recaps of U.S. dual class companies provide useful data as to relative value in the U.S.

Historical data are available as to premiums paid in acquisitions and in recapitalizations.[4] In about 85% of acquisitions and recapitalizations of U.S. dual class companies in the past 30 years, both classes received the same consideration. In this period, high-vote shares received a premium in an average of 1.1 transactions per year in the U.S. These transactions, although a small sample, provide relevant and useful data.

Why many high-vote shares have not received premiums. The high-vote shares might not receive a premium in an acquisition or recapitalization for several reasons:

3 If the nonvoting shares have a dividend preference, the risk-adjusted present value of the preference is a prior charge and should be excluded from the economic interest that the two classes share pro rata.

4 The benefits of control and the legal standards differ by country, so any analysis should be country-specific.

1. The by-laws require that high-vote shares may not be transferred unless they are converted into one-vote shares;

2. The by-laws provide that high-vote shares will automatically be converted into low-vote shares if transferred to a party not in the control group;

3. Prior to an IPO, high-vote shareholders made a commitment that all shareholders would receive the same consideration in an acquisition;

4. The by-laws provide that consent of the low-vote class was required for a merger;

5. Prior to a 2001 change in GAAP, an acquisition could be accounted for as a pooling of interests;

6. The control shareholder owns a similar percentage of each class; and

7. High-vote shares collectively own materially less than 50% of the total vote.

However, a few acquirers have paid premiums even though the high-vote shares are receiving a higher price to which they may not be entitled. Courts have sometimes failed to enjoin acquisitions by third parties who are paying a substantial premium for low-vote shares. In some cases where high-vote shareholders received a questionable premium, buyers have settled litigation by agreeing to make additional payments to low-vote shareholders, e.g., Affiliated Computer Services, Delphi Financial, and Robert Mondavi Corp.

In the recent sale of DreamWorks Animation SKG Inc. to Comcast Corp., co-founder Jeffrey Katzenberg received the same price per share as low-vote shareholders. The Class B shares have 15 votes, and the Class A shares have one vote. Katzenberg owns all of the DreamWorks' Class B stock and, with his Class A shares, owns 11.5% of the shares but 60% of the vote. DreamWorks' charter provides that minority shareholders should receive the same treatment in a merger as Katzenberg. However, he also received a "consulting agreement" that gives him a potentially highly lucrative participation in future profits of certain operations. Class action litigation is in progress.

U.S. transactions in which a premium was paid for high-vote shares. We have compiled a database of U.S. transactions since 1974 in which high-vote shares were offered more than low-vote shares and have calculated the premium in excess of economic interest for each transaction. Exhibit 1 summarizes the premiums by decades.

Exhibit 1. Premiums Paid for High-Vote Shares (Summary by Decade)

Period	Mean Premium	Median Premium	Transactions
1975-1989	14.0%	15.0%	5
1990-1999	2.8%	2.1%	16
2000-2009	3.8%	3.1%	11
2010-2017	1.4%	1.5%	7

Exhibit 2. Premiums in Excess of Economic Interest Received by U.S. High-Vote Shares

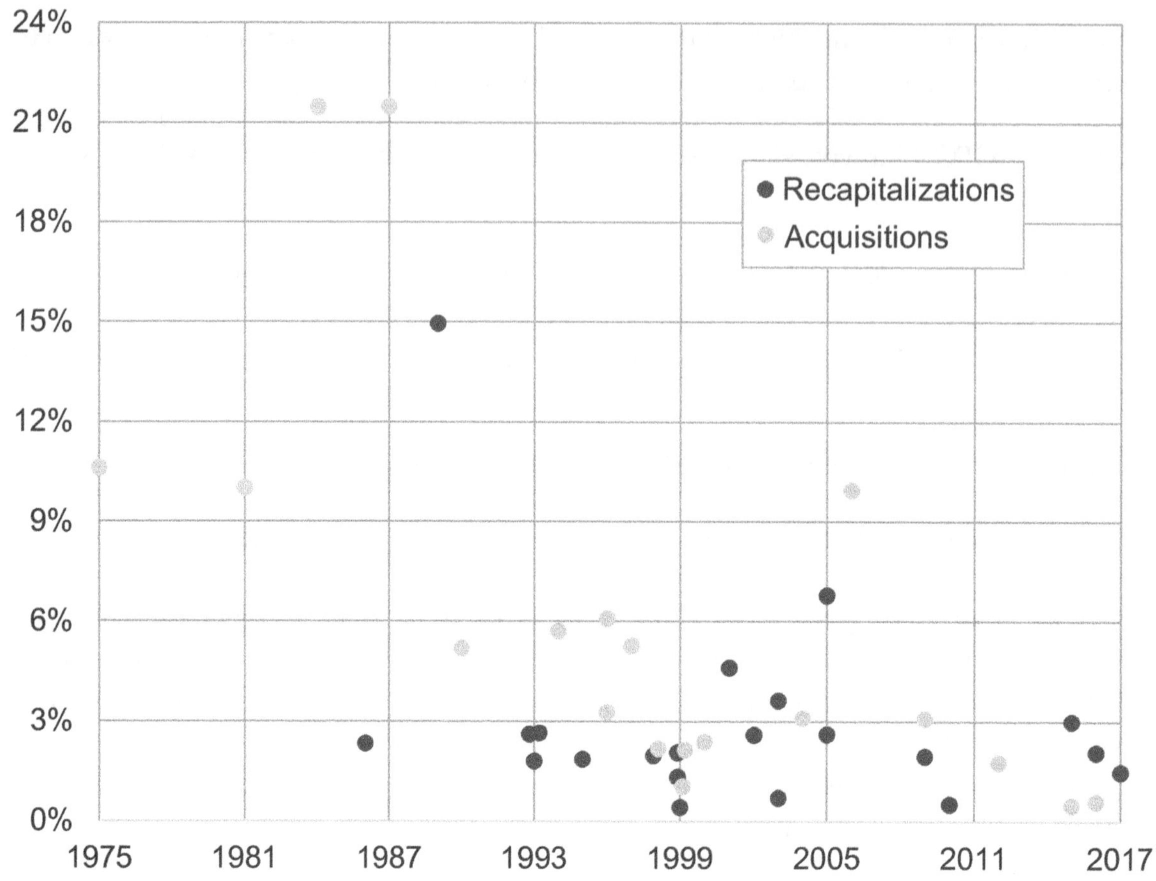

In the 1980s, extremely high premiums in excess of economic interest were paid for some high-vote shares. Since 1990, the median premiums are 2.3% and the means are 2.8%. On average, since 1990, premiums are about 1% higher for acquisitions than for recapitalizations. The data are summarized in Exhibit 2.

Can minority shares in a high-vote class be left out in the cold? Minority high-vote shareholders can be excluded from a premium paid to the control shareholders in an acquisition. The Delaware Court of Chancery—the primary venue for U.S. corporate litigation—decided in *Resorts International* [5] that minority high-vote shareholders were not entitled to a premium. It ruled that the minority's Class B shares were functionally and economically equivalent to the Class A shares, which had only 0.01 votes per share, because corporate control was in the hands of the shareholder who owned a majority of the Class B. The control shareholder had received $135 per share, and all other shareholders of both classes received only $36 per share. The Delaware Supreme Court upheld the decision, agreeing that the noncontrol high-vote shares had the same value as low-vote shares.

5 *In Re: Resorts International Shareholders Litigation,* 1988 Del. Ch. LEXIS 130 (Sept. 9, 1988); *aff'd,* 570 A.2d 259 (Del. 1990).

The *Simplot* case. Premiums for a high-vote class were addressed in a 1999 Tax Court case, in which the court concluded that a class of voting shares that owned less than 0.1% of the total equity was worth a premium of 3% of the total value of the subject company. J.R. Simplot Co. had 141,289 Class B nonvoting shares and only 76½ Class A voting shares (rounded). One family shareholder owned 22½ voting shares, and three (including the decedent) each owned 18 voting shares. The expert witnesses agreed that a premium was applicable to voting shares but disagreed as to the size of the premium. The Tax Court rejected the estate's position that the premium should be calculated on a per-share basis and stated that the premium for the voting rights "should be expressed in terms of a premium of the equity value."[6] It concluded, based on testimony as to publicly available information on transactions in which premiums had been paid for high-vote shares, that a 3% premium applied to the voting shares as a class.

The 9th Circuit rejected the premium the Tax Court applied because the decedent's minority block of shares did not have control. In a 2-1 decision, it decided that it was inappropriate to value a minority block of voting shares in relation to the value of the entire class, since the minority could not elect a director and could get no economic benefit. The majority decision did not discuss the Tax Court's determination that a premium is applicable to an entire class of voting shares. It valued the estate's block of voting shares as economically equal to nonvoting shares, stating:

> There was no basis for supposing that whatever value attached to complete control[,] a proportionate share of that value attached to each fraction of the whole.[7]

The Tax Court's view as to the possible "swing vote" value of the estate's 18 voting shares was dismissed as speculative. The dissenting opinion, however, argued that the estate's voting rights had incremental value even though the other family members collectively had control and concurred with the Tax Court.

> I do not believe that the majority's conclusion comports with economic reality.... The hypothetical buyer and seller of 18 [Class] A shares, reasonably informed of all relevant facts, would be aware of the interests of [the other shareholders], and would negotiate a price that would reflect them. Given these facts, ... I would affirm the Tax Court's decision.[8]

Courts have criticized directors and advisors for not considering relative fairness. The Delaware courts have criticized directors who did not consider relative fairness in transactions where high-vote shares received greater consideration than low-vote shares. They have similarly criticized financial advisors for not addressing the issue in their fairness opinions.

In 2002, *Reader's Digest* proposed a recap in which about half of the voting shares would be bought at premium and the balance would be exchanged for 1.24 shares of common. The Delaware Supreme Court said:

6 *Estate of Simplot*, 112 T.C. 130, 173 (1999). The writer was an expert witness for the IRS in this case.

7 *Estate of Simplot*, 249 F.3d 1191, 1195 (9th Cir. 2001).

8 Ibid. at 1195.

> [T]he Special Committee never sought, nor did its financial advisor, Goldman Sachs, ever tender, an opinion as to whether the transaction was fair to the Class A shareholders.... Given the obvious conflicting interests of the shareholder classes, the conceded absence of an evaluation of the fairness of the recapitalization on the Class A shareholders is significant.[9]

In 2005, Tele-Communications Inc. agreed to a transaction in which the 10-vote shares (TCOMB) would receive 10% more in cash than the one-vote shares (TCOMA). The Court of Chancery wrote:

> DLJ failed to opine upon the fairness of the TCOMB premium to the TCOMA holders.... The *Levco* Court mandated more than separate analyses that blindly ignore the preferences another class might be receiving ... [T]he premium received by the TCOMA holders ... must be balanced with the fairness and magnitude of the 10% TCOMB premium.[10]

The court explained:

> DLJ had opined "that, with respect to the holders of each series of [Tele-Communications] Common Stock ..., the Exchange Ratio relating to such series is fair to such holders from a financial point of view." ... Notably, the DLJ opinion does not discuss the effect of the TCOMB premium upon the TCOMA holders, *i.e.*, whether the TCOMB premium was fair to the TCOMA holders. Unfortunately for defendants, *Levco* appears to mandate exactly such an analysis: that the relative impact of a preference to one class be fair to the other class.[11]

Dual class—statutory appraisal. In Delaware and in most other states, common shareholders seeking appraisal are entitled to "fair value," i.e., a pro rata share of the company's equity with no discounts for minority interest or lack of marketability and no premium for control. Under a fair value standard, voting rights are not considered. Thus, no premium can be applied to high-vote shares in a statutory appraisal.

Sanity check. Valuations of high-vote and low-vote shares are a subset of valuations applying control premiums, minority discounts, and marketability discounts. Valuators should consider whether their conclusions as to the value of specific shares are consistent with the conclusions they would have reached had the company not had more than one class of shares. They should also ask themselves whether their conclusions reflect prices that are consistent with what a willing buyer might pay and a willing seller might accept for control.

***Gilbert E. Matthews**, CFA, is chairman of the board and a senior managing director of Sutter Securities Inc. (San Francisco) and can be reached at gil@suttersf.com. He has more than 50 years of experience in investment banking and has spoken and written extensively on fairness opinions, corporate valuations, and litigation relating to valuations.*

9 *Levco Alternative Fund, Ltd. v. Reader's Digest Assoc., Inc.* ("*Levco*"), 803 A.2d 428 (Del. 2002), 2002 Del. LEXIS 488 (Del. 2002) at *5-*6. The writer was an expert witness for plaintiff in this case.

10 *In re Telecommunications, Inc. Sh'h Litig.*, 2005 Del. Ch. LEXIS 206 (Dec. 21, 2005) at *54-*55.

11 Ibid. at *52-*53.

Key Valuation Considerations for Fairness Opinions

Fairness opinions are frequently finding their way into a courtroom, so it is important to have a grasp on both the legal and financial aspects. Craig Jacobson and Richard Peil, who are both with GlassRatner Advisory & Capital Group, and attorney Jeffrey Rothschild (McGuireWoods LLP) provide a valuable list of valuation and legal issues to consider when performing a fairness opinion,[1] which is summarized below.

Legal framework. At the outset, understand the legal framework for a fairness opinion assignment in the relevant jurisdiction. For example, the standard of value sometimes is fair market value, and sometimes it is not. In the Delaware Court of Chancery, where many stockholder disputes are adjudicated, there is a very specific definition of the fair value standard of value, which precludes consideration of three issues: (1) discounts for marketability; (2) discounts for lack of control; and (3) in appraisal actions, stockholders are not entitled to the synergistic benefits of any prospective transaction.

Due diligence. When you render a fairness opinion, you will likely give a presentation to the board or special committee. Make sure you have performed your due diligence procedures and analyzed the company and the transaction from a qualitative and quantitative point of view. You're probably going to be questioned during the presentation, so make sure you really know and understand the company's business and how it relates to the underlying valuation analyses supporting the fairness opinion. One question you will get is whether or not you interviewed management, so be ready to explain that. At the outset, make sure that you have adequate time to do your work and perform your due diligence.

Normalization adjustments. Consider normalization adjustments for discretionary expenses and nonrecurring items. One important thing is the normalization adjustments for nonrecurring charges must also be considered in the context of your guideline companies. Frequent examples of this are differences in accounting policies, such as for inventory. If your target company is a retailer, confirm that all the guideline companies in your peer group use the same inventory and accounting

1 Fairness Opinions: Best Practices + BVR Gives First Look at New Research Tool, BVR webinar (Aug. 10, 2017); sub.bvresources.com/bvstore/cd3.asp?pid=CD552.

method as the target company. When analyzing private M&A transactions, it will be more difficult to get data. However, to the extent possible, you must evaluate the factors that would lead you to confirm a selected transaction provides sufficient data to properly evaluate transaction multiples.

Discount rate and projections. Buyers are often thinking in terms of how much the target company is going to earn in the future, which is shown by a discounted cash flow (DCF) analysis. Projections are very important because they often reflect the analytical process by which buyers entering into a transaction take into consideration. A common valuation error is a mismatch of discount rates and the risk inherent in the projections. One must understand the discount rate is a long-term measure because a significant portion of risk, associated with a DCF analysis, is contained in the terminal value. For example, if using the Gordon growth or similar model to calculate the terminal value, the discount rate should reflect the target company's risk in perpetuity, not just the period of the discrete cash flow projections.

Guideline companies and transactions. A common mistake is that analysts don't choose the proper peer group companies. It is a significant problem because the choice of peer group companies is receiving an increasing amount of scrutiny in contested valuations. Analysts should be diligent in their selection process and dig deeper into available financial information, such as 10-Ks.

Analysts frequently evaluate the most basic valuation multiples of recent revenue or earnings. However, it's important to confirm there is a correlation between systematic market risk of the target company relative to the peer group companies. Regarding guideline M&A transactions, more recent transactions will be more relevant than older transactions. It is also important to understand certain other elements of a transaction, such as who was the buyer—was it a financial or strategic buyer? In addition, was the transaction due to the company's financial distress or other duress?

Industry and general economic data. No company exists in a vacuum, so make sure that you've considered the industry and general economic conditions in which the target company operates. This is especially important if there is uncertainty in securities prices. Don't ignore current asset prices when you're doing any kind of valuation assignment. That's particularly important when you're rendering a fairness opinion related to a transaction.

Discounts. Many fairness opinion valuation subjects are marketable interests. The definitions of fair value that might apply in a fairness opinion specifically preclude the marketability consideration. But it is important to consider, at the entity level, whether something might restrict the sale of the company as a whole. Also, consider the jurisdiction when developing discounts. For example, the Delaware Court of Chancery is frequently critical of a company-specific risk premium because it is regarded as overly subjective and subject to manipulation.

Fee structure. Contingency fees represent a potential conflict of interest in an opinion-only engagement. Confirm that your engagement letter states the fee is payable regardless of the conclusion and whether a transaction is consummated. In addition, your engagement letter should state the fee is due and payable when you are prepared to render an opinion, not when you actually render it.

This list touches on the highlights and is certainly not exhaustive. Jacobson, Peil, and Rothschild delve into much greater detail during a BVR webinar, Fairness Opinions: Best Practices + BVR Gives First Look at New Research Tool (Aug. 10, 2017). The new research tool is BVR's Fairness Opinion Research Service (see the sidebar for more information). You can access a recording of the webinar at sub .bvresources.com/bvstore/cd3.asp?pid=CD552.

New Database Debuts for Benchmarking Fairness Opinions

With the absence of regulation surrounding the issuance of fairness opinions, market practices become de facto standards. Business Valuation Resources (BVR) is launching its new product, the Fairness Opinion Research Service (FORS), that enables professionals to easily know "what's market" and benchmark their work against hundreds of board books, proxies, and fairness opinion letters filed at the SEC over the last five years.

"With FORS, practitioners access relevant documents through an efficient and intuitive interface that saves them countless hours spent tracking down filings," says Renaud Selmès, CTO of BVR. Most importantly, with FORS, users can screen this unique source of information using more than 40 criteria. Screening criteria include usual suspects such as target's industry, name, size, and location as well as participants such as counsel and opinion issuers. Profession-specific screening criteria include items such as multiples, WACC, and terminal value calculation methods.

"By using technology based on visualization and drag-and-drop, BVR provides practitioners with a premier user experience to instantly access fairness opinion data ranging from valuation summaries to advisory fees," says Selmès. For more information, go to www.bvresources.com/products/fairness-opinion-research-service.

Quantifying Personal Goodwill by Analyzing Customer Retention

By Claudia J. Stern and Carl S. Saba,
Hemming Morse (San Francisco and San Mateo, Calif., USA)

When a business is sold in an asset sale, an owner can derive substantial tax benefits if it can be proved that part of the sales price is personal goodwill instead of enterprise goodwill. Various lists of attributes help valuators determine whether the business itself or the deal structure provide support for personal goodwill. These are qualitative factors, such as whether there are personal relationships between the owner and the customers of the business or whether the buyer negotiated a covenant not to compete with the seller. However, quantifying the amount of personal goodwill can be more difficult.

In this article, we describe two valuation engagements where we used mathematical models to support our quantification of goodwill. These models link personal goodwill to quantifiable customer retention.

Engagement A. In the first engagement, the business was a provider of in-home care service. The owner was operating the business under a franchised brand. The key to this business was getting new clients as clients needed care for an average of 14 months. Clients either got better and no longer needed help or deteriorated to the point where they could no longer live in their homes.

At first, we thought the existence of a franchise would appear to be a contraindicator of personal goodwill. We thought that, like a McDonald's, the brand, not the owner's personal goodwill, would drive customer traffic. But the brand did not have much value in terms of getting new clients in the door. Rather, new clients were referred to the business through relationships that the owner had developed over approximately 20 years. The owner had transitioned some of these relationships to his sales force, which consisted of two people.

Customer analysis. We asked the owner for a list of new clients over the prior year. The list consisted of 140 clients, a large enough sample for us to use as a base for our calculations. The software the franchisor supplied allowed the owner to keep track of the referral source for each client.

We asked the owner to rate each referral source as to the amount the owner's reputation and work influenced the referral source to make the referral. We used a relatively simple rating scheme of 0% (no influence by the owner), 25%, 50%, 75%, or 100% (totally due to the owner's reputation and work). We described the rating scheme as follows:

- 0% due to the owner having no influence on the client's decision. An example would be referrals from the franchisor's internet presence.
- 25% due to the owner having some influence on the client's decision. An example would be where the owner had started a program and handed it off to his salespeople.
- 50% due to the owner being half the reason why a client chose the company.
- 75% due to the owner being most of the reason why a client chose the company. An example of this is senior housing communities where the owner had strong ties to the site managers and had set up programs to help keep seniors in their homes.
- 100% due to the owner, where he was completely responsible for the client choosing the company. An example of this is referrals from a senior resource center the owner created to help seniors navigate the complexities of aging.

We included in our report a list of the referral sources the owner rated 75% or 100% along with an explanation of why the owner's relationship with the referral source was so strong.

Using the rating system described above, we weighted the new clients from each referral. For example, if three clients came from a referral source the owner rated at 50% his efforts, the weighted client count from that referral source would be three times 50%, or 1.5 clients due to the owner. Of the total count of 140 clients, the weighted client count for the owner was 46, or approximately 33% of all new clients.

Using the same methodology, we also considered what would happen if the owner competed with the buyer and was able to take the existing sales team to his new business. This was a definite possibility as he had a strong relationship with his sales team. If we considered the sales team's relationships, in addition to the owner's relationships, the result was that approximately 46% of referral sources remain with the owner.

Allocation of goodwill. To assess the allocation between enterprise goodwill, the covenant not to compete, and the residual personal goodwill, we considered three scenarios:

1. The owner transfers his existing relationships with referral sources and his sales team to the new owner. The result would be a continued level of referrals and the business would continue to operate at its current level of performance.

2. The owner doesn't transfer the relationships and does not compete with the new buyer. The result would be a loss of some referral sources that are based on the owner's relationship with that referral source. In addition, there is a strong probability that one salesperson or both salespeople would leave the company. We conservatively estimated that 25% of the existing referral sources would be lost under this scenario based on our sample of 33% of new clients attributable to the owner and our discussions with the owner.

3. The owner does not transfer his relationships and competes with the new buyer. The result would be that conservatively 35% of existing referrals would go with the owner. As described above, if he took the sales team and competed, it would increase the loss of referrals to 46%.

The value of Scenario 3 is the enterprise value of the existing business. It is that business that is not due to the owner personally but is attributable to the business such as the franchisor's marketing efforts. This value was allocated to the tangible and identified intangible assets transferred, with the remainder being the enterprise goodwill.

The difference between Scenario 2 and Scenario 3 is the value of the covenant not to compete, as that is the only difference contemplated between these two scenarios. We note, however, that it is not probable that the owner would compete with the new buyer. Therefore, we adjusted the value of the noncompete by multiplying it by a probability that the owner would compete absent such an agreement. We assessed a probability of competing at 25% based on our conversations with the owner.

For Scenario 1, we used a capitalized cash flow model based on the current performance of the business. The estimated value of the business was $5 million. For Scenario 3, we used a discounted cash flow model for the first 14 months, then capitalized the remaining cash flows as a terminal value. For this same scenario, we assumed that the level of clients that would be lost would decline linearly over 14 months, which is the average length customers use the service. As clients leave, they would be replaced at 65% of the current level given that the referral sources were not fully, effectively transferred to the new owner (35% followed the seller). For Scenario 3, we estimated the value at $3 million. Of this, $2.7 million was allocated to enterprise goodwill and $300,000 was allocated to tangibles and identified intangibles.

For Scenario 2, we used a discounted cash flow (over 14 months, like Scenario 3) and a terminal value to estimate the value of the business under Scenario 2. The difference in value between Scenario 2 and Scenario 3 was $200,000, or the value of the noncompete before probability weighting. We then multiplied the value by the probability that the owner would compete to get the probability weighted value of the noncompete agreement. The resulting value was $50,000 for the noncompete agreement. Personal goodwill of $1.95 million was then the value of Scenario 1 ($5 million for a full transition) less the value of Scenario 3 ($3 million) less the probability weighted value of the noncompete ($50,000).

Engagement B. The business in this engagement was an occupational therapy treatment center. The owner, a physician, had established then grown his practice. The owner had strong relationships with insurers in the area as well as with large employers.

The total purchase price was $3.1 million. The price was first allocated to the identified assets that were transferring (valued at $100,000), leaving $3 million to be allocated to a noncompete, an earn-out based on retaining customers in the first year, enterprise goodwill, and personal goodwill. The parties had valued the noncompete at $300,000, and the earn-out (based on the existing customer list) was valued at $600,000.

Customer analysis. We first looked at the customer base during 2012 and assessed its retention. The idea behind testing customer retention was to assess the loyalty of customers, whether to the practice or the owner. Our analysis went as follows:

- We split the clients into three groups: clients billing less than $1,000 per year, clients billing more than $1,000 per year but not over $10,000 per year, and clients billing over $10,000 per year.
- The bulk of clients (62% of all clients) fell into the lowest billing range, which accounted for only 10% of billings by dollar volume. The highest billing group (5% of all clients) accounted for 49% of the dollar volume.
- Clients billing over $10,000 per year had exceptionally high retention rates. All but two of the 110 customers had billings in 2014.
- Clients in the midrange were less likely to remain clients than the highest billing group. However, those that stayed increased their average billings. This indicates that higher billers were likely to remain with the practice.
- Finally, those in the lowest billing range, $1,000 per year and under, had very low retention rates. Nearly two-thirds did not bill in 2014.
- Clients who had billings in 2012 billed over $5 million in 2014, or 85% of total 2014 billings.

The results indicate exceptional loyalty to the practice at the high end.

We then looked at the top 100 customers for 2014. We asked the clinic's manager to rank the top 100 customers into three groups based on their loyalty to the owner. Customers ranked "one" were very loyal to the owner and were highly likely to leave the practice if he left or opened a competing practice; customers ranked "three" had no relationship with the owner and would not leave just because the owner left. Customers ranked "two" were in the middle and, on average, had some relationship with the owner but would be as likely to stay or go if the owner left.

A Few Questions About a Model for Quantifying Personal Goodwill

The accompanying article that describes an approach for quantifying personal goodwill by analyzing customer retention sparked a few follow-up questions. So *BVU* asked the authors, Claudia J. Stern and Carl S. Saba, both with Hemming Morse, to respond to a few of our queries.

Q: *What is the origin of this approach?*

A: This is an approach or methodology that Carl Saba developed given the particular nature of the business under consideration.

Q: *Why do you use this approach over other approaches?*

A: We are unaware of any other approach that attempts to quantify personal goodwill that breaks the quantification down to specific aspects of the business, such as the owner's relationship with referral sources.

Q: *Some experts may view the customer rankings and ratings as subjective.*

A: We agree that we are still basing the valuation on the subjective judgment of the owner. However, what is different is that we are trying to force the owner to think about it on a customer-by-customer basis or referral-source basis, which hopefully reduces some of the subjectivity. In both cases, however, we can see quantifiable factors such as the number of referrals or amount of billing per client, which helps quantify the "stickiness" of the relationship over extended periods.

Q: *The engagements you describe are for tax purposes. I assume you also use this for other purposes, e.g., divorce?*

A: We have not attempted to use this in family law, but that's a very clever idea to extend it to that. Family law is so state-specific that we would have to be careful about saying anything about applying it to family law.

Q: *What are the rules/regulations applicable to the situations you describe? Are they the same rules in both situations?*

A: Yes, the rules/regulations are based on the federal tax code, which permits different tax treatment on personal goodwill versus the remaining gain on a sale of a business. The question addressed in the article is how much of the payment for the business can be associated with personal goodwill, which has preferential tax treatment as compared to the remaining gain. The idea is that personal goodwill (or some portion thereof) can be transferred to the buyer by cooperation from the seller. We estimate that amount, some of which is in the form of a noncompete agreement.

Q: *You mention there are "various lists of attributes that help valuators determine whether the business itself or the deal structure provide support for personal goodwill." What lists do you have in mind? Are these factors based on a tax regulation (federal or state?), case law, or industry practice?*

A: BVR developed the attribute list that we use. This is the footnote we include in our reports: "The indications of personal and enterprise goodwill are sourced from *BVR's Guide to Personal v. Enterprise Goodwill*. BVR (Business Valuation Resources) is a widely recognized source of both data and practice aids for valuation professionals (see bvresources.com)." The list BVR developed is based on consideration of a number of articles that have been written on personal goodwill valuation and relevant court case rulings.

Q: *Did you get pushback on your analysis? If so, by whom and what were/are the counterarguments?*

A: Actually, there was no pushback either from the clients or the IRS. There was a long vetting process by the client and acquirer in the second case study described in the article.

Feedback wanted. If anyone has any questions or comments on this approach, please send them to andyd@bvresources.com.

The results of our analysis were:

- The top 100 customers represented 50% of total billings for 2014. This is consistent with the 2012 billing analysis above, where the top 110 customers were 49% of 2012 billings.
- By dollar volume, 60% of the sample were ranked one—those with a very strong relationship with the owner. This represented 40% of total 2014 billings.
- By dollar volume, 20% were ranked two. This represented 15% of total 2014 billings.
- By dollar volume, 20% ranked three—those with no relationship with the owner.

Allocation of goodwill. Based on these findings, at a minimum, the owner was personally responsible for 40% of all billings (the total billings of those ranked one divided by total 2014 billings). At the maximum, he could be responsible for 80% of all billings if the ranking for the entire customer list mirrors that of the top 100 customers. In addition, he is likely responsible for half of those with a ranking of two. In summary, the minimum amount he is responsible for is 47.5% (40% plus 7.5%, half of the 15% ranked two), and, at a maximum, he would be responsible for 87.5% (80% plus 7.5%).

We estimated his personal goodwill at 50% of the total goodwill, which is slightly higher than the minimum level of 47.5% but substantially less than the maximum level of 87.5%. We used 50% to allocate the goodwill between personal goodwill at $1.5 million ($3 million multiplied by 50%) and enterprise goodwill.

Included in the personal goodwill is the value of the noncompete agreement ($300,000) and one-half of the value of the customer list arising from the earn-out payment ($300,000, or 50% of $600,000). The $300,000 was defined by the buyer during contract negotiations and is part of personal goodwill, as discussed in the first engagement above. We allocated the customer list to personal and enterprise goodwill by the same 50% ratio that we allocated the total goodwill. Based on our analysis, the majority of visits that would trigger achievement of the earn-out payment would be from existing customers, and, therefore, their composition and relationship to the owner would be similar to the overall customer base.

The engagements described above were actual sales that were consummated. As far as we are aware, there have been no challenges to the tax position taken based on our work.

Author note: The actual percentages and dollar values have been changed to protect client confidentiality.

Claudia J. Stern, *CPA/BVA/CFF, is a principal in the Forensic and Financial Consulting Services Group at Hemming Morse, a national accounting and financial consulting firm based in California. She can be reached at sternc@hemming.com.* ***Carl S. Saba,*** *MBA, CVA, is a partner in the Forensic and Financial Consulting Services Group at Hemming Morse. He can be reached at sabac@hemming.com.*

Using a Restricted Stock Study Quintile Analysis for a DLOM

Editor's note: Restricted stock studies are often used when developing a discount for lack of marketability (DLOM). However, certain characteristics of the issuer of the restricted stock can impact the discounts in the studies. This article presents pages 388 to 395 from the VPS DLOM Guide and Toolkit *(see sidebar following article) as an excerpt that illustrates additional analysis designed to adjust for those characteristics in order to develop a relevant sample for the subject company. The hypothetical case study involves valuing a 20% noncontrolling ownership interest in a non-dividend-paying company.*

Median discounts on restricted securities in these studies have generally ranged from about 10 percent to 50 percent over the study periods. The discounts, however, have also ranged significantly within the studies (variation not shown above) based upon the restrictions applicable to the securities in the sample and the underlying fundamental characteristics of the issuers.

VALTIP

Analyses of the restricted stock studies have shown that the discounts can be strongly affected by issuer characteristics such as size, profitability, dividends, and volatility, as well as the holding-period restrictions applicable to the specific transactions.[1]

Because discounts vary from company to company, and since the studies encompass many different regulatory environments with different holding-period restrictions, additional analysis was performed to develop samples that are most comparable to the subject company.

VPS DLOM Toolkit Analysis

To develop a relevant sample for the subject company, we elected to use a quintiles analysis of the FMV RSS Database,[2] one of the largest restricted stock study databases available. A quintiles analysis involves matching the subject company to a group of restricted stock transactions in the FMV data with similar fundamental characteristics (i.e., revenue, market value, etc.) as that of the subject. The median discount from each quintile is then utilized as a proxy for a discount

1 For a detailed discussion of the restricted stock studies, see Chapter 10, "Factors Affecting Restricted Stock Discounts."

2 Since the *VPS DLOM Toolkit and Guide* was published, the FMV RSS Database has been renamed the Stout RSS Database.

Figure 05 Discounts by Quintile Based on Subject Company Fundamental Data

Model Inputs		Summary Output	
Subject Company Fundamentals ($ in 000s)	User Inputs	Quintile	DLOM
Market Value of Equity (Marketable)	7,500	5th Quintile	25%
Total Revenues	20,000	3rd Quintile	14%
Total Assets	5,000	5th Quintile	28%
Book Value of Equity	4,500	4th Quintile	26%
Market to Book Ratio	1.70	4th Quintile	14%
Net Profit Margin (After-Tax)	6.00%	1st Quintile	11%
Volatility	58%	4th Quintile	13%

applicable to the subject company.[3] These discounts are then further analyzed and adjusted for qualitative differences between the samples and the subject company. This analysis relied upon the *VPS DLOM Toolkit* Model.

Figure 05 summarizes the indicated discounts from each quintile based upon the Company's market value, revenue, total assets, total equity, market-to-book ratio, net profit margin, and volatility.[4]

The discounts from the quintile analysis ranged greatly, from a low of 11 percent (based upon net profit margin) to a high of 28 percent (based upon total assets). However, because each quintile contains a different sample of companies with different underlying characteristics, an analysis was performed to identify the sources of variation in the discounts and to ensure comparability to the subject business. For example, a particular quintile may be overpopulated by high volatility securities, which could bias discounts high for that quintile. Additional analysis was performed to investigate average characteristics of each quintile before selection of the discounts. Figure 06 illustrates pertinent summary statistics for each of the quintiles relied upon.

The issuer characteristics vary significantly among quintiles. For example, the volatility quintile has a smaller fraction of unprofitable firms (59 percent) versus that of the total assets quintile (86 percent). More importantly, variation in issuer characteristics helps explain the variation in the observed discounts across quintile baskets, particularly volatility and holding periods. In Figure 06, the data are sorted by declining level of volatility.

3 The quintiles analysis is a recommended methodology of FMV Opinions. The data for each quintile were downloaded from the FMV RSS Database.

4 Total assets, equity, and market value are exclusive of excess cash of $7,000,000. The volatility for the subject company was estimated by examining the median volatility for all non-financial, profitable, and non-dividend-paying U.S. companies trading on a U.S. exchange with annualized revenues between $10 million and $50 million, market capitalization less than $50 million (ADRs were excluded), and share price greater than $2. Securities with 0 percent volatility were excluded. The sample of 54 companies indicated median volatility of about 58 percent, rounded. Data obtained from Bloomberg.

Figure 06 Summary Statistics of Quintiles Relied Upon for DLOM

Summary Statistics of Samples						
Indicator	DLOM	Volatility	% Not Profitable	% Dividend Paying	% Reg. Rights	Avg. HP
Total Assets	28%	104%	86%	0%	22%	1.35
Market Value of Equity (Marketable)	25%	89%	67%	4%	29%	1.33
Book Value of Equity	26%	86%	75%	0%	34%	1.37
Total Revenues	14%	73%	62%	5%	42%	1.31
Market to Book Ratio	14%	69%	51%	19%	51%	1.19
Volatility	13%	59%	59%	7%	49%	1.30
Net Profit Margin (After-Tax)	11%	55%	0%	29%	63%	1.18
Median	**14%**	**73%**	**62%**	**5%**	**42%**	**1.31**

The discounts in each quintile are strongly correlated with the volatility of the quintile; that is, as the median volatility of the quintiles decreases, the discounts have a tendency to decrease. Further notice that the average volatility of the samples is quite high at 73 percent, many of the firms are unprofitable, the median holding period across samples is only about 1.31 years, certain samples have a high fraction of securities issued with registration rights, and that the fraction of firms paying dividends is quite low. Because of these differences several adjustments must be made in order to develop a meaningful discount, particularly in relation to the subject business.

Recall that our subject business is highly profitable and is not expected to distribute any net income in the form of dividends. Moreover, based upon our analysis of other non-dividend-paying and profitable small firms, we determined that the volatility of the subject business might be about 58 percent, as compared roughly to the 73 percent median volatility of the quintiles.

At the same time, however, the holding period of the transactions is only 1.31 years, and many securities are subject to registration rights. This suggests that the transactions are relatively liquid. However, Bill Smith has indicated that a liquidity event for the minority shareholders may not be realized for the next 5 to 10 years. Thus, an upward adjustment is warranted for differences in the expected liquidity horizon.

To account for these differences, the reported discounts should be normalized for differences in volatility, holding periods, and other factors. We will begin with the issue of volatility. Studies that have grouped the FMV RSS Database by volatility suggest that a 1.0 percent reduction in the

Figure 07 FMV RSS Database: Relationship of Volatility and DLOM

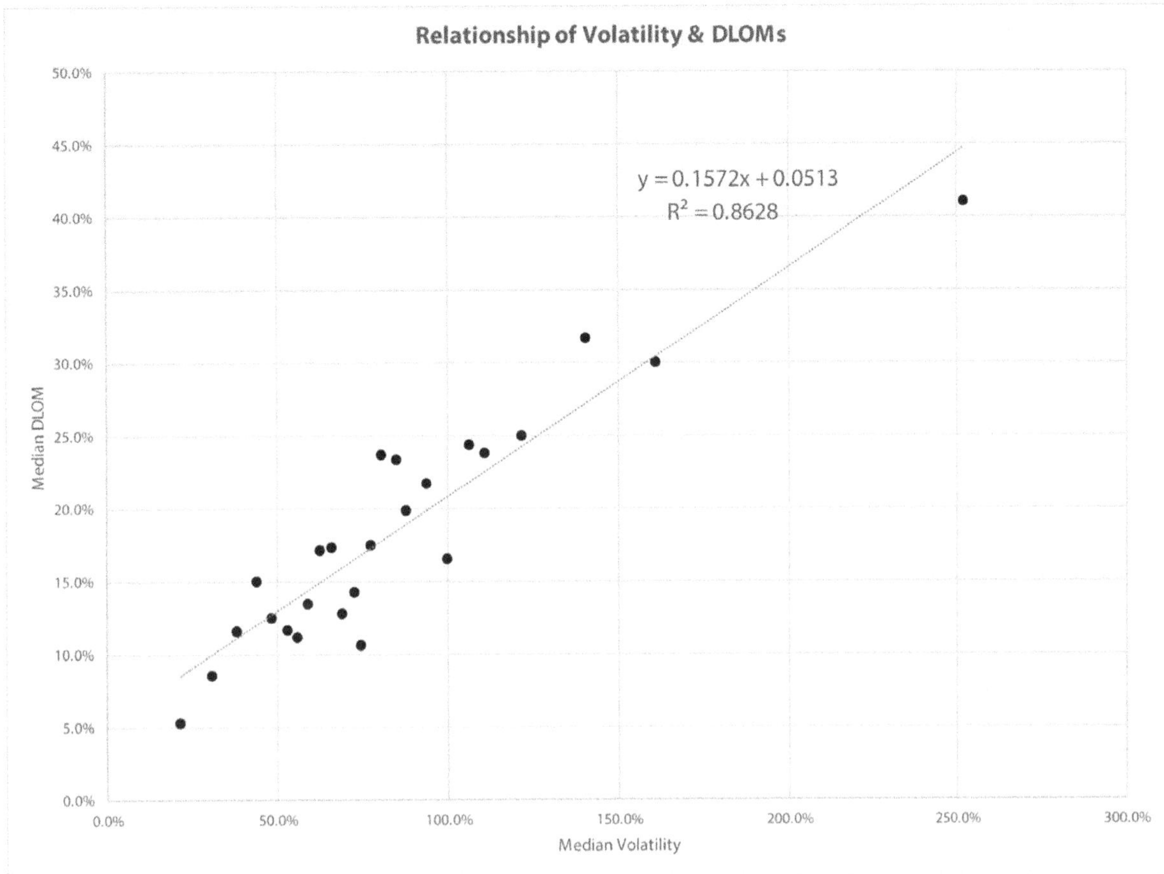

volatility of the security will translate into a 0.1572 percent reduction in the discount for lack of marketability, as presented in Figure 07.[5] The analysis is based on a subset of transactions from the FMV RSS Database at the case study valuation date, which is why the volatility regression analysis is slightly different from the example presented in Chapter 10, "Factors Affecting Restricted Stock Discounts."

Our analysis of profitable, non-dividend-paying publicly traded companies indicates that the subject company might be expected to have an annualized volatility of about 58 percent. Therefore, assuming the relationship between volatility and discounts holds, the volatility-adjusted discounts for the subject company are presented in Figure 09.[6]

5 This relationship is based upon a simple linear regression of median volatility against median discounts for 25 equally sized portfolio baskets from the FMV RSS Database grouped by volatility (See Chapter 10, "Factors Affecting Restricted Stock Discounts"). Please note, however, that there are some statistical issues with this approach because we do not explicitly control for other variables across portfolio baskets. Therefore, the slope coefficients may be biased due to the omission of other explanatory variables. However, we include this approach because it represents a somewhat objective way of adjusting discounts for volatility. Alternatively, the appraiser could use judgment to adjust the discounts for volatility.

6 For example, the total assets row indicates volatility of 104%. Therefore, the expected discount would be (104% – 58.0%)*15.72% = 7.2 percentage points lower, given the subject company's volatility of only 58%.

Figure 09 Determination of the Volatility Adjustment

Determination of Volatility Adjustment							
Indicator	Reported DLOM	Median Vol. of Quintile	Vol. of Subject	Difference in Vol.	Vol. Adj. Factor	Volatility Adjustment	Vol. Adj. DLOM
Total Assets	28%	104%	58%	-46%	15.72%	-7.2%	21%
Market Value of Equity (Marketable)	25%	89%	58%	-31%	15.72%	-4.8%	20%
Book Value of Equity	26%	86%	58%	-28%	15.72%	-4.4%	22%
Total Revenues	14%	73%	58%	-15%	15.72%	-2.4%	12%
Market to Book Ratio	14%	69%	58%	-11%	15.72%	-1.7%	13%
Volatility	13%	59%	58%	-1%	15.72%	-0.1%	13%
Net Profit Margin (After-Tax)	11%	55%	58%	3%	15.72%	0.5%	12%
Median	**14%**	**73%**	**58%**	**-15%**	**15.72%**	**-2.4%**	**13%**

The volatility should account for some of the differences in characteristics between the subject company and the restricted securities. However, further analysis using a *Mandelbaum*-style analysis is provided at the end of this section.

Next, the discount indications were adjusted for differentials in the expected holding period of the subject investment and the restricted stock transactions. The subject company's expected holding period is approximately 5 to 10 years, but the median holding period of the sample was approximately 1.31 years, and approximately 40 percent of the transactions were issued with some form of registration rights. Analysis of the FMV RSS Database suggests that transactions issued with registration rights have their shares registered and declared effective by the Securities and Exchange Commission in 85 days (average), or approximately 0.23 years.[7] Therefore, transactions issued with registration rights have considerably shorter expected holding periods than transactions issued without registration rights. We should, therefore, expect the quintiles populated with many transactions with registration rights to bias the discounts low. Moreover, they will affect the true expected holding periods of the investors.

The expected holding period was calculated for each quintile, taking into consideration the fraction of the quintile that was issued with registration rights. We assume securities issued with registration rights have holding periods equal to the average term to register the shares of 0.23 years (rounded). Therefore, if a quintile has an average holding period of 1.31 years, but 40 percent of the quintile is issued with registration rights, we would compute an effective holding period for

7 This statistic is based upon the median number of days to register for all transactions issued with registration rights in the FMV RSS Database as of May 1, 2015, excluding large block data, negative discount transactions, and companies in SIC Division H.

Figure 010 Determination of Adjusted Holding Period

Determination of Adjusted Holding Period					
Indicator	Vol. Adj. DLOM	% Registration Right	Holding Period	HP Adjusted Factor	Adjusted HP
Total Assets	21%	22%	1.35	0.23	1.11
Market Value of Equity (Marketable)	20%	29%	1.33	0.23	1.00
Book Value of Equity	22%	34%	1.37	0.23	0.98
Total Revenues	12%	42%	1.31	0.23	0.86
Market to Book Ratio	13%	51%	1.19	0.23	0.70
Volatility	13%	49%	1.30	0.23	0.78
Net Profit Margin (After-Tax)	12%	63%	1.18	0.23	0.58
Median	**13%**	**42%**	**1.31**	**0.23**	**0.86**

*Total may not sum exactly due to rounding. HP-adjusted factor is actual 0.231647 to the 6th decimal place.

that quintile of 1.31*(1-40%) + 0.23*40% = 0.88 years (rounded).[8] Figure 010 summarizes the effective holding periods for the quintiles (sorted by effective holding period) and the volatility-adjusted DLOM for each quintile.

Notice that the volatility-adjusted discounts are correlated with the effective holding periods; that is, as the effective holding periods decline, the discounts have a tendency to decrease. Observe that a simple comparison of unadjusted holding periods is not sufficient. For example, the volatility quintile has an unadjusted holding period of 1.30 years, but, since 49 percent of that sample was issued with registration rights, the effective holding period of the sample is only 0.78 years. It is no surprise that the volatility-adjusted discount of this sample is low relative to some of the other samples. Overall, the median effective holding period of the sample is 0.86 years. Thus, the inherent level of liquidity from this data is much greater than one would expect for the subject business.

Three types of analyses were performed to normalize the discount data for differences in holding periods:

- Adjusted DLOM was calculated using Finnerty's average-strike put option model.
- Adjusted DLOM was calculated using FMV Opinions adjusted restricted stock equivalent discount adjustment factor.
- DLOM was adjusted based on data from restricted stock studies on the impact of changes in holding period.

8 Other factors, such as block size, could affect the holding period. These factors are not addressed in computing the effective holding period, as they are not easy to determine.

Figure 011 Determination of Holding-Period Adjusted DLOM

Determination of Holding-Period Adjusted DLOM					
Indicator	Vol. Adj. DLOM	Adjusted HP	Expected Holding Period	HP Adjust. (Option Model)	HP Adjusted DLOM
Total Assets	21%	1.11	7.50	15%	35%
Market Value of Equity (Marketable)	20%	1.00	7.50	15%	36%
Book Value of Equity	22%	0.98	7.50	16%	37%
Total Revenues	12%	0.86	7.50	16%	28%
Market to Book Ratio	13%	0.70	7.50	17%	30%
Volatility	13%	0.78	7.50	17%	30%
Net Profit Margin (After-Tax)	12%	0.58	7.50	18%	30%
Median	**13%**	**0.86**	**7.50**	**16%**	**30%**
Average	**16%**	**0.86**	**7.50**	**16%**	**32%**
Standard Deviation	**5%**	**19%**	**0%**	**1%**	**4%**
Coefficient of Variation	**0.29**	**0.22**	**0.00**	**0.08**	**0.11**
*Totals may not sum exactly due to rounding.					

Finnerty's Average-Strike Put Option Model

Finnerty's average-strike put option model was used to determine the expected increase in discounts for an increase in holding period. Arithmetic average-strike put options are financial instruments that can be used as proxies to quantify some of the opportunity costs of illiquidity.[9] These option models have been shown to result in similar discounts as incurred on transactions of restricted stocks. They allow mathematical measurement of discounts utilizing certain assumptions, including holding periods.

Using Finnerty's average-strike put option model, we computed the increase in discounts for a security with annualized volatility of 58 percent (i.e., the estimated volatility of the subject company) as one moves from the effective holding period indicated by each quintile to 7.5 years (the mid-point of the 5- to 10-year expected liquidation period for the subject company). Figure 011 presents a summary of the results.

Adjusting the discounts for holding-period differences results in much better discount estimates, dropping the coefficient of variation by almost two thirds. The adjusted discounts suggest a range of 28 percent to 37 percent, with a median discount of 30 percent.

Large Block Adjustment

As additional evidence for the holding-period adjustment, we considered FMV Opinions' suggested adjustment to the restricted stock discount. Some authors contend that large blocks of restricted

9 See Chapter 19, "Option Pricing Models," for a detailed discussion on option pricing models.

securities are inherently more illiquid than small blocks of restricted securities because the dribble-out rules of SEC Rule 144, as well as general supply and demand constraints, make selling large blocks of restricted securities into the marketplace prohibitively expensive.[10] Based on analysis by the authors of this *Guide*, at the time of publication, discounts on all large block data in the FMV RSS Database (defined as those transactions wherein more than 30 percent or more of the outstanding stock is placed) command discounts approximately 2.71x higher than small block data (defined as all transactions where less than 30 percent of the outstanding stock is placed). This factor may be different at other dates, depending on data in the FMV RSS Database. Therefore, applying this adjustment to the median volatility-adjusted discount of 13 percent (see Figure 011), would suggest holding-period-adjusted discounts of about 35 percent (i.e., 13.0*2.71 = 35.0%). One must be careful in applying such analysis, however, as large block data may reflect factors unrelated to illiquidity, such as managerial entrenchment, monitoring costs, or risk.[11] Therefore, this may be viewed as an upper bound of the discount.

Restricted Stock Study Data on Holding Periods

Finally, studies that have grouped transactions by holding period suggest that discounts in the most restrictive two-year holding-period environments have discounts approximately 6 to 10 percentage

10 See the *FMV Opinions Companion Guide* for additional details.

11 For additional information on factors that contribute to the discounts on large block data, see Chapter 10, "Factors Affecting Restricted Stock Discounts," and Appendix G: FVLE Issue 34, "FMV Opinions Restricted Stock Database: Before You Rely on Restricted Stock Block Size to Determine an Incremental DLOM Applicable to Private Equity, Know the Facts," by Jim Hitchner, which can be found at www.valuationproducts.com.

Figure 012 Summary of Discount Adjustments

Summary of Discount Adjustments					
Indicator	Unadjusted DLOM	Volatility Adjust.	Vol. Adj. DLOM	HP Adjust.	HP Adj. DLOM
Total Assets	28%	-7%	21%	15%	35%
Market Value of Equity (Marketable)	25%	-5%	20%	15%	36%
Book Value of Equity	26%	-4%	22%	16%	37%
Total Revenues	14%	-2%	12%	16%	28%
Market to Book Ratio	14%	-2%	13%	17%	30%
Volatility	13%	0%	13%	17%	30%
Net Profit Margin (After-Tax)	11%	1%	12%	18%	30%
Median	14%	-2%	13%	16%	30%
Average	19%	-3%	16%	16%	32%
Alternative HP Adjustment					
Large Block Data	14%	-2%	13%	22%	35%
Holding Period Data	14%	-2%	13%	14%	27%
*Totals may not sum exactly due to rounding.					

points[12] higher than discounts subject to a one-year holding-period environment. Furthermore, transactions subject to a one-year holding-period environment have median discounts approximately 5.0 percentage points higher[13] than transactions subject to a six- month holding-period environment. More importantly, the collective spread in median discounts from the six-month holding-period data to the most restrictive two-year holding-period data suggests an aggregate discount increment of about 14 percent.[14] If one assumes that an investor would require at least the entire 14-percentage-point increment to compensate for additional holding-period risk, the holding-period-adjusted discount would be approximately 27 percent,[15] (i.e., median discount of 13% and incremental adjustment 14% = 27%).

Figure 012 summarizes the results of the holding-period normalizations.

12 Calculated by authors of this *Guide* using data from the FMV RSS Database. Statistics may vary based on the period of time over which the data are analyzed.

13 Ibid.

14 Ibid.

15 Some analysts may wonder why a higher holding-period adjustment was not applied in this scenario. After all, restricted stock studies suggest a 14-percentage-point increase in discounts for a 1.5-year increase in holding period, or approximately 9.33 percent per year. Since the median holding period of the sample is about one year, and the expected liquidation period of the subject business is 7.5 years, one might have simply assumed that a 60.65 percent holding-period adjustment should have been made (i.e., 9.33 * (7.5-1) = 60.65 percent). The problem with such analysis is that it assumes that the relationship between discounts and holding periods is linear. However, Amihud and Mendelson (1986) have suggested that the compensation for liquidity exhibits diminishes marginal returns; that is, investors require lower incremental compensation for each 1 unit increase in illiquidity (as measured by bid-ask spread in their study). Thus, much of the compensation for illiquidity occurs in the early years of the restriction period. In the appraiser's judgment, the incremental adjustment for reducing liquidity by an additional four years would have not greatly exceeded the incremental compensation observed for transactions with holding periods of six months to two years.

Tax Affecting S Corporations: It's Not a Matter of Whether. It's a Matter of When

By Alan Zipp (Rockville, Md., USA)

The propriety of tax affecting S corporations is not a question of right or wrong; rather, the question is *when* it is appropriate to tax affect S corporations in business appraisals. The standard of value required determined the answer. Under the fair market value standard, as required by the tax law, the courts have decided it is not appropriate to tax affect S corporations in tax valuations. Under equitable value standards, including fair value, courts have decided that tax affecting the S corporation is appropriate, and, in some cases required, such as in divorce valuations, shareholder litigation, economic damages calculations, and the like. In general terms, valuations under the tax law do not permit tax affecting S corporations, while valuations under equitable value standards do permit tax affecting S corporations.

As business appraisers, because so much of our work requires subjective judgment in analyzing the facts of the case, whenever possible, we appreciate bright-line rules to guide us. This article will provide some bright-line rules about tax affecting S corporations based on court decisions involving a variety of valuation cases. These court decisions represent authoritative guidance to provide some bright lines based on the purpose and function of the appraisal and the requisite standard of value.

The key to answering the question as to when it is appropriate to tax affect an S corporation is to identify the standard of value required and the purpose and function of the appraisal. For example, when the purpose and function of the appraisal is to comply with federal tax laws, the Tax Code and Treasury Regulations mandate the standard of value as "fair market value."[1] When the purpose and function of the appraisal is for equitable purposes, the standard of value is based on an equitable standard, such as fair value. In appraisals involving an equitable standard of value, case law provides guidance as to when it is appropriate to tax affect the S corporation.

1 Income tax 26 U.S.C. § 1001(a); 26 U.S.C. § 1014(a); 26 U.S.C. § 1015(a); Estate tax 26 C.F.R. § 20.2031-1(b); Gift tax 26 C.F.R. § 25.2512-1. The U.S. Supreme Court said that fair market value is the standard for determining the value of property for federal tax purposes. *United States v. Cartwright*, 441 U.S. 546, 550-551 (S.Ct. 1973).

Fair market value under the tax law denies tax affecting. Under the Internal Revenue Code, S corporations are not subject to income taxes as are C corporations.[2] Tax affecting an S corporation, consequently, requires the application of a hypothetical expense at the corporate level, which is not actually payable under the Internal Revenue Code. According to the Tax Court in the 1999 *Gross* case, "the principal benefit that shareholders expect from an S corporation election is a reduction in the total tax burden imposed on the enterprise. The owners expect to save money, and we see no reason why that savings ought to be ignored as a matter of course in valuing the S corporation."[3] More than a decade later, the Tax Court continued that position in *Estate of Gallagher*, stating, "[the expert] has advanced no reason for ignoring such a benefit, and we will not impose an unjustified fictitious corporate tax rate burden on [the S-Corporation's] future earnings."[4] In *Estate of Adams*, the Tax Court stated that "it is appropriate to use a zero corporate tax rate to estimate net cash flow when the stock being valued is stock of an S-Corporation."[5] In a 2011 partnership valuation case, *Estate of Giustina*, the expert reduced the cash flows by 25% to account for the income taxes the owner of the partnership interest would owe on that owner's share of the partnership's income. The Tax Court rejected that adjustment and said: "Thus [the expert's] cash flow estimates must be recomputed to eliminate the 25% discount for income tax liability."[6]

The issue of tax affecting in valuations for estate tax purposes is not new. A 1972 estate claimed that fair market value should be determined taking into consideration income tax payable on property of the estate. In *Estate of Robinson*, the Tax Court did not agree, pointing out that a hypothetical buyer is not a specific buyer and said the estate tax regulations are "explicitly clear in providing that property … is to be valued, for estate tax purposes, under an objective approach applying the willing buyer-willing seller test. There is no support in the law or regulations for petitioner's approach which is designed to arrive at the value of the transfer as between the individual decedent and his estate or beneficiaries.… Under that approach, every determination of fair market value for estate tax purposes would require consideration of possible income tax consequences as well as a myriad of other factors that are peculiar to the individual decedent, his estate, or his beneficiaries.… We hold that petitioner is not entitled to a discount of this value on account of the possible income tax payable."[7]

---

2 26 U.S.C. § 1363(a) "Except as otherwise provided in this subchapter, an S corporation shall not be subject to the taxes imposed by this chapter."

3 *Gross v. Commissioner*, T.C. Memo 1999-254.

4 *Estate of Gallagher v. Commissioner*, T.C. Memo 2011-148.

5 *Estate of Adams v. Commissioner*, T.C. Memo 2002-80.

6 *Estate of Giustina v. Commissioner*, T.C. Memo 2011-141.

7 *Estate of Robinson v. Commissioner*, 69 T.C. 222 (1977). "Although petitioner's theory may, at first blush, appear strong, its broad ramifications demonstrate its frailty. For instance, under that approach, every determination of fair market value for estate tax purposes would require consideration of possible income tax consequences as well as a myriad of other factors that are peculiar to the individual decedent, his estate, or his beneficiaries. Consideration would have to be given in a case such as the instant one, for example, as to when the estate is likely to distribute the note to the beneficiaries, and thereafter, to each beneficiary's unused capital loss carryovers, his possible tax planning to reduce future taxes on the gain included in each installment, his tax bracket both currently and in the future, his marital status, and other factors. The willing buyer-willing seller test, though it may not be perfect, provides a more reasonable standard for determining value, and it must be followed."

The recent history of tax cases is unanimous in denying an adjustment for imputed income taxes in valuing S corporations for federal tax purposes.[8] Tax cases base their decisions on the federal tax law definition of fair market value in the estate tax regulations: "The fair market value is the price at which the property would change hands between a willing buyer and a willing seller, neither being under any compulsion to buy or to sell and both having reasonable knowledge of relevant facts."[9] Revenue Ruling 59-60 further elaborated on the classification of the willing buyer and willing seller as being hypothetical and said: "Court decisions frequently state in addition that the hypothetical buyer and seller are assumed to be able, as well as willing, to trade and to be well informed about the property and the market for such property."[10]

For federal tax purposes, "[w]hen assessing hypothetical transactions between hypothetical buyers and sellers, it is improper to ascribe motivations that are personal and reflective of the idiosyncrasies of particular individuals.... Rather, it is necessary to view such persons as economically rational actors possessing all relevant information and seeking to maximize their gains."[11] "The buyer and seller are hypothetical, not actual persons, and each is a rational economic actor, that is, each seeks to maximize his advantage in the context of the market that exists at the date of valuation."[12] "The subjective intention or idea of this particular plaintiff corporation ... is irrelevant.... To hold otherwise would be to command future juries to wade into the thicket of personal corporate idiosyncrasies and non-market motives as part of their valuation quest."[13] "The hypothetical willing buyer and seller are presumed to be dedicated to achieving the maximum economic advantage."[14]

The Tax Court is a court of limited jurisdiction established under Article I of the U.S. Constitution as a legislative court to adjudicate controversies between taxpayers and the Commissioner of Internal Revenue.[15] The Tax Court is subject to review by the U.S. Courts of Appeal, and the standard for reversal is a finding that "the decision of the Tax Court is not in accordance with law."[16] The U.S.

---

8 *Gross v. Commissioner*, 272 F.3d 333 (6th Cir. 2001); *Wall v. Commissioner*, T.C. Memo 2001-75; *Estate of Heck v. Commissioner*, T.C. Memo 2002-34; *Estate of Adams v. Commissioner*, T.C. Memo 2002-80; *Dallas v. Commissioner*, T.C. Memo 2006-212; *Estate of Giustina v. Commissioner*, T.C. Memo 2011-141; *Estate of Gallagher v. Commissioner*, T.C. Memo 2011-148.

9 26 C.F.R. § 20.2031-1(b) Estate tax regulations.

10 Rev. Rul. 59-60, 1959-1 CB 237. "Courts have said the willing buyer and willing seller are hypothetical." In *United States v. Simmons*, 346 F.2d 213, 217, (5th Cir. 1965), the court said that "the willing buyer and seller are a hypothetical buyer and seller having a reasonable knowledge of relevant facts. In *Rothgery v. United States*, 475 F.2d 591, 594, (Ct.Cl. 1973), the Court of Claims said, "The notion of the willing seller as being hypothetical is also supported by the theory that the estate tax is an excise tax on the transfer of property at death and accordingly that the valuation is to be made as of the moment of death and is to be measured by the interest that passes, as contrasted with the interest held by the decedent before death or the interest held by the legatee after death."

11 *Holman v. Commissioner*, 601 F.3d 763 (8th Cir. 2010).

12 *Estate of Jameson v. Commissioner*, 267 F.3d 366 (5th Cir. 2001).

13 *Estate of Curry v. United States*, 706 F.2d 1424 (7th Cir. 1983).

14 *Estate of Newhouse v. Commissioner*, 94 T.C. 193, 218 (1990); see also *Estate of Davis v. Commissioner*, 110 T.C. 530, 535 (1998), "The willing buyer and the willing seller are hypothetical persons, rather than specific individuals or entities, and the individual characteristics of these hypothetical persons are not necessarily the same as the individual characteristics of the actual seller or the actual buyer. The hypothetical willing buyer and the hypothetical willing seller are presumed to be dedicated to achieving the maximum economic advantage."

15 26 U.S.C. 7441. "There is hereby established, under article I of the Constitution of the United States, a court of record to be known as the United States Tax Court."

16 26 U.S.C. 7482(c)(1).

Supreme Court has long held that "[t]he Internal Revenue Code, not general equitable principles, is the mainspring of the Board's jurisdiction."[17] According to the U.S. Supreme Court, "[t]he Tax Court is a court of limited jurisdiction and lacks general equitable powers."[18] The Tax Court itself recognizes its lack of equitable jurisdiction, as it said, "Petitioners ask us to consider their economic hardship. We are not a court of equity, however."[19]

Fair market value is a legal standard of value under the tax law. The definition of the fair market value standard is clearly a legal determination made by federal courts, including the Tax Court. The cases interpreting and applying the fair market value standard are based on legal, rather than equitable, principles of statutory construction. As a result, clear guidelines have developed with regard to tax affecting S corporations in valuations for tax purposes.

Under the fair market value standard, as interpreted and applied for federal tax law purposes, it is not appropriate to tax affect the S corporation in making a business appraisal. Based on numerous federal tax cases, a bright-line rule has emerged that precludes tax affecting S corporations under the fair market value standard. The rationale for this rule is that the fair market value of an S corporation should be measured to a hypothetical investor based on the enterprise's rate of return available to the hypothetical investor, not the after-tax rate of return to a particular investor.

Equitable valuation permits tax affecting S corporations. Fair market value is not the only standard of value used in business appraisals. Where the purpose and function of the appraisal is equitable, many courts have accepted tax affecting as an appropriate adjustment in the valuation of an S corporation. Equitable cases involving the value of an S corporation include shareholder disputes, marital property valuations in divorce, lost profits claims, and business damages litigation, to name a few. Under an equitable standard of value, such as fair value, intrinsic value, investment value, divorce value, value to the holder, etc., it may be appropriate to tax affect the S corporation depending on the jurisdiction and the purpose and function of the appraisal.

It is a fundamental principal of business valuation to define the standard of value before making the appraisal. The Uniform Standards of Professional Appraisal Practice requires the identification and definition of the standard of value in every appraisal.[20] It is also a fundamental principal of business valuation to understand the purpose and function of the appraisal. It is well known that different standards of value can result in differing appraised values; hence, applying the proper

17 *Commissioner v. Gooch Milling & Elevator Co.*, 320 U.S. 418, 64 S. Ct. 184 (1943).

18 *Commissioner v. Robert McCoy, Executor*, 484 U.S. 3, 108 S. Ct. 217 (1987).

19 *Coppin v. Commissioner*, T.C. Memo 2009-191. See also *Paxman v. Commissioner*, 50 T.C. 567, 576, "Not only is the Tax Court not a court of equity but petitioners, in effect, are asking us to legislate changes in the statute as enacted by Congress."

20 USPAP Standards Rule 10-2(a)(v) requires that the appraisal report "state the purpose of the appraisal, including the standard of value (definition) and its source." The Appraisal Standards Board of The Appraisal Foundation promulgates the Uniform Standards of Professional Appraisal Practice. The Appraisal Foundation, authorized by the Congress as the source of appraisal standards and appraiser qualifications, develops, publishes, interprets, and amends the Uniform Standards of Professional Appraisal Practice on behalf of appraisers and users of appraisal services. The Financial Institutions Reform, Recovery and Enforcement Act of 1989 mandates the use and application of USPAP standards in appraisals involving federally insured bank lending activities (www.uspap.org).

standard of value can be critical. Often, the purpose and function of the appraisal determines the proper standard of value.

For example, when the purpose of the appraisal is to comply with the federal tax law, the required standard of value is fair market value, as provided in Treasury Regulations, 26 C.F.R. § 2512-1. In contrast, when the purpose of the appraisal is to comply with state corporation law involving shareholder rights statutes, the required standard is fair value. Fair value is an equitable standard of value. Under the Model Business Corporation Act, adopted by a majority of states, fair value is the appropriate standard of value in shareholder oppression suits, derivative litigation, and similar business actions.[21] Under the Model Business Corporation Act, the definition of fair value states that valuation discounts for lack of marketability or minority status are inappropriate both because most transactions that trigger appraisal rights affect the corporation as a whole and because such discounts give the majority the opportunity to take advantage of minority shareholders who have been forced against their will to accept the appraisal-triggering transaction. The official comment to the act makes it clear that the intent is to award a shareholder his or her proportional interest in the corporation after valuing the corporation as a whole, rather than the value of the shareholder's shares when valued alone. Fair value, under the act, is measured personally to the specific shareholder and is not measured to a hypothetical willing buyer.

In contrast to the fair value standard prohibiting discounts for lack of marketability and minority interest, under the tax law's fair market value standard, both lack of marketability and minority interest discounts are applicable to S corporations.[22]

The Delaware Supreme Court said, "An appraisal proceeding is a limited statutory remedy. Its legislative purpose is to provide *equitable* relief for shareholders dissenting from a merger on grounds of inadequacy of the offering price."[23] The Vermont Supreme Court said, "A fair value determination is necessarily a fact-specific process. The weight to be given to particular evidence is a matter within the sound discretion of the trial court."[24] Cases relating to shareholder rights under the appraisal statutes of the Model Business Corporation Act are equitable in nature and are intended to permit the courts great latitude in determining value and fashioning an appropriate equitable award; hence, courts have wide discretion to consider income taxes, as well as all other relevant considerations, on a case-by-case basis. Fair value is markedly different from fair market value.

21 Section 13.01 Model Business Corporation Act defines "fair value" to mean the value of the corporation's shares determined: (i) immediately before the effectuation of the corporate action to which the shareholder objects; (ii) using customary and current valuation concepts and techniques generally employed for similar businesses in the context of the transaction requiring appraisal; and (iii) without discounting for lack of marketability or minority status except, if appropriate, for amendments to the articles pursuant to Section 13.02(a)(5).

22 *Estate of Gallagher v. Commissioner*, T.C. Memo 2011-148. "We agree that a minority discount is appropriate in valuing decedent's 15% minority interest in PMG ... we determine a 23% minority discount to the equity value of PMG.... We find a 31% lack of marketability discount to be appropriate." *Gross v. Commissioner*, T.C. Memo 1999-254. "We find that an appropriate lack of marketability discount for the gifted shares on the gift date was 25 percent."

23 *Paskill Corporation v. Alcoma Corporation*, No. 321, 1999 (Del. 2000). "The dissenter in an appraisal action is entitled to receive a proportionate share of fair value in the going concern on the date of the merger, rather than value that is determined on a liquidated basis."

24 *In re 75,629 Shares of Common Stock of Trapp Family Lodge, Inc.*, 725 A.2d 927, 1999.

Shareholder appraisal cases. A good illustration of tax affecting the S corporation in a fair value case is *Delaware Open MRI Radiology Associates, P.A. v. Kessler.*[25] Applying the equitable standard of value, the Delaware court said, "This case is another progeny of one of our law's hybrid varietals: the combined appraisal and entire fairness action. In this case, the key question is whether the minority stockholders of Delaware Open MRI Radiology Associates, P.A., received fair value in a squeeze-out merger." According to the court, "The resolution of this case is complicated by the presence of both an *equitable* entire fairness claim and a statutory appraisal claim.... Put simply, I must determine the fair value of Delaware Radiology's shares on the merger date.... Fair value is, by now, a jurisprudential concept that draws more from judicial writings than from the appraisal statute itself.... In simple terms, to reach a fair value award, I must determine Delaware Radiology's value as a going concern on the merger date and award the Kessler Group the percentage of that value that tracks its members' pro rata interest in Delaware Radiology on that date." As a fair value case, the court did not apply discounts for either a lack of marketability or minority interest of the Kessler Group. The court, however, did tax affect the value of the S corporation to reflect the value actually taken from the Kessler group of stockholders.

The *Delaware Radiology* court explained the equitable nature of the case when it said, "Unlike a statutory appraisal action, the success of an *equitable* action premised on the assertion that a conflicted merger is unfair ultimately turns on whether the court concludes that the conflicted fiduciaries breached their duties.... Under Delaware law, an appraisal petitioner is entitled to be paid for that which has been taken from him." The court emphasized that the equitable nature of the case requires measuring the precise value that was taken from the specific shareholders. The court said, "To capture the precise advantage of the S-Corporation structure to the Kessler Group, it is necessary to use a method that considers the difference between the value that a stockholder of Delaware Radiology would receive in Delaware Radiology as a C-Corporation and the value that a stockholder would receive in Delaware Radiology as an S-Corporation. By using that method, I can make my best estimate of the value that is relevant in this case—the going concern value in an S-Corporation that was taken from the Kessler Group in the merger."

The court recognized that the Kessler group of stockholders has been forcibly denied the future benefits of S corporation status and should receive compensation for those expected benefits, not an artificial value that disregards the favorable tax treatment available to them. The court said, "But the minority should not receive more than a fair S-Corporation valuation. Refusing to tax affect at all produces such a windfall." The court acknowledged that the Internal Revenue Code[26] requires that the taxable income of the S corporation be taxed at the individual tax rates of the stockholders. The court said, "Affording a remedy to the Kessler Group that denies the reality that each shareholder owes taxes on his proportional interest in Delaware Radiology would result in the Kessler Group receiving a higher per share value from the court than it could ever have realized as a continuing shareholder." The court said that the amount that should be the basis for an appraisal

25 *Delaware Open MRI Radiology Associates, P.A. v. Kessler, et al.*, 898 A.2d 290 (Del. 2006).

26 26 U.S.C. § 1366.

or entire fairness award is the amount that estimates the company's value to the Kessler group as S corporation stockholders paying individual income taxes at the highest rates—an amount that is materially more in this case than if Delaware Radiology was a C corporation.

The Delaware court sought to identify the particular injured shareholders and provide an equitable remedy that relates to the specific value taken from them based on the realities of the facts and circumstances of the case. The court observed that the minority shareholders "are comprised of affluent physicians who pay at the highest marginal rate." The court determined that the primary tax benefit of the S corporation is the avoidance of the dividend tax otherwise payable by the shareholders if the company was a C corporation. The court said assessing corporate taxes to the shareholder at a personal level does not affect this benefit. The court held: "To ignore personal taxes would overestimate the value of an S-Corporation."

The court did not apply the highest individual or corporate tax rate in calculating the value of the S corporation's earnings. Instead, the court said, "The issue, though, is that tax affecting Delaware Radiology at a 40% level (or C-Corporation level) would not recognize any S-Corporation value that flowed to the Kessler Group or compensate the Kessler Group for its involuntary removal as shareholders in a profitable S-Corporation. To be consistent with Delaware law, I must tax affect Delaware Radiology's future cash flows at a lower level that recognizes the full effect of the Kessler Group's ability to receive cash dividends that are not subject to dividend taxes. In order to accurately capture the value to the Kessler Group of Delaware Radiology's S-Corporation status, I have estimated what an equivalent, hypothetical 'pre-dividend' S-Corporation tax rate would be. This calculation allows me to treat the S-Corporation shareholder as receiving the full benefit of untaxed dividends, by equating its after-tax return to the after-dividend return to a C-Corporation shareholder. I will, therefore, apply an effective tax rate of 29.4% to the earnings of Delaware Radiology to measure with the greatest practicable precision the fair value of the Kessler Group's interest in the going concern value of Delaware Radiology."

The court said, "The results of this analysis not only serve as the foundation for my appraisal award but as the basis for a conclusion that the merger was not financially fair to the squeezed-out minority, the Kessler Group, as a matter of *equity*."

The *Delaware Radiology* case has been cited numerous times in equitable valuation cases, particularly in marital property valuation cases. In a tax case, *Dallas v. Commissioner*, the *Delaware Radiology* method of tax affecting was soundly rejected as the Tax Court said: "The Court of Chancery did not decide the price that a hypothetical willing buyer would pay a hypothetical willing seller ... that we used in this case." The Tax Court determined: "Fair value in minority stock appraisal cases is not equivalent to fair market value."[27]

27 *Dallas v. Commissioner*, T.C. Memo 2006-212. "In *Del. Open MRI* the court of chancery used a method to estimate the fair merger price that considered the difference between the value that a stockholder of Delaware Radiology would receive in Delaware Radiology as a C-Corporation and the value that a stockholder would receive in Delaware Radiology as an S-Corporation and applied a type of tax-affecting. However, the court of chancery did not decide the price that a hypothetical willing buyer would

The 8th Circuit Court of Appeals, in a minority shareholders' appraisal proceeding, *Swope v. Siegel-Robert, Inc.*, discussed the history, operations, and fair value of the statute. The issue before the court was the "fair value" of the minority shares rather than the "fair market value," which would have included market considerations such as minority status and the lack of willing buyers. The court said, "Because 'fair market value' is irrelevant to the determination of fair value, market forces, such as the availability of buyers for the stock, do not affect the ultimate assessment of fair value in an appraisal proceeding. Because of this difference, we determined that an IRS appraisal prepared for estate tax purposes was not relevant in the context of that appraisal proceeding. Regardless, appraisals for estate tax purposes are not relevant to the determination of fair value pursuant to a dissenters' appraisal proceeding."[28]

Divorce cases. A 2007 case of first impression in Massachusetts, *Bernier v. Bernier*,[29] provides important insight into the nature of equitable business valuations in divorce and the appropriateness of tax affecting S corporations. Although the *Bernier* court used the term "fair market value" throughout its opinion, it is clear that such reference was not intended to reflect the strict definition of fair market value applied under the federal tax law. The court distinguished equitable distribution of marital property from arm's-length hypothetical buyers and sellers, where it said: "As a preliminary matter, where valuation of assets occurs in the context of divorce, and where one of the parties will maintain, and the other be entirely divested of, ownership of a marital asset after divorce, the judge must take particular care to treat the parties not as arm's-length hypothetical buyers and sellers in a theoretical open market but as fiduciaries entitled to *equitable* distribution of their marital assets."

This case illustrates the fundamental difference between "law" and "equity" in the valuation of property. Where the valuation is made under principles of "law," the premise of value is based on the hypothetical willing buyer and seller. Where the valuation is made under principles of "equity," the premise of value is based on the fiduciary relationship the specific parties have to each other.

The *Bernier* court looked to the *Delaware Radiology* case as relevant to its interpretation of Massachusetts family law. The court found that the *Delaware Radiology* case concerned a closely held S corporation where fiduciary considerations constrained the dealings between the majority and minority stockholders. The court quoted from its long-standing position that "[w]e hold

---

pay a hypothetical willing seller, both having reasonable knowledge of all the relevant facts and neither being under compulsion to buy or to sell that we used in this case."

28 *Swope v. Siegel-Robert, Inc.*, 243 F.3d 486 (8th Cir. 2001). "In our review of that opinion, we held it was not appropriate under Missouri law, in the context of unwilling minority sellers' appraisals, to discount the value of shares due to lack of marketability or due to minority shareholder status. The issue before the court was the 'fair value' of the minority shares rather than the 'fair market value,' which would have included market considerations such as minority status and the lack of willing buyers. Because 'fair market value' is irrelevant to the determination of fair value, market forces, such as the availability of buyers for the stock, do not affect the ultimate assessment of fair value in an appraisal proceeding. Because of this difference, we determined that an IRS appraisal prepared for estate tax purposes was not relevant in the context of that appraisal proceeding. Regardless, appraisals for estate tax purposes are not relevant to the determination of fair value pursuant to a dissenters' appraisal proceeding."

29 *Bernier v. Bernier*, 449 Mass. 774 (2007). "This appeal ... presents us with the novel question whether it is proper to discount the value of an S-Corporation ... by "tax affecting" income at the rate applicable for C-Corporations, where one spouse will receive ownership of all shares of the S-Corporation after the divorce and the other will be required to relinquish all ownership in the business.... Also presented by the wife's appeal are whether the judge erred in discounting the fair market value of the S-Corporations at issue here by applying 'key man' and 'marketability' discounts."

that stockholders owe one another substantially the same fiduciary duty in the operation of the enterprise that partners owe to one another ... [that standard of duty being defined as] the 'utmost good faith and loyalty.'"[30] The *Bernier* court said that "[h]ere too, the property division between the husband and wife is constrained by fiduciary considerations."

The *Bernier* case involved an S corporation that the trial court valued using a C corporation tax rate. The Supreme Judicial Court of the State of Massachusetts took exception to that valuation method and, instead, adopted the *Delaware Radiology* methodology as the rule for equitable valuations in Massachusetts. According to the court, "On the issue of tax affecting, we conclude that the judge erred in adopting the valuation of the husband's expert witness that tax affected the fair market value of the parties' S-Corporation at the 'average corporate rate,' in the words of the husband's expert, of a C-Corporation.... Further, careful financial analysis tells us that applying the C-Corporation rate of taxation to an S-Corporation severely undervalues the fair market value of the S-Corporation by ignoring the tax benefits of the S-Corporation structure and failing to compensate the seller for the loss of those benefits. On the other hand, in the circumstances of this divorce action, we agree with a recent decision of the Delaware Court of Chancery that failure to tax affect an S-Corporation entirely artificially will inflate the value of the S-Corporation by overstating the rate of return that the retaining shareholder could hope to achieve."

The *Bernier* court cited *Delaware Open MRI Radiology Associates v. Kessler* and referred to it in its opinion as the *Kessler* court. The court said, "Our review of the scant case law and the pertinent literature on the issue leads us to adopt generally the metric employed by the *Kessler* court ... which most closely achieves the parties' stated intention in this case to divide the value of their S-Corporations equally.... We also conclude that, where the husband testified that he planned to retain control of the S-Corporations after the divorce, the judge erred in applying key man and marketability discounts, discounts that assume the possible sale of the asset." The *Bernier* court said, "We conclude that the metric employed by the *Kessler* court provides a fairer mechanism for accounting for the tax consequences of the transfer of ownership of the supermarkets from one spouse to the other in the circumstances of record. On remand on the issue of valuation, the judge is to employ the tax effecting approach adopted in *Kessler*."

On the issue of discounts for key man and marketability, the *Bernier* court reversed the trial court and said: "This discount was not warranted in light of the husband's testimony negating any possibility of a sale. The subject companies will continue as going concerns and are not being converted to cash.... Applying a marketability discount in light of the husband's intended, and presumed, acquisition of the supermarkets unfairly deflated their value." The court cited the New Jersey *Brown v. Brown* case, which applied the fair value standard in divorce valuations of business interests.[31]

30 *Donahue v. Rodd Electrotype Co. of New England, Inc.*, 367 Mass. 578, 593 (1975).

31 *Brown v. Brown*, 348 N.J. Super. 466, 474-476 (2002). "Neither marketability nor minority discount should be applied absent extraordinary circumstances.... Close corporations by their nature have less value to outsiders, but at the same time their value may be even greater to other shareholders who want to keep the business in the form of a close corporation."

Following the *Bernier* decision, Massachusetts trial courts routinely tax affected pass-through entities, including S corporations and partnerships, in divorce valuations. The Massachusetts Supreme Court acknowledged this as the rule in Massachusetts when it said, in *Adams v. Adams*, "The Special Master was certainly correct to tax affect the transfer of the wife's portion of the present value of the partnership interest."[32]

On appeal, however, the court took exception to the methodology applied in tax affecting the partnership for equitable distribution purposes as well as the valuation methodology itself. According to the court, "What constitutes proper valuation methodology and the valuation of a business interest is a question of fact." The trial court's special master tax affected the capitalized partnership value by combining and applying the current federal capital gains tax rate (rather than the income tax rate). The court rejected the use of the federal capital gains tax rate as well as the capitalized earnings valuation method.

The court acknowledged that the direct capitalization of earnings is a generally accepted business valuation method. The court said, "This method is the preferred accounting formula for valuing corporations, stocks, and similar interests. It is appropriate for the valuation of interests in corporations, in particular, because the formula presumes the perpetuity of a future income stream, and corporations are defined, in part, by their infinite existence." The court said, "It was, however, error to use that method in this case because the husband's partnership interest was delimited by a finite period of cash flow." Partnerships do not have perpetual existence. The court found that the husband planned to retire in 14 years and his partnership profit distribution would cease when he leaves the partnership. His cash flow following retirement would be limited to his withdrawal payment, payable over 10 years pursuant to the partnership agreement.

As a result, the court rejected the capitalization of earnings method of valuation and said, "On remand, the judge (or special master) should recalculate the present value of the husband's partnership interest, applying consistent figures to … both the distributions and the withdrawal payments." The court discussed the discounted cash flow method and the capitalization of earnings method and concluded that the discounted cash flow methodology should be used for a partnership that lacks the perpetual existence of a corporation. The court said, "In our view, this methodology is better suited for valuing an individual's interest in a partnership. Unlike the direct capitalization of income approach, which assumes a perpetual stream of income, the discounted cash flow method uses a more complex equation to reduce a finite period of future income (here, fourteen years of distribution before retirement, and ten years of withdrawal payments thereafter) to present valuation.… The special master, and the judge adopting his findings, should have employed that methodology here."

The court took exception to the use of capital gains tax rates in tax affecting the partnership income. The court said, "The character of all items constituting the partner's distributive share is

32 *Adams v. Adams*, 459 Mass. 361 (2011).

determined as if each item were realized directly from the source from which realized by the partnership, or incurred in the same manner as incurred by the partnership. Therefore, distributions from a partnership are not uniformly subjected to either an ordinary income tax rate or a capital gains tax rate, but are itemized, with each item treated appropriately for tax purposes.... It is not necessarily error that the special master tax affected at a rate different from the rates advanced by both experts.... However, in rejecting the opinion of both experts as to the applicable tax rates, the special master and the judge were still obligated to provide a reasonable explanation, and here, they failed to offer a cogent explanation of their choice.... Nonetheless, it is not clear from the special master's brief treatment of the issue, (1) why he applied a combined capital gains tax rate in lieu of the effective income tax rates suggested by both the husband's and the wife's experts, or some amalgamation of all applicable rates, as this court ordered in *Bernier*, in the context of the transfer of an interest in a close corporation.... On remand, the judge should provide a clearer explanation of which rates are applicable in tax affecting this transfer of a share of the present value of the husband's partnership interest to the wife."

In 2013, the Appeals Court of Massachusetts decided the case of *Gralton v. Gralton.*[33] The court restated the rules of Massachusetts as: "The Supreme Judicial Court decided *Adams v. Adams*, 459 Mass. 361, 388-389 (2011), which makes clear that where, as in this case, an interest in a pass-through entity is valued using the income method, the value must be 'tax affected' utilizing the approach described in *Bernier v. Bernier*, 449 Mass. 774, 790 (2007). The tax-affected valuation of the interest must be used unless it is materially at odds with the totality of the circumstances or ... at variance with the requirements of the *equitable* distribution statute.... In this case, the judge did not tax affect the husband's interest in the S-Corporation, nor did he determine whether a tax-affected valuation would be at odds with the circumstances or the requirements of the statute. Consequently, that aspect of the judgment valuing the interest in the S-Corporation must be vacated and the case remanded.... While we note that this court in *Bernier*, utilized the dividend tax rate as of the date of valuation in tax affecting the value of the interest in the S-Corporation there, we also note that we do not read *Bernier* or *Adams* to require invariably the use of a 29.4 percent tax affecting rate in tax affecting the value of the interest in circumstances like those before us where the dividend tax rate on the date of valuation was the same (fifteen percent) as the dividend tax rate in the *Kessler* decision relied on in *Bernier*.... So much of the amended judgment as sets the distribution of marital property in reliance upon the valuation of the S-Corporation is vacated, and that aspect of the case is remanded for proceedings consistent with this memorandum and order."

As the Massachusetts cases demonstrate, equitable relief requires that tax affecting is appropriate in the valuation of S corporations for equitable distribution purposes in divorce. The history of this position shows that it is derived from the fair value standard of value used in shareholder litigation under the Model Business Corporation Act, as applied in *Delaware Radiology*.

33 *Gralton v. Gralton*, No. 12-P-1220 (Mass. May 29, 2013).

Economic damages. The calculation of economic damages is another category of equitable relief using business valuation. Historically, most liability cases were tried in state courts where income taxes were not a major consideration.[34] Then the U.S. Supreme Court ruled that income taxes are an important consideration in cases involving equitable considerations.[35] Following that decision, federal courts began routinely requiring that adjustments for income taxes be made in calculating economic damages. In applying the Supreme Court tax affecting decision, two adjustments were necessarily made. First, the stream of future earnings must be reduced from a gross amount to a net after-tax amount to reflect the amount that would be available to the plaintiff and his family. Next, the future earnings are discounted to their present value. The 9th Circuit Court of Appeals went further in applying the Supreme Court decision and held that a lump-sum damage award should be increased by the amount of income tax that would have to be paid on the earnings of the total award.[36]

S corporations present several problems in lost profits cases. Arguments were made that, because the S corporation paid no taxes, it had no net profits because all of its income is treated as the personal income of the shareholders. As a result, the courts were without a base to calculate lost profits damages. The argument was that the plaintiff S corporation, having no profits at the corporate level, cannot show lost profits for a tort committed against it or for breach of a contract that it entered into. Any damages the individual shareholders suffer would be irrelevant as they were not the injured party. The corporation was the injured party. The 11th Circuit Court of Appeals rejected that argument and remanded the case for the S corporation to consider reasonable compensation for the shareholder-employees in calculating its lost profits.[37]

Conclusion. The answer to the question of whether it is appropriate to tax affect an S corporation is, yes, under the appropriate circumstances. The standard of value required to be applied and the purpose and function of the appraisal will generally determine when it is appropriate to tax affect the S corporation.

---

34 *Hall v. Chicago & N.W. Railway Company*, 125 N.E.2d 77 (Ill. 1955). "It is a general principle of law that in the trial of a lawsuit the status of the parties is immaterial. Thus, what the plaintiff does with an award, or how the defendant acquires the money with which to pay the award, is of no concern to the court or jury. Similarly, whether the plaintiff has to pay a tax on the award is a matter that concerns only the plaintiff and the government. The tortfeasor has no interest in such questions."

35 *Norfolk and Western Railway Company v. Liepelt*, 444 U.S. 490 (1980), "It is his after tax income, rather than his gross income before taxes, that provides the only realistic measure of his ability to support his family.... We therefore reject the notion that the introduction of evidence describing a decedent's estimated after tax earnings is too speculative or complex for a jury. Respondent argues that if this door is opened, other equally relevant evidence must also be received. For example, she points out that in discounting the estimate of future earnings to its present value, the tax on the income to be earned by the damage award is now omitted. Logically, it would certainly seem correct that this amount, like future wages, should be estimated on an after tax basis."

36 *Shaw v. United States*, 741 F.2d 1202 (9th Cir. 1984). The court stated: "We have indeed noted that, since income taxes on lost compensation should be deducted, a lump sum damage award should correspondingly be increased by the amount of income tax that would have to be paid on the earnings of the total award."

37 *Ad-Vantage Telephone Directory Consultants, Inc. v. GTE Directories Corp.*, 849 F.2d 1336 (11th Cir. 1987). See also *Hospital Products, Inc. v. Sterile Design, Inc.*, 923 F.2d 859 (8th Cir. 1990); and *Bova v. Gary*, 843 N.E.2d 952 (Ind. App. 2006). Plaintiff president and sole shareholder of S corporation injured in automobile accident can offer evidence of corporation's lost profits resulting from his inability to work as probative of the value of plaintiff's lost earning capacity.

Feedback Wanted on Tax Affecting Article

The accompanying article, "Tax Affecting S Corporations: It's Not a Matter of Whether. It's a Matter of When," presents the author's view on why the IRS and Tax Court have rejected tax affecting of pass-through entities. We invite readers to submit comments and feedback on this article.

We have already seen some comments on this article, some agreeing with the author and others taking issue. In the latter group, commenters are united in their view that this matter is *not* settled law. The Tax Court cases cited in the article are memorandum decisions, which are not precedent—a point that Judge David Laro of the Tax Court has also made in the past. Judge Laro also stated that the IRS's position of no tax affecting "contradicts sound valuation practices" and that "the final chapter on tax affecting has not yet been written" at the 2015 AICPA FVS conference in Las Vegas.

At the time of this writing, two cases are pending in Tax Court that may help to write this final chapter, depending on the outcomes. The cases are *Cecil et al. v. Commissioner of Internal Revenue* and the other is the Michael Jackson estate tax case. In the *Cecil* case, the valuation experts for both the taxpayer and the IRS use tax affecting. In the *Jackson* case, the court denied the IRS's motion to exclude testimony concerning tax affecting, with the judge writing: "It is highly likely that the proper use of the discounted cash flow method will be an important issue in this case. Whether and how to take tax effects into account in that valuation will likely be crucial to the final numbers."

What do you think? Is there a bright-line rule that precludes tax affecting S corporations under the fair market value standard? Let us know your thoughts—you can email them to the editor at andyd@bvresources.com.

There is a difference between business valuations made for "law" purposes and business valuations made for "equity" purposes. Under the federal tax law, it is not appropriate to tax affect the S corporation. For business valuations made for equitable purposes, such as shareholder litigation, marital property determinations, economic damages measurements, and similar fiduciary relationship issues, it may be appropriate to tax affect the S corporation business valuation depending on the jurisdiction and required standard of value.

As stated by the Tax Court: "Fair value is … not equivalent to fair market value."[38]

Alan Zipp *is an attorney, certified public accountant, accredited in business valuation, certified valuation analyst, certified business appraiser, and certified fraud examiner. He has been providing tax and financial planning advice to individuals and small businesses since 1970. He is an author, lecturer, and discussion leader for the American Institute of Certified Public Accountants. In addition to tax matters, he has developed a specialty in the area of divorce tax and financial planning and related litigation support services. He is located in Rockville, Md., and can be reached at alanzipp@aol.com.*

38 *Dallas v. Commissioner*, T.C. Memo 2006-212

A Reflection on Low Risk-Free Interest Rates

By Matthew Crane, Marshall & Stevens Inc. (New York, N.Y.)

Although business appraisals often do not concern themselves with the details of monetary policies, given the current low-interest-rate environment, it's useful for appraisers to have a historical perspective, in addition to understanding some of the relevant economic theories regarding the outlook for changes in interest rates. Under these economic theories, interest rates may either stay at low levels for the foreseeable future or return to normal levels, where real rates above inflation will exist for Treasury investments. Where inflation exceeds the stated rate, investors are currently incurring economic losses. Therefore, appraisers should consider whether or not willing buyers and sellers or market participants would choose to earn a negative real return or perhaps contemplate normalizing adjustments. The risk-free rate is the starting point for valuations, yet, given the current low spot rates, the issue arises that, if the starting point is meant to encompass inflation expectations, perhaps the use of a spot rate that has a negative real return may not make sense.[1] Exhibit 1 details the spread between inflation and the 10-, 20-, and 30-year Treasury bond rates.

1 Duff & Phelps (2016), page 3-3.

Exhibit 1. Spread Between Inflation and the 10-, 20-, and 30-Year Treasury Bond Rates

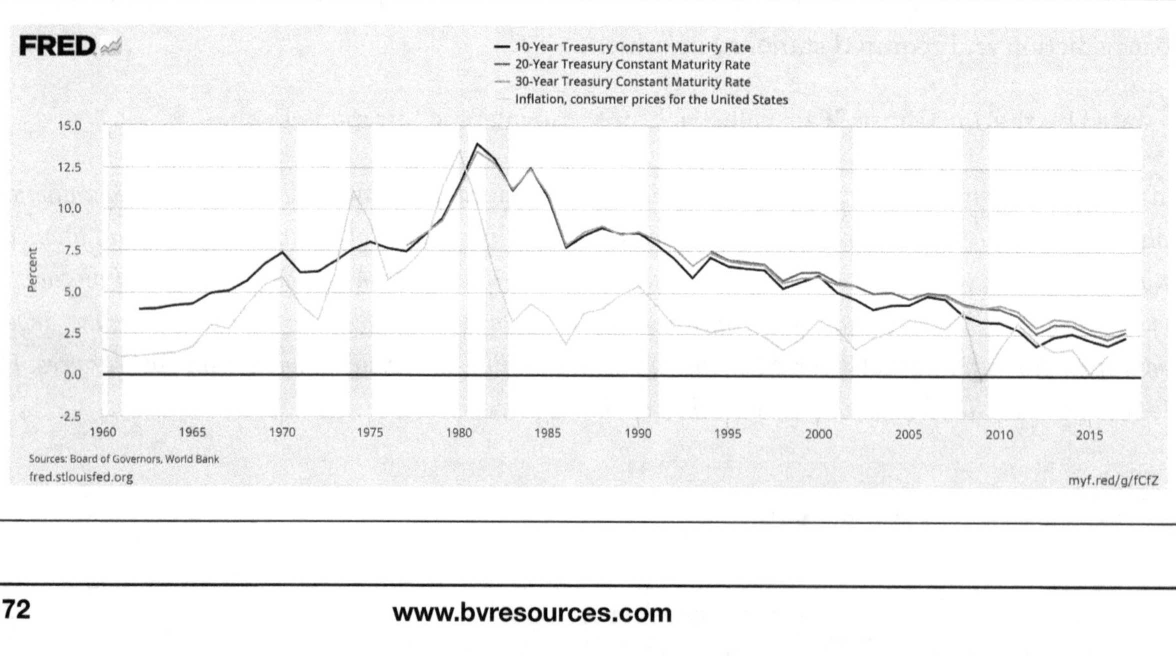

Exhibit 2. Debt to GDP for the United States, Japan, and Germany

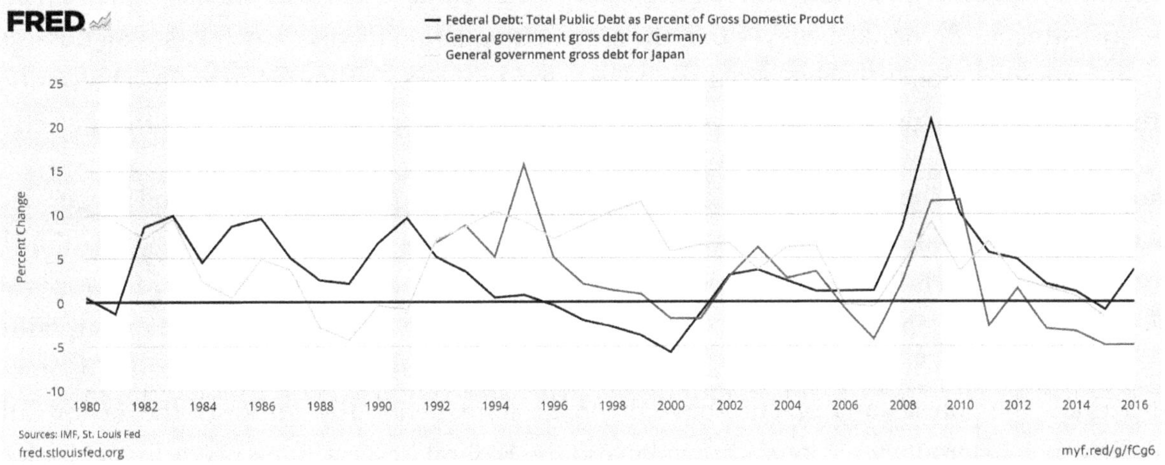

As indicated in Exhibit 1, the decrease in the spread between the rate of inflation and risk-free rates has been ongoing since the early 1980s and there are minimal differences in the yields to compensate investors for differences in holding periods between the 10-, 20-, and 30-year Treasury bonds. So what is going on here? In the current decade, the spreads between inflation and the risk-free rates have sunk to current lows. Is this phenomenon a new development? Secular stagflation is one theory that declares it is.

Secular stagflation is the result of low equilibrium interest rates being exported to other economies, lead to capital outflows and currency depreciation, shifting demand toward Europe and Japan from the United States.[2] In simplistic terms, the contagion of low interest rates spreads throughout economies. According to Larry Summers (2010), "The first priority for policy should not be financial engineering in either the private sectors or the public sector but a concerted effort to identify and find the means of financing the most productive investment opportunities globally." This theory tends to espouse that the low-interest-rate environment is a new normal and could continue for some time. In simplistic terms, the United States is not immune from low interest rates in other economies, and the relative risk-reward comparison globally is ongoing, whereby the rates are susceptible to the global markets—a "flight to quality." For monetary policy to attain stabilization, the old rules may not apply and intervention is needed to bring the rates back up to normal levels.

To further examine the relationship between different countries, the debt to GDP for the United States, Japan, and Germany are presented in Exhibit 2.

One can see the similar leveraging and deleveraging during the financial crisis that occurred in the 2008 and 2010 period, with all three economies showing a steep deleveraging and Germany's ratio going negative for an extended period. So it would appear that this relationship between countries is cause for concern.

2 Olivier Blanchard, Raghuram Rajan, Kenneth Rogoff, and Larry Summers (2010), page 562.

Ben Bernanke (2015) also suggests a related theory to secular stagflation, which is the global savings glut. Under this theory, too much capital has been set aside and "there is a global excess of savings over investment." Bernanke believes that the secular stagflation theory only focuses on domestic capital formation, domestic household spending, and reduced population growth. The solution to the global savings glut is foreign investment and monetary policies that support that objective.

The debt super cycle theory predicates low interest rates on the expansion of public and private debt, a temporary condition, which is currently being corrected. According to Kenneth Rogoff (2010), the cure for the situation is for monetary policy to adopt measures that focus on "heterodox" responses pointing to deleveraging, instead of the orthodoxy currently in place such as inflation targeting.[3] This theory tends to believe interest rates will increase in the future and the old rules do apply, but perhaps the policies and practice have diverged. John Taylor, the author of the Taylor Rule, cites that such heterodoxy responses are valid and the Federal Reserve Bank needs to "get back on track" with the rules-based policies instead of the interventionist types of measures implemented. In essence, stable policies create stable results. Intervention creates havoc.

So now the question is how these theories may affect an appraisal. In practice, the 20-year Treasury bond rate generally is considered the starting point for developing a discount rate—Roger Grabowski (2010). The principal reason is to consider the longer-term view of an investment horizon. However, where real rates are negative, one has to question the relevance of the choice of which risk-free security or whether the spot rate is valid. If an appraiser is to normalize the risk-free rate, the appraiser would have to select a period that the normalization process should occur and methodology. Methodology is beyond the scope of this article, but the choice of time frame really depends on how long the appraiser may believe these low risk-free rates will continue.

To give some perspective on what time frame may be appropriate, Exhibit 3 puts a picture to the historical perspective of the risk-free rates.

Extended data for the 20-year Treasury bond (T-Note) is not as available as shorter-term treasuries, such as the three-month Treasury bill (T-Bill). Consequently, an extensive analysis of the T-Note is not possible. Exhibit 3 shows a dramatic rise in the T-Bill occurring in the 1960s that continued through the 1980s. The T-Note shows a related decline in rates trending with the T-Bill. Both the T-Note and T-Bill rates are at lows, but these lows also occurred for the T-Bill during the late 1930s and 1940s, which included the Great Depression and World War II.

According to the St. Louis Federal Reserve's "Fred" database, the minimum T-Bill of 0.01% occurred on several dates: January 1940 and subsequently September 2011, November 2011, and December 2011, after the financial crisis and the federal government's subsequent intervention by instating the Troubled Assets Relief Program (TARP). The maximum rate of 16.30% occurred in May 1981. As of April 2017, the T-Bill rate is 0.80%. The median T-Bill rate based upon the entire data set is 3.04%.

3 Ibid, page 370.

Exhibit 3. Historical Perspective of the Risk-Free Rates

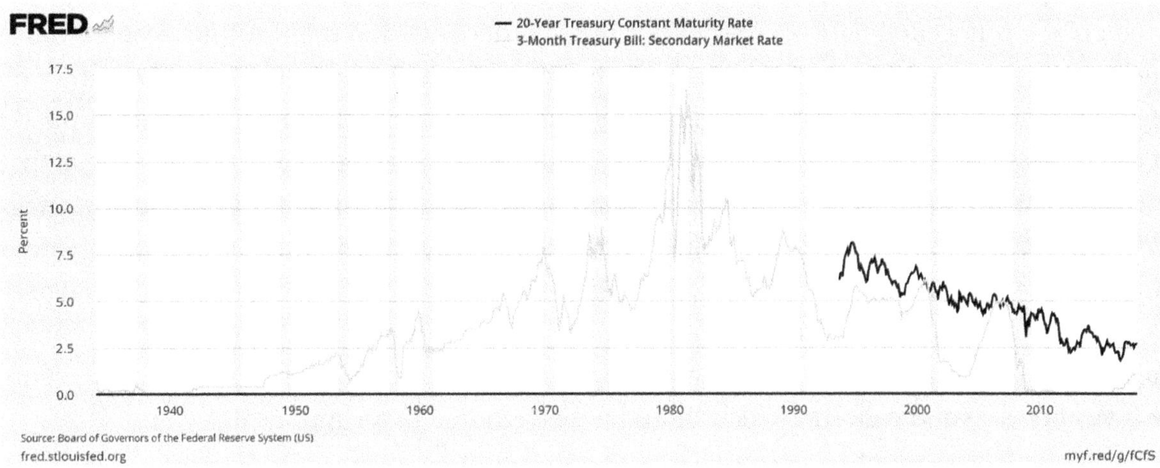

Looking at several breakpoints in the data is useful. For instance, the T-Bill rate was 1.0% or less at three periods. The first period encompasses the beginning of the data, January 1934, until approximately 14 years later, February 1948. The second period began June 2003 and ended less than a year later, in April 2004. The third period began in October 2008 and continues to the present, approximately eight and one half years later. So, based upon the data, T-Bill rates under 1.0% are unusual but not uncharted territory. Risk-free rates have been low before, and it appears that a general range of this occurrence is eight to 14 years, so an assumption of 10 years may be useful, which would indicate, as of the date of this article, we are coming to the tail end of this phenomenon. It is noteworthy to state that data for the T-Bill is not available prior to 1934, so it's difficult to say whether the first period lasted longer than 14 years, but it is safe to say it is possible these low rates may continue. Currently, the T-Note and T-Bill rates indicate that the direction is changing toward increased rates. Consensus is the rates will increase modestly and will not decline further.

The monetary policies the Federal Reserve Bank has at its disposal are focused on the discount (interest) rate, reserve requirements, and open-market policies. An example of the Fed's influence on the discount rate is inflation targeting, which essentially sets an interest rate above or below expected inflation. Reserve requirements dictate to the banks what types of deposits are required. Quantitative easing is an example of open-market policies, or the printing of monies to buy back government debt is another tool that the Federal Reserve Bank has applied in recent history. Quantitative easing is a form of "asset purchases" by the federal government. At this juncture, given the Fed chairperson's inclination to consider future inflation targeting[4] and/or asset purchases, the expectation is that low interest rates will not continue and that interest rates will only go up, but others also believe that such actions by the Fed may be ineffective and these new interest rates are a "new normal." So appraisers have to decide for themselves whether this is a new normal or a temporary condition.

4 See recent speech by Janet Yellen www.federalreserve.gov/newsevents/speech/yellen20170303a.htm.

Conclusion. My personal viewpoint is that the debt super cycle theory holds validity and the secular stagflation seems improbable, while the global savings glut makes intuitive sense. There is too great a connection between the leveraging of economies and the resulting response in low interest rates. Although it would be logical that the effects of stagflation on one large economy would affect another, evidence points to a different conclusion. Japan's decline in GDP has continued for an extended period, during periods when the United States economy has grown. Perhaps that is evidence that a contagion can be immunized and prevented. In closing, I believe that low interest rates will continue but that this phenomenon is a temporary condition and not a "new normal." However, the appraiser still has to make a judgement call based upon today's rates. A suggested measure would be to look at inflation and the real rates of return over a period of 10 years and make a comparison to the spot rate to determine the reasonableness. The issue of negative returns for investors is a valid concern, which should not be ignored in an appraisal.

***Matthew Crane,** ASA, CPA, CEIV, is a director at Marshall & Stevens Inc. and leads the financial valuation practice at its New York City office. He can be reached at mcrane@marshall-stevens.com.*

Caveat: Matthew Crane prepared this article in his personal capacity. The opinions expressed in this article are the author's own and do not reflect the view of this publication or Marshall & Stevens, the author's employer.

References:

Ben Bernanke, "Why Are Interest Rates So Low, Part 3: The Global Savings Glut," Brookings, 2015.

Olivier Blanchard, Raghuram Rajan, Kenneth Rogoff, and Larry Summers, "Progress and Confusion: The State of Macroeconomic Policy," MIT Press (2016).

Duff & Phelps, *2016 Valuation Handbook - Guide to Cost of Capital,* John Wiley & Sons, Inc., 2016.

Roger Grabowski, "Developing the Cost of Equity Capital: Risk-Free Rate and ERP During Period of Flight to Quality," *Business Valuation Review,* page 173, 2010.

John Taylor, "Getting Back on Track: Macroeconomic Policy Lessons From the Financial Crisis," Federal Reserve Bank of St. Louis Reserve, May/June 2010.

Inside *Pratt's Stats:* Impact of Entity Form on Selling Price (Part 1)

By Eric J. Barr (Marks Paneth) and
Peter L. Lohrey (Montclair State University)

Editor's note: This is a two-part article that explains how transaction size and the entity form of the buyer and seller support the existence (and the magnitude) of the "pass-through entity premium" where the buyer is able to take advantage of the pass-through status of the seller. This article is based on the results of various statistical analyses of Pratt's Stats *transactional data.*

Several database providers provide information about private-company transactions. One of the largest and most detailed databases is *Pratt's Stats*™ in which:

> Data is gathered primarily from business intermediaries such as the International Business Brokers Association, the Certified Business Counselors, and other business intermediaries. *Pratt's Stats* is the only private company database that includes balance sheets and income statements for the companies sold.[1]

The purpose of this article is to provide information regarding the content of the *Pratt's Stats* database, which is one of the most widely used databases when developing a conclusion (or calculation) of value of an ownership interest under the guideline transactions method.

We analyzed the Feb. 29, 2016, version of the *Pratt's Stats* database containing more than 24,000 private-company transactions (it now has over 28,000 transactions). This database now includes almost 150 data fields for each transaction,[2] including:

- SIC and NAICS;
- Business description;

1 Shannon P. Pratt, *The Market Approach to Valuing Businesses*, 2nd edition, Hoboken, N.J., John Wiley & Sons Inc., 2005, p. 65.

2 BIZCOMPS, another database that provides information on private-company transactions, contains approximately 14,000 transactions with 21 data fields per transaction (available at www.bvresources.com/bizcomps).

- Franchise;
- Development stage company;
- Real estate;
- Age of target;
- Employee count;
- City, state, region, country;
- Acquirer type;
- Date of income statement;
- Income statement data;
- Balance sheet data;
- Purchase price date;
- Intangible asset data;
- MVIC price and debt terms;
- Transaction type;
- Assumed lease, renewal options, and lease length;
- Noncompete agreements and terms;
- MVIC as a percentage of different operating statistics; and
- Profitability, liquidity, and capitalization ratios.

A sample transaction can be obtained at the *Pratt's Stats*™ webpage,[3] available from Business Valuation Resources.[4]

Pratt's Stats defines sales price as the market value of invested capital[5] (or MVIC).

This article describes the specific data that are included in *Pratt's Stats:*

3 www.bvresources.com/prattsstats.

4 The Market Approach, page 327.

5 MVIC is defined as the market value of equity plus the market value of interest-bearing debt.

Exhibit 1. Number of Asset and Equity Sales Transactions by MVIC Price Category

Sales Price (MVIC)		# of Transactions			Cumulative % of Transactions			Annual % of Transactions		
From	To	Asset Sales	Equity Sales	Total	Asset Sales	Equity Sales	Total	Asset Sales	Equity Sales	Total
$0	$250,000	9,896	198	10,094	40.6%	0.8%	41.4%	98.0%	2.0%	100.0%
$250,001	$500,000	3,139	195	3,334	12.9%	0.8%	13.7%	94.2%	5.8%	100.0%
$500,001	$1,000,000	1,888	287	2,175	7.8%	1.2%	8.9%	86.8%	13.2%	100.0%
$1,000,001	$2,000,000	1,010	377	1,387	4.1%	1.5%	5.7%	72.8%	27.2%	100.0%
$2,000,001	$5,000,000	787	701	1,488	3.2%	2.9%	6.1%	52.9%	47.1%	100.0%
$5,000,001	$10,000,000	496	680	1,176	2.0%	2.8%	4.8%	42.2%	57.8%	100.0%
$10,000,001	$20,000,000	397	800	1,197	1.6%	3.3%	4.9%	33.2%	66.8%	100.0%
$20,000,001	$50,000,000	425	1,008	1,433	1.7%	4.1%	5.9%	29.7%	70.3%	100.0%
$50,000,001	$100,000,000	229	606	835	0.9%	2.5%	3.4%	27.4%	72.6%	100.0%
$100,000,001	$500,000,000	221	688	909	0.9%	2.8%	3.7%	24.3%	75.7%	100.0%
>$500,000,000		73	258	331	0.3%	1.1%	1.4%	22.1%	77.9%	100.0%
Totals		**18,561**	**5,798**	**24,359**	**76.2%**	**23.8%**	**100.0%**	**76.2%**	**23.8%**	**100.0%**

Source: *Pratt's Stats* database, Feb. 29, 2016

- Asset vs. equity transactions;
- Actual mix of buyers;
- Transactions by NAICS code;
- Number of transactions by year; and
- Number of transactions by seller, buyer, and type of transaction.[6]

Asset sales and equity sales. The data contained in *Pratt's Stats* summarizes MVIC sales prices by size categories. *Pratt's Stats* reports two types of MVIC sales transactions: asset sales and equity sales. Exhibit 1 summarizes the number of each type of transaction by MVIC size category.

Our investigation found that the greater the MVIC price, the greater the likelihood that the transaction would be an equity sale. For example, approximately 96% of the transactions of $1 million or less were asset sales, while approximately 69% of the transactions greater than $10 million were equity sales.

Entity form of purchaser. *Pratt's Stats* discloses whether the purchaser is a private company or a public company.[7]

6 A discussion of the actual mix of sellers by entity form can be found in Part 2 of this two-part article, which will appear in the next issue.

7 Private companies can be classified for federal taxation purposes as either pass-through entities (PTE) such as limited liability corporations, partnerships, or "C" corporations—where the entity pays corporate income taxes before shareholders pay personal income taxes on any proceeds they receive from the business.

The transactions that private- and public-company buyers completed for each MVIC sales price category are summarized in Exhibit 2. Certain transactions were excluded from Exhibits 2, 3, 4, 10, and 11. These transactions were: (1) foreign company sellers; (2) transactions where accurate information regarding the selling entity form or buyer entity form was not provided; or (3) transactions lacking information with respect to equity or asset sale structure. Hence, the total number of transactions noted in Exhibit 2 (and the exhibits that follow) does not match the total number of transactions in Exhibit 1.

Exhibit 3 presents the number of transactions by private-company buyers by each MVIC category.

Exhibit 2. Number of Transactions by Private- and Public-Company Buyers

Sales Price (MVIC)		# of Buyers			
From	To	Private	Public	Totals	% of Totals
$0	$250,000	8,964	60	9,024	41.4%
$250,001	$500,000	3,014	83	3,097	14.2%
$500,001	$1,000,000	1,913	181	2,094	9.6%
$1,000,001	$2,000,000	955	341	1,296	5.9%
$2,000,001	$5,000,000	587	784	1,371	6.3%
$5,000,001	$10,000,000	225	789	1,014	4.6%
$10,000,001	$20,000,000	107	934	1,041	4.8%
$20,000,001	$50,000,000	60	1,171	1,231	5.6%
$50,000,001	$100,000,000	20	678	698	3.2%
$100,000,001	$500,000,000	8	720	728	3.3%
>$500,000,000		-	214	214	1.0%
		15,853	**5,955**	**21,808**	**100.0%**

Source: *Pratt's Stats* database, Feb. 29, 2016

Exhibit 3. Number of Transactions by Private-Company Buyers

Sales Price (MVIC)		Private Buyer Transactions		
From	To	Number	% of Total	Cumulative %
$0	$250,000	8,964	56.5%	56.5%
$250,001	$500,000	3,014	19.0%	75.6%
$500,001	$1,000,000	1,913	12.1%	87.6%
$1,000,001	$2,000,000	955	6.0%	93.6%
$2,000,001	$5,000,000	587	3.7%	97.4%
$5,000,001	$10,000,000	225	1.4%	98.8%
$10,000,001	$20,000,000	107	0.7%	99.4%
$20,000,001	$50,000,000	60	0.4%	99.8%
$50,000,001	$100,000,000	20	0.1%	99.9%
$100,000,001	$500,000,000	8	0.1%	100.0%
>$500,000,000		-	0.0%	100.0%
		15,853	**100.0%**	

Source: *Pratt's Stats* database, Feb. 29, 2016

As noted in Exhibits 2 and 3, approximately 88% of all private-company transactions consisted of MVIC transaction values of $1 million or less. Of the 15,853 private-buyer transactions, only 1,962 involved MVIC sales prices of more than $1 million.

Exhibit 4 presents the transactions public-company buyers completed. We found that approximately 76% of all public-company transactions involved MVIC transaction prices of $5 million or more. Of the 5,955 purchases public buyers made, only 1,449 involved MVIC prices less than $5 million.

Number of transactions by NAICS code. We next turned to *BVU*, which contains an article indicating *Pratt's Stats* MVIC/revenue trends. One of the exhibits included provides MVIC/revenue interquartile range by business sector. The industries by NAICS code included in this exhibit are:

- Agriculture, forestry, fishing, and hunting (100000 to 199999);
- Mining, utilities, and construction (200000 to 299999);
- Manufacturing (300000 to 399999);
- Transportation and warehousing; wholesale trade; and retail trade (400000 to 499999);
- Information, finance, and insurance; real estate rental and leasing; professional, scientific, and technical services; management of companies and enterprises; and administrative and support and waste management and remediation services (500000 to 599999);
- Educational services; and healthcare and social assistance (600000 to 699999);

Exhibit 4. Number of Transactions by Public-Company Buyers

Sales Price (MVIC)		Public Buyer Transactions		
From	To	Number	% of Total	Cumulative %
$0	$250,000	60	1.0%	1.0%
$250,001	$500,000	83	1.4%	2.4%
$500,001	$1,000,000	181	3.0%	5.4%
$1,000,001	$2,000,000	341	5.7%	11.2%
$2,000,001	$5,000,000	784	13.2%	24.3%
$5,000,001	$10,000,000	789	13.2%	37.6%
$10,000,001	$20,000,000	934	15.7%	53.3%
$20,000,001	$50,000,000	1,171	19.7%	72.9%
$50,000,001	$100,000,000	678	11.4%	84.3%
$100,000,001	$500,000,000	720	12.1%	96.4%
>$500,000,000		214	3.6%	100.0%
		5,955	**100.0%**	

Source: *Pratt's Stats* database, Feb. 29, 2016

- Arts, entertainment, and recreation; and accommodation and food services (700000 to 799999);
- Other services (800000 to 899999); and
- Public administration (900000 to 999999).

Exhibit 5 presents the number of transactions by NAICS code, and Exhibit 6 presents the same information on a common-sized basis as a percentage of MVIC transaction price.

Exhibit 5. Number of Transactions by NAICS Code

Sales Price (MVIC)		Pratts' Stats # of Transactions by NAICS Codes									
From	To	100000-199999	200000-299999	300000-399999	400000-499999	500000-599999	600000-699999	700000-799999	800000-899999	900000-999999	Totals
$0	$250,000	7	275	663	2,470	1,823	560	2,706	1,587	3	**10,094**
$250,001	$500,000	10	189	387	953	622	274	518	376	2	**3,331**
$500,001	$1,000,000	7	146	357	620	481	223	181	159	1	**2,175**
$1,000,001	$2,000,000	5	87	298	313	395	162	65	59	2	**1,386**
$2,000,001	$5,000,000	2	97	375	256	559	116	57	24	1	**1,487**
$5,000,001	$10,000,000	2	68	340	152	520	45	30	16	2	**1,175**
$10,000,001	$20,000,000	5	62	353	140	542	48	34	12	1	**1,197**
$20,000,001	$50,000,000	6	78	455	152	644	52	32	13	1	**1,433**
$50,000,001	$100,000,000	6	46	268	105	343	25	30	10	1	**834**
$100,000,001	$500,000,000	49	340	-	98	365	31	14	6	2	**905**
>$500,000,000		2	33	126	37	125	-	4	2	2	**331**
Totals		**101**	**1,421**	**3,622**	**5,296**	**6,419**	**1,536**	**3,671**	**2,264**	**18**	**24,348**

Source: *Pratt's Stats* database, Feb. 29, 2016

Exhibit 6. Common-Sized Number of Transactions by NAICS Code

Sales Price (MVIC)		*Pratts' Stats* # of Transactions by NAICS Codes										
From	To	100000-199999	200000-299999	300000-399999	400000-499999	500000-599999	600000-699999	700000-799999	800000-899999	900000-999999	Totals	Cumulative Totals
$0	$250,000	0.0%	1.1%	2.7%	10.1%	7.5%	2.3%	11.1%	6.5%	0.0%	41.5%	**41.5%**
$250,001	$500,000	0.0%	0.8%	1.6%	3.9%	2.6%	1.1%	2.1%	1.5%	0.0%	13.7%	**55.1%**
$500,001	$1,000,000	0.0%	0.6%	1.5%	2.5%	2.0%	0.9%	0.7%	0.7%	0.0%	8.9%	**64.1%**
$1,000,001	$2,000,000	0.0%	0.4%	1.2%	1.3%	1.6%	0.7%	0.3%	0.2%	0.0%	5.7%	**69.8%**
$2,000,001	$5,000,000	0.0%	0.4%	1.5%	1.1%	2.3%	0.5%	0.2%	0.1%	0.0%	6.1%	**75.9%**
$5,000,001	$10,000,000	0.0%	0.3%	1.4%	0.6%	2.1%	0.2%	0.1%	0.1%	0.0%	4.8%	**80.7%**
$10,000,001	$20,000,000	0.0%	0.3%	1.4%	0.6%	2.2%	0.2%	0.1%	0.0%	0.0%	4.9%	**85.6%**
$20,000,001	$50,000,000	0.0%	0.3%	1.9%	0.6%	2.6%	0.2%	0.1%	0.1%	0.0%	5.9%	**91.5%**
$50,000,001	$100,000,000	0.0%	0.2%	1.1%	0.4%	1.4%	0.1%	0.1%	0.0%	0.0%	3.4%	**94.9%**
$100,000,001	$500,000,000	0.2%	1.4%	0.0%	0.4%	1.5%	0.1%	0.1%	0.0%	0.0%	3.7%	**98.6%**
>$500,000,000		0.0%	0.1%	0.5%	0.2%	0.5%	0.0%	0.0%	0.0%	0.0%	1.4%	**100.0%**
Totals		**0.4%**	**5.8%**	**14.9%**	**21.8%**	**26.4%**	**6.3%**	**15.1%**	**9.3%**	**0.1%**	**100.0%**	

Source: *Pratt's Stats* database, Feb. 29, 2016

Exhibit 7. Number of Transactions by Year

Sales Price (MVIC)		*Pratts' Stats* # of Transactions/ Year of Transaction																
From	To	Pre-2000	2000	2001	2002	2003	2004	2005	2006	2007	2008	2009	2010	2011	2012	2013	2014	2015
$0	$250,000	733	288	358	453	407	572	611	579	624	887	589	733	678	677	696	683	524
$250,001	$500,000	243	88	119	138	137	194	208	204	242	294	191	183	209	231	215	254	182
$500,001	$1,000,000	163	62	100	91	95	116	117	141	164	162	111	112	133	147	158	180	121
$1,000,001	$2,000,000	188	73	63	90	68	80	88	85	111	92	71	64	53	47	68	73	72
$2,000,001	$5,000,000	382	98	53	48	75	96	88	77	98	73	48	54	73	61	45	82	37
$5,000,001	$10,000,000	398	81	43	41	43	67	75	73	68	62	25	31	46	35	23	43	22
$10,000,001	$20,000,000	443	80	46	29	31	60	72	74	82	52	47	39	24	36	21	42	19
$20,000,001	$50,000,000	484	108	59	45	40	62	88	100	95	66	35	49	55	50	37	47	11
$50,000,001	$100,000,000	240	69	26	22	35	45	52	48	67	35	11	45	30	29	35	25	21
$100,000,001	$500,000,000	50	62	44	24	44	62	74	93	82	50	30	52	79	52	38	52	21
>$500,000,000		6	15	7	4	6	10	23	21	29	15	10	38	35	35	25	32	18
Totals		**3,330**	**1,024**	**918**	**985**	**981**	**1,364**	**1,496**	**1,495**	**1,662**	**1,788**	**1,168**	**1,400**	**1,415**	**1,400**	**1,361**	**1,513**	**1,048**
Source: *Pratt's Stats* database, Feb. 29, 2016																		

Exhibits 5 and 6 show that approximately 48% of all the transactions in the *Pratt's Stats* database had NAICS codes from 400000 to 599999. Our exhibits indicate a limited number of transactions greater than $1 million for NAICS codes 700000 to 999999.

Transactions by year. From 1990 through Dec. 31, 2015, the U.S. economy experienced three cycles of recession and recovery. These sequences impacted the marketability of certain businesses, created a compulsion for certain business owners to sell, limited the availability of capital to finance purchase transactions, and affected median MVIC price by transaction price category. Exhibit 7 summarizes the number of transactions by year for each MVIC category. During years of recession (i.e., 2001 and 2009), the number of transactions decreased substantially compared to the immediately preceding prerecession years. Exhibit 8 summarizes the median MVIC price for each category by year.

Combinations of buyer, transaction type, and seller. *Pratt's Stats* provides, among other things, transactional data with respect to: (1) type of buyer (private buyer or public buyer[8]); (2) type of transaction (sale of assets or sale of equity); and (3) federal taxation entity form of seller (C corporation, S corporation, or partnership).[9] The three federal taxation categories of business entity result in 12 different combinations of transactions. See Exhibit 9.

Preliminary findings. For each of the 12 combinations of buyer, transaction type, and seller in Exhibit 9, we can make some preliminary findings regarding transactional data. For a buyer who is purchasing assets, we expect that transactions less than $2 million will be: (1) completed more frequently by private-company buyers than public-company buyers; and (2) there will be more asset transactions

8 Private companies consist of both pass-through entities and C corporations—*Pratt's Stats* does not provide a breakdown of each.

9 For analysis purposes, the category of partnership includes general partnerships, limited partnerships, joint ventures, limited liability companies, limited liability partnerships, and sole proprietorships.

Exhibit 8. Median MVIC Price by Year

Sales Price (MVIC)		*Pratts' Stats* Median MVIC Price/ Year of Transaction								
From	To	Pre-2000	2000	2001	2002	2003	2004	2005	2006	2007
$0	$250,000	115,000	118,160	108,250	112,500	110,000	109,000	120,000	120,000	117,350
$250,001	$500,000	344,043	332,000	380,000	347,800	336,000	350,000	340,500	342,500	360,000
$500,001	$1,000,000	692,055	700,000	675,000	700,000	675,000	686,577	650,000	720,000	700,000
$1,000,001	$2,000,000	1,500,000	1,473,000	1,374,681	1,441,417	1,400,000	1,435,508	1,450,000	1,324,000	1,400,000
$2,000,001	$5,000,000	3,333,232	3,278,786	2,852,313	3,000,000	3,028,000	3,250,544	3,000,000	3,150,000	3,033,423
$5,000,001	$10,000,000	7,036,550	7,390,441	7,006,694	7,201,232	7,381,000	7,000,000	6,928,741	7,500,000	7,042,500
$10,000,001	$20,000,000	14,000,000	15,562,500	12,700,000	15,000,000	15,355,728	14,375,835	14,000,000	14,247,914	13,356,848
$20,000,001	$50,000,000	30,000,000	29,250,000	32,562,500	36,500,000	31,118,750	32,500,000	32,010,000	31,140,000	30,067,000
$50,000,001	$100,000,000	68,000,000	66,800,000	65,500,000	69,550,000	70,500,000	76,349,000	70,302,966	73,461,500	67,711,000
$100,000,001	$500,000,000	146,500,000	182,750,000	184,100,000	234,700,000	199,085,128	189,630,500	164,289,500	194,154,000	198,152,500
>$500,000,000		731,850,000	678,186,000	847,423,500	754,500,000	1,007,360,500	757,500,000	1,460,000,000	925,500,000	1,104,386,000

Sales Price (MVIC)		*Pratts' Stats* Median MVIC Price/ Year of Transaction								
From	To	2008	2009	2010	2011	2012	2013	2014	2015	
$0	$250,000	110,000	100,000	105,000	100,000	109,000	110,000	99,900	118,250	
$250,001	$500,000	350,000	353,000	350,000	350,000	350,000	345,143	350,000	355,000	
$500,001	$1,000,000	692,000	695,494	717,876	675,000	681,666	681,456	670,000	675,000	
$1,000,001	$2,000,000	1,400,000	1,300,000	1,425,000	1,275,000	1,380,000	1,325,000	1,500,000	1,400,000	
$2,000,001	$5,000,000	3,200,000	3,219,500	3,000,000	3,158,000	2,600,000	2,990,000	2,652,500	3,200,000	
$5,000,001	$10,000,000	6,946,000	7,134,892	7,426,000	7,632,043	6,755,357	6,766,000	6,900,000	6,262,500	
$10,000,001	$20,000,000	14,270,500	14,241,000	14,702,000	14,009,890	15,120,000	14,000,000	13,905,000	15,250,000	
$20,000,001	$50,000,000	33,680,500	32,729,000	28,600,000	30,000,000	35,119,500	32,100,000	32,544,000	27,669,980	
$50,000,001	$100,000,000	70,831,000	74,000,000	70,531,000	72,259,500	68,085,000	82,528,745	73,516,000	79,678,746	
$100,000,001	$500,000,000	192,950,000	183,525,000	211,850,000	195,000,000	188,500,000	158,000,000	214,911,500	158,101,000	
>$500,000,000		753,384,000	871,500,000	1,000,000,000	960,000,000	1,092,917,500	840,647,000	831,679,000	1,425,107,000	

Source: *Pratt's Stats* database, Feb. 29, 2016

than equity transactions. For transactions greater than $2 million, the reverse should generally hold true. Exhibit 10 confirms our expectations .

Exhibit 11 displays the median MVIC for each combination in each size category. We found that median MVIC may vary significantly by sales price range depending on the type of combination.

Greater returns for smaller companies. We believe that small public companies should experience higher returns than larger public companies for the following reason:

Exhibit 9. Twelve Combinations of Buyer, Transaction Type, and Seller

	Buyer	Transaction Type	Seller
1	Private	Asset	C corp
2	Private	Asset	S corp
3	Private	Asset	Partnership
4	Private	Equity	C corp
5	Private	Equity	S corp
6	Private	Equity	Partnership
7	Public	Asset	C corp
8	Public	Asset	S corp
9	Public	Asset	Partnership
10	Public	Equity	C corp
11	Public	Equity	S corp
12	Public	Equity	Partnership

Valuation analysts know that small firms have risk characteristics that differ from those of large firms. For example, large firms may have greater ability to enter the market than a small firm and obtain market share. Large companies have more resources to "weather the storm" in economic downturns. Large firms can spend more on R&D, advertising, and often have greater ability to hire the "best and brightest." Large firms may have greater access to capital, broader management depth, and less dependence on only a few customers. A greater number of analysts follow large firms than small firms, so there is more information available about large firms. Small firms have fewer resources to fend off competition and redirect themselves after changes in the market occur.

Any one of these differences (not an all-encompassing list) would tend to increase investors' required rate of return to induce them to invest in small companies rather than investing in large companies.[10]

For these reasons, we expect that median MVIC-to-revenues ratios will increase as MVIC prices increase. MVIC to revenues is a pricing ratio that is frequently utilized when applying the market approach. Our findings in the second part of this article confirmed this expectation.

10 Duff & Phelps, *2016 Valuation Handbook - Guide to Cost of Capital,* page 4-2. (available at www.bvresources.com/products/index).

Exhibit 10. Number of Transactions for Each Buyer, Transaction Type, and Seller Transaction—By Size Category

Sales Price (MVIC)		*Pratt's Stats* # of Transactions												
		Buyer	Private						Public					
		Trans.	Asset			Equity			Asset			Equity		
From	To	Seller	C Corp [1]	S Corp [2]	Partnership [3]	C Corp [4]	S Corp [5]	Partnership [6]	C Corp [7]	S Corp [8]	Partnership [9]	C Corp [10]	S Corp [11]	Partnership [12]
$0	$250,000		1,171	4,499	3,140	56	68	30	13	11	6	13	10	7
$250,001	$500,000		545	1,612	715	79	49	14	19	17	10	23	11	3
$500,001	$1,000,000		383	1,004	347	85	68	26	38	25	17	60	23	18
$1,000,001	$2,000,000		227	468	127	82	42	9	68	40	26	126	56	25
$2,000,001	$5,000,000		97	273	76	76	60	5	142	110	49	308	136	39
$5,000,001	$10,000,000		34	93	17	42	31	8	162	102	48	298	137	42
$10,000,001	$20,000,000		7	37	11	30	18	4	158	99	52	402	179	44
$20,000,001	$50,000,000		9	11	6	15	15	4	172	121	64	552	195	67
$50,000,001	$100,000,000		2	1	1	8	5	3	128	36	34	350	68	62
$100,000,001	$500,000,000		4	-	-	2	-	2	115	28	30	407	66	74
>$500,000,000			-	-	-	-	-	-	35	-	13	134	10	22
Totals			2,479	7,998	4,440	475	356	105	1,050	589	349	2,673	891	403

Source: *Pratt's Stats* database, Feb. 29, 2016

Exhibit 11. Median MVIC Prices by Size and Combination Category

Sales Price (MVIC)		*Pratt's Stats* Median MVIC Price						
		Buyer	Private					
		Trans.	Asset			Equity		
From	To	Seller	C Corp [1]	S Corp [2]	Partnership [3]	C Corp [4]	S Corp [5]	Partnership [6]
$0	$250,000		125,000	120,000	98,000	146,325	124,189	123,100
$250,001	$500,000		350,000	350,000	330,000	353,000	350,000	351,500
$500,001	$1,000,000		683,000	682,000	660,000	695,000	672,367	695,000
$1,000,001	$2,000,000		1,320,000	1,400,000	1,400,000	1,458,385	1,422,728	1,500,000
$2,000,001	$5,000,000		2,700,000	2,850,000	2,600,000	2,855,457	2,911,795	3,750,532
$5,000,001	$10,000,000		6,456,500	6,844,000	7,050,000	6,750,000	7,829,000	7,850,000
$10,000,001	$20,000,000		16,000,000	12,857,000	12,500,000	13,734,560	12,850,000	12,887,500
$20,000,001	$50,000,000		26,200,000	29,000,000	29,084,691	30,600,000	32,000,000	32,750,000
$50,000,001	$100,000,000		60,400,000	58,028,870	66,350,000	57,052,668	72,000,000	73,811,000
$100,000,001	$500,000,000		226,250,000	n/a	n/a	300,942,000	n/a	124,649,000
>$500,000,000			n/a	n/a	n/a	n/a	n/a	n/a
Totals			**2,479**	**7,998**	**4,440**	**475**	**356**	**105**

Sales Price (MVIC)		*Pratt's Stats* Median MVIC Price						
		Buyer	Public					
		Trans.	Asset			Equity		
From	To	Seller	C Corp [7]	S Corp [8]	Partnership [9]	C Corp [10]	S Corp [11]	Partnership [12]
$0	$250,000		108,000	182,753	149,500	198,970	170,500	168,902
$250,001	$500,000		328,157	376,014	355,750	376,000	380,800	357,500
$500,001	$1,000,000		705,000	793,750	800,000	768,266	819,364	733,500
$1,000,001	$2,000,000		1,635,872	1,406,250	1,476,563	1,500,000	1,423,469	1,500,000
$2,000,001	$5,000,000		3,300,000	3,369,476	2,949,673	3,500,000	3,330,462	3,600,000
$5,000,001	$10,000,000		7,000,000	7,300,500	7,180,179	7,080,750	7,036,100	7,126,182
$10,000,001	$20,000,000		13,517,788	14,525,393	13,855,060	14,250,000	13,994,000	14,285,001
$20,000,001	$50,000,000		31,375,000	30,150,000	30,033,500	32,000,000	30,000,000	30,800,000
$50,000,001	$100,000,000		70,000,000	72,331,882	81,050,000	70,000,000	67,628,673	69,520,966
$100,000,001	$500,000,000		200,000,000	138,169,000	158,000,000	191,034,000	178,097,500	180,350,000
>$500,000,000			838,358,000	n/a	760,000,000	930,000,000	800,658,000	805,500,000
Totals			**1,050**	**589**	**349**	**2,673**	**891**	**403**

Source: *Pratt's Stats* database, Feb. 29, 2016

Summary. When relying on a business transaction database, it is important for business appraisers to understand the information that is compiled. This article provides users of the *Pratt's Stats* database with a better understanding of the data sorted by MVIC size categories, asset vs. equity transactions, actual mix of buyers, transactions by NAICS code, and number of transactions each year. It also summarizes data for each of the 12 combinations of buyer, seller, and transactions. In Part 2, we will explain further how transaction size and entity form impact selling price.

Eric J. Barr, *CPA/ABV/CFF, CVA, CFE, is the partner in charge of valuation services at Marks Paneth LLP. He has more than 40 years of public accounting experience and has testified as an expert in the areas of business valuation, commercial litigation, forensic accounting, and lost profits analysis. He is a frequent public speaker in connection with the valuation of closely held and family-owned businesses, is a member of the editorial board of* The Value Examiner, *and has written articles for various professional publications. His book,* Valuing Pass-Through Entities, *was published in 2014 by John Wiley & Sons Inc. He can be reached at EBarr@markspaneth .com.*

Peter L. Lohrey, *Ph.D., CVA, CDBV, is an assistant accounting professor at Montclair State University. He has more than 20 years of experience in litigation services, valuation, mergers and acquisitions, loan workouts, and expert witness matters. Dr. Lohrey specializes in commercial damage calculations and business valuation for tax, litigation, and forensic purposes. He can be reached at lohreyp@mail .montclair.edu.*

The authors wish to acknowledge Tianyuan (Tina) Ren and James A. DiGabriele for their contributions to this article.

Inside *Pratt's Stats:* Impact of Entity Form on Selling Price (Part 2)

By Eric J. Barr (Marks Paneth) and Peter L. Lohrey (Montclair State University)

Editor's note: This is the second part of a two-part article that explains how transaction size and the entity form of the buyer and seller support the existence (and the magnitude) of the "pass-through entity premium" where the buyer is able to take advantage of the pass-through status of the seller. This article is based on the results of various statistical analyses of Pratt's Stats *transactional data.*

Based on our statistical analyses of *Pratt's Stats* transactional data, this article explains how: (1) transaction size; and (2) buyer and seller entity form support the existence (and the magnitude) of the "pass-through entity premium" where the buyer is able to take advantage of the pass-through status of the seller. Our results were taken from a statistical analysis of *Pratt's Stats'* data.[1]

Several database providers supply details on private-company transactions. One of the largest and most detailed databases is *Pratt's Stats*™, which contains more than 24,000 private-company transactions and more than 100 data fields for each transaction.[2] The birth year of the *Pratt's Stats* database was 1995, with the earliest transaction contained in the database occurring during 1990.[3] The data contained in the *Pratt's Stats* database summarize the market value of invested capital (MVIC)[4] transaction price by the size categories presented in Exhibit 1.

Exhibit 1. *Pratt's Stats* MVIC Price Categories

MVIC Price	
From	To
$0	$250,000
$250,001	$500,000
$500,001	$1,000,000
$1,000,001	$2,000,000
$2,000,001	$5,000,000
$5,000,001	$10,000,000
$10,000,001	$20,000,000
$20,000,001	$50,000,000
$50,000,001	$100,000,000
$100,000,001	$500,000,000
>$500,000,000	

Source: *Pratt's Stats* database, Feb. 29, 2016

1 *Pratt's Stats* database as of Feb. 29, 2016. It now contains over 28,000 transactions and close to 150 data fields.

2 BIZCOMPS, another database that provides information on private-company transactions, contains approximately 14,000 transactions with 21 data fields per transaction.

3 www.bvresources.com/prattsstats.

4 MVIC is defined as the market value of equity plus the market value of debt.

Our results reveal there is an inverse relationship between the size of the MVIC price category and the number of sales transactions. For example, approximately 41% of all transactions have a MVIC price of $250,000 or less and approximately 64% of all transactions have an MVIC price of $1 million or less. Accordingly, the database is heavily concentrated with relatively small MVIC sales price transactions ($1 million or less). Only approximately 24% of the transactions have a MVIC sales price greater than $5 million.

Exhibit 2 illustrates the number of transactions within each MVIC size category.

C corporations and pass-through entity (PTE) sellers in *Pratt's Stats* database. Revenue Ruling 59-60 effectively requires that consideration must be given to: the value of the subject interest to the hypothetical seller and the hypothetical buyer, the hypothetical pool of buyers and the relative negotiating strength of each party. The value of the subject interest to the hypothetical seller is the floor value—where the hypothetical seller who is under no compulsion to sell would not accept a price less than this value. Similarly, the value of the subject interest to the hypothetical buyer is the ceiling value—where a hypothetical buyer under no compulsion to purchase the subject interest would not pay a price greater than this value. Hence, consideration must be given to the entity status of both the seller and the buyer. The reason that the entity status of the hypothetical buyer is important is that the hypothetical buyer would not pay for any PTE tax benefit it would not receive.[5,6]

5 An example of a PTE tax benefit is that the owner of a C corporation incurs two levels of income taxes, one at the entity level and a second time at the individual level, when income is distributed as dividends; an owner of a PTE incurs only one level of taxation at the owner level.

6 For detailed discussions on the income approach and fair market value, and fair market court decisions, see Chapters 8 and 9, respectively, in *Valuing Pass-Through Entities* (Eric Barr, Wiley).

Exhibit 2. Number of Transactions by MVIC Price Category

MVIC Price		# of Transactions		Common Sized # of Transactions	
From	To	By Category	Cumulative	By Category	Cumulative
$0	$250,000	10,094	10,094	41.4%	41.4%
$250,001	$500,000	3,334	13,428	13.7%	55.1%
$500,001	$1,000,000	2,175	15,603	8.9%	64.1%
$1,000,001	$2,000,000	1,387	16,990	5.7%	69.7%
$2,000,001	$5,000,000	1,488	18,478	6.1%	75.9%
$5,000,001	$10,000,000	1,176	19,654	4.8%	80.7%
$10,000,001	$20,000,000	1,197	20,851	4.9%	85.6%
$20,000,001	$50,000,000	1,433	22,284	5.9%	91.5%
$50,000,001	$100,000,000	835	23,119	3.4%	94.9%
$100,000,001	$500,000,000	909	24,028	3.7%	98.6%
>$500,000,000		331	24,359	1.4%	100.0%
Totals		24,359	24,359	100.0%	100.0%

Source: *Pratt's Stats* database, Feb. 29, 2016

These factors are also referenced in a Job Aid the Internal Revenue Service published dated Oct. 29, 2014, titled "Valuation of Non-Controlling Interests in Business Entities Electing to Be Treated as S Corporations for Federal Tax Purposes"[7] (the Job Aid). This Job Aid states that "the conceptual foundation provided by Revenue Ruling 59-60 underscores the fact that the isolation of a single variable, such as the choice by a business entity of pass-through status, without simultaneously addressing all of the above factors, will likely lead to erroneous conclusions in a practical application."[8]

The Internal Revenue Service publishes an updated version of the IRS Data Book annually. The IRS Data Books contain a table noting the number of tax returns filed each year on federal Forms 1120 (C corporations), 1120S (S corporations) and 1065 (partnerships, limited partnerships, general partnerships, joint ventures, limited liability companies, and limited liability partnerships, which are collectively referred to herein as "partnerships"). S corporations and partnerships are collectively referred to herein as pass-through entities (PTEs). Exhibits 3 and 4 summarize the data from Table 2 of the IRS Data Books for tax years 2003 through 2015.

Based on the IRS Data Book data for tax years 2003 through 2015, we expect to find that 20% to 30% of all sellers would be C corporations, with the balance being partnerships and S corporations.

Exhibit 3.
IRS Data Book Data
Table 2—Summary of Number of Business Entity Income Tax Returns (in Thousands)

		Pass-Through Entities			
Year	Total	Total	Partnership	S Corporation	C Corporation
2015	10,816	8,600	3,883	4,717	2,216
2014	10,663	8,442	3,799	4,643	2,221
2013	10,500	8,252	3,686	4,566	2,248
2012	10,469	8,206	3,626	4,580	2,263
2011	10,432	8,119	3,574	4,545	2,313
2010	10,373	8,017	3,509	4,508	2,356
2009	10,537	8,061	3,565	4,496	2,476
2008	10,285	7,747	3,307	4,440	2,538
2007	9,704	7,196	3,097	4,099	2,508
2006	9,052	6,598	2,773	3,825	2,454
2005	8,793	6,299	2,665	3,634	2,494
2004	8,566	6,025	2,521	3,504	2,541
2003	8,271	5,711	2,381	3,330	2,560

Source: IRS Data Books; tax years 2003-2015

Exhibit 4.
IRS Data Book Data Derived From
Table 2—Summary of Number of Business Entity Income Tax Returns (Percentage of Total)

		Pass-Through Entities			
Year	Total	Total	Partnership	S Corporation	C Corporation
2015	100.0%	79.5%	35.9%	43.6%	20.5%
2014	100.0%	79.2%	35.6%	43.5%	20.8%
2013	100.0%	78.6%	35.1%	43.5%	21.4%
2012	100.0%	78.4%	34.6%	43.7%	21.6%
2011	100.0%	77.8%	34.3%	43.6%	22.2%
2010	100.0%	77.3%	33.8%	43.5%	22.7%
2009	100.0%	76.5%	33.8%	42.7%	23.5%
2008	100.0%	75.3%	32.2%	43.2%	24.7%
2007	100.0%	74.2%	31.9%	42.2%	25.8%
2006	100.0%	72.9%	30.6%	42.3%	27.1%
2005	100.0%	71.6%	30.3%	41.3%	28.4%
2004	100.0%	70.3%	29.4%	40.9%	29.7%
2003	100.0%	69.0%	28.8%	40.3%	31.0%

Source: IRS Data Books; tax years 2003-2015

7 Job Aid, page 8.

8 Job Aid, page 9.

When analyzing the *Pratt's Stats* data, we initially excluded the following transactions: (1) foreign company sellers; (2) transactions where accurate information regarding the selling entity form or buyer entity form was not provided; or (3) transactions lacking information with respect to equity or asset sale structure. This led to 2,600 out of approximately 24,400 transactions being excluded. Exhibit 5 summarizes the number of transactions of C corporation and PTE[9] sellers, by MVIC sales price size category, according to the *Pratt's Stats* database. We found that, after the exclusions, approximately 69% were PTEs, which reasonably approximates our expectation.

Valuation hierarchy expectations. Among the more than 100 data fields, *Pratt's Stats* provides transactional data with respect to: (1) type of buyer (private buyer or public buyer[10]); (2) type of transaction (sale of assets or sale of equity); and (3) entity form of seller. These three types of fields result in 12 different potential combinations of transactions. See Exhibit 6.

Next, we developed a valuation hierarchy with respect to certain types of combinations. We assumed that most public-company purchases were strategic acquisitions, or they possessed synergistic benefits. Accordingly, deal structure and the seller's entity type were assumed to be less important in our valuation hierarchy for Combinations 7 through 12. Private-company buyers often have different types of motivations and less access to capital, among other factors, that distinguish them from public-company buyers. Hence, only private transactions were considered.

9 For analysis purposes, the category of partnership includes general partnerships, limited partnerships, joint ventures, limited liability companies, limited liability partnerships, and sole proprietorships.

10 Private companies consist of both pass-through entities and C corporations. *Pratt's Stats* does not provide a breakdown of each.

Exhibit 5. Number of Transactions by C Corporation and Pass-Through Entity Sellers

Sales Price (MVIC)		# of Sellers				
					% of Totals	
From	To	C Corp	PTEs	Totals	C Corp	PTEs
$0	$250,000	1,253	7,771	9,024	13.9%	86.1%
$250,001	$500,000	666	2,431	3,097	21.5%	78.5%
$500,001	$1,000,000	566	1,528	2,094	27.0%	73.0%
$1,000,001	$2,000,000	503	793	1,296	38.8%	61.2%
$2,000,001	$5,000,000	623	748	1,371	45.4%	54.6%
$5,000,001	$10,000,000	536	478	1,014	52.9%	47.1%
$10,000,001	$20,000,000	597	444	1,041	57.3%	42.7%
$20,000,001	$50,000,000	748	483	1,231	60.8%	39.2%
$50,000,001	$100,000,000	488	210	698	69.9%	30.1%
$100,000,001	$500,000,000	528	200	728	72.5%	27.5%
>$500,000,000		169	45	214	79.0%	21.0%
		6,677	**15,131**	**21,808**	**30.6%**	**69.4%**

Source: *Pratt's Stats* database, Feb. 29, 2016

When looking at Combinations 1 through 6, we expected Combinations 5 (private buyer, equity transaction, S corporation seller) and 6 (private buyer, equity transaction, partnership seller) would have larger valuation multiples than Combination 4 (private buyer, equity transaction, C corporation seller) because a private PTE buyer would pay just one level of income taxes (at the owner level) with respect to the earnings of the subject company. For Combination 4 (where equity of C corporations was acquired), the buyer would be required to pay two levels of income taxes (at the entity level and again at the owner level when dividends are distributed). We expected that the additional tax to the buyer of Combination 4 would lower the valuation multiple for this combination as compared to Combinations 5 and 6.

Exhibit 6. Twelve Combinations of Buyer, Transaction Type, and Seller

	Transaction		
	Buyer	**Type**	**Seller**
1	Private	Asset	C corp
2	Private	Asset	S corp
3	Private	Asset	Partnership
4	Private	Equity	C corp
5	Private	Equity	S corp
6	Private	Equity	Partnership
7	Public	Asset	C corp
8	Public	Asset	S corp
9	Public	Asset	Partnership
10	Public	Equity	C corp
11	Public	Equity	S corp
12	Public	Equity	Partnership

Criteria for determining the sample to be tested. To test these expectations, the following items were used to conduct our analysis:

- Identification of exclusions and outliers;
- Selection of independent variables;
- Selection of dependent variables; and
- A comparison of the independent and dependent variables, net of exclusions and outliers.

The following transactions were excluded:

1. All public-company buyers (Combinations 7 through 12).
2. Combinations 1, 2, and 3, which involved asset sales.
3. Financial service companies (SIC code 6). Those companies in finance, insurance, or real estate are excluded because some of the financial data used are difficult to apply to companies in the financial sector.[11]
4. Transactions where the target companies had a net loss or negative EBIT in the year preceding the transaction.[12]

11 These are the same criteria utilized in developing the Risk Premium Report Portfolios in the *2017 Valuation Yearbook,* pages 7-2 and 7-4.

12 Ibid., page 7-2.

We also eliminated outliers that did not meet parametric parameters. The data were arranged to identify the first quartile (Q1), median, mean, and third quartile (Q3). If a data point was less than *Q1 - [1.5 × (Q3 - Q1)]*, it was considered an outlier. In addition, if a data point was greater than *Q3 + [1.5 × (Q3 - Q1)]*, it was also considered an outlier.

We selected Combinations 4, 5, and 6 as independent variables and the MVIC price-to-revenue ratio as the dependent variable. Based on these criteria, we developed the sample size in Exhibit 7 for testing.

It was necessary to determine an appropriate sample for the number of transactions in each MVIC size category because not all MVIC sizes for Combination 6 contained a sufficient number of observations. The cut-off used for testing expectations was 35 transactions or more (transactions that were less than this are highlighted in Exhibit 7). Size Categories 6 through 11 had fewer transactions than the minimum number of 35 transactions and were not included in the tests noted below.

Exhibit 7. Transaction Count Net of Exclusions and Outliers Combinations 4, 5, and 6

Size	Combination	Transaction Count
1	4	34
1	5	46
1	6	22
2	4	47
2	5	35
2	6	10
3	4	58
3	5	50
3	6	13
4	4	63
4	5	31
4	6	7
5	4	66
5	5	47
5	6	4
		Scope: 35+ count

Source: *Pratt's Stats* database, Feb. 29, 2016

Testing the hypothesis. To test the hypothesis that the MVIC price-to-revenue ratio for Combinations 5 and 6 would exceed Combination 4 for Size Categories 1 through 5, we performed the following tests:

1. H01: Compared the median MVIC price-to-revenue ratio for Combinations 4, 5, and 6 within each of the first five size categories;
2. H02: Multiple regression analyses were then performed using dummy variables; and
3. H03: Analysis of variance (ANOVA) tests were performed using a log normal distribution.

The results of these tests were then compared to the implied PTE premium assuming three different scenarios:

1. Maximum C corporation tax rates;
2. $0 tax affecting adjustment; and
3. Modified Delaware MRI model (MDMM).

Median MVIC-to-revenue ratio for Combinations 4, 5, and 6 within each of the first five size categories. The median MVIC-to-revenue ratio for each size (1 through 5) and combination (4, 5, and 6) with 35 transactions or more were calculated. The median MVIC-to-revenue multiples of Combination 5 was greater than Combination 4. With respect to Combination 6, no samples contained 35 transactions or more. These findings support our hypothesis that the MVIC-to-revenue multiples for Combination 5 would exceed Combination 4. The next step was to determine the applicable PTE premium of the MVIC-to-revenue ratio relative to the C corp MVIC-to-revenue ratio. Assuming that the ratio of PTE to C corporation buyers of private companies matched the mix of PTE to C corporation sellers per Exhibit 5, the PTE premium for each size-combination factor was calculated. See Exhibit 8.

The population of tested transactions indicates that the mean PTE premium was approximately 17% and the median PTE premium was approximately 15%.

Exhibit 8. Median MVIC-to-Revenue Multiples Comparison of C Corporation, S Corporation, and Partnership Equity Transactions for Different Size Categories

		Exclusions & Outliers			Exhibit 5			Exclusion & Outlier Calculations			
Size	Combination	Count	Median	Expected	C Corp	PTE	Totals	Formula	PTE Multiple	C Corp Multiple	PTE Premium
1	4	34	0.2935	Base	13.90%	86.100%	100%				
1	5	46	0.3687	Yes	13.90%	86.100%	100%	.2935*13.9%+X*.861 = .3687	0.38084	0.2935	1.29758
1	6	22	n/a	n/a							
2	4	47	0.4066	Base	21.50%	78.500%	100%				
2	5	35	0.4266	Yes	21.50%	78.500%	100%	.4066*.215+x*.785 = .4266	0.432078	0.4066	1.06266
2	6	10	n/a	n/a							
3	4	58	0.4993	Base	27.00%	73.000%	100%				
3	5	50	0.5328	Yes	27.00%	73.000%	100%	.4993*.27+ x*.73 = .5328	0.054519	0.4993	1.091909
3	6	13	n/a	n/a							
4	4	63	0.5920	Base	38.80%	61.200%	100%				
4	5	31	n/a	n/a							
4	6	7	n/a	n/a							
5	4	66	0.6093	Base	45.40%	54.600%	100%				
5	5	47	0.6790	Yes	45.40%	54.600%	100%	.6093*.454 + x*.546 = .679	0.736956	0.6093	1.20951
5	6	4	n/a	n/a							
										Mean	1.165416
		Scope: 35+ count								Median	1.150711

Exhibit 9. Multiple Regression Using Dummy Variables Determination of PTE Premium

			Exclusions & Outliers								Exclusion & Outlier Calculations			
Size	Combination		Count	P-value	Confidence Level	Estimated Value	Expected	C Corp	PTE	Totals		PTE Multiple	C Corp Multiple	PTE Premium
1	4		34	Base	0.05	0.28988		13.9%	86.1%	100%				
1	5	[1]	46	<.05	0.05	0.41891	Yes	13.9%	86.1%	100%	.28988*.139+x*.861 = .41891	0.439740627	0.28988	1.516975
1	6		22	<.001	0.05	0.45817	Yes	13.9%	86.1%	100%				
[1] Fitted model for 4, 5, and 6: MVIC to sales = 0.28988 + .012903*D(1) + 0.16829*D(2), where D(1) = {1, if group 5; 0, others} and D(2) = {1, if group 6; 0, others}														
[2] Highly reliable findings due to small P-value and confidence level of 0.05														
2	4		47	Base	0.05	0.39722		21.5%	78.5%	100%				
2	5	[3]	35	0.148	0.05	0.45509	Yes	21.5%	78.5%	100%	.39722*.215+x*.785 = .45509	0.470939745	0.39722	1.185589
2	6		10	0.238	0.05	0.47081	Yes							
[3] Fitted model for 4, 5, and 6: MVIC to sales = 0.39722 + .05787*D(1) + 0.07359*D(2), where D(1) = {1, if group 5; 0, others} and D(2) = {1, if group 6; 0, others}														
[4] Findings not highly reliable due to size of P-value														
3	4		58	Base	0.05	0.51804		27.0%	73.0%	100%				
3	5	[5]	50	0.235	0.05	0.58342	Yes	27.0%	73.0%	100%	.51804*.27+x*.73 = .58342	0.607601644	0.51804	1.172888
3	6		13	0.524	0.05	0.57376	Yes							
[5] Fitted model for 4, 5, and 6: MVIC to sales = 0.51804 + .06538*D(1) + 0.05572*D(2), where D(1) = {1, if group 5; 0, others} and D(2) = {1, if group 6; 0, others}														
[6] Findings not highly reliable due to size of P-value														
4	4		63	Base	0.05	0.60966		38.8%	61.2%	100%				
4	5	[7]	31	0.109	0.05	0.47834	No	38.8%	61.2%	100%				
4	6		7	<0.001	0.05	1.23996	Yes							
[7] Fitted model for 4, 5, and 6: MVIC to sales = 0.60966 - .13132*D(1) + 0.63030*D(2), where D(1) = {1, if group 5; 0, others} and D(2) = {1, if group 6; 0, others}														
5	4		66	Base	0.05	0.72158		45.4%	54.6%	100%				
5	5	[8]	47	0.707	0.05	0.75024	Yes	45.4%	54.6%	100%	.72158*.454+X*.546 = .75024	0.774070842	0.72158	1.072744
5	6		4	0.171	0.05	1.00398	Yes							
[8] Fitted model for 4, 5, and 6: MVIC to sales = 0.72158 + .02866*D(1) + 0.28240*D(2), where D(1) = {1, if group 5; 0, others} and D(2) = {1, if group 6; 0, others}													Mean	1.237049
[9] Findings not highly reliable due to size of P-value													Median	1.179239

Multiple regression analyses were performed with dummy variables. The results of the dummy variable regression analyses, and the calculated PTE premium for each combination, are presented in Exhibit 9.

The mean PTE premium was approximately 24%, and the median PTE premium was approximately 18%. It should be noted that only Size 1 contains statistically significant results.

ANOVA tests performed using a log normal distribution. ANOVA tests were then performed using log normal function. These ANOVA tests:

1. Compared the MVIC-to-revenue ratios for each of the tested combinations;

2. Determined the difference between means of the MVIC-to-revenue ratios; and

3. Determined the confidence levels for each size comparison of Combinations 4, 5, and 6.

Exhibit 10 presents the results from the ANOVA tests.

Except for Size 4, with Combinations 4 and 5, all other combinations supported our hypothesis that the MVIC-to-revenue multiples for Combinations 5 and 6 would exceed Combination 4.

Limitations of the study. The analyses presented in Exhibits 8, 9, and 10 examine whether the expectation that the MVIC-to-revenue pricing multiples of Combinations 5 and 6 exceeds Combination 4. The potential limitations of this study are:

1. Thirty-five transactions may be deemed to be either too high or too low for Exhibits 8 and 9. The results may differ when using a higher or lower range.

2. Due to scope limitations, no Combination 6 transactions were included in determining the PTE premium calculated in Exhibit 8.

3. In the multiple regression analysis presented in Exhibit 9, only the first sized set of transactions has highly reliable findings due to small p-values and a confidence level of 95%. Combinations 2, 3, and 5 had relatively high p-values, which decrease the reliability of these findings in relation to the first combination.

Exhibit 10. The ANOVA Procedure Comparing Combinations 6 and 4, and 5 and 4

Size	Level Comparison	Difference Between Means	Consistent With Expectations	Confidence Level
1	6 > 4	0.16829	Yes	95%
1	5 > 4	0.12903	Yes	95%
2	6 > 4	0.07359	Yes	50%
2	5 > 4	0.05787	Yes	50%
3	6 > 4	0.05572	Yes	20%
3	5 > 4	0.06538	Yes	50%
4	6 > 4	0.6303	Yes	95%
4	4 > 5	0.13132	No	70%
5	6 > 4	0.2824	Yes	60%
5	5 > 4	0.02866	Yes	50%

4. The ANOVA procedures summarized in Exhibit 10 indicated that, for Size 4, the valuation multiple of Combination 4 exceeded that of Combination 5, which contradicts our expectations.

Notwithstanding these limitations, the use of three different models—with each model yielding similar results—provides sufficient evidence that the valuation analyst can rely on the PTE premia presented in Exhibits 8, 9, and 10.

The calculated PTE premia for each test was compared to the size premia derived from various tax-affecting models. This relationship was used to determine whether the findings noted in the foregoing analysis of *Pratt's Stats* data corroborates or contradicts the PTE premium resulting from the different tax-affecting models.

Summary and conclusions. Exhibit 11 analyzes the tax savings benefit of PTE status assuming:

1. C corporation income tax rates;
2. $0 company income taxes (the IRS position as articulated in the IRS Job Aid); and
3. Application of the modified Delaware MRI model (MDMM).[13]

As noted in the top half of Exhibit 11, company net income equaled $660 (C corporation model), $1,000 (assuming no tax-affecting adjustment), and $787 (under the MDMM). These are three frequently applied methodologies that are used to determine the income subject to capitalization under the income approach. *The primary question that needs to be answered is which model is most appropriate based on the analysis of* Pratt's Stats *data described herein? In other words, does the PTE premia derived from the aforementioned tests more closely match the PTE premia assuming: (1) C corporation income tax rates; (2) a $0 tax-affecting adjustment; or (3) the PTE premia derived by using the MDMM?*

Exhibit 11. Comparison of Findings to Multiple PTE Valuation Models

	C Corp	PTE	MDMM
Pretax income	$1,000	$1,000	$1,000
Corporate income taxes	(340)	-	(213)
Company net income	660	1,000	787
Dividend tax	(130)	-	(187)
Individual income tax	-	(400)	-
Net after-tax income	$530	$600	$600
Premium vs. C corp		1.52	1.19
Assumptions:			
Corporate income tax	34%		
Individual income tax	40%		
Dividend tax	24%		
Exhibit 8, after exclusions and outliers:			
Mean	1.17		
Median	1.15		
Exhibit 9, dummy variable multiregression analysis:			
Mean	1.24		
Median	1.18		

13 The MDMM is based on the model that the court applied in *Delaware MRI Radiology Associates, P.A. v. Howard B. Kessler* but modified to allow for other factors not present in the case. It effectively "reverse-engineers" the appropriate income tax rate to be applied to a PTE when using C corporation valuation multiples under the income approach. For more information, go to valuingptes.com.

The calculated mean and median PTE premia, after exclusions and outliers in Exhibit 8 are 17% and 15%, respectively. The calculated mean and median PTE premia using a dummy variable multiregression analysis in Exhibit 9 are 24% and 18%, respectively. These findings, based on an analysis of actual transactional data during the period 1990 through 2015, reasonably approximate the 19% PTE premium derived when applying the MDMM. *These data strongly support the use of the MDMM when valuing PTEs; they also strongly reject the appropriateness of using corporation income tax rates or a $0 tax-affecting adjustment when valuing PTEs.*

Eric J. Barr, *CPA/ABV/CFF, CVA, CFE, is the partner in charge of valuation services at Marks Paneth LLP. He has more than 40 years of public accounting experience and has testified as an expert in the areas of business valuation, commercial litigation, forensic accounting, and lost profits analysis. He is a frequent public speaker in connection with the valuation of closely held and family-owned businesses, is a member of the editorial board of* The Value Examiner, *and has written articles for various professional publications. His book,* Valuing Pass-Through Entities, *was published in 2014 by John Wiley & Sons Inc. E-mail: EBarr@markspaneth.com.*

Peter L. Lohrey, *Ph.D., CVA, CDBV, is an assistant accounting professor at Montclair State University. He has more than 20 years of experience in litigation services, valuation, mergers and acquisitions, loan workouts, and expert witness matters. Dr. Lohrey specializes in commercial damage calculations and business valuation for tax, litigation, and forensic purposes. E-mail: lohreyp@mail.montclair.edu.*

The authors wish to acknowledge Tianyuan (Tina) Ren and James DiGabriele for their contributions to this article.

Section II.
Industry-Specific Valuation

An Investor's View of the Valuation of Alternative Space Firms

A very exciting and interesting industry is the alternative space sector that consists of space commercialization companies. These firms are involved in such activities as launch services, satellite and rocket manufacturing, recovery of minerals on asteroids, as well as space tourism for the superwealthy.

Michael Blake (Arpeggio Advisors) has been performing appraisals of space commercialization companies and investment funds for over five years. The need for valuation typically arises in a 409a context (lots of stock options are being issued), the raising of capital, and gifts or transfers. He recently interviewed Stephen Fleming (Boostphase), who is a venture capitalist active in the alternative space industry with a hands-on management background as well. Fleming is an investor in six private aerospace companies, making his first space-related private-sector investment in 2000.

What we are now seeing in this industry, Fleming explains, is that, although people were making space-based private-sector investments as early as the late 1970s, the wider world realized just a few years ago that this business does not have to be the exclusive domain of nation states. Technology is at the point where private companies can have significant and substantial businesses in launching and exploiting and working in space without having to be under the authority of NASA. NASA does not even have to approve this activity. "There are some people at NASA who are a little bit upset about this, but that is the legal truth," says Fleming.

Michael Blake: *What features tend to separate successful space companies from less successful ones?*

Stephen Fleming: There are no successful startups in the space industry. There are some space imaging startups that are seeing some success, and obviously telecom satellites are a huge industry. So you have United Launch Alliance (ULA), a very successful firm, but it was a shotgun marriage of Boeing and Lockheed Martin assets. You have Elon Musk's SpaceX, which builds and launches rockets. It's winning the PR wars, but two launch failures have damaged the brand and savaged its cash flow. And you have Blue Origin, a famously secretive firm, so no one has any idea of its finances. After those three, you have everybody else.

In general, the more successful space companies are targeting a particular market need and are not trying to be all things to all people. Boeing does a good job of that, so the feeling is to let Boeing do it.

MB: *When we are appraising a space company, what are the key things to be looking for that are going to value a company higher or lower?*

SF: Of course, one of the key issues is the terminal value, which in this industry is most likely to be zero. Traditionally, most of these companies have failed. There have been literally dozens of space-related startups that have simply gone bankrupt or have been acquired just for the engineering team. I have done that. So there is extraordinary volatility in terms of what the result is going to be.

There really have not been any unquestionable successes yet. Elon Musk with SpaceX is probably the closest. He has certainly accomplished remarkable things. I think he will continue to accomplish remarkable things, but by no means is that an attainable model as yet. It has been heavily dependent on government grants and government contracts. I should be fairer—government contracts are more legitimate. But, if you are looking for who is going to be a Facebook or Apple in this industry, there isn't one of those yet. I think there are a lot of people who are very optimistic when you look at the fundamental drivers of the industry. There are a lot of waves of technology floating in the right direction, so I and others believe there is going to be a way to make a lot of money.

I think that in a particular company you have to accept the fact that their business model today is probably wrong. But we simply don't know in what way it is wrong. As an investor, not a valuation consultant, I am looking to bet on that team and to see whether I think this team is nimble enough to surf those waves and find value coming out the door. That being said, the launch startups are very definitely high risk in many ways. There are some imaging companies that have done quite well. There has actually been one exit of a company, and I think it was the only private transaction exit in this area.

MB: *It was $500 million for SkyBox by Google.*

SF: Yes, there has been a significant transaction. I think it is the only one that actually happened where you can see that people put money in, they built something, and they took money out. So we have one—just one of those in the whole industry. Obviously, there are the telecom satellites that have been out there for 50 years, and that is a huge business.

As an investor, if I am looking to start up, I want to understand a market dynamic that explains why this is going to be successful, why now is the right time to exploit it, and why you, the management team, are the right people to make it happen. So, in some ways, they are like any other startup, just higher risk.

MB: *So, in terms of common themes of investments gone bad, you told me amateurs talk propellants and professionals talk insurance. What does that mean?*

SF: That became a line around the space industry probably a decade ago. You would go to conferences and you would have these brilliant rocket scientists talking about their fabulous new propellants or their terrific new rocket nozzle design or their incredible new architecture for a launch system or for a satellite transmission. Whatever it is, they never talked about the overall business model.

For example, whether you are launching satellites, whether you are launching people, you need insurance. You need some level of financial controls. You need some level of a human resource strategy. You need a sales channel. You need integration policy. You need a lot of things that to the rocket scientist are kind of boring. They don't really want to talk about what it is going to cost to insure this. I just want to make sure that it goes up.

But, as an investment, it really becomes less and less relevant whether your technology is special, but rather whether your business model is special. That is where I think a lot of these startups ran themselves into the weeds. They were being run by the founding engineers, who thought like engineers and focused on the engineering problems. But, at the end of the day, they hadn't attended to the business.

MB: *You can't really accept the science projects.*

SF: It was very much the science projects.

MB: *So is anyone other than billionaires investing in these?*

SF: Yes, there are some. Billionaires get a lot more attention because people like reading about billionaires. But there are some firms that are attracting either straight annual investment, which is XCOR, which I have been involved with for almost 17 years now. That is terrifying. They are still a startup at 17 years. They can almost vote! Some firms are attracting honest-to-goodness venture capital fund investment. Vector is a new company. There is also Rocket Labs out of New Zealand.

Then there are the smallsat (small satellite) companies that have actual business models. If data can be delivered on a consistent basis to farmers or to seismologists or to whatever market segment we are looking at, then there is an honest-to-goodness revenue stream there. You are seeing financial investors starting to notice those companies. That didn't happen a few years ago.

MB: *Not a lot of acquisitions are happening yet in this sector. What is going to make a company attractive to an acquirer?*

SF: I think you are going to see that the big firms will get bigger. Some of the big companies may be new companies. For example, SpaceX is a big company and so is Blue Origin, which likely is bigger. United Launch Alliance is big, but it traces its history back to Boeing in the 1920s. But the big companies are going to be looking to be more comprehensive and complete in their product lines, so in some cases they will acquire what they need.

If a firm can demonstrate projected cash flow, then you could get a purely financial acquisition. Whether it is for a launch or a satellite, you may have, say, 10,000 farmers around the country paying $1.95 a week for crop data. That kind of order book demonstrates the company's ability to generate a revenue stream.

MB: *From your perspective in terms of looking at a potential investment, what in your mind makes you think that a particular space company is worth more or what makes it worth less?*

SF: Looking at the new industry sector, there are a lot of new people investing in the industry. No one was doing this 30 years ago, and most people weren't investing 10 years ago. So with that you get some herd behavior that you don't get in more mature industries because in a more mature industry you will have people who have lived through cycles before and they know what cycles look like. They were there for the disk drive bubble of the 1980s, and they know how to live through one of those.

In a new industry, you don't have those people, so you get a situation where—well, a positive circumstance, such as Congress passing the Space Commercialization Act in 2015. Suddenly, it's raining soup, and everyone is running out to buy buckets, so let's invest in bucket manufacturers. People have a kind of herd behavior—they all plunge in. Or a negative circumstance can happen. SpaceX had a rocket blow up on the launching pad. Virgin Galactic lost a vehicle in an atmospheric test flight three years ago. Because investors are new, they apply that lens to everybody in the industry, even though it might be completely unrelated technologies, completely unrelated market sectors, completely unrelated engineering situations. That can depress valuations all across the board. The truth is it is never as good as you think it is and it is never as bad as you think. In more mature markets, some of those betas get damped out, but that has not happened yet in the space industry.

What has happened is that you are getting fits and starts of people thinking that either it's like the Gold Rush, or the cost is too high, and the government is going to come in and make it illegal. That has been a valuation driver pulling in both directions for as long as I have been around.

Learn more: Blake and Fleming conducted a webinar, Down-to-Earth Considerations for Appraising Private Space Commercialization Companies, in December 2016. You can access a recording at sub.bvresources.com/pastevents.asp.

NYSSCPA Symposium Highlights Valuation and Other Challenges of the Legal Marijuana Industry

The legal marijuana business is the fastest growing industry in the U.S., and, if the momentum toward legality includes all states by 2020, U.S. retail marijuana sales could reach $35 billion. This past December, *BVU* attended the Marijuana Symposium: Business, Tax and Legal Implications, sponsored by the New York State Society of CPAs. New York is one of 28 states that have legalized marijuana for medical purposes, but it is not among the eight states that have legalized recreational marijuana.

Regulatory hurdles. New York State Senators Diane Scavino and Liz Krueger talked about the regulatory hurdles legal marijuana businesses face. In her keynote address, Scavino said many problems stem from the fact that the drug remains on the federal government's Schedule 1 status as a dangerous substance that has no accepted medical treatment use. Therefore, there is no insurance coverage for medical marijuana, banks will not open accounts for these firms, they cannot pay tax with marijuana proceeds, and they are not allowed to deduct normal business expenses. For the industry to truly thrive, marijuana must be descheduled, she said.

Krueger agreed, and noted that criminalization has already done too much damage to New York communities. The state has some of the most "draconian" drug laws in the country. "It's time to legalize, tax, and regulate," she said.

When the New York medical marijuana bill was signed into law in 2014, it created a program that was smaller and narrower than what was originally envisioned. For example, the original legislation allowed medical marijuana to be prescribed for post-traumatic stress disorder and chronic pain, but these conditions were cut in the final version due to concerns about abuse. Because the program is so narrow, it faces significant obstacles before it can sustain itself. Scavino pointed out, for instance, that there are only five licenses for up to 20 dispensaries in a state with a population of almost 20 million people. This can make access problematic, she said, particularly for patients upstate who may have to drive 400 miles to the nearest dispensary to get the brand of marijuana they need. Also, other drugs can be delivered through the mail, but federal regulations do not allow marijuana to be sent through the mail or through any private courier service.

There is also a great concern that the nominee for U.S. attorney general, U.S. Senator Jeff Sessions, who has come out heavily against marijuana legalization, for both medical and recreational use, will crack down and stifle industry growth. If he becomes the nation's top law enforcer, it could mean the end of the "Cole Memo," a set of guidelines the Department of Justice issued to federal prosecutors about how to enforce marijuana laws under the Controlled Substances Act. If these guidelines no longer exist, it could throw the legal marijuana industry "in disarray," Scavino said. New York and other states use the Cole Memo to shape their own programs and business processes.

Business owner perspective. One of five licensed operators in New York for medical marijuana is Etain Health. Hillary Peckham, one of the firm's co-founders, told of the struggles to get the business up and running. Part of being in the marijuana industry, she says, is being an activist and promoting education. "There needs to be more awareness and involvement to better ensure operator compliance," she says. "We've had several accountants tell us they don't want to get involved in the marijuana business because they don't think they are allowed to, so it's a lot more difficult to find that kind of help than most people think."

The Arkley Accounting Group is one firm that counts business owners in the cannabis industry among its clients. The firm's owner, Todd Arkley, is a former landscaper who got into accounting after he agreed to keep the books for one of his customers. Arkley points to federal taxation problems this industry faces in terms of the inability to take tax deductions for normal business expenses. IRC Section 280E does not allow the deductions because marijuana is illegal under federal law. There have been several court cases on this issue, and the industry is now able to deduct COGS, but it is still faced with effective tax rates of 60% to 80% because of the inability to claim business expense deductions. An audience member pointed out that there is a case pending in Tax Court that argues that Section 280E should not apply to businesses that are legal under state law. The case involves Harborside Healthcare Center, the country's largest cannabis dispensary ($30 million in sales), which is facing a $2.4 million back tax bill from the IRS.

Peckham also says it has been challenging to access banking services. "We found that state banks were more likely to work with us, but branches of national banks either would not or could not," she says. Etain Health did what a lot of marijuana companies do and that is to split the company up into different operations, with each entity handling a specific task. This at least protects some parts of the overall operation in terms of being allowed access to banking.

She also described the limits on the business in New York, where a firm is only allowed to make extracts and not sell flowers or buds. A firm must grow the plants, formulate products, send them out for third-party testing, and run dispensaries. "No operator is profitable yet in New York and no one has shown yet that you can make it profitable," she says. "Minnesota has the same program in New York (extracts only, heavy regulation) and nobody is profitable there." New York's approach is to take a very small program and open it up step by step as opposed to some other states that have opened up with a large program and then tried to rein it in through regulation. "I think New York's approach is the right approach, because you can actually prove benefits to the public," she says.

Valuation angles. "In my 30 years of doing business valuation I thought I had seen everything until I got involved in this industry," says **Ron Seigneur** (Seigneur Gustafson LLP), calling the appraisal of a legal marijuana firm the "ultimate challenge." His practice is based in Colorado, one of the first states to legalize adult recreational marijuana, and he has done about 20 valuations so far.[1] Of course, risk is a major factor, he pointed out, with company-specific risk premiums ranging from 30% to 40%. He also advised that when valuing a cannabis firm, focus on the "four L's": license rights, lease, location, and legislative environment.

A dearth of comparable transactional data from the market means that appraisers must rely on the income approach. Revenue projections can be especially tricky, but Seigneur uses management interviews and site visits to examine the size of the facility and the nature of the technology in use. Drawing from his experience in this industry, Seigneur is then able to estimate potential production. Using third-party resources, such as Cannabis Benchmarks, which tracks national prices, and the number of harvests (average of 5.5 per year), you can project out the revenue side.

Ground floor. "The rewards of early involvement may be quite significant," says corporate cannabis lawyer Neil Kaufman (Kaufman & Associates), talking about accountants getting involved in this industry. Of course, this is of interest to any professional service provider, such as valuation experts. "The tide has turned," he says, referring to the changing public opinion and the pressing fiscal needs of state governments. "There's an inexorable march around the world towards the legalization, regulation and taxation of marijuana products," he says. If a state can generate significant tax revenues, then this industry will not be ignored. And states that are already involved will not want to give up those revenues.

While medical marijuana will continue to be a part of the market, it will be dwarfed by the huge increase in the recreational market, Kaufman says. This has already been seen in Colorado, and it will soon happen in California. "When the California recreational market opens up, it's expected to change the entire dynamics of the industry," he says. In November 2016, it was reported that a shipment of marijuana was seized while on its way from California to Mexico—instead of the other way around. "That may be a harbinger of things to come."

Amid all of the political and economic challenges, panel moderator Debra Borchardt (Forbes) asked if there was anything positive about going into this business. "We now have about 50 children who used to have 100 seizures a day and after using our product are now down to about one seizure a month," Peckham said to an audience that burst into applause. "They've gone from incapacitated to all smiles."

1 Seigneur is a contributor to a new edition of a BVR special report, *What It's Worth: Value and Business Challenges in the Budding Cannabis Industry*, available at www.bvresources.com/publications.

A Case Study of Valuing Distressed Assets in the Energy Sector

By Doug Peterson,
Valuation Research Corp. (Atlanta, Ga., U.S.A.)

In 2015, oil prices plummeted from a high above $60 per barrel to below $40 per barrel. By late 2015, no one expected prices to return to the $80-to-$100-per-barrel level that was the norm over most of the last decade.

Obviously, oil prices had a profound effect on the value of exploration and production companies as well as their underlying assets. In addition to the financial distress this caused companies with high levels of debt, the low price outlook affected the economics of operating an existing well and/or building a well, which ultimately would have an impact on the expected timing and volumes of production from the acquired reserves. Thus, the pricing forecast had a significant impact on the value of the tangible assets, from a standpoint of production volume and its impact on utilization levels, and the acquired reserves from a sales standpoint (price per barrel and volume) and its influence on realized cash flows.

When production utilization is lower, the economic viability of the tangible assets (i.e., return on investment) falls into greater question. Additionally, when prices are lower, it becomes prohibitive to extract value from oil and gas reserves, which are dependent on the stage of the reserves development, or reserve classification, which include:

- Proved developed producing (PDP);
- Proved developed nonproducing (PDN);
- Proved undeveloped (PUP);
- Probable (PRB); and
- Possible (POS).

All classifications except PDP require some level of investment to begin generating production volume.

Client situation. An energy production company whose subsidiary had acquired certain distressed assets from an energy and production company retained VRC's Mexico-based affiliate Grupo NASSA. The acquired company was in Chapter 11 bankruptcy protection after the precipitous drop in oil prices in 2015. VRC was engaged to determine the fair value of certain tangible and intangible assets of the acquired company. This property included:

- Three oil platforms;
- Machinery and equipment;
- Production wells;
- Ship and barge anchoring systems;
- Two additional platforms under construction; and
- All oil and gas reserves.

Grupo NASSA valued other ancillary assets such as vehicles.

To perform the valuation of the energy reserves, we coordinated with multiple parties operating in different languages and valuing assets at several locations. This included our U.S.-based staff, our Grupo NASSA affiliate, the acquiring company and its subsidiary, the acquired company, and our expert geologists. The valuation included on-site evaluation of the acquired oil platforms as well as oil reserves and wells—some developed, some undeveloped—off the coast of Peru.

In selecting a valuation methodology, we needed to consider the significant divergence in the enterprise value of the business versus the undiscounted value of the assets given the dramatic drop in commodity prices at the time.

The solution. VRC employed a cost approach to determine the value of the tangible assets. The value of the tangible assets required the calculation of a significant economic obsolescence factor given their low utilization. To determine the value of the oil and gas reserves, we employed a multiperiod excess earnings method (MPEEM).

In estimating the fair value of the personal property, the cost approach was used because it provided the most accurate reflection of the asset's value to the owner-user on an ongoing basis. A company or investor purchases equipment for future use. Therefore, the valuation should reflect the remaining value to the company in its use of the assets, not the value of the assets in exchange on the market. Thus, the assets are viewed as service property. In this case, the value conclusion was arrived at by obtaining information from the used equipment market, making any necessary adjustments regarding comparability where information was sufficient to identify and compare with the subject, and adding all costs that would be required to convert an idle piece of equipment to an integral part of an operating unit.

Determining an economic obsolescence on the tangible assets was challenging given fluctuating energy prices and uncertain production projections. As of the valuation date, production volume from each of the operating wells ranged from 10% to 30% capacity. Economic obsolescence was determined based on aggregate prevailing production levels of the three platforms relative to their aggregate rated capacity. At the time, the platforms were only running at 14.7% of their rated capacity on a combined basis. This information helped to determine an economic obsolescence factor for the property associated with the platforms and the construction in-process.

To value the intangible reserve assets, we addressed valuation issues relative to the reserve interests. At the client's direction, valuation of the POS reserves was excluded from the scope of the valuation analysis due to both their relative uncertainty and because it was assumed these would be uneconomical given the prevailing price levels and the amount of capital and operating expenditures required to begin extracting the reserves and, ultimately, generating production. For each of the proved reserve classes and the probable reserves assets that were producing, or could be anticipated to produce in the determinable future, the appropriate premise of value was determined to be market value-in-use. Both the income approach to value and a modification of the sales comparison approach to value (considered a market approach) can be appropriate in valuing such assets. The cost approach was considered to be inapplicable because depleted assets such as oil and natural gas reserves cannot be reproduced or placed at their location.

In using the income approach, the results of the financial models were developed using the MPEEM. MPEEM is a form of a discounted cash flow analysis whereby an operating model is first constructed to forecast revenues and expenses derived from the business enterprise associated with the assets being valued. When other assets are required to produce this cash flow, then portions of the total cash flow attributable to these contributory assets must be identified and deducted from the total cash flow. As a result, the values of the tangible assets and the oil and gas reserves are highly interdependent since the MPEEM is heavily reliant on the valuation of the tangible assets used to produce the oil since the use of the tangible assets is considered a contributory asset (the higher the value of tangible assets, the higher the contributory asset charge to the reserves, and the lower the value of the reserves). The remaining cash flow stream, or excess earnings, is attributable to the asset being valued. An appropriate discount rate is then selected, and the present value for the excess earnings stream is derived to yield the value for the subject assets.

The market approach is based on a multiplier of a designated increment of forecast income prospective purchasers use when valuing such interests. Multipliers can be established through interviews with persons knowledgeable of the market for such interests providing an alternate indication of value. This approach has historically been used in valuing producing oil and natural gas interests.

While participants used this method for rough estimations, the more sophisticated industry participants typically use a discounted cash flow method to determine values used in transactions. VRC believed that a multiple of income would not in itself represent the fair value, so this technique was not used.

Conclusion. Valuing distressed assets in the energy sector presented many challenges. Certain methodologies and assumptions resulted in several "decision points" about the economic viability of the assets that had a significant impact on the concluded values of the various assets. Accordingly, the consideration and determination of the appropriate methodologies and assumptions were paramount.

Doug Peterson *is a managing director in the Atlanta office of Valuation Research Corp. Prior to joining VRC, he held valuation positions with Duff & Phelps (Chicago) and KPMG (Chicago and Atlanta).*

Key Value Drivers and Valuation Issues for Solar Power Firms

Editor's note: This is an excerpt from the latest in the series of BVR's What It's Worth *guides:* Valuing Oil, Gas, and Alternative Energy Assets. *It contains perspective from experts on the challenges, key valuation drivers, and opportunities in oil, gas, and alternative energy sectors. It also provides in-depth analysis of important court cases.*

There are several reasons to value solar power companies, such as for leaseback transactions or interests in "yieldcos"—pooling arrangements of residential installations into one investment fund. During a BVR webinar,[1] Rick Daubenspeck of BDO addresses the key value drivers and unique issues that ultimately affect a solar company's risk rate.

Solar power installations generate revenue based upon the ability to sell the electricity they generate, and most sell their electricity under power purchase agreements (PPAs). Under a PPA, a buyer, or offtaker, will purchase the electricity generated at a contractual price over an indicated length of time. The buyer could be the business or tenant where the system is located, a local utility, or a local municipality. Most business enterprises consume all of the produced energy, but many residential programs allow the tenant to sell excess electricity to the local utility for distribution to its customers.

Daubenspeck points to the key factors that have driven growth in solar energy generated in the U.S.:

- Economic incentives under the investment tax credit (ITC);
- Incentives on the state level, such as renewable energy credits (REC) and performance-based incentives (PBI), which can help contribute to the value of the solar power producer depending on its location and services offered;
- Renewable portfolio standards (RPS) committed to by a number of states;
- Improvements in component performance and installation designs; and

1 Alternative Energy: Understanding Critical Business Valuation Issues, BVR webinar (February 2016). Available on demand at www.bvresources.com/pastevents.asp.

- The decline in the cost of key components, such as photovoltaic (PV) modules and inverters.

"The ITC is key to the economic viability of solar installations," says Daubenspeck. In 2005, the Energy Policy Act created a 30% tax credit for commercial solar installations. The act was set to expire on several occasions but was extended each time. Currently, the ITC will remain at 30% through the end of 2019, dropping to 26% for 2020, then 22% for 2021, and ultimately remain at 10% as of the beginning of 2022.

Valuation approaches. The income approach is most commonly applied for valuing a solar installation because it captures the impact of a system's revenue-generating ability based on forecasted capacity factors. The approach also enables the modeling of tax credit impacts. "You model what it is going to produce in Year 1, including the contracted PPA rate and any federal or local financial incentives. Then you run it out at a degradation rate over the system's economic useful life while including the costs associated with operating the system," Daubenspeck explains.

The market approach is considered but typically not used in valuing solar companies, given the lack of comparable transactions in the market. "The people who buy and sell used modules, inverters, and so on purchase components from smaller installations like houses," Daubenspeck says. In other words, they are small parts, not modules from large installations. People do not normally buy a large number of modules at one time.

The cost (net asset) approach is a calculation of value. "We consider it, but the approach only captures the initial cost outlay and not the added benefit of the tax credit and the PPA," explains Daubenspeck. However, business appraisers need to ask whether the value is in the individual components or in the ability to generate revenue and income as an operating system.

Developing an opinion of value. The most widely accepted method for developing an opinion of value for a solar installation is a discounted cash flow (DCF). Daubenspeck describes the critical items of information that valuators need to consider with a DCF as follows.

1. *Overall capacity of the system.* Overall capacity determines much of the operating expenses and overall installation costs. A lot of the expenses—operating maintenance, the overall cost, insurance—will be based on the system's size and capacity, i.e., 500 kilowatts (kW), 2 megawatts (mW), or 10 mW.

2. *Estimated amount of electricity that will be generated in the first year of operation.* "This is critical in calculating the annual revenue of the system; it will decline approximately 0.5% annually," says Daubenspeck. Typically an engineer can estimate the amount from a model based on size, location, etc.

3. *Components that make up the system.* The key component is PV modules, followed by inverters, racking, wiring, combiner boxes, transformers, etc. Some of the components will need to be replaced during

the system's lifetime. Appraisers need to determine what the components are in addition to the rate, the term, and the offtake under the PPA. All of these issues will come into play in the valuation.

4. *Expenses related to operating the system.* Appraisers also need to determine the expenses relating to operating and maintenance, site lease, insurance, interconnection fee, management fees, etc.

The life of a system is driven by all of its parts, but primarily the one part that has the longest life. Currently, there are economic useful lives of solar installations of up to 40 or 45 years. "Some people think this is crazy, but if a module degrades at 0.5% a year, after 20 years, it still has 90% of its energy-generating capability," says Daubenspeck. It doesn't make economic sense to buy a new system if the current one is running well. There are fully paid-for systems that are 20 years old and running at 90% capacity. In fact, a couple of systems have been in place for over 40 years and are running at about 50% or 65% efficiency.

5. *Rate per kW generated, term, and offtake under the PPA.* The offtaker—the consumer or utility purchasing the energy—is critical, especially if the offtaker is a utility the purchases at a discount. "For example, a number of years back, utilities in California were required to buy energy off the grid," Daubenspeck relates. They challenged the court, which resulted in an agreement that allowed the utilities to pay less on a per-watt basis than a retailer. As such, a utility bill has two components: the generation amount and the distribution amount. The utilities buy at the generation amount because they have to distribute it, and they want revenue from that service.

This arrangement will factor into the rate paid under the PPA, which should be similar to a market rate. However, some arrangements may have an escalator, e.g., 2% annually. "Again, operation and maintenance, and additional costs such as interconnection and management fees, will factor into this," explains Daubenspeck.

6. *System location.* The average cost for electricity varies among customers (residential, commercial, and industrial) for each of the 50 states. The average market rate and annual increase following the PPA term will vary based upon the location of the system.

The site lease could be very important when valuing a system for a transaction. "What happens if an existing ground lease expires before the installed system reaches the end of its economic useful life?" Daubenspeck asks. What are the average ground lease rates in that area? The Department of Energy publishes average cost-per-watt data by state for a residential, a commercial, an industrial, and oftentimes transportation, and consumer.

There are other factors to consider that may or may not impact the overall value of the system under a DCF, including the following:

- *Any additional state incentives that the system may be eligible for* such as renewable energy credits (RECs), performance-based incentives (PBIs), state tax credits based upon cost to construct, etc. You can find policies and incentives by state with the Database of State Incentives for Renewables & Efficiency (www.dsireusa.org).

- *Additional requirements specific to a sale/leaseback structure or a flip structure.* You want to know what type of structure you have: leaseback or flip. Flip structures have been predominant in the wind sector.

- *Purchase option dates under the PPA.*

Conclusion. As the solar industry continues to grow, so will the opportunities for business appraisers. "Appraisers have to consider each of the valuation approaches, but the income approach, in my opinion, is the only way to value a solar company," says Daubenspeck.

For more information, see *What It's Worth: Valuing Oil, Gas, and Alternative Energy Assets,* available at www.bvresources.com/publications. ***Rick Daubenspeck,*** *ASA, MRICS, a managing director at BDO Consulting, can be reached at 602-293-2366 or rdaubenspeck@bdo.com.*

Valuation Approaches and Special Considerations for Home Healthcare Businesses

By Alan B. Simons,
Security Risk Advisors (Philadelphia, Pa.)

Editor's note: This is an excerpt from a chapter in the recently released book, the BVR Guide to Ancillary Healthcare Services Valuation.[1] *The article goes into much more detail about the home healthcare industry and its associated risks. This excerpt discusses the valuation approaches and special situations with respect to these types of entities.*

Home health and hospice care is a subset of all healthcare providers (such as hospitals, physicians, senior care, and so on) that further breaks down into the following five major service lines:

- Home health—skilled nursing, physical therapy, occupational therapy, speech therapy, aid service, and medical social work provided to patients in their home;
- Home hospice—care provided for terminally (life expectancy of six months or less) ill patients and their families in their homes (can also be provided at other care sites);
- Private duty and staffing services—personal care and supportive services that a home care aid primarily provides;
- Home medical and respiratory equipment—durable medical equipment such as walkers, beds, wheelchairs, and oxygen concentrators; and
- Home infusion—intravenous therapies such as parenteral nutrition, antibiotics, and chemotherapy.

The goal of home healthcare is to provide a continuum of services designed to allow disabled or older individuals to stay in their homes for support and treatment as an alternative to assisted

1 Mark O. Dietrich, *BVR Guide to Ancillary Healthcare Services Valuation*, Business Valuation Resources, 2016. Includes contributions of 15 of the top U.S. healthcare valuation experts. Available at www.bvresources.com/publications.

living, nursing homes, and hospital facilities. Proponents of home healthcare believe it is less expensive and a better care alternative for most people.

These services, when combined, would represent a very comprehensive home healthcare business. But, more often than not, the appraiser will be valuing businesses with fewer service lines, and often the business may be comprised of only one service line.

A unique set of variables drive the profitability and risks associated with each of these service lines, making it difficult to make global assumptions about the home healthcare business. The appraiser needs to develop an understanding of each service line and how these service lines interact if the subject business operates in two or more.

In some organizations, each service line can stand on its own as an independent, financially viable business. When this is the case, each business has a broad source of patient referrals independent of the other service lines. Under this scenario, each service line and the business as a whole would have more value than when service lines are interdependent upon each other for referrals.

For example, a service line might have no value to a potential buyer if all or most of its business was dependent on a previously related entity. If the service line is sold without the related entity, there is no guarantee that referrals (and therefore, the business) will continue. This can happen when a home health business or service line is a "captive" of a hospital or nursing home. It can also happen when a service line gets most or all of its referrals because of its relationship or proximity to one or more other related service lines. Generally, a home health business is a core business or service line when it has a broad base of referral sources, and other service lines are added to enhance its profitability. In this case, most or all of the value may reside in the core business.

Appraisers need to understand the relationship among the service lines and referral sources to determine where the value resides. This is particularly important when the business is a captive or when not all of the service lines are being sold together.

In addition, the Affordable Care Act (ACA) is challenging home health service lines to develop quality measures that will impact future payments. An appraiser needs an understanding of the evolving changes in value-based payment plans that will increase payments for positive performance and decrease payments for negative performance. Another ACA challenge for home health service lines will be the bundling of payments based on an acute episode of care. New bundled payment plans for hip and knee replacements started in 2016. The bundled payment is paid to the acute care hospital, and the hospital is responsible for providing the care the patient needs for 90 days after discharge.

The appraiser will want to have a discussion with management about the changes that are occurring in the home health provider's community. Are there new entities such as accountable care organizations (ACOs) that are being established to manage the care of individuals in the community? Will these ACOs contract with any willing home healthcare provider or are they going to limit the number of providers? What will be the factors and measurements used to select a home healthcare provider?

Valuation Approaches

Income approach. The income approach, and more specifically the discounted cash flow method, is the valuation approach and method most appraisers prefer to value profitable operating businesses. This method can be difficult to use for marginally profitable or unprofitable businesses if there is inadequate cash flow to provide a reasonable return on the business's assets. In that case, methods under the market or asset approach may be more appropriate.

Under an income approach, it is important to determine whether the forecasted cash flows are reasonable and achievable. If the appraiser thoroughly understands the business and the industry (as previously discussed), he or she should be able to reasonably make this determination and factor it into the development of a discount rate applicable to the cash flows forecasted for the subject company.

When evaluating forecasted cash flow growth rates, the appraiser needs to consider imminent changes and proposed changes to reimbursement, opportunities for the subject company to expand, population growth, age demographics, and age-cohort specific use rates where data might be available.

Looking at the specific operational issues affecting the company, its historical operations, and by making comparisons to industry data, the appraiser should be able to evaluate the reasonableness of future working capital needs and capital expenditure requirements.

Care must be used in developing an equity discount rate that results in a risk-adjusted rate of return necessary to attract buyers to invest in the subject company. Appraisers need to ensure that they understand the operating characteristics (for example, size, growth rates, margins, product, and service mix) of the business or businesses from which discount rates and equity risk premiums are derived and make appropriate company-specific risk adjustments to reflect differences between the subject company and the source of these rates or premiums. In addition, there could be other changes such as new legislation, proposed or enacted, that was unknown when the market-derived discount rates or premiums were published.

Most home healthcare businesses are not capital-intensive. (One exception would be a hospice with an inpatient and residential facility.) As a result, they generally do not incur (nor do they have a need to incur) significant long-term debt. The appraiser must consider this and other factors when determining a debt-to-equity ratio for a weighted average cost of capital (WACC) assumption. Caution should be used in automatically using debt-to-equity ratios derived from publicly traded companies because they may not be "pure plays"[2] and the subject company may have significantly

2 A pure play is a company that is only in one line of business. Many public companies are in multiple lines of business.

different operating characteristics and growth opportunities. Under the fair market value standard, the debt-to-equity ratio, used in the WACC, should be one that is reasonably achievable by the subject company and likely to provide the returns anticipated to debt and equity investors from the anticipated cash flows used in the forecast.

Appraisers need to ensure that risk-adjusted rates of returns used match the earnings stream being valued. It is generally acknowledged that most discount rates are derived from public-company transactions on an after-tax basis. When valuing healthcare businesses for regulatory purposes (for example, under the anti-kickback statute and transactions involving nonprofit IRC 501(c)(3) entities), it is generally accepted that controlling interests must be valued on an after-tax basis (including pass-through entities) under the assumption that the most likely buyer is a commercial C corporation. One rationale for this is that, without having to pay taxes, nonprofit organizations could theoretically afford to pay more than a comparable for-profit organization for the same business. Valuing after-tax cash flows also keeps after-tax discount rates derived from public companies consistent with the subject company's earnings stream. Appraisers need to consider adjustments to the discount rate or methodology that might be required for nonregulatory valuation engagements and for engagements involving minority interests in pass-through entities to maintain consistency between the discount rate and the earnings stream.

Market approach. Methods under the market approach can be useful but difficult to use correctly when valuing home healthcare businesses because it is always hard to find publicly traded companies and sales transactions for companies that are truly comparable to the subject company. Unless the comparable company is publicly traded, it is almost impossible to adequately evaluate a comparable company's operating characteristics.

Some comparable sales transactions may predate current reimbursement levels, economic changes, or not have anticipated proposed legislation, which might result in an erroneous conclusion about a current transaction. Furthermore, a significant number of comparable sales transactions represent acquisitions by existing healthcare companies that may recognize economic synergies resulting in an investment or synergistic standard of value (not fair market value if that is the standard desired).

Despite these limitations, a thorough analysis of publicly traded companies and comparable sales transactions is extremely useful in developing an understanding of the marketplace, value drivers, who the most likely buyers are, and in determining a reasonable range (low to high) to test values indicated under other approaches.

The market approach can also be useful when operating income and cash flows are indeterminable because of poor records or commingled operations or in the case of the mismanagement of an otherwise sound company. In those cases, market-derived valuation multiples that are not tied to earnings can be useful. Assuming you have reliable revenues and daily census data for the subject company, price-to-revenue multiples or price-to-average-daily-census multiples from guideline publicly traded companies or comparable sales transactions are useful in estimating an indicated range of potential values.

For example, buyers within the industry will frequently use a multiple of patient average daily census (ADC) data to benchmark the value of these businesses. If the benchmark is $50,000 per ADC and the ADC is 200 patients, the business might be worth $10 million.

However, remember that, when choosing a revenue multiple or census multiple, you are implicitly assuming that the subject company has all of the operating characteristics from which the revenue or census multiple was derived. So appraisers must be extremely careful when relying primarily on market multiples.

Developing a significant understanding of the subject company and the industry can go a long way toward overcoming the shortcomings inherent in the market approach. For example, if you can benchmark a company's revenue and direct labor costs relative to its peers, you may become more comfortable in choosing a revenue or daily census multiple.

Methods under the market approach appear simple and intuitive and, therefore, have great appeal. But these methods need to be used judiciously and generally in conjunction with other approaches.

Aside from traditional public-company research and general sales transaction databases, Irving Levin Associates Inc. (www.levinassociates.com) publishes *The Senior Care Acquisition Report,* which includes information about publicly announced home healthcare transactions.

Asset approach. Methods under the asset approach are rarely used as the primary method to value operating companies such as home healthcare unless the business is unprofitable or marginally profitable whereby cash flows do not produce an adequate return on assets. However, methods under the asset approach should still be considered to ensure that values under other approaches (primarily the income approach) exceed values that would be developed under an asset approach, which is usually viewed as the lowest or floor value.

Under an income or market approach, the premise of value is almost always a going concern. When using an asset approach, the premise of value is sometimes more difficult to determine, but the valuation methods used must be applied consistent with the premise chosen.

Special Situations Affecting Home Healthcare Value

Management's integrity. Healthcare is arguably the most highly regulated industry in the country. Many of the regulations facing providers today were enacted to address years of providers abusing the system and profiting illegally and unethically under government programs, such as Medicare and Medicaid, and private insurance programs.

Today, there are significant fines, penalties, and the possibility of prison for violating federal and state regulations governing the healthcare industry and nonprofit organizations. While enforcement has helped to curb abuses, they still exist.

While appraisers generally are not performing due diligence, it is important for them to do a high level assessment of management's integrity. Appraisers who understand the home healthcare industry and the associated regulations also understand many of the illegal schemes and can evaluate management's integrity fairly effectively through benchmarking the company against its peers (looking for anomalies) and interviewing management (looking for inconsistencies).

The risk associated with management's integrity can impact whether a hypothetical buyer who may not be willing or able to operate the business illegally or unethically can maintain revenue levels and profitability. The appraiser should always require that the organization being valued disclose any and all correspondence and external audit findings that have been conducted by state licensure agencies, Medicare-certifying organizations, Medicare and Medicaid fiscal intermediaries, focused medical review audits and findings, and any past or ongoing notifications from the Office of the Inspector General (OIG) including past or current corporate integrity agreements (CIAs). Other useful tools to test the operational integrity of the organization is whether a compliance plan is in place that is modeled after the OIG's suggested format as well as internal audit committee reports and findings that would be a component of the compliance plan.

The appraiser's assessment of management's integrity may create the need for normalizing adjustments and should have a direct effect on risk-adjusted rates of return used under an income approach as well as judgments the appraiser made using methods under other approaches.

Certificate of need (CON) states. States may restrict or limit new home health businesses though CON legislation. Typically, these states limit CON application to service lines that are "skilled in nature" and heavily dependent on Medicare and Medicaid certification and reimbursement such as home health and hospice. However, some states also have regulations that govern establishment of new "licensed-only" providers that will not be Medicare-certified but will obtain reimbursements from Medicaid.

To start a new home healthcare business in a CON state, you generally need to demonstrate adequate demand and need. Depending on the state, the CON process can be time-consuming and expensive. Generally, home healthcare businesses in CON states will be worth more compared to a similar business in a state without a CON. However, each state's CON rules may be more or less restrictive, and the appraiser should research the state's current plan for home healthcare services to determine whether there is opportunity for new businesses to enter the market. Even if the business is no more profitable in the CON state, the lack of new competition will generally reduce risk compared to businesses in non-CON states.

In states where CONs are very restrictive, the CON alone can be worth a significant amount of money, even without an operating business, and, as a result, sometimes CONs are valued independent of the operating business.

Appraisers need to consider the effect on the discount rate when valuing home healthcare businesses in CON states versus non-CON states. When valuing a CON alone (without an operating business), appraisers should generally rely on the income approach (relief from royalty method) or possibly the cost approach, unless comparable transaction data for the CONs in the state are available. If using a relief from royalty method, consider what percentage of the expected operating margin should be allocated to the CON when doing a pretax royalty rate calculation. For example, if agencies are expected to earn 12% in that market, the pretax royalty rate for the CON valuation calculation might be 3% (or 25% of the 12% operating margin, for example) of the forecasted revenues expected if the CON were used in an operating business.

Provider-owned business. Home healthcare businesses owned by hospitals or nursing homes are unique because they generally will not have their own financial statements or tax returns and will almost never have a balance sheet. They generally only track costs directly applicable to departments or service lines such as home health services (for example, direct supplies, direct compensation, and benefits) but allocate indirect overhead (such as telephone, security, maintenance, rent, utilities, human resource, and information systems) from the parent entity's total overhead. As a result, operations for provider-owned home healthcare businesses are generally not comparable to stand-alone businesses.

Without objective financial statements (and particularly balance sheets), it is usually impossible to develop meaningful financial ratios and analysis. However, a number of operational benchmarks, such as revenue per visit, average daily census, or visits per employee, can still be developed and compared to industry benchmarks to evaluate the quality of operations.

Another potential problem in valuing a provider-owned home healthcare business is that sometimes it is not motivated by profit. In some cases, the lack of profit motivation may be because home health is not a core part of the overall business and may contribute little to overall operations. In other cases, the business may be viewed solely for its contribution to the parent entity's mission or as part of a continuum of care. While lack of profitability is not inconsistent with being a nonprofit organization, management sometimes uses its nonprofit mission to rationalize underperformance. Appraisers need to understand that marginal profitability, or even losses in the hands of management, doesn't necessarily mean these businesses cannot be run profitably in the hands of profit-motivated management.

To value provider-owned businesses, historical and forecasted operations need to be normalized and made comparable to non-provider-owned or stand-alone businesses. Great care must be exercised in doing this to ensure that only controllable costs are adjusted and uncontrollable costs, which may be unique to that marketplace, are not changed. Care must also be exercised to ensure that, under the fair market value standard, adjustments are not unique to a particular buyer.

Appraisers need to develop a reasonable understanding of industry benchmarks for home healthcare businesses to support or evaluate the assumptions that will be necessary to convert the hospital-owned business into a non-hospital-owned business.

Some questions typically asked during these assignments are:

- How much space (square footage) does the business really need?
- Is the rent too high and location too expensive for the needs of the business?
- Is the business sharing management with other departments and how are those costs allocated?
- Are the parent entity's labor costs and benefits comparable to a non-provider-based business?
- Are there costs and other administrative functions that are only required because they are part of the larger entity (for example, Joint Commission accreditation)?
- How are patients referred for home healthcare services?

How referrals are made to a provider-owned business can have a significant impact on its value—and, of course, referrals are a key regulatory risk area. For example, there is less risk of losing referrals if they come from a variety of physicians as opposed to only physicians employed by or on the staff of the parent entity. While this is a typical risk associated with a concentration of customers, it may be more prevalent for provider-owned businesses. In valuing the business under a fair market value standard, the appraiser should evaluate what would change if the business were not part of, or reliant upon, the parent entity.

Real estate and nonoperating assets. Most home healthcare businesses are not capital-intensive (an exception might be a hospice that has an inpatient or residential facility). As a result, real estate and other nonoperating assets can create special problems in determining value. In particular, cash flows from the operating business often will not provide an adequate return on the real estate and nonoperating assets.

Generally, these assets should be excluded from the value of the operating business and valued separately if they are, in fact, going to be acquired as part of the transaction. These assets should be removed from the balance sheet, and their historical costs should be removed from the income statements. For those assets, such as real estate, that are used in the business, fair market value rent expense (assuming a fair market value standard) should be substituted for the cost of owning and operating the real estate. Fair market value rent for the operating business should be consistent with rents that other home care businesses would pay for only the square footage needed to operate a similar business within the subject company's market. Fair market value rent could be more or less than rents paid historically or agreed to prospectively.

If the valuation is being done for regulatory purposes, rent that is below or above fair market value is a potential issue that a healthcare attorney familiar with applicable regulations should evaluate.

Conclusion. Valuing home healthcare businesses is not unlike valuing other businesses except that appraisers should have a significant understanding of their operating characteristics and the industry. Changes in future reimbursement can significantly affect earnings and value. Accountable care organizations and bundled payments may completely change providers' business models and cost structures and the way they are reimbursed. As a result, it is incumbent on appraisers to be familiar with the effect these changes may have on the business. In addition, for any healthcare engagement, appraisers should have a reasonable understanding of regulations affecting healthcare providers and nonprofit organizations and a grasp of the current changes that Congress and state legislatures may enact.

Alan B. Simons, *CPA/ABV, CFF, CMPE, DABFA, is head of operations at Security Risk Advisors. Prior to this, he was principal-in-charge of CliftonLarsonAllen's national healthcare valuation practice and the business valuation and litigation support practice for the Philadelphia office.* *The author would like to thank Ron Clitherow, MPH, and Gary R. Massey, CPA, for their significant contributions to this article.*

Challenges and Common Errors in Valuing Electrical Contractors

Electrical contracting is a mature industry characterized by a large number of companies, in which relatively low capital requirements have encouraged entry of many small-scale operators. The electrical contracting industry is highly dependent on the national and regional economy, as well as the disposable income of the population. "It is also a very fragmented industry in terms of revenue mix with categories including new residential, nonresidential, government, municipalities, installation, retrofit, green installation and services, and maintenance and repair," explains Erin Hollis, financial valuation and consulting director in the Chicago office of the valuation, transaction, and advisory firm Marshall & Stevens Inc. She and Matthew Crane, a director also with Marshall & Stevens, outline the potential challenges when valuing these firms.[1]

1. Workforce. The industry requires a specialized workforce but faces issues of employee turnover and an aging employee population. Valuation professionals need to assess not only the availability of skilled and experienced labor, but also the impact of the presence (or absence) of labor unions. "Technological advances in the industry may strain the workforce demand in some areas," Hollis says.

2. Backlog of work. Backlog is comprised of the uncompleted contracts that the contractor is currently working on and will continue to work on, which may or may not be of a long-term nature. "For purposes of valuation, all other things being equal, an electrical contractor with a significant backlog is more valuable than another available contractor without the backlog. So, in my opinion, it is worthwhile to look at a contracting company's backlog of work," Crane explains.

3. Underlying contracts. Also critical are the underlying contracts themselves. Electrical contracting is a highly competitive business and not one that enjoys high margins. This means that bidding on contracts is critical and therefore usually done by key people within the firm. "So, if you are performing a valuation of an electrical contractor," Crane advises, "you probably want to look at some of the larger contracts that they have in hand and are working on at the time of the valuation date."

1 This is an excerpt from a special report, *What It's Worth: Valuing Electrical Contracting Companies*, BVR, 2017 (www.bvresources.com/publications).

4. Underfunded pension liability. Another potential valuation issue, especially in many metropolitan areas, is the unionization of electrical contractors. "If contractors want to perform work in certain metropolitan areas, for example, they have to do a deal with the union," explains Crane.

Along with that comes the union pension. "Not too many years ago, I was valuing an electrical contractor with an underfunded pension liability. The deal with pension liabilities is that, if the contractor wants to exit the business—either liquidate or sell the business to a third party—he or she has to settle with the union any underfunding of the pension liability on the day he or she wants to transact with another party."

This limits the pool of buyers, Crane points out, because any buyer interested in acquiring that electrical contractor has to look at the underfunded pension liability. "Does the seller really have the ability to settle this pension liability? The buyer doesn't necessarily want to assume it. Maybe the buyer will simply rather let them go out of business and just pick up the employees from the union hall."

How do you account for underfunding on a pension when conducting a valuation? "The way that I will handle the underfunding on the pension," says Crane, "is, when the valuation process starts and you get the documents from the client, ask the client to go to the union and learn what exactly is the underfunding at this particular date. That is something the client has to do."

"Then they may come back with this answer: 'Well, according to our analysis, the pension is underfunded by $10 million.' There is not necessarily a dollar-for-dollar deduction off the valuation in this case because there is a possibility that the stock market will turn around and it might be overfunded at some date, but, if you are valuing the business using the concept of highest and best use and this is a contingent liability, you will have to deduct some dollar amount from the invested capital."

How do you do that? "You might run some different scenarios," advises Crane. "Could a buyer potentially turn that problem around in a certain amount of time? Could you run a discounted cash flow of the liability or even another scenario? It is my belief that some deduction has to come off of the value." Crane also advises valuation specialists read the paper "How Does the Market Value Underfunded Pension Liabilities?" (available for download at www.nber.org/papers/w1602).

5. Bonding. The company's ability to get bonding in some markets is a big issue. "You might value smaller electrical contractors that don't have that requirement, and, if that is the case, it's obviously not an issue," explains Crane.

How should you treat the absence of bonding as a valuation issue when it is not legally required? "If a company can't get bonded for whatever reason," says Hollis, "and this, say, prevented it in the past from expanding into a different market, then that is a negative that heightens the risk of the company. On the other hand, if a company could get bonding but has not so far, that might represent an opportunity that could be included in the forecast or increase its potential value in the eyes of a third-party buyer."

6. Leasing. "Electrical contractors don't have a high need for capital investments, but they do need lifts, trucks, temporary space, and other items that they may not necessarily want to own. So they might enter into long-term leases, which may or may not be at market rates, so you should look into what the leases are at the valuation date," advises Crane.

7. Key person risk. This is an issue of particular concern to small contractors, where the owner generally does all the estimating and bidding and has all the relationships with the clients. "So, if you are valuing an electrical firm for gift and estate tax purposes, for example, you should consider key person risk, or personal goodwill at any rate," Crane counsels.

8. Nonoperating assets and discretionary expenses and/or salaries. "Electrical businesses are quite often run by families," notes Crane, "and they take on expenses on a somewhat discretionary basis. The shareholders determine who gets paid what, and how, and if there are any other benefits in the company that they can take out."

With these specific issues as a backdrop, Hollis and Crane point out what they've seen as the common errors in valuing electrical contractors (see sidebar on next page).

Common Valuation Errors: Electrical Contractors

Errors commonly made in valuing electrical contractors include the following:

- Overlooking inventory obsolescence;
- Not considering excess or deficit in working capital;
- Not considering union concerns;
- Overlooking employee turnover issues;
- Not considering revenue mix (or lack of):
  - Clientele;
  - Services; and
  - Employee contribution (key person, either in experience or management/bidding).

"In regard to inventory obsolescence, for example, some contractors tend to stock up on their inventory of cables if they are installing VoIP in buildings," Crane says. "They pile up the inventory because, when a job comes around, they need it." Some inventory may consist of specialized items for which there is a lag time when ordering, so the contractor may tend to buy in mass, and meanwhile technological advances have made it obsolete.

Another common error is not considering an excess or deficit in working capital. "If you don't factor that in and there is an excess or deficit, and you are valuing controlling interest, then you are missing the boat," Crane warns.

The valuation professional may be overlooking union concerns, such as unfunded pension benefits.

Employee turnover is another area that can be easily missed. "The average age of electricians is rising," Crane notes, "and not a lot of people are necessarily going into the field today. The aging of the electrical workforce makes it harder for companies to identify good workers. They need stability, and it is a problem, or it could be a problem within a valuation, so you need to consider it."

Another common error is to fail to consider the revenue mix of clientele, services, and employee contribution. "Often, I have met with electrical contractors in doing valuations for estate tax purposes and learned that it is a family business, and sometimes you need to consider that within the valuation. You particularly need to consider who is in charge of doing the bidding," Crane says.

The mix of services and clientele are also key issues to look at. What is the direction of the contracting firm? Does it really want to go more into repair work and buildings, or is it staying away from that area? Maybe it doesn't bid on government jobs. Maybe it stays away from that kind of business, so it is important not to just look at the financials in isolation.

(Source: *What It's Worth: Valuing Electrical Contracting Companies*, BVR, 2017, www.bvresources.com/publications).

Latest Trends That Affect Auto Dealership Valuations

In some respects, automobile dealerships are different than other traditional industries. When the industry is in its "up cycle," dealerships often sell at numbers that make the rates of return difficult to justify in a traditional income approach. Often, buyers pay a hefty price for a good franchise even though the dealer is losing money. It's difficult to explain that by normalizing.

During a recent webinar,[1] Timothy York and Adam Lawyer, both with Dixon Hughes Goodman, gave an update on industry trends and reflected on the way dealerships are valued for actual transactions. Here are some highlights.

Industry economics. Auto dealership volume, earnings, and price tags arguably are still near all-time highs. The franchise is the most important driver of value for auto dealerships, followed by real estate and facilities. While luxury imports are still the most desirable auto franchise, they are losing steam to high-end domestics. The value of a dollar of earnings of an automobile dealership is dramatically affected by the franchise that is generating those earnings. The strongest franchises continue to be the luxury imports, according to the Haig Report.[2] Porsche maintains its "blue sky" multiple range of 7.5x to 9.0x, the highest range of all auto franchises. "Blue sky" is the amount paid for dealerships over and above the value of the tangible assets.

Some observations from York and Lawyer on certain franchises:

- Volkswagen and Audi resolved "Dieselgate" and are gaining market share.
- Jaguar and Land Rover had a mid-20% sales increase in 2015 and 2016; they have new and exciting product gaining desirability among buyers.
- Lexus is a historic powerhouse but has struggled the last several years with few new models and declining sales; dealers still love the brand, but for how long?

1 Valuing Auto Dealerships: Applicable Methods, Value Drivers, and Current Economic Environment, BVR webinar (Aug. 31, 2017); sub.bvresources.com/bvstore/cd3.asp?pid=CD556.

2 Haig Report, Second Quarter 2017; www.haigpartners.com.

- Subaru is gaining steam with consumers and dealers, especially in Sun Belt states.

Regulatory. The Trump administration is generally good news for auto dealerships due to reduced regulations, particularly in the Consumer Financial Protection Bureau (CFPB). Also, increases to EPA requirements have been rescinded, allowing dealers to sell more high-profit trucks and SUVs. Healthcare costs may decline assuming Washington gets its act together on this. Tax reform is gaining steam, especially the cuts in corporate rates, meaning higher levels of after-tax income available to owners, which should boost dealership value.

Disruptors. The top three auto dealership disruptors to keep in mind are:

- *Direct sales (Tesla).* While York has not necessarily seen tremendous disruption at this point in time that has had a significant effect on current dealers, this is something to watch. If Tesla were to become more successful in direct selling and attacking the existing franchise model, it certainly could impact how you look at valuation, operations, and so forth. He notes that Ford and GM tried selling direct years ago, but they quickly disbanded their efforts and went back to just making cars, not selling them.

- *Ride sharing (Uber, Lyft).* Some dealers are experimenting with this concept with their own fleets and trying to determine what the impact will be. Does everyone really want to own a vehicle all the time? This is unchartered territory, but there are thoughts that this will help the business evolve.

- *Self-driving cars.* Along with Waymo (Google) and Tesla, which get a lot of press, not many people realize that Ford, GM, Toyota, and others (including Apple) are also investing heavily in this space. Many people think that we are a lot closer than is typically realized because some autonomous vehicles are being tested in cities such as Pittsburgh and a few in California. But the manufacturing complexities are so severe that we may be decades away from fully autonomous vehicles being sold and purchased regularly.

Valuation method. In this industry, the blue sky multiple continues to be the most commonly used method for determining the value used in actual dealership transactions. Several years ago, York and Lawyer's firm, Dixon Hughes Goodman, developed the "current industry market indicator" (CIMI) method, which is essentially the blue sky multiple method.[3] The CIMI method estimates the fair market value of a dealership by multiplying the expected pretax earnings by an appropriate multiple to determine the amount of blue sky (intangible asset value) and then adding the adjusted net assets to get the fair market value of the entire company.

Blue sky multiples are often reported in ranges for a given franchise, and the analyst must use judgment regarding where in the published range the subject dealership would likely fall or if for

3 The CIMI method, among other auto dealership valuation considerations, is also covered in the special report, *What It's Worth: Automobile Dealership Value* (www.bvresources.com/products/what-it's-worth-automobile-dealership-value).

some reason the dealership falls outside the published ranges. According to Kerrigan Advisors, there are four key drivers of blue sky variability: (1) earnings growth expectation; (2) buyer demand; (3) real estate (rent and nature of facilities); and (4) market preference (franchise suitability). When determining the appropriate blue sky multiple, analysts typically start with the average and adjust up or down depending on how the subject dealership fares with the four drivers.

For example, here's how a multiple may be selected using the CIMI method. Assume a dealership with two franchises, Toyota and Subaru.

- Rural operating location *(adjust multiple downward);*
- Toyota image-compliant facilities *(adjust multiple upward);*
- Subaru facilities need renovation *(adjust multiple downward);*
- Stable earnings, low expected growth *(adjust multiple downward);*
- Toyota—70% of sales, multiple range 5.0-6.5;
- Subaru—30% of sales, multiple range 4.0-5.0;
- Selected multiple:

Toyota: 5.75 × 70%	= 4.03
Subaru: 4.0 × 30%	= 1.20
Combined	= 5.23
Rounded	= **5.25**

As a sanity check, blue sky multiples can be translated into a rate of return on equity (investment). For example, a multiple of five times pretax earnings equals a 20% rate of return. The implied rate of return derived from the CIMI method can be converted to an after-tax rate of return and compared to the capitalization or discount rates used in the income approach.

Although auto dealership valuations are complex, accepted valuation methodologies combined with specific industry knowledge can result in a reasonable and supportable estimate of value.

Section III.
Legal, Regulatory, Standards

The 10 Most Important Valuation Cases of 2016

Because valuation and damages are key components of most lawsuits, there is no shortage of cases addressing issues of interest to appraisers and financial experts. For several years now, *BVLaw* has provided a list of the cases that stood out during a given year. Here are our nominees for the most impactful cases of 2016.

1. ***In re Appraisal of Dell Inc.*, 2016 Del. Ch. LEXIS 81 (May 31, 2016)** In the most controversial statutory fair value decision of the year, the Chancery found the sales process in this management buyout led to unquantifiable mispricing, which meant the deal price did not equal fair value. The court relied on a post-transaction DCF analysis for its fair value determination.

2. ***Wagner v. Wagner*, 2016 Ida. LEXIS 128 (April 27, 2016)** Providing a Western state perspective on the use of discounts in statutory fair value proceedings, the Idaho Supreme Court decided that discounts "are just another fact that a court may consider in determining fair value." They are not mandatory, the court made clear.

3. ***Perez v. Bruister*, 2016 U.S. App. LEXIS 8046 (May 3, 2016)** In reviewing a gnarled ESOP case, the 5th Circuit Court of Appeals upheld most of the district court's liability and valuation determinations. The 5th Circuit agreed with the district court that rescission was too drastic a remedy because it was possible to determine overpayment by averaging and weighting the valuations of three equally credible trial experts.

4. ***In re DFC Global Corp.*, 2016 Del. Ch. LEXIS 103 (July 8, 2016)** In a statutory fair value decision that includes a deep discussion of beta, the Chancery's chief judge, Bouchard, decided that it was futile to rely on a single valuation method to determine fair value where the company's future and, by extension, its projections were riddled with uncertainty. The court said blending the results of three "imperfect" (common) valuation methods achieved a reliable indicator of value.

5. ***In re Cole*, 2016 Bank. LEXIS 932 (March 24, 2016)** This divorce-meets-bankruptcy case explains the importance of knowing the standard of value that applies in a given context. As the Bankruptcy Court noted, a Chapter 7 trustee must "reduce to money the property of the bankruptcy estate,

clearly contemplating a sale or other disposition of the property. This is different from determining the intrinsic value … in a divorce proceeding."

6. *Washington v. Kellwood Co.*, 2016 U.S. Dist. LEXIS 92309 (July 15, 2016) (*Kellwood II*), and *Washington v. Kellwood Co.*, 2016 U.S. Dist. LEXIS 136612 (Sept. 30, 2016) (*Kellwood III*) This damages case made our list last year when the court found the plaintiff expert's dodgy yardstick-based damages analysis was admissible under *Daubert*. Post-trial, the court did a 180-degree turn, striking down the jury's multimillion-dollar lost profits award based on the very expert opinion the court earlier had admitted. The court also reversed its earlier decision to allow for a new trial on lost business value.

7. *Fish v. Greatbanc Trust Co.*, 2016 U.S. Dist. LEXIS 137351 (Sept. 1, 2016) In a second, high-profile ESOP case, two well-known experts were asked to assess the process and valuations the ESOP trustee's prominent financial advisor had undertaken before finding the contested transaction was fair to the ESOP. In concluding there was no overpayment and clearing the defendants of all liability, the court relied exclusively on "credible and persuasive" defense expert testimony.

8. *In re ISN Software Corp. Appraisal Litig.*, 2016 Del. Ch. LEXIS 125 (Aug. 11, 2016) It's not unusual for the Chancery to lament the chasm between the value determinations the parties' trial experts propose. But, according to the court, this case took the prize for generating judicial skepticism regarding valuation. One petitioner expert claimed the fair value was eight times the value the DCF analysis of the company's expert implied. The court performed its own DCF analysis to arrive at fair value.

9. *Wisniewski v. Walsh*, 2015 N.J. Super. Unpub. LEXIS 3001 (Dec. 24, 2015) (*Wisniewski II*) An appellate decision emerging from New Jersey at the cusp of 2015 sparked a spirited discussion over the role (if any) and size of DLOM in statutory fair value proceedings. In its earlier ruling, the court had ordered a DLOM to punish the plaintiff (seller) for engaging in conduct harmful to the other shareholders. In its third (and likely final) ruling, the court found the plaintiff expert's DCF analysis did not specifically adjust for lack of marketability and applied a 25% DLOM.

10. *Verghetta v. Lawlor*, 2016 N.Y. Misc. LEXIS 845 (March 9, 2016) Another statutory fair value decision out of New York did little to clarify the jurisdiction's inconsistent attitude toward DLOM. The court confronted testimony from two very unevenly matched valuation experts and a gaping difference in values. In trying to make sense of the conflicting financial evidence and achieve a pragmatic resolution, the court declined to apply a marketability discount and rejected tax affecting.

Main Lessons for Appraisers in the IPEV 2015 Valuation Guidelines

By Andrew Strickland,
Scrutton Bland (Colchester, U.K.)

The valuation of private equity investments brings with it special challenges. Despite this fact, interim appraisals are needed regularly because investors in private equity funds require transparent information from the managers. The "International Private Equity and Venture Capital 2015 Valuation Guidelines"[1] are designed to satisfy this requirement, so they are therefore focused on fair value for financial reporting purposes.

The guidelines embrace a great many areas of business appraisal. In doing so, they do not shy away from giving guidance on some contentious areas. They therefore carry lessons for us all.

Background. The term "private equity" is used in the guidelines in a broad sense to include investments in early-stage ventures, management buyouts, management buy-ins, infrastructure, mezzanine capital, and similar transactions and growth or development capital.

The guidelines are considered to be consistent with U.S. GAAP and also with IFRS and are to be used to determine fair value. *Accounting Standards Codification* (ASC) Topic 820, *Fair Value Measurement,* as issued by the Financial Accounting Standards Board (FASB), and IFRS 13, *Fair Value Measurement,* as issued by the International Accounting Standards Board (IASB), determine the measurement of fair value under U.S. GAAP and IFRS. Fortunately, they share the same definition of fair value.

The IPEV Board has entered into an understanding with the International Valuation Standards Council (IVSC) with the objective of promoting consistency between them.

A recurring theme is that the valuation expert should view fair value from the position of the market participants transacting in their economic best interests. This is consistent with the measurement guidance articulated in both ASC Topic 820 and IFRS 13: "An entity shall measure the Fair Value

1 The IPEV 2015 guidelines (and the 2012 version) are available at www.privateequityvaluation.com.

of an asset or liability using the assumptions that Market Participants would use when pricing the asset or liability, assuming that Market Participants act in their economic best interest."

Looking forward and back. The god Janus supposedly faced in two directions, looking back over the previous 12 months and also to the year that was to come. These guidelines give pride of place to the two concepts of calibration and backtesting, both of which are seen as powerful tools. They both use evidence in the past as a means of appraising value in the present and future.

Calibration is based on the premise that the price paid for an initial investment in an orderly transaction captures the impact of control and liquidity and other inputs on valuation. Calibration can be used under both the market and the income approaches. The guidelines explain:

> [T]he valuation techniques that are expected to be used to estimate Fair Value in the future should be evaluated using market inputs as of the date the investment was made.

The concept applied is that the single-period earnings multiple or the cost of capital implicit in the purchase price should inform the appraiser at future valuation dates.

Backtesting is to be used as a learning experience for the appraiser so as to be prepared for the next assignment. Backtesting is the reconciliation between the actual exit price and the previous assessment of fair value. It should enable inherent appraisal biases, such as overly conservative assumptions, to be identified and addressed.

The guidelines assume that the appropriate method of valuation will likely be the determination of the enterprise value and the addition of any surplus assets. This is then followed by the deduction of those elements of debt ranking above the instrument being valued.

Entry price and recent investment price. The actual prices private equity businesses pay to acquire stakes in the relevant business in an orderly transaction are clearly very strong evidence of value at that point. It is therefore considered fitting that such a price (excluding transaction costs) is used initially but only for a limited period. The guidelines do not provide rules as to the length of such limited period but recognize that values may well change rapidly in fast-moving sectors of the economy.

The guidelines do recognize the peculiar difficulties of valuing early-stage investments. They state:

> The "Price of Recent Investment" valuation technique is commonly used in a seed, start-up or an early-stage situation, where there are no current and no short-term future earnings or positive cash flows.

In early-stage investments, there are often several funding rounds. These may therefore refresh the price of the recent investment over the early years.

Control values. The private equity funds frequently either have direct control or have invested together with other investors in order to have collective control. In such a circumstance, the sale of the enterprise normally maximizes the value at exit. If this is the case, this should also be the valuation basis.

The guidelines recognize that in some situations this may not be appropriate. For example, if a minority stake is being valued and the other owners' interests are not aligned, it may not be appropriate to assume a sale of the enterprise and allocation of value as described above.

The 2015 version of the guidelines repeat word for word the view on values in the public markets that was in the 2012 version:

> While there is an argument that the market capitalization of a quoted company reflects not the value of the company but merely the price at which "small parcels" of shares are exchanged, the presumption in these Valuation Guidelines is that market based multiples are indicative of the value of the company as a whole.

This therefore agrees with the exposure draft from The Appraisal Foundation "The Measurement and Application of Market Participant Acquisition Premiums," which was issued for its second exposure on Sept. 1, 2015. Here is added support for the concept that appraisers should not misinterpret bid premiums as control premiums.

DLOL and DLOM. The estimation of fair value assumes that the period required to consummate a transaction hypothetically began at a point in time in advance of the measurement date, reaching the crescendo of the notional exchange of contracts at that measurement point. This is a simple truth in business valuation—we must value on the cusp of the notional transaction taking place. However, in undertaking that valuation, it is important to recognize all the factors that a buyer would take into account, including the costs of future sales transactions.

The guidelines state that a discount for lack of marketability (DLOM) is not appropriate if it relates to the time required to achieve a sale. However, the valuer should include a discount for lack of liquidity (DLOL) if it reflects the frequency of transactions.

Valuation methods. Despite some softening of view, the guidelines remain wary of discounted cash flow techniques due to the subjectivities of some of the inputs. (They do however advocate the use of DCF in earn-out arrangements, as explained below.) They are also concerned with valuers moving too far away from the valuation techniques actual market participants use:

> Unlike derivatives and debt markets, mathematical option pricing models have not seen wide usage in the private equity marketplace. Such models are rarely used by Market Participants to determine the transaction price for an Investment. However, for certain early stage Investments, option pricing models (OPM) or probability-weighted expected return models (PWERM) are deemed by some to provide a reliable indication of Fair Value where a limited number of discrete outcomes can be expected.

Deferred 'contingent consideration.' The guidelines recognize the increasing appearance of possible additional sales proceeds based on future events as part of the strategy for exit:

> The contractual right to future consideration can be very beneficial, especially for deals encircled with uncertainty; where significant potential value of a business lies in the outcome of future events. The contractual right to future consideration is often described as "contingent consideration."

There is normally no uncertainty as to the contractual right in such circumstances; the uncertainty is limited to the potential amount that might be received.

The guidelines then give strong direction to the approach that should be followed in estimating the likely amounts to recognize:

> Due to the unique aspects of these types of rights, it is likely that an income approach (discounted cash flow) will be the best tool to estimate Fair Value using cash flows which have been appropriately probability weighted for expected outcomes. The expected cash flows are then discounted using an appropriately chosen discount rate. Most likely cash flows, in their simplest form, are determined by assessing the probability and amount of payment at various points in time.

Endorsement. The IPEV 2012 valuation guidelines were endorsed by 28 entities throughout the world, including the following entities:

1. U.S. National Venture Capital Association;
2. Canada's Venture Capital and Private Equity Association;
3. Mexican Private Equity Association; and
4. British Private Equity and Venture Capital Association.

Similar endorsement is expected for the 2015 version of the guidelines, which were issued in December 2015.

Andrew Strickland, *for many years a corporate partner at Scrutton Bland, is now a consultant to the firm. He is a member of the valuation committee of the Institute of Chartered Accountants in England and Wales (ICAEW) and is on the board of the International Institute of Business Valuers.*

Strong Pushback of Sec. 2704 Regs at IRS Hearing

An unprecedented number of speakers testified at the December 1 IRS hearing to fight the controversial proposed Section 2704 regulations. The regs, designed to curb estate valuation discounts for minority interests, are so broad and convoluted that they should be withdrawn permanently, speakers urged. In total, 37 witnesses appeared and not just valuation experts, but also attorneys, wealth planners, trade groups, and family business owners. About 175 people appeared to be in the audience to see and hear the goings on. It was an amazing turnout in force to derail these controversial regs.

Tough talk. The regs were anticipated for a long time, but it was expected that they would target perceived abuses by aggressive estate planning tactics that yield overly large valuation discounts for family limited partnerships that hold marketable securities. Speakers decried the fact that the regs are so broad that they ensnare family operating businesses in the net—businesses formed for legitimate reasons as opposed to tax avoidance. Witness after witness implored the IRS to carve out a safe harbor for these family firms, which they say the regs as written would devastate.

Revising the regs, however, can't be done, witnesses agreed. They are so complicated that they're beyond repair. One veteran valuation expert and thought leader told *BVU:* "Every time I read them they get more confusing." Speakers said that, if the IRS won't withdraw them for good, the agency should go back to the drawing board and come out with a new version—and allow for another comment period.

Hearing logistics. *BVU* could not find anyone in attendance, including speakers, who had appeared or attended a hearing such as this before. Of course, Washington, D.C., is an impressive place and the massive stone IRS building can be intimidating. After going through airport-like security, you need to be escorted everywhere—even to the restrooms. The cafeteria was off-limits to the public, and there was no lunch break during the full-day hearing, just a few 15-minute breaks.

The hearing was held in an auditorium that held 210 seats. The panel was seated at the front, and there was a podium stage right for the witnesses, who came up one at a time when their names were called. Witnesses have 10 minutes to speak, and there is a traffic light-type device on the witness stand with green, yellow, and red lights. When the light turns from green to yellow, you'd better start wrapping up. Red means stop. If you don't stop, you get cut off.

Valuation experts appeared on behalf of themselves and also as members of the various valuation professional organizations (VPOs). The AICPA, ASA, and NACVA all had witnesses testifying on their behalf. There were four panelists for the government: Charlotte Chyr, IRS special counsel to the associate chief counsel; Leslie H. Finlow, IRS senior technician reviewer; John D. MacEachen, IRS senior trial attorney (and principal author of the proposed regs); and Catherine Hughes, attorney-advisor at the Treasury. The panel remarked that, since there were so many speakers, they would keep their questions to witnesses to a minimum. However, they felt compelled to make some remarks in response to the strong concerns of the witnesses on a number of points.

Six-month put right. A common issue speakers brought up was the so-called "implied put right" that exists in the proposed regs. This is the ability of each member of the entity to force the company to buy back his or her interest for cash equal to a minimum value within six months of exercising the right. No such right exists in the real world, speakers told the panel, and it should be removed from the regs.

"It is not our intention for the regs to contain a put right," said Chyr. This appeared to put this matter to rest and short-circuited some comments by subsequent speakers. However, it needs to be clarified that it is not in there because, if the perception persists that it is indeed in there, "judges may rule on it and then we're stuck with case law," said Stephanie Loomis-Price (Winstead PC) on behalf of the American College of Trust and Estate Counsel.

Redefining fair market value. The proposed regs remove the hypothetical willing buyer and willing seller assumption from the definition of fair market value—and also the notion of an arm's-length transaction. This goes against almost 100 years of court precedent and valuation theory that uses the standard definition of fair market value as we all know it.

Lance Hall (FMV Opinions), in his testimony, commented on the removal of those key elements from the definition of fair market value. "That's like asking Michelangelo to paint the Sistine Chapel without the color blue," he said. Michelle Gallagher (Gallagher Valuation & Forensics PLC), testifying on behalf of the AICPA, used an analogy of a Snickers candy bar. "If you take the peanuts out of the Snickers bar, what do you have? Something different … something with a different taste, a different market, a different value to consumers." She finished her testimony by handing out Snickers to the panel members.

Three-year rule. Another recurring theme was the three-year rule, which would nullify discounts taken for certain transfers that occurred within three years of the transferor's death. The "bright line" nature of the three-year rule drew criticism. "While I understand Treasury's perception of abuses associated with third-party owners inasmuch they may affect the inability to liquidate an ownership interest or the entity, I am again concerned that inflexible, 'bright-line' rules may be potentially abusive, too," said Chris Treharne (Gibraltar Business Valuations). "I encourage Treasury to identify and adopt alternate, more flexible language that accomplishes its goals of preventing taxpayer abuse without imparting inflexible constraints on legitimate ownership structures and strategies."

Along those lines, John Porter (Baker Botts LLP) suggested using the terminally ill standard and actuarial tables to address the deathbed transfer issue. Porter served as lead counsel for the taxpayers in *Kerr v. Commissioner* in Tax Court and the 5th Circuit Court of Appeals.

Speakers were also concerned that the rule would apply to transfers that occurred prior to the regs being finalized. As written, the regs are unclear on this. "The three-year lookback rule will not be retroactive," Chyr told the audience. It would only affect transfers made after the date the final regs are published.

New meaning of control. The proposed regs also change the definition of control to "at least 50%" ownership. This, of course, is, "technically, and practically, incorrect," said Peter Agrapides (Western Valuation Advisors), testifying on behalf of NACVA. A "more than 50%" ownership has been the threshold of control used by all of the business valuation standards as well as in a legal context. To say that two 50% owners have equal control does not make economic sense and results in the "creation of an artificial value," he said.

Hypothetical appraisals. The proposed regs conflict with the Treasury's own definition of "qualified appraisal," said Mark Hanson (Schenck SC), also testifying on behalf of NACVA. That definition includes that the appraisal is consistent with USPAP. The 2016-17 edition of USPAP states (in Standards Rule 9-4(d)): "An appraiser must, when necessary for credible assignment results, analyze the effect on value, if any, of the extent to which the interest appraised contains elements of ownership control and is marketable and/or liquid." The failure to consider discounts is not in accordance with this or other valuation standards and thus would render the value as hypothetical.

The implied put right in the proposed regs is an assumption that the appraiser would have to disclose. Also, the appraiser would have to state that the valuations are hypothetical in nature, which is not consistent with the fair market value standard. Bottom line, the proposed regulation "requires the business valuator to arrive at a fair market value of interests under hypothetical assumptions that are known to be untrue, in conflict with governing legal documents and state law, and possibly, may even be commercially unviable," he said.

Family attribution. The idea of treating minority owners who are family members as having control just because they are family has been struck down in Tax Court a number of times. But here are the family attribution rules back again in an attempt to reduce or eliminate valuation discounts for intrafamily transfers. William Frazier (Stout Risius Ross), on behalf of the ASA, pointed out that IRS Revenue Ruling 93-12 was repealed, which means that discounts for lack of marketability or control cannot be denied simply because the interest in a family-controlled business is passed from one family member to another.

Family harmony. The proposed regs use a new definition of value that assumes that all members of a family-owned business, including a husband and wife, will act in accord with each other in the best interests of the family. The divorce rate in the U.S. is over 50%, so can you imagine all of these divorcing spouses acting in accord? Does anybody know any family that always gets along? Robert Weinstock (Strategic Valuation Group LLC), in bringing up this issue, pointed out: "Just look at the Kardashians!"

Regs hit home. While most of the speakers talked of technical legal and tax issues and appraisers discussed valuation theory and practice, the speakers representing family businesses, farms, and ranches added poignancy to the proceedings. When Clarene Law was called to testify, there was a hush in the audience. As the frail, elderly lady faced the audience and the IRS, she said, "I guess I'm the one you're all talking about." Of course, she was referring to all of the testimony about the ruinous effect the regs would have on family firms. She said she had borrowed her parents' life savings to open a small motel in 1962. She and her husband struggled to build the business from nothing into a thriving concern with four generations of family members running multiple locations. Law has "high hopes" to pass on the family legacy to the next generation, some of whom own minority stakes. "The proposed regulations will severely disrupt the plans that are so dear to my heart," she said, trying to maintain her composure. "We may have to sell out if minority discounts are compromised." As her voice wavered, she said to the panel: "We had the opportunity to pursue the American Dream. Please let our children have the same chance."

Another speaker, Keith Miller (Coalition of Franchisee Associations), is a Subway franchise owner, who pointed out that franchises operate under extremely restrictive rules set forth in the franchise agreement. For example, not all franchises automatically renew, so their value "goes down every day," he said. Also, there are many restrictions on the sales of franchises. To ignore these restrictions, as the proposed regs require, would hit franchises especially hard.

Also on the minds of family business owners is the fate of workers. Estimates vary, but family businesses, farms, and ranches provide over 50% of jobs in this country. Hannay Reels in upstate New York is a fourth-generation firm with 165 employees. "Up until now, we've been able to hand it down through the generations," said Roger Hannay. "But if Section 2704 happens, we may be forced to consider selling it to non-family business bidders. There will be no guarantee that our workers will be able to stay on."

Robert Grossman (Grossman Yanak & Ford LLP), testifying on behalf of NACVA, stressed that the IRS has consistently supported valuation discounts. Its own recent job aids (one on DLOM itself and the other on S corps) clearly state the need and reasoning for a DLOM for a noncontrolling interest as "reflected by market data and accepted by all of the major business valuation credentialing organizations as per the provisions of Revenue Ruling 59-60."

"We will make it clear that these regs will not eliminate minority discounts," said Hughes. Audience members were happy to hear that, to some extent. Of course, this doesn't mean that discounts won't be significantly reduced, which they will be under the regs as written.

We must point out that not all of the witnesses were against the regs. A speaker from Americans for Tax Fairness fully supports the regs, saying they will close loopholes the wealthy use to avoid estate taxes. Everyone agrees that some abuses are going on that should be stopped, but why not focus the regs on those egregious cases without hurting the family business that was formed for legitimate reasons?

Recommendations. Witnesses opposing the regs all agreed they should be withdrawn permanently. Barring that, they need to be revised and reissued because of all of the complicated language that would make interpretation difficult. "Our great fear is that IRS agents will interpret these regs without proper guidance," said Frazier. "The result would be chaos."

Here is a summary of the main recommendations the speakers made:

1. Do not redefine fair market value and do not replace it with a new artificial concept called "minimum value." Continue to use the accepted definition of fair market value as the standard of value for estate and gift purposes and allow for appropriate discounts for lack of marketability and control.

2. Although the IRS said it would not be in the final regs, speakers reiterated their call to delete the implied six-month put option from the regs. There is no basis in market reality for an implied put option, and the final regs should make it explicitly clear that no such right is implied.

3. Do not define "control" as "at least 50%," but instead use "at least 50%" in order to be consistent with business valuation and legal principles.

4. The regs should have an exception or safe harbor for operating businesses. The carve-out should also include entities that hold assets for those businesses, suggested Keith Schiller (Schiller Law Group).

What's next: The IRS will "seriously consider" the comments made at the hearing—and those about 10,000 people submitted on the IRS website. It is highly unlikely the IRS will finalize the proposed regs as written because of remarks officials made at the hearing. Some observers think the regs will be tweaked and rushed through before the Trump administration moves in, otherwise they will have little chance to see the light of day. Stay tuned!

BVU applauds the incredible efforts of the valuation community, the legal profession, family business owners, and other stakeholders in coming together to speak in a strong and compelling voice on these controversial regs.

IACVA Readies Exposure Draft for Peer Review of Valuation Services

Citing the need to enhance the professional standards of valuation worldwide and give valuation professionals more control over the practices within their own field, the International Association of Consultants, Valuers & Analysts (IACVA) is creating an exposure draft on how peer review can work within the valuation industry.

Risk of regulation. IACVA President William Hanlin detailed the peer review plan at a recent conference in Atlanta that IACVA co-sponsored with the Southeast Chapter of Business Appraisers (SECBA). Hanlin suggests that institution of a peer review process for valuation is a way for the profession to set standards that help to measure and ensure that valuers deliver quality work, as well as to potentially head off attempts to increase the regulation.

Hanlin cited increasing indications by the U.S. Securities and Exchange Commission (SEC) that the business valuation market was "confusing." That led to the American Institute of Certified Public Accountants (AICPA), the American Society of Appraisers (ASA), and the Royal Institute of Chartered Surveyors (RICS) to begin work with the SEC on potential mandatory standards for valuation professionals working in fair value for financial reporting for public companies.

This has led to another credential being rolled out (Certified in Entity and Intangibles Valuation, or CEIV), with a proposal for potentially 3,000 hours of fair value experience required, Hanlin says. One way for the valuation industry to proactively address that is through peer review for valuation professionals, which gives the industry a better chance to police itself, which Hanlin suggests may be even more important as the need for valuation services expands in other countries.

Better differentiation from accounting. Similar to the manner in which AICPA, ASA, and RICS try to claim purview over business valuation before the SEC, as more countries see growth in the valuation profession, accounting societies are pushing for business valuation to belong to them, in terms of control over credentials and standards. But, unlike the United States and Canada, most countries have nowhere near the maturity of the business valuation profession or the number of professionals with any type of credential.

Hanlin estimates that 35,000 to 40,000 people in the United States have gone through some sort of business valuation training, with about 10,000 being in some sort of active practice. Conversely, in the past seven years, IACVA has trained approximately 7,000 people in the rest of the world, without a sense of how many of them are making a career from it. It's one of the main reasons Hanlin touts more credentialing specifically controlled and administered by business valuation professionals and peer review standards that mean that valuers have their work assessed by other valuers every few years as a way that enables the industry to better represent the quality and consistency of its own work.

It also enables the industry to create standards that police itself, as opposed to arguing over the quality of valuation work before a judge who may not fully understand how valuation works. Further, when it's held that the valuation professional made a mistake—regardless of the merits of the finding—that becomes a published finding. It is better for the industry to develop its own way to essentially weed out bad work and give aggrieved customers a mechanism to resolve quality disputes—not fee disputes—in a way that isn't as adversarial as the courts, Hanlin adds.

How peer review works. Peer review would be modeled on the approach accountants use. Mandatory peer review has been around for about 25 years, Hanlin says. Essentially, for accountants who issue financial statements, another accountant from a different firm comes in and ensures that the published financial statements meet professional standards.

Hanlin argues that business valuers have to ask themselves if they consider themselves to be professionals in need of standards, and define the standards that ensure quality work, especially before accountants without specialized understanding of the valuation markets try to do it for them. In the United States, valuation is a mature, well-defined profession with different subsets, such as financial reports, tax, litigation, and merger and acquisition, which are still new concepts in many parts of the world. Now consider the progress of the valuation industry here, Hanlin continues. In the late 1980s, a valuation expert would suggest a number and the judge would approve it. Now, there is no admissible valuation information in court proceedings without a complete report from the valuer that can be examined and cross-examined.

Meanwhile, in India, there are a total of five certified valuers, Hanlin says, even though Chartered Accountants got a law passed in that country three years ago that says valuers will eventually have to be registered to practice in that country. But, even in estimates of the numbers worldwide of business valuation professionals, there is often not a distinct number that's focused on business valuation, as opposed to the very different world of appraising tangible goods.

One country with robust peer review for valuers is China, potentially because the state holds interest in so many industries and has a vested interest in ensuring they are being properly valued as portions are sold to private ownership. In that country, if you want to do valuation, you submit to peer review.

Finally, as valuation expands worldwide, standards and peer review can help differentiate it from fair value assessments, Hanlin argues. A fair value assessment is different from a valuation because the seller has no say in the definition of "fair value." It is rooted in what the buyer will pay. The challenge is that "fair value" valuations have their own set of circumstances, and the valuer must often explain to the auditor how valuation works, to get the auditor to sign the audit report, much in the way that something needs to be explained to a judge, Hanlin says.

Peer review helps to build more professionalism and standards for business valuation and gives valuers another way to argue that the work they're doing meets specific quality control standards, Hanlin said in his presentation.

What to do. Read the IACVA Quality Control Standards[1] and submit ideas for implementation of a peer review system that will be remedial and inspiring. Watch for the exposure draft on peer review procedures and be sure to submit comments.

It's expected that IACVA's peer review process will be voluntary but ultimately implemented by regulators in other countries who see the public benefit of increased confidence in valuation, a better way for valuers to gain entry to the field at a younger age, and more reliability and professionalism, Hanlin says.

1 Proposed Quality Control for Valuation & Appraisal Practice, sub.bvresources.com/pdfs/QCValuationandAppraisal.pdf.

AICPA BV Chair Nathan DiNatale Discusses the New CEIV Credential

A new valuation credential related to fair value for financial reporting has been developed under a joint effort of the AICPA, ASA, and RICS. These groups want to bring more consistency to the profession and reduce the number of questions auditors raise about the valuations. The new credential is Certified in Entity and Intangible Valuations™ (CEIV™), and it focuses on business entities and intangible assets.

Credential holders will be required to comply with a mandatory performance framework (MPF), which is designed to make sure that the valuation expert adequately documents his or her work and thought processes. This will help make auditors more comfortable with valuation estimates, especially for intangibles. The MPF has recently been finalized, so the stage is now set for the launch of the CEIV credential.

BVU had the pleasure of talking with Nathan DiNatale (SC&H Group), chair of the AICPA Business Valuation Committee, about the new credential.

BVU: *What is the current status of the CEIV credential launch date?*

Nathan DiNatale: CPAs and financial professionals can start working now on the training requirements for the CEIV credential. The credential exam will be ready to take early this year.

BVU: *Did the mandatory performance framework (MPF) go through material changes during the exposure draft process?*

ND: We received some excellent commentary from numerous parties through the exposure draft process for the mandatory performance framework. What we found was that the mandatory performance framework and the uniform guidance that it provides were well-received. The feedback from those commenting was that it made sense for the valuation profession, clients, investors, auditors, and regulators. Those comments will be made available on the VPOs' websites at some point in the future and should make for interesting reading.

BVU: *Will the MPF require a credential holder to do more work than before?*

ND: The mandatory performance framework provides uniform guidance to valuation professionals on how much documentation is necessary to support their fair value measurement results in company financial statements. Most of this work is being done as part of the fair value measurement process, but it isn't always being documented in a consistent and transparent manner. The CEIV credential and its mandatory performance framework addresses those issues in a way that I believe will become best practice for the valuation profession.

BVU: *Does the CEIV credential apply only to public-company engagements?*

ND: The CEIV credential is focused on entity and intangible asset valuations for financial reporting purposes. It applies to public companies, as well as privately held entities that issue financial statements in accordance with U.S. GAAP and other organizations that use fair value measurement to provide values in their financial statements.

BVU: *Is the education process a common process or are all three VPOs doing their own programs? Is that two different things? Is the exam the same for all VPOs?*

ND: Each organization will offer training to fit the needs of its members. The contents covered in the training will be consistent among all three VPOs. The two-part CEIV exam will be the same for any credential candidate regardless of which organization they work with to obtain the CEIV credential.

BVU: *There is a minimum of 3,000 hours of FV experience—is that in billable time?*

ND: Not always. Experience related to fair value measurements may include any number of activities. For instance, an auditor/specialist valuation review of fair value measurements prepared by a third party and a firm's internal review of fair value measurements prepared by the firm's valuation team are relevant experiences. Signing valuation reports, supervising or managing fair value measurement engagements, developing thought leadership, and training staff on fair value measurement matters also can count toward the 3,000-hour minimum. A current or past partner or supervisor will be required to attest to a candidate's experience. If a partner or supervisor is not available, then peer attestation will be acceptable. There will not be any exceptions to experience attestation.

BVU: *If one has a valuation credential from another group (not the ASA or RICS), does that fulfill some of the CEIV requirements? The ASA has a streamlined path for CFAs to obtain the CEIV credential. Any similar offering from the AICPA?*

ND: Reciprocity for other valuation credentials will vary depending on the VPO. Generally, professionals with ABV, MRICS, FRICS, ASA, ASA-AM, CFA, and CBV credentials will have some training and examination requirements for the CEIV credential waived by AICPA. This should shorten the time it takes to progress through the pathway for the CEIV credential.

BVU: *How many AICPA members are expected to obtain the credential?*

ND: We don't have a hard estimate to share right now. I think it is fair to say that many valuation professionals that do perform fair value measurements for financial reporting purposes will be obtaining this credential from AICPA. It's going to be a credential that their clients will look for because it provides a consistent and transparent method of how to document fair value measurements for review by auditors and regulators. As AICPA members, these professionals will have their expertise backed by the world's largest member association representing the full accounting ecosystem, including auditors, management accountants, and valuation experts.

BVU: *Do you need to have an AICPA membership to get a CEIV from AICPA?*

ND: Yes. Financial professionals who want to get a CEIV credential from AICPA will either have to be an AICPA member or join the organization.

BVU: *Is there any requirement to submit a report in order to receive the credential? If not, why not?*

ND: CEIV credential holders will be required to participate in an annual, proactive quality monitoring program. The goal of this program is to provide confidence to markets and regulators that CEIV credential holders are performing high-quality valuations in compliance with the uniform guidance provided by the mandatory performance framework. Submission of a report eventually will be part of this monitoring program.

BVU: *Is the quality control process carried out by each VPO, or are there common reviewers and panels?*

ND: Each VPO will carry out a similar quality control process as part of the quality control monitoring program to ensure the expected level of quality, consistency, and transparency in the work product of credential holders.

BVU: *What specific sanctions can be imposed if there are significant deficiencies? (What is the definition of "significant deficiency"?)*

ND: Not following the uniform guidance and other requirements of the mandatory performance framework is an example of what would be considered a significant deficiency. The sanctions to be imposed will vary. For instance, sanctions could range from requiring additional education to revocation of the CEIV credential.

BVU: *Can other VPOs become a part of the CEIV credentialing process? How?*

ND: For now, the CEIV credential can be obtained from AICPA, ASA, or RICS.

BVU: *Do you feel that the CEIV credential will eventually be expanded to outside of the U.S.?*

ND: Yes, I do because the valuation profession is going to demand it. The uniform guidance and quality monitoring offered by the CEIV credential will ensure the consistency, quality, and transparency of the work in fair value measurement undertaken by CEIV credential holders. That was one of the goals that AICPA, ASA, and RICS identified when they joined forces and decided to develop one credential that provides a consistent set of requirements for fair value measurement.

Fair value measurement is fast becoming an accepted part of developing financial statements by companies around the world. The consistency of training and qualifications provided to financial professionals who obtain the credential, combined with the uniform guidance and ongoing monitoring of credential holders, are going to be critical to increasing investor and regulatory confidence in the valuation profession globally.

I anticipate that companies, no matter where they are in the world, will want to see the new framework provided by the CEIV credential applied to fair value measurement processes used to develop values for their company financial statements. This will be driven by a desire for the enhanced quality, consistency, and transparency that will be provided.

BVU: *What is the status of the similar credential in the works for financial instruments?*

ND: Right now, all of us are focused on a successful introduction of the CEIV credential to the valuation profession.

For more information: A special website has been set up at ceiv-credential.org/ that has more details on the credential and its requirements.

Fair Value Experts Offer Their Insights on ASC 805

Editor's note: The launch of the new Certified in Entity and Intangibles Valuation, or CEIV, credential has thrust the issue of fair value into the spotlight. This article presents an overview of ASC 805 on business combinations from the perspective of two experts on fair value, and it is excerpted from a new guide to purchase price allocations to which they generously contributed.

ASC 805 describes the proper accounting treatment an acquirer should use in business combinations. Originally issued as SFAS 141(R), ASC 805 supersedes APB 16 (1960) and SFAS 141 (2001). It applies to business combinations with an acquisition date on or after the beginning of the first annual reporting period beginning on or after Dec. 15, 2008 (Dec. 15, 2009, for acquisitions by not-for-profit entities).

Purpose. "ASC 805 provides a broader definition of business, which we never had in the past," says Nathan DiNatale, who leads the Business Valuation & Litigation Support Group for SC&H Group LLC, "and requires the use of the acquisition method. It recognizes assets acquired and liabilities assumed at fair value as defined in ASC 820."

DiNatale explains that, under ASC 805, all business combinations are accounted for by applying the acquisition method, which requires:

- Identifying the acquirer;
- Determining the acquisition date and the fair value of the acquisition price;
- Recognizing the identifiable assets acquired, liabilities assumed, and noncontrolling interests at accounting date fair value; and
- Recognizing goodwill, or, in the case of a bargain purchase (see below), a gain.

"The acquisition method," says Mark Zyla, managing director of Acuitas Inc., an Atlanta-based valuation and litigation consultancy firm, "is based on the concept that there are really fair value measurements in a business combination, understood broadly. First, you have fair value of the consideration paid—cash, stock, contingent consideration, earn-outs—that have to be measured as relative fair value. The second broad fair value measurements arise from what you are getting—the entire business enterprise. Third, it is the fair value of the individual assets that acquires part of the transaction liabilities assumed. Then the fourth and last part of the acquisition method is residual value, which is goodwill."

Zyla explains that this is referred to as the acquisition method and it is distinct from purchase accounting. "We no longer have purchase price allocations. We have the acquisition method—even though for many of us it is still common in the vernacular to call 805 business combinations purchase price allocations."

"Under the acquisition method," Zyla adds, "we measure contingent consideration of fair value, any assets and liabilities that are contingent in nature. That includes warranties, environmental liabilities, anything that can be estimable and reasonably determinable that is of a contingent nature. All these must be measured at fair value."

Under ASC 805, all business combinations are accounted for by the acquisition method, which requires identifying the acquirer. "The process of identifying the acquirer," says DiNatale, "begins with the determination of the party that obtained control. You have to look at the actual transaction and, based on the consolidation standards, determine what party gained control." These standards, referenced in ASC 810 for U.S. GAAP, generally stipulate an acquisition of 50% or more.

"The date the acquisition takes place is physically the date on which the party obtains control," DiNatale notes, "which is usually the asset purchase date. This involves recognizing identifiable assets acquired, liabilities assumed, all at fair value as of the acquisition date, and recognizing goodwill."

What if there's no intention to use a particular asset? "I get this question a lot," says DiNatale. "For example, I'll hear: 'We acquired a company. We are not going to use the trade name. We don't need to value the trade name.' Well, that is not true."

"Yes, an acquirer for competitive or other reasons may not use an acquired asset, or may plan to use the asset in a way that may not be its highest and best use," he says. "For example, you pull in a trade name, which you consider irrelevant since you're going to use your own better-known trade name. However, you still need to value that trade name because, for other market participants, there may be a value to that trade name. The standard specifies that the intended use of the asset by the acquirer does not affect its fair value, so keep that in mind when you are thinking through the assets you chose to acquire or not acquire. They all will most likely need to be valued."

What identifies an asset as an asset under ASC 805? In other words, what are the "recognition criteria"?

DiNatale says that an asset is *identifiable* if it either:

- Is separable, that is, capable of being separated or divided from the entity and sold, transferred, licensed, rented, or exchanged, either individually or together with a related contract, identifiable asset, or liability, regardless of whether the entity intends to do so; or
- Arises from contractual or other legal rights, regardless of whether those rights are transferable or separable from the entity or from other rights and obligations.

"The actual FASB guidance provides a lot of different examples of what can be and what cannot be separately recognized intangibles," he notes.[1]

Key points. ASC 805 defines a "business combination" as follows: "A transaction or other event in which an acquirer obtains control of one or more businesses." It defines a "business" as "an integrated set of activities and assets that is capable of being conducted and managed for the purpose of providing a return."

"Anybody who does this type of work needs to read through the FASB definition and what the standards say about it because it really is important," DiNatale emphasizes. "I had a client who bought what was really a contract, but under the FASB definition, that contract qualified as a business. It had inputs and employees working on the contract. It had laptops and working capital. It was a long-term government contract, and as a result it was considered to be a business. So you really need to understand what the defined terms included in ASC 805 mean. It is critical to go through the asset purchase agreement or stock purchase agreement to understand what is really happening."

A business consists of inputs and processes applied to those inputs that have the ability to create outputs. Although a business usually has outputs, outputs are not required to qualify as a business.

"For example, development-stage enterprises have no revenues," says DiNatale, "but they may still be considered businesses—even though they are not producing a product or servicing customers yet." To determine whether a development-stage enterprise is a business, he recommends asking the following questions:

- Does the enterprise have planned principal operations and have they started?
- Do they have employees, intellectual property, other inputs, and processes present?
- Is the enterprise researching and developing?
- Do they have a plan to produce outputs and they are pursuing that plan?

1 On Dec. 23, 2014, the Financial Accounting Standards Board (FASB) issued Accounting Standard Update (ASU) 2014-18, Business Combinations (Topic 805): Accounting for Identifiable Intangible Assets in a Business Combination (a consensus of the Private Company Council). The document can be downloaded at fasb.org/jsp/FASB/Document_C/DocumentPage?cid=1176164674146&acceptedDisclaimer=true.

"If the answer to all or even some of these questions is affirmative, then that development-stage enterprise is clearly a business," he explains. "Generally, development-stage enterprises that have employees capable of developing a product would be considered a business, even though you are valuing something that really doesn't have cash flow at the moment. So you are really trying to figure out the value of these intangibles, which can be much more difficult to value than traditional businesses."

Measuring the fair value of the business combination. The fair value of the business combination is measured at the fair value of the consideration transferred. DiNatale explains that consideration could come in several different ways including cash, notes payable, transfer of equity interest, and contingent consideration.

Under ASC 805, transaction-related costs are expensed, rather than—as was formerly the case—capitalized. "I have seen people use a flow of funds to determine the consideration transferred—be careful with that," DiNatale cautions. "Flow of funds typically have some reimbursement for transaction expenses or it may include sell side, M&A fees, or other fees, so you are not really capturing the true amount. Don't just look at the number. Make sure you understand every dollar in the flow of funds and make sure that you understand how they are flowing and whether they should be included as consideration or not. This is really important."

Allocation of assets and liabilities. Assets and liabilities that are of a contingent nature will be recorded at their relative fair values if "reasonably determinable," under ASC 805.

DiNatale explains that ASC 805-20-25—Allocation of assets and liabilities—requires that all identifiable assets and liabilities acquired, including the identifiable intangible assets, be assigned a portion of the purchase price based on their fair values. The value of the business acquired is usually measured as the sum of the acquisition-date values (measured at fair value with a few exceptions) of the following:

- Consideration transferred for the acquiree;
- Equity interests in the acquiree the acquirer held immediately before the acquisition date (for an acquisition achieved in stages, also known as a step acquisition); and
- Noncontrolling interests in the acquiree third parties (in a partially owned subsidiary) held.

"There is some language in FASB's guidance on how to value the noncontrolling interest," says DiNatale. "Whenever you have a noncontrolling interest that is either transferred or exists, it is very important to understand how those are handled."

"Total consideration transferred is allocated among the fair value of the tangible and the intangible assets," DiNatale explains. "Goodwill is considered a residual amount that represents the future economic benefits arising from the other assets acquired in a business combination that have not met the criteria for being individually identified and separately recognized. If the fair value of net assets acquired is less than the total consideration paid for the acquired entity, the difference is recorded as goodwill."

The exhibit illustrates the formula.

Goodwill	=	**Consideration transferred** + **Fair Value** of any noncontrolling interest + Acquisition date **Fair Value** for the acquirer's previously held equity interest - **Net amount** of acquisition-date amounts of assets acquired and liabilities assumed

Contingent consideration. Contingent consideration, commonly referred to as an earn-out, represents an obligation of the acquirer if future events or conditions are met. All contingent consideration is included in business combination accounting and is measured at its fair value as of the acquisition date.

"Contingent consideration represents this obligation of this acquirer for future events or conditions if they are all met," says DiNatale. "The presence of contingent consideration depends on the deal structure, company, and industry. It is not always a component of consideration, but make sure that when it is, you understand how to value it."

DiNatale explains that, typically, the fair value of contingent consideration is determined by probability weighting specific well-supported outcomes via a Monte Carlo simulation model or similar risk-simulation tool. "Some of those that are more complicated need to be modeled under Monte Carlo, especially if you are working with the Big Four. They want to see a more robust way of developing contingent consideration besides just determining percentages."

In regard to contingent consideration, DiNatale advises, make sure you have specific relevant projections. "Management should prepare multiple sets of projections that rely on independent future outcomes," he says. "These projections are weighted to determine the most appropriate probability-weighted outcome for the contingent consideration expected to be paid. ASC 805-30-35 states that changes resulting from events after the acquisition date, such as meeting an earnings target, reaching a specified share price, or reaching a milestone on a research and development project, are not measurement period adjustments."

The acquirer, as stated in ASC 805-30-35, "shall account for changes in the fair value of contingent consideration that are not measurement period adjustments as follows:

- "Contingent consideration classified as equity shall not be remeasured and its subsequent settlement shall be accounted for within equity; and

- "Contingent consideration classified as an asset or a liability shall be remeasured to fair value at each reporting date until the contingency is resolved. The changes in fair value shall be recognized in earnings."

"This language provides an outline of how to handle contingent consideration moving forward," notes DiNatale. "Typically, the changes in this are on a period-by-period basis and are recognized in earnings. Once you have a measurement—if it is a fairly long earn-out—you will be required to update that on an annual basis to make sure that it is consistent with the current assumptions in the earnings projections."

Bargain purchase. In some cases, an acquirer may make a bargain purchase—a business combination where the acquisition-date amounts of identifiable net assets acquired, excluding goodwill, exceed the sum of the value of consideration transferred. This standard requires the recognition of a gain for a bargain purchase.

Paragraph ASC 805-30-25-4 requires the acquirer to reassess whether it has correctly identified all of the assets acquired and all of the liabilities.

"A bargain purchase," explains Mark Zyla, "occurs when the fair value of the assets acquired and liabilities assumed is greater than what was paid for it. If it is greater than what was paid for it, a situation which the FASB believes should be rare, the FASB suggests that you go back and check your work to see if your assumptions are consistent with one another."

DiNatale reinforces the point: "I rarely ever see a bargain purchase. Usually if you arrive at a bargain purchase it means you did something wrong, but not necessarily." If, after checking all your assumptions and making sure you didn't miss anything, you have a bargain purchase gain, DiNatale explains, "the new standards require disclosure of the amount of the gain, the line item where the gain is recognized, and a description of the reasons why the transaction resulted in this bargain purchase gain. The key here is that after you review the calculation and you determine that you still have a bargain purchase, it should be recognized in earnings and attributed to the acquirer."

The objective of the review is to ensure that the measurements appropriately reflect consideration of all available information as of the acquisition dates assumed before recognizing a gain on a bargain purchase.

Additional terminology. DiNatale provides the following additional terminology regarding ASC 805:

- PFI—prospective financial information;
- IRR—internal rate of return;
- WARA—weighted average return on assets;

- BEV—business enterprise value;
- TAB—tax amortization benefit;
- MPEEM—multiperiod excess earnings method; and
- NCI—noncontrolling interest.

For more information. DiNatale and Zyla are contributors to a newly released report, *Case Studies in Purchase Price Allocations,* which is now available at www.bvresources.com/publications.

Final IVS 2017 Seeks to Standardize Conduct and Approach to Global Valuation

The International Valuation Standards Council (IVSC) has released IVS 2017, its latest set of standards that aim to bring more consistency to valuation practices across the world. IVS 2017 was launched in mid-January, following initial releases in April 2016 and June 2016 and the consideration of more than 100 industry comments in response to those releases. The IVSC will push for worldwide adoption of the standards (see sidebar).

IVS 2017 is not about telling valuers what they can and can't do as professionals but is about telling members what they can and can't do to claim compliance with IVS 2017, says Adam Smith, director of valuation standards for IVSC. Smith's comments came in an interview with Michael

IVSC Pushes for Worldwide Adoption of IVS 2017

The release of the final version of IVS 2017 comes amid new efforts by the IVSC to push for worldwide adoption. IVSC chairman Sir David Tweedie has said that "valuation is not a profession. If valuers wish to become a profession, and continue with self-regulation, then VPOs must adopt IVS and enforce compliance—no exceptions." IVS 2017 adoption becomes mandatory this July, according to the IVSC website.

New IVSC structure. The IVSC has created a new Standards Review Board that will amend and approve the international valuation standards going forward. The new board will have two focused subject matter expertise boards reporting to it: a Tangible Assets Standards Board (covering real estate, plant and machinery, and personal property) and a Business Valuation Standards Board. Now that IVS 2017 has been finalized, the new boards are now operational, and it is expected that the first meetings will take place March 2017.

In its efforts to promote worldwide adoption, the IVSC and the World Association of Valuation Organisations (WAVO) strengthened their ties by signing a memorandum of cooperation (MOC) in 2016 to jointly promote the importance of adopting the standards. Also, The Appraisal Foundation released a document, "A Bridge From USPAP to IVS," that connects the two sets of standards to help make appraisals compliant with both sets of standards. This was a significant step toward establishing a set of globally accepted ethical and professional standards for valuation.

Badham, executive director of the International Institute of Business Valuers (iiBV), and addressed concerns with the previous version of the standards that allowed a valuer to release a report that was technically in compliance with the standards as long as it stated the areas where it was not in compliance with the printed standards.

New configuration. One step that IVSC took in the creation of IVS 2017 was to bring some basic organization to the layout of the standards. The idea is to add flexibility in the update process so that standards or paragraphs can be added when appropriate as opposed to a wholesale rewriting of the standards. IVS 2017 is divided first into five general standards: (1) scope of work; (2) investigations and compliance; (3) reporting; (4) bases of value; and (5) valuation approaches and methods. Six asset standards follow: business and business interests, intangible assets, plant and equipment, real property interests, development property, and financial interests.

IVS 2017 doesn't mandate a particular report format, but it makes clear that a valuation report must be clear on the scope of the work that was performed, how it was done, what the inputs and assumptions used were, and provide a clear conclusion about how the valuation was completed. "We would consider it a failure if we wrote standards that prevented a valuation professional from doing something right or required them to do something wrong," Smith points out. "So that was our guiding principle—that we should only require the right things."

Word distinctions better defined. Another revision made for IVS 2017 was an attempt to make the mandates under the standards more clear by using and defining three consistent words throughout: "must," "should," and "may."

When "must" is used, it means that the valuer must fulfill that requirement whenever it applies to the valuation. There is no way to get out of compliance if the valuer intends to say that the work is IVS compliant. The use of "should" means that the requirement is presumptive, as Smith explains. It means that, whatever the policy, it must be done unless it can be demonstrated that the valuer was able to achieve the objective of the standards without that particular action. The term "may" means the requirement is something that the valuer is to consider but is not required to do in order to be compliant with IVS or to state that the valuation follows IVS 2017.

Similar words such as "shall" and "might" were used in the draft standards, but commenters pointed out that they were confusing, so they were dropped in the final version.

Framework for type of valuation. The new chapter on valuation approaches and methods sets a framework for the selection of the appropriate valuation and method for the valuation being done, Smith says. When the "should" language is used in this chapter, there is a presumption that the valuation approach specified is to be used. The use of "may" allows for more flexibility. The change is driven by the market. A common grievance from stakeholders is that, if they hired two different valuation professionals to do a valuation, there was no confidence that the valuers would use the same approach. To be clear, stakeholders didn't expect that each valuer would arrive at the same number but were frustrated that it wasn't approached in the same way, Smith notes.

For example, this chapter states that the market approach should be applied and afforded significant weight when the subject asset has recently been sold in a transaction appropriate for consideration under the basis of value, the subject asset or substantially similar assets are actively publicly traded, and/or there are frequent and/or observable transactions in substantially similar assets.

The chapter also notes, however, that certain types of approaches, such as Monte Carlo, are not included or detailed in the section. Also, there was in a change to the final version, that valuers should consider the use of multiple approaches and methods and that more than one approach should be considered when there are insufficient factual or observable inputs for a single method to reach a reliable conclusion.

The idea is not only to create a framework for a consistent approach to valuation when certain facts were in place, but also to allow for judgment to continue to be able to be used as circumstances warranted, Smith says.

Responsibility for information in report. An additional change makes clear that it is the valuer's responsibility to assess whether the information provided for the valuation is reliable. This responsibility extends to circumstances such as when the client is giving all of the information to the valuer or whether it is coming from a website, blog, Wikipedia, or the like. Valuers cannot blindly use information provided and must assess whether it is reasonable to use the information provided.

In IVS 2013, a valuer could theoretically be compliant taking all of the calculations from the client and using those numbers, but more diligence will be required under IVS 2017.

Other key changes. Several redlined changes were made to the final version of IVS 2017, based on comments received in response to draft releases. Among them:

- The definition of a valuer was revised to be defined as "an individual, group of individuals, or a firm possessing the necessary qualifications, ability and experience to undertake a valuation in an objective, unbiased and competent manner."

- It's made clear that the valuer must have the technical skills, experience, and knowledge to understand, interpret, and utilize the work of any specialists.

- Legislative, regulatory, and other authoritative requirements take precedent over IVS requirements.

- A final valuation report or conclusion must be established.

- It's made clear that the valuation record must also include the basis for which all of the conclusions were reached.
- The valuer's choice of bases should consider instructions and input from the client and/or representatives, but regardless of those instructions the valuer should not use a basis or bases of value that are inappropriate for the intended purpose of the valuation.
- Market value presumes a price negotiated in an open and competitive market where the participants act freely. The market could be international or local and can have numerous or limited participants.
- The nature and source of valuation inputs must be consistent with the basis of value, which must have regard to the valuation purpose. An example offered is that various approaches and methods could be used to arrive at an opinion of value provided they use market-derived inputs. To indicate market value, the income approach should be applied with inputs and assumptions that participants would adopt. Market value using the cost approach should be indicated with the cost of an asset of equal utility, and the analysis of market-based costs and depreciation should determine the appropriate depreciation.
- When calculating market rent, the valuer must consider that the terms and conditions of a lease are appropriate unless they are illegal or contrary to legislation and, when a market rent is not subject to a lease, the assumed terms and conditions are the terms typically agreed to in a market for the type of property on the valuation date between market participants.
- The control premiums area is clarified to note that, while all else being equal, participants would generally prefer to have control over a subject asset and willingness to pay a control premium or a discount for lack of control will be a factor in whether the ability to exercise control enhances the economic benefits available to the owner of the subject asset.
- When a probability weighted expected cash flow is used, the valuer does not have to consider distributions of all possible cash flows using complex models and techniques but may develop a limited number of scenarios and probabilities to capture the array of possible cash flows. Valuers also must consider seasonality and cyclicality in cash flow analyses.
- Valuers should only apply the market approach to intangible assets when both information is available on arm's-length transactions involving similar or identical assets on or near the valuation date *and* sufficient information is available to allow the valuer to adjust for all significant differences between the subject intangible asset and those involved in the transactions.
- Contributory assets are those used in conjunction with the subject intangible asset in the realization of prospective cash flows associated with the subject intangible asset. Assets

that don't contribute to the prospective cash flows associated with the subject intangible asset are not contributory assets.

- Contributory asset charges for elements of goodwill should not be mechanically applied when circumstances do not warrant it. The valuer should assess the relevant facts and circumstances of the situation.

What to do. Many valuation firms are likely to believe that the valuation work they're doing is likely to be pretty compliant with the standards already, while others may have to make changes to their approach, Smith says. He suggests reading IVS 2017 from front to back and comparing it to internal procedures and looking at how valuation conclusions are reported. The final published version of IVS 2017 has been made available to members and sponsors. Others can access it at www.ivsonline (subscription required).

ASA BV Chair Discusses Recent Changes to New FV Rules and CEIV

After several years in the works, the new valuation credential related to fair value for financial reporting is now being rolled out. Education and training is underway, and the exam, at the time of this writing, was being finalized. This effort represents the first significant collaboration of major valuation professional organizations (VPOs): the AICPA, ASA, and RICS. Behind the new credential, the Certified in Entity and Intangible Valuations™ (CEIV™), is a mandatory performance framework (MPF), a set of best practices designed to make sure that the valuation expert adequately documents his or her work and thought processes.

Several changes have been made to the MPF and the CEIV credential, and there are also some key points to emphasize. To get a better understanding, *BVU* talked with William Johnston (Empire Valuation Consultants LLC), chair of the ASA's BV committee. He is also the ASA's CEIV program development representative and an instructor in the ASA's first CEIV training course.

BVU: *As I recall, the MPF originally was applicable only to work done for public companies. That has changed?*

WJ: Yes. Originally the focus of the MPF was public companies partly because the original impetus for change was from regulators, such as the SEC, and their comments related to public companies. But, as time progressed, the question became: Why shouldn't this apply also to private companies? You can have a multibillion-dollar private company with U.S. GAAP financial statements, so there's no reason why that company should have a more lax standard in terms of fair value for financial reporting. Therefore, the finalized MPF applies to fair value engagements for public companies and also private companies that issue financial statements under U.S. GAAP.

BVU: *There was also a change in terms of the education and training for the CEIV credential?*

WJ: Yes. There is no longer an exemption from part of the education requirements for experienced professionals. The CEIV education consists of two parts: The first part is a body of knowledge on general accounting and valuation issues related to financial reporting, and the second part is education related to the MPF. Under the original rules, individuals with a certain level of fair value experience would not have to take the body of knowledge part of the education. They would just have to take the new MPF training but then take the two-part exam that covers everything. The thinking was that these individuals had so much experience that it seemed unnecessary for them to go through the basic education part of it, although they would still be tested on it. But then we realized that, while that may be true for some individuals, it may not be true for everyone. We want to make sure that everyone is on the same high level in terms of the education and training for this new credential. We're trying to raise the bar here, and we want to make sure everybody is up-to-date on current developments. Therefore, the exemption was eliminated, and the final rules require everyone to take the same two-part education course.

BVU: *Can you describe the ASA's CEIV course?*

WJ: The ASA's new CEIV course is BV401, which lasts for three days and covers both the body of knowledge and the MPF. Then, there is a two-part exam with separate questions for both parts. The exam is a timed, online exam. The course is available online and on demand and will also be offered in a live classroom setting, which is also streamed online. (*Editor's note: The ASA's first live class (which was also streamed online) was held from February 27 to March 1 in Phoenix).*

BVU: *The CEIV course is separate and apart from qualifying in the first place to apply for the credential.*

WJ: Yes, getting the CEIV credential is a two-part process that I compare to getting your undergraduate degree and then a graduate degree. As an undergrad, you have to achieve a base level of business valuation education. If you already have a business valuation credential from the ASA, AICPA, or RICS, then you're all set in that regard. For those individuals, it makes sense to get the CEIV credential from the organization to which you already belong. But if you don't have a credential from either of the three groups, you have to join one of them and then meet their specific BV education requirements.

If you have certain other credentials from another organization, some equivalency credit may be given. For example, at the ASA, if you have a CFA credential and five years of business valuation experience, you can qualify for a fast track to CEIV accreditation by joining the ASA and meeting some other requirements, such as ethics training.

After you complete the "undergraduate" phase, then, for what I call the "graduate degree" part, you need to meet the experience and education requirements specific to fair value and the CEIV credential. This part of the process is the same for all three VPOs. You need 3,000 hours of fair value experience over the past five years and take the two-part course and pass the two-part exam.

BVU: *Going back to the MPF, do the rules apply for anyone doing fair value work for financial reporting purposes regardless of whether you have the credential or not?*

WJ: An individual who has the CEIV credential is required to comply with the MPF. For those without the credential, the rules say the MPF "should" be considered best practice when doing fair value measurements for financial reporting purposes. The word "should" is defined in the MPF glossary as almost meaning "must" or, at a bare minimum, is more stringent than I thought that term would be.

BVU: *It's been said that the MPF does not require more work than before. Is that your understanding?*

WJ: I don't necessarily agree that there's less work involved under the MPF. It's not a matter of people not doing the work properly but rather the degree of rigor involved in the documentation that's now required. The MPF requires a very extensive level of documentation that must be included in the work file. Not everyone is documenting their work to this extent, so, in that case, the MPF would require more work.

BVU: *Is there a specific area where it's perceived that more work may be needed?*

WJ: One area is in terms of management projections. Some experts may be hesitant to question projections from management because of various reasons. They may not want to ruffle feathers, or they feel that management knows the company best, so why question the projections. The MPF discusses "professional skepticism," which emphasizes very strongly the need to apply skepticism to information that you get from management and third parties, especially projections. So that is a key component of the finalized MPF.

BVU: *If someone is currently in compliance with existing standards to the letter, would he or she be in compliance with the MPF?*

WJ: No. The MPF is a different set of standards than any existing standard. It doesn't focus on how to perform the work but rather how much needs to be done. There is some overlap to other standards, but the MPF supplies a more detailed list of documentation you need in the work file. It also gives a certain amount of flexibility in terms of what to include in the report or in the work file. It specifies what the report has to contain and what the work file has to contain.

BVU: *What about enforcement? How will it be determined that credential holders are adhering to the requirements?*

WJ: A new quality control process will be established that includes a required review of a work file for each credential holder initially and then periodically thereafter. This will be a proactive process as opposed to a reactive one that, for example, is initiated by a complaint.

BVU: *The CEIV covers entity and intangibles valuation but also inventory. What about other tangible assets, such as M&E and real estate? Shouldn't this type of framework apply to that piece of the pie?*

WJ: Yes, I absolutely agree with that. We were trying to keep the scope focused on a certain area and certain types of things and then, if this is successful, to expand it. I think tangible assets could benefit substantially by some of these standards. While it's not required, I could see other appraisers in other disciplines, such as M&E and real estate, starting to follow these standards now. Also, auditors may follow them in other areas as well even though they are not required at this point.

BVU: *Are regulators concerned only with the BV side and not so much about the hard asset side?*

WJ: That's a good point. The concerns were primarily focused on BV including intangibles so that's why the efforts surrounding the CEIV credential have been in that area. But, on an overall basis, you certainly have to be concerned about the whole picture.

BVU: *There can be wide variations on the hard asset side, so I assume that's a concern.*

WJ: Yes, in most valuations, there will be a range of values no matter what type of asset you're talking about. I'm not an M&E appraiser, but different methods and assumptions in valuing these tangible assets will produce a range of values.

BVU: *What are the plans for the future in terms of this overall initiative to improve fair value measurement?*

WJ: There is nothing in concrete, but the hope is that, if this is successful, it would be extended to apply to other assets such as financial instruments and tangibles.

BVU: *If someone does not have a BV credential from one of the three VPOs, why would one choose the ASA for the CEIV credential?*

WJ: The ASA, AICPA, and RICS are all officially approved to offer the CEIV credential. Getting it through the ASA offers several benefits. The ASA is the only one of the three organizations that is solely focused on valuation. ASA is also a leader in financial reporting and fair value education, and we are the only organization that offers a specialty designation for intangible assets. We also offer regional fair value conferences as well as webinars and tracks at our national conference. To maintain the CEIV credential, there is an ongoing education requirement, and ASA is a leader in that education.

Feedback Wanted on Potential Refinements to International Valuation Standards

Now that the International Valuation Standards Council (IVSC) has released the 2017 International Valuation Standards (IVS 2017), the organization is seeking industry feedback on an Agenda Consultation Paper[1] for input on how best to refine the standards in the coming years. The comment period ends Aug. 15, 2017, and all comments will be posted on the IVSC's website. This is part of the IVSC's major new efforts to continually evolve IVS instead of issuing completely revised standards every few years.

Why it matters. Some U.S. practitioners may wonder why IVS 2017 is relevant to them. First of all, business valuation is a global profession and companies are increasingly operating across borders. For any engagements where the Big Four are involved in auditing your work, they will consider IVS 2017 in their review. IVS 2017 adoption becomes mandatory July 2017, according to the IVSC website, and they are a good resource for appraisers no matter where they are located.[2]

The Invitation to Comment (ITC) is focused on two areas: valuation topics that the IVSC should address under its current agenda and additional valuation topics that stakeholders feel should be added or prioritized as part of the agenda. IVSC has also identified major valuation topics to include in the ITC. These topics are:

- Nonfinancial liabilities;
- Discount rates;
- Early-stage valuation;
- Biological assets;
- Extractive industries; and

1 www.ivsc.org/files/file/view/id/859.

2 Available in print or PDF at www.bvresources.com/products/international-valuation-standards-2017.

- Inventory.

For each of these areas, a framework is laid out that includes a summary of the valuation topic. The summary includes relevant history, stakeholder concerns, and a board rationale for why it considers standards necessary for the topic. Then, there is a list of potential standard-setting alternatives that includes approaches the IVSC can take for the standards development and any methodologies. Finally, there are specific questions for commenters to respond to on each topic. For example, in the section on early-stage valuation, IVSC asks commenters to consider the following questions:

- Question 3.1: Are additional standards for the valuation of early-stage companies a critical area that should be addressed by the IVSC? Please explain why.

- Question 3.2: In which areas of the valuation of early-stage companies do you see the greatest diversity in practice? Are there additional areas of concern not noted above in this ITC? If so, please discuss.

- Question 3.3: Of the potential Standard Alternatives outlined above (A, B, C), which do you prefer and why?

The section notes that there are issues related to early-stage valuations, including no revenue and limited expense history; or potentially substantial expense history related to product development, yet no revenue; or product development and expense for a product near completion, yet no revenue. The enterprise could have orders and be operating at a loss still or some revenue with achievement of early financial milestones or profitable operations and cash flow. All of these variables could impact how the entity would be valued and might not sync up to traditional valuation methods.

In addition, the IVSC will make improvements to IVS 2017 on its own, including sections on control premium and discount for lack of control, capital structure considerations, and development value. IVSC considers these changes to be minor, so it is not seeking comments on these topics.

Future potential topics. The IVSC has also identified topics for future projects. The IVSC board considers these topics to have limited application, and the future projects may include exposure drafts, discussion papers, or guidance notes. These topics are:

- Analysis of commercial lease transactions;

- Specialized public service assets;

- Sustainability and renewable energy;

- Automated valuation models and data analytics;

- Valuation of personal property including art and antiques;

- Recovery and resolution;
- Price versus value;
- Distressed situations;
- Valuation in markets susceptible to change;
- Privatization; and
- Alternative financing arrangements.

"Our IVS Agenda reflects the outcome of initial meetings of IVSC's Tangible Assets, Business Valuation and Standards Review Board, where we distilled the main findings of our own gap analysis and collated the many valuable suggestions for revisions to IVS from stakeholders in previous consultations," according to Mark Zyla (Acuitas), chairman of the IVSC Standards Review Board (see sidebar).

IVSC to Form New Board on Financial Instruments

BVU recently attended the ASA's 12th Annual Fair Value Conference where Kevin Prall of the International Valuation Standards Council (IVSC) told the audience the organization is moving forward with the formation of a Financial Instruments Board.

This past April, the IVSC hosted a financial instruments roundtable in New York. Participants included some of the world's leading regulators, banks, data providers, valuation firms, external audit firms, accounting standards setters, and valuation professional organizations (VPOs). "There was broad consensus on the need to further develop standards in this area," said Prall. He also mentioned that the IVSC is currently taking applications for members of the Financial Instruments Board and supplemental members to the Standards Review Board (go to www.ivsc.org).

The Financial Instruments Board will be in addition to the other boards that were recently set up and had their first meetings this past March. The Standards Review Board will amend and approve international valuation standards and is chaired by Mark Zyla (Acuitas). This board has two focused subject matter expertise boards reporting to it: a Tangible Assets Standards Board (covering real estate, plant and machinery, and personal property), chaired by Ben Elder (RICS), and a Business Valuation Standards Board, chaired by Andreas Ohl (PwC). Although the first meetings were closed, future meetings will be public. The boards produced the Agenda Consultation Letter that proposes areas where IVS can evolve, and they are soliciting comments from interested stakeholders (see main article).

"We are looking forward to receiving views and recommendations on our IVS Agenda from practitioners, valuation professional organizations, academics, corporations, and regulators and working collaboratively with them to improve IVS," Zyla continued.

Comments are being accepted through Aug. 15, 2017. They can be emailed to aaronsohn@ivsc.org or kprall@ivsc.org, using File Reference IVSC Agenda Consultation 2017. To view the complete Invitation to Comment, visit www.ivsc.org/files/file/view/id/859.

Work File Checklist for Discount Rates Under New Fair Value Regulations

Under the new requirements for fair value for financial reporting, valuation experts will be expected to have a certain amount of documentation in their work files. For holders of the new CEIV credential, a work file will be reviewed within the first year they receive the credential and then periodically after that. For those without the CEIV credential, they will be expected to comply with the new requirements, which are designed as overall best practices. In other words, anyone doing fair value for financial reporting should comply with these new rules.

The new requirements are contained in the Mandatory Performance Framework (MPF), which is designed to make sure that the valuation expert adequately documents his or her work and thought processes. The guidance does not explain "how to" perform a valuation but rather "how much" documentation is required.

Practice aid. A handy tool to use for compliance is a work file checklist of what the MPF requires for all the different aspects involved in fair value measurement. On page 85, we present a checklist for the documentation of prospective financial information (PFI), an area of particular concern and scrutiny. Here, we present a checklist for what you need at a minimum in terms of documenting how you came up with the discount rate.

This checklist is a recasting and summary of what is contained in the MPF, so you need to read the document (and the companion document, the Application of the Mandatory Performance Framework) for further explanation and information. You can download these documents at a special website set up for the CEIV credential (www.ceiv-credential.org).

Focus on CSR. Of all the items in the checklist, the one that will require the most extensive amount of documentation is the adjustment for company-specific risk. It is not enough to provide qualitative support or say the CSR premium is based on your professional judgment or those used in other valuations or in a recent purchase price allocation. You need to provide quantitative support that backs up your adjustment. As we said, the MPF does not give you guidance on "how" to do something, so you'll have to look to other guidance for that.

The MPF also notes that a number of discount rate models exist, so you need to carefully assess which one is best for a particular task and "ensure that rationale is well documented in the engagement work file."

Work File Checklist: MPF Requirements for Documenting the Derivation of a Discount Rate

The valuation professional, at a minimum, must document the following in writing within the work file, if applicable:

Cost of equity

☑ The reasons why you selected the discount rate model(s) you used.

☑ The source of the risk-free rate you used and why you selected it.

☑ The source or calculation of the equity risk premium and rationale for its use.

☑ An explanation of the calculation of beta of the guideline public companies (or other industry risk adjustments) and the rationale for the method used when using CAPM (or rationale for the use of another source of beta).

☑ The rationale for selecting the specific beta when using CAPM, including "adjusted betas."

☑ An explanation of the size premium including the amount, source of the premium data, and the rationale for selecting the concluded premium (even if zero).

☑ The amount of company-specific risk adjustment (if any), the rationale for application of the adjustment, and the objective and quantitative data sets used to develop the specific concluded adjustment.

☑ The amount of country-specific risk adjustment the source of the adjustment data (if applicable) and the rationale for selecting the concluded adjustment (even if zero).

☑ Any other significant assumptions should be clearly explained and documented as well as other inputs that may apply depending on the models chosen.

Cost of debt

☑ The sources of data used and the rationale for their use (for example, spot market YTM on bonds with a debt rating commensurate with the creditworthiness of the subject entity).

☑ The rationale to support the selection of the pretax cost of debt and any additional source documents.

☑ The rationale for the statutory tax rate used to adjust the pretax rate to an after-tax rate.

Capital structure

☑ The capital structures of the guideline public companies, industry sector, or subject company and rationale for selection of the time frame over which they are measured, as applicable.

☑ The market participant capital structure selected in the calculation of the WACC and rationale for its selection.

Checklist continued on next page.

Other

☑ When other discount rate models are used instead of CAPM or WACC, the work file must contain details on:

- The model specification;
- Inputs chosen and the sources of those inputs:
- Submethodological selections made; and
- Why, if applicable, any adjustments were made to the model results.

(Source: This checklist is derived from the document "Application of the Mandatory Performance Framework for the CEIV." The information in this checklist has been summarized and adapted. See the actual document for additional explanation and requirements at www.ceiv-credential.org).

What You Should Know About FASB Changes to Revenue Recognition and Lease Accounting

By Michael Mathieson,
Valuation Research Corp. (Chicago, Ill., USA)

When accounting rules change, many business appraisers believe that there will be no impact to valuation. This is sometimes true because the changes may just affect how the financial statements are presented and don't change important variables that impact valuation, such as cash flow. But the recent changes to the accounting rules for revenue recognition and leases deserve the attention of valuation experts because of how sweeping the changes are and because they may have an effect on certain valuation analyses.

In 2016, the Financial Accounting Standards Board (FASB) issued accounting updates on two significant topics: revenue recognition and lease accounting. Companies should begin to plan now on how to incorporate the new standards and update procedures.

Revenue recognition. In 2014, FASB and the International Financial Reporting Standards (IFRS) converged to issue a standard for revenue recognition that would increase comparability across industries. This new standard marked a significant change and was meant to reduce complexity and standardize revenue recognition regardless of industry.

Many perceived the prior guidance, which varied under generally accepted accounting principles (GAAP) and IFRS, to be too complex and inconsistent among industries. Companies had to meet different requirements depending on the industry or type of transaction.

FASB's new guidance will address inconsistency and weakness in the existing revenue requirements, create a new framework to address revenue issues, improve comparability across entities and industries, provide more information and improved disclosure on financial statements, and simplify the preparation of financial statements by reducing the number of requirements. The new revenue recognition guidelines are premised on the following principle:

> Recognize revenue in a manner that depicts the transfer of goods or services to customers in an amount that reflects the consideration to which the entity expects to be entitled in exchange for those goods or services.[1]

The rule is effective for public companies for the first interim reporting period for fiscal years *beginning* after Dec. 15, 2017. Nonpublic companies have an additional year and will begin *adopting* after Dec. 15, 2018. The changes are significant and in many cases expected to allow companies to recognize revenue earlier. It will take time for companies to adopt and transition to the new standard. For most, the transition has already started, and entities that have not begun the transition process are running out of time to properly complete the necessary steps.

Following are the FASB revenue recognition steps:

1. *Identify the contract with the customer.* Other arrangements such as leases will be accounted under different standards (see below).

2. *Identify the performance obligations.* Performance obligations are the promises or deliverables in the contract. They can be accounted for separately if the goods or services are distinct. An obligation is distinct if the consumer can benefit from it on its own.

3. *Determine the transaction price.* The transaction price needs to be allocated to each of the separate performance obligations in the contract. It should reflect the amount of payment one could expect in exchange for the delivery of goods or services.

4. *Allocate the transaction price to the performance obligations in the contract.* If there is more than one obligation, then the transaction price should be allocated to each obligation identified in the contract.

5. *Recognize revenue when (or as) the reporting satisfies the performance obligation.* This happens when control of the promised good or service is transferred to the customer.

Implementation. As companies implement this new approach to revenue recognition, they need to focus on the following:

1. Developing and implementing the appropriate processes and controls.

2. Working with information systems to adopt the new standard and change processes to reflect the new revenue recognition model.

3. Analyzing any needed change to pricing strategies.

4. Revising any measures tied to revenue such as sales incentives, debt covenant ratios, or compensation plans.

1 "What You Need to Know About Revenue Recognition," *FASB Outlook*, 2014 Q1 issue; FASB.org.

5. Working with auditors to review these new processes and controls. Allow enough time for both auditor review and revision. It is important to bring auditors in early as they will need to agree with how you plan to allocate revenue to each step in the revenue recognition process.

6. Seeking to understand the likely impact on financial results.

7. Being prepared to communicate the likely impact both internally and externally.

Practical implications. In practice, we anticipate the new rules will have several implications.

- There could be an unexpected impact on a company's post-transaction statements from valuation of deferred revenues and the implied reduction.

- Some industries will encounter more challenges through revenue recognition than others. A consumer goods producer that manufactures and sells product is unlikely to see a significant impact. Others, such as technology companies, have ongoing obligations including support services. For these companies, the new rules will have potentially significant implications on the timing as performance obligations may cover an extended period.

- Expect audit staff to scrutinize and possibly challenge the revenue recognition model. Valuation Research Corp. (VRC) anticipates many companies will need to go through several rounds of review to develop an acceptable approach.

- Some companies may see an adoption-year impact of increased or decreased revenues. This should even out over time.

FASB and IASB created a joint transition resource group for revenue recognition. Practitioners can visit the resource group to learn more.[2]

Lease accounting. In early 2016, FASB issued an Accounting Standards Update related to the financial reporting of leasing transactions. Many companies are transitioning to the new rules. Under the new standard, companies will include leased assets and the related obligation on their balance sheets, in addition to classification changes to the income and cash flow statements.

FASB implemented the new standard to respond to requests from investors and financial statement users for a better representation of an organization's leasing activities and transactions as well as to end what the SEC and some stakeholders believe can be a form of off-balance sheet accounting.

The new model affects both financing leases (such as the current capital lease) and operating leases. It will not only change the lessee accounting for all leases. It will impact how financial statements

2 www.fasb.org/cs/ContentServer?c=Page&pagename=FASB%2FPage%2FLandingPage&cid=1176164065747.

will be presented and affect key financial metrics such as debt covenants or performance indicators tied to compensation.

The effort involved in the adoption of this new leasing standard should not be underestimated. The identification of all leasing arrangements for many companies will be a large exercise involving judgment and robust data collection. In addition, the new accounting standard may require changes to systems and the related control environment. It is also likely to affect financial statements and could impact the way investors analyze a company's financial condition and operating results.

FASB established its intended adoption date to be required for fiscal years and the related interim periods beginning after Dec. 15, 2018, with retroactive application to the previous two fiscal years. This means companies should have complete adoption effective Jan. 1, 2019, and retroactive application to 2017 and 2018 for both annual and interim financial statements. For nonpublic companies, the required adoption date is for fiscal years beginning after Dec. 15, 2019. Early adoption is permitted upon issuance of the new standard.

Valuation impacts. Changes to revenue recognition rules will likely result in the continuing evolution of valuation approaches for the resulting haircut to deferred revenue and the assigning of value to separately identified performance obligations.

In terms of any analysis that valuation experts may do, some industries could see revenue growth rates change after implementing the revenue recognition rules. These changes may be material, so valuation analysts need to take this into account when looking at historical trends in order to forecast future revenue growth. Of course, this also applies when looking at the performance of peer companies that the changes may or may not affect. Margins may also change because the new rules affect both revenue and expenses. Also, if revenue changes, certain multiples will change, so keep this in mind when doing a peer analysis—other firms may be recognizing revenue differently.

Michael Mathieson, *CPA, serves as senior advisor to Valuation Research Corp., advising VRC and client personnel on valuation accounting and business implications. For a more in-depth conversation about these new rules and their impact on valuations, please feel free to contact him at MMathieson@ValuationResearch.com or at 312-957-7491.*

Tale of the Tape: Different BV Standards Do Not Conflict

There has been some criticism in the past concerning the fragmentation of the business valuation profession. Indeed, a casual observer may look at the various sets of BV standards that different credentialing and standard-setting organizations have issued and get the idea that they are at odds with each other. But that is not the case.

New analysis. All of the standards are essentially addressing the same issues and do not conflict with each other, according to a new side-by-side analysis of the five sets of North American and three sets of international standards. A chart that compares the North American standards was presented at the annual conference of the National Association of Certified Valuators and Analysts (NACVA). The chart compares the standards of NACVA, IBA, AICPA, ASA, and USPAP. The authors are Mark Hanson (Schenck SC), Mark Kucik (The Kucik Valuation Group LLC), and Carl Steffen (WSRP LLC). Hanson is the incoming chair of NACVA's standards board, and Steffen is the outgoing chair. A short excerpt from this chart is in the accompanying exhibit, and the entire chart is available free on BVR's website.[1] The authors are finalizing a similar chart of the international standards (IVS, Canada, and RICS).

The perceived differences in the standards can be attributed to the fact that each organization writes its standards for its own members, who have different needs and levels of education in business valuation. For example, the AICPA's standard is written for its entire membership of CPAs, many of whom have no formal education in business valuation. On the other hand, the NACVA standard is written for its members who have all gone through courses in business valuation. Not surprisingly, the AICPA standards are longer than the NACVA standards because the CPA needs a lot more background about valuation methodologies and approaches. When you boil it all down, the principles are all basically the same.

Of course, the standards have some subtle differences, but these can be interpreted as being covered in one of the other standards but worded a little differently. Because of these nuances, practitioners still need to read and interpret what the different standards say about a particular aspect of practice in order to be in compliance.

1 The full version of the Business Valuation/Appraisal Standards Comparison Chart is available on BVR's website at www.bvresources.com in the Free Resources section under Articles and Webinars.

Business Valuation/Appraisal Standards Comparison Chart (Excerpt)

This excerpt is from a chart that compares the standards set by NACVA, IBA, AICPA, ASA, and USPAP. The full chart is available on the BVR website at www.bvresources.com in the Free Resources section. The standards are summarized in three broad categories: ethics, development, and reporting, which is the way the chart is organized. It reveals that all of the five sets of standards are essentially addressing the same issues and do not conflict with each other. The differences noted in some cases can be interpreted to be covered or implied in other sections.

Scope of Services

				AICPA-SSVS-VS Sec. 100	
NACVA	IBA	USPAP	ASA	Calculation	Valuation
A. Applicability					
These Standards are applicable when valuing ***a business, business ownership interest, security, or intangible asset.*** The General and Ethical standards apply to all professional services performed by members.	X	Preamble	ASA Business Valuation Standards (BVS) General Preamble (F8) BVS-I, Preamble BVS-I, Sections II A and B	Intro and Scope Secs./ Sec. .01	Intro and Scope Secs./Sec. .01
B. Valuation Services					
A member may express either a Conclusion of Value or a Calculated Value. When performing such Valuation Services, members shall comply with these Development and Reporting Standards. Valuation Services are:	X	Standards 9 and 10 and look at Advisory Opinion ("AO") 21 There are two levels of service for Appraisal Practice, which is a subset of Valuation Services: Appraisal and Appraisal Review (F4)	BVS-I, Section II C Refers to three categories: Appraisal, Limited Appraisal, and Calculation (F9)	Intro and Scope Secs./Sec. .02/.04/.21b	Intro and Scope Secs./Sec. .02/.04/.21a
1. Valuation Engagement					
A Valuation Agreement requires that a member apply valuation approaches or methods deemed in the member's professional judgment to be appropriate under the circumstances and results in a Conclusion of Value; or	X	SR 9-1	BVS-I, Section II C 1		Secs. .21a/.23/ .24/.26

Table continues on next page.

				AICPA-SSVS-VS Sec. 100	
NACVA	IBA	USPAP	ASA	Calculation	Valuation
2. Calculation Engagement					
A calculation engagement occurs when the client and member agree to specific valuation approaches, methods, and the extent of selected procedures and results in a Calculation Value.	X	SR 9 (See Scope of Work Rule) and (F4)	BVS-I, Section II C 3	Sec. 21b	
C. Other Services					
Any service provided by a member of the NACVA should be done so in an ethical and competent manner that does not negatively impact the valuation profession in general or the NACVA in particular.	X IBA STD	Ethics Rule/ Competency Rule	PAPCE Par. 2.1, 3.4, and 4.2	Ethics Rules/Secs. .05-.09	Ethics Rules/Secs. .05-.09
D. Jurisdictional Exception					
These Standards may differ from published governmental, judicial, accounting, or other authority that specifies valuation development or reporting procedures. In that event, the member should follow the applicable published authority or stated procedures. The other parts of these Standards shall continue in full force and effect.	X	Jurisdictional Exception Rule		Secs. .01/.03/.10	Secs. .01/.03/.10

Hong Kong Cracks Down on Valuations in Wake of Scandal

The recent arrests of senior management of two valuation firms in Hong Kong by government anti-corruption forces has led the Securities and Futures Commission (SFC) to issue a Guidance Note[1] on directors' duties in the context of valuations in corporate transactions involving listed companies. The SFC also issued a circular to financial advisers regarding valuations in corporate transactions together with a statement on the liability of valuers for disclosure of false or misleading information.

Office raids. *BVU* visited Hong Kong back in April, and, not long after we left the offices of the valuation firm Roma Group, anti-corruption forces of the government raided the place, and the CEO was arrested. The next day, the executive director at asset appraisal and advisory firm GreaterChina Professional Services Ltd. was also arrested—part of a probe by Hong Kong's Independent Commission Against Corruption (ICAC). The two firms are connected—they are joint shareholders in asset valuation firm Greater China Appraisal Ltd.

Kelvin Luk, chairman and CEO of Roma Group, was arrested for his "alleged personal involvement in a transaction of one of the clients of the Group," according to a company statement referred to in a report[2] in Reuters. Luk has resigned from Roma. No details were given on the arrest of David Yip, executive director at GreaterChina Professional Services Ltd., according to a report[3] in Bloomberg. Yip is also chairman of a Hong Kong-based company that said it had a deal to buy the English Premier League soccer team Hull City. Luk told Bloomberg that his arrest was related to a personal matter and was not connected to Greater China Appraisal.

In talking with various valuation professionals in Hong Kong, there was concern in the profession over the quality of valuation work. There are no official local standards and no formal oversight of the profession. Regulators had put some pressure on the profession several years ago, but that died down. This recent action by the government has revived the efforts for the local profession to get its house in order.

1 www.sfc.hk/edistributionWeb/gateway/EN/circular/openFile?refNo=17EC25.

2 www.reuters.com/article/roma-group-probe-idUSL3N1HT06L.

3 www.bloomberg.com/news/articles/2017-04-21/chairman-of-hull-city-bidder-greaterchina-arrested-in-hong-kong.

BV snapshot. In our talks with auditors and several valuation firms, here's a look at the BV picture in Hong Kong:

- There is no valuation professional organization (VPO) that has taken hold, and the perception is that "anybody" can do business valuation. Because of that, it's difficult to get a handle on the number of valuers in Hong Kong. Estimates range from 200 to 500.
- The most prevalent and respected credential here for BV experts is the CFA, who get BV-specific training. There is also a CPA designation from a Hong Kong group. There are some ASA members here, but it's tough to recruit new members as there's no strong incentive to join.
- Appraisers use the typical data: Duff & Phelps, Bloomberg, Cap IQ. No data are available on private companies here, but some appraisers feel they can use U.S. data and adjust it.
- The valuation books we saw on the office shelves are the same as you'd see in the U.S. The English language is prevalent here, so translation is not an issue. Hong Kong appraisers look to the U.S. for methodology if they don't know how to handle a particular issue.
- Credentials are not listed on business cards here—it's considered "boastful." More important is the relationship with clients.
- Fair value engagements are common, such as purchase price allocations and impairments.
- Not much litigation work is done here related to valuation. Shareholder disputes are few as many firms—including the listed firms—are family-owned without wide ownership. There is not much damages work, we're told. There is no requirement for fairness opinions here, but, with large deals, an independent valuation is needed.

There have been attempts to set up a VPO in Hong Kong. In the wake of the internet bubble, the concerns of local regulators triggered efforts by the valuation community to organize and bring the profession to a higher level. The Hong Kong Business Valuation Forum (HKBVF) was formed, but it was mostly real estate-centric. It did, however, issue standards for the valuation of businesses and intellectual property. But then the concerns of the regulators dissipated and the effort fizzled. Recently, the Hong Kong Institute of Financial Valuers (HKIFV) was set up to take up where the other organization left off. Before this latest scandal broke, Michael Li (Roma Group), a member of the working committee of the HKIFV, told us the group was about to issue a discussion draft and approach the regulators to get their blessing. Some veteran valuators in Hong Kong said they doubted that the regulators would give the HKIFV their seal of approval. Also, the group did not have the backing of the Big Four. Now, with this latest government crackdown, renewed efforts to set up a VPO will likely emerge in some shape or form.

Warning. In issuing the new Guidance Note, the SFC reminds directors that they are the guardians of their listed companies' assets and must ensure that acquisition targets are properly considered and investigated. The SFC also mentioned that valuers are expected to exercise the degree of skill and care reasonably competent members of their profession ordinarily exercise. They should not knowingly or recklessly accept any assumption that is not reasonable and fair. Valuers may be liable if their valuation reports contain any materially false or misleading information. The SFC will take appropriate actions against those companies, directors, advisers, and valuers who fail to comply with their duties.

Key Differences Remain Between Certain Sections of GAAP and IFRS

Valuation professionals involved in valuation for financial reporting need to know the key differences between the International Financial Reporting System (IFRS) and U.S. generally accepted accounting principles (GAAP), according to Mark Weston, a valuation partner with Davidson & Co. LLC (Vancouver, B.C.).[1] It's especially important as efforts continue to find convergence within the two approaches, he says. The U.S. will likely face a dual GAAP environment as the International Accounting Standards Board, which is responsible for IFRS, and the Financial Accounting Standards Board, which is responsible for GAAP, pursue their own agendas, Weston adds.

Weston pinpoints three components of IFRS and GAAP to show areas where they converged and areas where they are different (see the sidebar for a listing of the standards discussed here).

1. ASC 805 vs. IFRS 13

"As a valuer, you're dealing with financial reporting and valuation for financial reporting—fair value. We are all somewhat familiar with that. It is an exit concept," Weston says. "I am not concerned with what the client has paid—I am concerned with what the client would receive if it sold the asset or what the client would pay if, in fact, it had to transfer the liability."

U.S. GAAP and IFRS Standards Discussed in This Article

U.S. GAAP	*IFRS*
ASC 350, Intangibles—Goodwill and Other	IAS 36, Impairment of Assets
ASC 360, Property, Plant, and Equipment	IAS 38, Intangible Assets
ASC 805, Business Combinations	IFRS 3, Business Combinations
ASC 820, Fair Value Measurements and Disclosures	IFRS 13, Fair Value Measurement

1 Weston made his remarks during a panel discussion in a recent webinar, Tour de Value: Team iiBV Tours the Global Valuation Landscape, BVR, July 11, 2017. Archive recording available at www.bvresources.com/products/training.

Weston believes that the GAAP and IFRS standards for fair value measurement are converged, noting that some analysts describe them as "absolutely converged," although he prefers the term "highly converged."

The areas of high convergence include:

- The price received to sell an asset or paid to transfer a liability between market participants at the measurement date;
- An exit price definition of fair value that would result from the market participants' behavior;
- The valuation technique is appropriate in instances where sufficient data are available that maximize use of relevant observable inputs and minimize the use of unobservable inputs; and
- Includes concepts such as highest and best use for nonfinancial assets, principal (most advantageous) market, and fair value hierarchy-based on inputs.

2. ASC 820 vs. IFRS 3

"IFRS 3 and ASC 820 are highly converged, and effectively a purchase price allocation is essentially the same under both standards," Watson says. He first asks whether a business combination has occurred when asked to do a purchase price allocation. If it's not considered a combination, he allocates the purchase proceeds to the asset, and there is no goodwill.

The areas of high convergence include:

- The acquisition of assets that don't constitute a business is not a business combination;
- The acquiring entity allocates the cost of the acquisition to the acquired assets and liabilities;
- Accounted for using the acquisition method and the date of the acquisition is the date the acquirer gains control;
- Considered measured at fair value at the date of the acquisition, with contingent consideration recorded as a liability or asset remeasured based on fair value until settlement;
- Identifiable assets acquired, and liabilities assumed are recognized separately from goodwill;
- Exceptions regarding the recognition of contingent liabilities, deferred tax assets and liabilities, indemnification assets, and others;

- Goodwill measured as a residual and recognized as an asset, and negative goodwill (bargain purchase) recognized in profit or loss after reassessing values used in acquisition accounting; and
- One area of minor distinction is that U.S. GAAP defines control slightly differently than IFRS, which defines control as a business combination in which an acquirer gains control of one or more businesses.

3. ASC 350/ASC 360 vs. IAS 38/36

"Although there is some convergence, there are still significant issues that exist. Under IAS 36, effectively, it is just a one-step test. IAS 36 deals with all intangible assets and says that, for indefinite-lived intangible assets, one has to test them annually or when an indication of impairment exists. For finite-lived assets, the testing is done only when certain triggers exist," Weston points out.

"The test is a bit different in the U.S. You compare the carrying amount of the asset with its recoverable amount. The recoverable amount is actually defined as the higher of the fair value less cost to sell, or something called the value in use. This, of course, is the first test under ASC 350, our standardized two-step test."

Areas of partial convergence between ASC 350 and IAS 38 include:

- An intangible asset is a nonmonetary and nonfinancial asset without physical substance and considered identifiable when it is separable or arises from contractual or legal rights;
- Goodwill is only recognized in a business combination, and goodwill as well as identifiable intangible assets are not subject to amortization and are subject to impairment testing, but the test is different; and
- Finite-level intangible assets are amortized over their useful lives.

Areas where ASC 350/360 and IAS 36 differ:

- Intangible assets that are not yet available for use are tested for impairment only when an indication of impairment exists, as opposed to annually;
- Assets are tested as individual assets, groups of assets, or at reporting unit levels;
- Determination or assessment of cash generating units (CGUs) and reporting units are the responsibility of auditors or management, not the valuer; and
- Long-lived assets subject to depreciation are tested for impairment on a stand-alone basis if possible, otherwise on an asset group basis.

For the impairment of goodwill, ASC 350 uses a two-step test that first compares the fair value of a reporting unit to the carrying amount. If the fair value is less, the second step calculates the impairment charge by comparing the implied value of the goodwill with the carrying amount. However, FASB eliminated the second step, which aligns GAAP more closely to IFRS.

Final point. As IFRS continues to be adopted globally, the impact on multinational U.S. businesses will increase and valuation experts will have to become more financially bilingual.

Work File Checklist for Fair Value Overview Under New Regulations

Anyone doing fair value for financial reporting should comply with the requirements under the new CEIV credential whether they hold the credential or not. CEIV holders will have a work file reviewed within the first year they receive the credential and then periodically after that. Those without the CEIV credential will be expected to comply with the new requirements, which are designed as overall best practices.

The new requirements are contained in the Mandatory Performance Framework (MPF), which is designed to make sure that the valuation expert adequately documents his or her work and thought processes. The guidance does not explain "how to" perform a valuation but rather "how much" documentation is required.

Practice aid. A handy tool to use for compliance is a work file checklist of what the MPF requires for all the different aspects involved in fair value measurement. On page 274 is a checklist for the documentation of prospective financial information (PFI), an area of particular concern and scrutiny. That topic is included in the "General Valuation Guidance" section of the MPF companion document, the "Application of the Mandatory Performance Framework."

Here, we present a checklist for the other two topics in that section: (1) an overview of fair value measurement (initial and subsequent measurement dates); and (2) the selection of valuation approaches and methods. This checklist will give you what you need at a minimum in your work file and is based on what is contained in the two MPF documents, which you can download from a special website set up for the CEIV credential (www.ceiv-credential.org).

Checklist follows on next page.

Work File Checklist: MPF Requirements for Documenting Fair Value Measurement and the Selection of Valuation Approaches and Methods

Fair Value Measurement (Initial and Subsequent Dates)

☑ The valuation professional, at a minimum, must document the following in writing within the work file, if applicable:

☑ The valuation professional's own assessment of fair value at the initial transaction (if applicable) and subsequent measurement dates;

☑ An indication that it is not assumed that the transaction price equates to fair value at or near the transaction date;

☑ An assessment of management's selection of calibrated inputs used to value the subject interest on subsequent measurement dates;

☑ Assessment of fair value of the subject interest at the initial transaction (for example, consideration of unit of account, principal market, market participants, and methods and inputs used to determine fair value);

☑ The relevance of all calibrated inputs used to estimate fair value on subsequent measurement dates;

☑ The evaluation of all inputs used to estimate fair value on subsequent measurement dates;

☑ The evaluation of management's rationale and support for the inputs used to estimate initial fair value of the subject interest and its FASB ASC 820 hierarchy classification (for example, Level 1, Level 2, or Level 3); and

☑ The rationale for any changes in valuation approaches or methods used for subsequent measurement dates as compared to the initial transaction.

Selection of Valuation Approaches and Methods

The valuation professional, at a minimum, must document the following in writing within the work file, if applicable:

☑ The process and rationale for selecting the valuation method(s) or excluding potentially relevant valuation methods to estimate the fair value of the subject interest;

☑ The process and rationale for selected weighting (or emphasis on) each approach and the method in reconciling various indications of value to reach the final conclusion of value (if more than one approach or method is used);

☑ A reconciliation of the results should include these, among other things:

- ☑ A supporting narrative about the applied methods and their applicability and usefulness to the valuation assignment, the reliability of the underlying data used in their preparation, and an explanation of inputs and assumptions;
- ☑ An assessment of the reliability of the results obtained and whether any of the results used to reach a conclusion of value are deemed more or less probative of fair value based on information gathered throughout the engagement *(Note: The extent of documentation should be commensurate with the level of judgment and qualitative analysis involved in supporting the positive assertion.)*; and
- ☑ A clear explanation discussing any apparent inconsistencies in the analysis relative to external or internal documentation or data (for example, contrary evidence), which may then take the form of mathematical calculations when using quantitative weighting.

☑ An explanation, based on the results of the first three items above, that identifies whether the conclusion of value is based on the results of one valuation approach and method or based on the results of multiple approaches and methods.

Future checklists will go into specifics of fair value documentation requirements for various methods, inputs, and assets/liabilities.

(*Source*: This checklist is derived from the document, "Application of the Mandatory Performance Framework for the CEIV." The information in this checklist has been summarized and adapted. See the actual document for additional explanation and requirements at www.ceiv-credential.org).

AICPA Fields Questions About New CVFI Credential

Efforts to improve the quality in fair value for financial reporting continues with the introduction of a new credential by the AICPA: Certified in Valuation of Financial Instruments (CVFI). An exposure draft[1] of a "disclosure framework" has been issued that establishes parameters of documentation requirements. *BVU* recently spoke with Jeff High, AICPA senior manager—fair value measurements, and asked some questions about the new credential.

BVU: *What is the goal of the CVFI credential efforts?*

Jeff High: The goal of the CVFI is to improve the quality and reviewability of valuations of financial instruments. Namely, the idea is to produce greater transparency and trust in valuations. The credential is designed to ensure that those who perform, review, or audit those valuations are qualified to do so and namely to follow a procedure and performance that allows for greater reviewability and transparency in those calculations.

BVU: *Do you see this as a global credential? Will it embody not only U.S. GAAP, but international standards as well, such as IFRS and IVS?*

JH: Yes, the CVFI is a global credential intended to provide greater clarity and consistency in valuations in the global financial market. Whether in New York, London, or Hong Kong, to be proficient in valuations of financial instruments and related financial reporting, one should have an understanding of both U.S. GAAP and IFRS.

BVU: *What is the current status of the launch date for the CVFI credential?*

JH: We are aiming to launch the credential in 2018. CPAs and valuation professionals can sign up to receive information and updates on the credential at www.aicpa.org/Membership/Pages/financial-instruments-form.aspx.

BVU: *What is the disclosure framework related to the CVFI credential?*

1 Available at www.aicpa.org/InterestAreas/FairValueMeasurement/Resources/DownloadableDocuments/AICPA_FI_Framework_Exposure_Draft.pdf (Comments due Sept. 26, 2017).

JH: The Financial Instruments Framework (aka Disclosure Framework of Financial Instruments Performance Framework) is the guiding document for those who hold the CVFI. It lays out the guiding principles of behavior and performance by which a CVFI credential holder is expected to abide.

BVU: *Will the disclosure framework require a credential holder to do more work than before?*

JH: The amount of work credential holders following the disclosure framework would do depends entirely on the valuation professional firm/organization for which they work or the client they are reviewing and the legal environment in which they operate. Some organizations and professionals operate under significant documentation requirements with high degrees of transparency and reporting.

Indeed, the framework and credential are designed to create greater transparency and efficiency in the valuation and review process. By simply showing their work, or creating a common framework, we expect more clarity and a more streamlined process for reviewing financial instrument valuations.

BVU: *Can you reveal any of the comments you've received so far on the exposure draft? Anything in particular that the comments are focusing on?*

JH: We'll undertake a thorough review of all the comments we've received at the conclusion of the comment period. This feedback from stakeholders will be used to help shape the finalized disclosure framework.

BVU: *The disclosure framework application document includes a blue-shaded sidebar (the only one in the entire document) that talks about the importance of scrutinizing prospective financial information from third parties. Have you identified this issue as one aspect of fair value that needs to be improved on?*

JH: Yes, we believe the guidance that will be set forth for CVFI credential holders will help to improve the means in which third-party financial information is taken into account during the financial instrument valuation process.

BVU: *Does the CVFI credential apply only to public company engagements?*

JH: The CVFI applies to everyone involved in the valuation of financial instruments for financial reporting purposes.

BVU: *How is the CVFI different from the CFA?*

JH: The CFA and CVFI are complementary and independent designations. The CVFI is designed to create a foundation for those who perform, review, and audit financial instrument valuations. Per the CFA Institute, the CFA program provides a strong foundation of advanced investment analysis and real-world portfolio management skills (www.cfainstitute.org). CFA charterholders who are analyzing securities will have greater certainty and confidence in the valuations a CVFI credential holder performs.

BVU: *Please describe the education/training process and requirements.*

JH: To obtain the CVFI credential one must:

1. Have obtained three years of experience in the field of financial instrument valuation;
2. Completed the AICPA-approved education (roughly 35 hours of online-delivered education);
3. Passed the CVFI exam delivered by the AICPA;
4. Maintain the credential with eight hours of continuing education per annum;
5. Continue with ongoing quality monitoring and follow the Financial Instruments Framework;
6. Be a member or associate member of the AICPA; and
7. Abide by the AICPA Code of Professional Conduct.

BVU: *Will there be any grandfathering for individuals with a great deal of experience?*

JH: No, each individual must follow the process to obtain the CVFI credential.

BVU: *Does one need a valuation credential to qualify?*

JH: The CVFI credential does not require anyone to obtain another valuation credential beforehand.

BVU: *If one has a valuation credential from another group (not the AICPA), does that fulfill some of the CVFI requirements?*

JH: The process to obtain the CVFI credential is uniform for all valuation professionals.

BVU: *Do you need to have an AICPA membership to get the CVFI?*

JH: One must be or become a member or associate member of the AICPA to obtain the credential.

BVU: *Is there a requirement to submit a valuation report in order to receive the credential?*

JH: That is not a requirement for the credential.

BVU: *Can you describe the quality control process? Will it be a proactive process? What sanctions can be imposed for significant deficiencies?*

JH: CVFI credential holders will be required to participate in an annual proactive quality monitoring program. Details of the quality monitoring program are still being determined.

SEC Settlement Over Fair Value Signals Shift of Focus

The recent settlement between KPMG and the SEC over alleged overvaluations of assets marks a shift in the agency's enforcement focus. Until now, the SEC primarily targeted policies, procedures, and internal controls. But, in this case, the SEC set its sights on the actual valuation of assets. The SEC order[1] is important in that it gives you an overall sense of where the agency will be focused in the future.

Significant matter. The case involves allegations of improper professional conduct and security law violations by KPMG and its audit partner relating to the review and audit of financial statements of Miller Energy, an oil and gas company based in Tennessee. During its fiscal year 2010 (ending April 30), Miller Energy acquired certain oil and gas interests in Alaska for $4.5 million. In its fiscal 2010 financial statements, the company reported these assets at $480 million. The SEC alleged that the valuation violated GAAP and overstated the assets by hundreds of millions of dollars. KPMG was hired for the next fiscal year's audit and also issued an audit report that gave an unqualified opinion to the company's 2011 financial statements that included as an opening balance sheet item the inflated $480 million.

After an investigation (apparently triggered by a critical financial blog), KPMG agreed to pay more than $6.2 million to settle SEC charges that it failed to properly audit the financial statements of Miller Energy. Specifically, the failures involved management's fair valuations of unproven oil and gas reserves and related fixed assets. Allegations included misuse of industry expert reports on reserves and tangible assets, a double counting of fixed assets, inadequate testing of assumptions, the auditor's lack of industry experience, and an inadequate disclosure of the work of the valuation specialists, which contributed to the improper valuations, according to the SEC order. KPMG and the audit partner on the engagement agreed to settle without admitting or denying any of the allegations, but they agreed to certain remedial acts and sanctions.

Here are the main points that valuation experts need to take away from this case.

1 *In the Matter of KPMG LLP and John Riordan, CPA*, SEC Release No. 81396 (Aug. 15, 2017). Available on BVR's website in the Free Resources area (Articles and Webinars section) at sub.bvresources.com/defaulttextonly.asp?f=downloads.

Bargain purchase red flag. Miller Energy paid $4.5 million for oil and gas assets that it then booked at $480 million. Under ASC 805, that's a bargain purchase, which standard setters expect to be rare. True, the buyers could have gotten a great deal, but, if it appears that a bargain purchase has been made, you need to apply some extra scrutiny. The SEC made it a point to say KPMG should have checked its work.

Lack of industry experience. The SEC criticized the fact that the in-house business valuation group that was assisting the audit team was taking its direction from an audit partner who did not have experience in the oil and gas industry. The SEC order mentions an expert's reserve report for the supplemental oil and gas disclosures that was used as the evidence for fair value measurement. The report stated that it was not giving a determination of fair value or fair market value of the reserves. It was a generic analysis that had problems, such as using only one discount rate when some reserves were more riskier. Someone with oil and gas expertise should have picked up on this, the SEC says.

Replacement cost issue. The valuation team also used as evidence of fair value an insurance broker's report on what the replacement cost would be ($46 million) for the hard assets (pipelines, facilities, and operating platforms). The SEC criticized the inclusion of those hard assets, saying:

> Due to their remote and desolate location, a willing buyer and seller would not have agreed on replacement cost as the price for the assets. This was particularly true of the underground pipelines that connected the various oil production facilities, which, in order to value them separately, KPMG deemed as surplus assets that were not needed to generate cash flows in the reserve report. Using management's numbers, EDS (which was the KPMG internal business valuation group) estimated that replacing the pipelines would cost up to $46 million, about half the proposed value of the fixed assets.

The SEC went on, making the bold statement that it was "highly unlikely that any market participant would pay $46 million for pipelines that were assumed to be extraneous to the production of oil and gas from nearby fields."

Insufficient evidence. The SEC found that KPMG failed to obtain sufficient competent evidence regarding the impact of the opening balances on the current year's financial statements despite knowing that management had performed no proper fair value assessment in the prior year. Further, KPMG procedures failed to appropriately consider facts leading up to the acquisition of those assets, which included multiple offers received for those assets that fell through. Later, when Miller Energy was in bankruptcy, it asked to abandon the assets because, at least in the opinion of that owner at the time, it would have cost more to get the oil out of the ground than what it could otherwise realize upon the sale of that oil.

Inadequate disclosure. The SEC criticized the audit team for failing to clearly state the valuation specialist's findings. The SEC thought that it was incumbent upon KPMG to document in its work papers exactly what the business valuation group did and to memorialize that. It found that to be a deficiency.

For more information. The SEC order gives you a sense of where the SEC will be focusing as to the use of and work by valuation specialists, whether internal or external. A copy of the SEC order can be found on BVR's website in the Free Resources area (Articles and Webinars section). Also, the matter was discussed during a BVR webinar, Fair Value and Valuation: Understanding the SEC, PCAOB and Key Case Law, with Yvonne Williams-Wass (Eversheds Sutherland), Peter J. Anderson (Eversheds Sutherland), and Mark Zyla (Acuitas). The webinar contains 100 minutes of insights into the current regulatory landscape of fair value.

Work File Checklist for Growth Rate and Terminal Value

The requirements under the new credential for fair value for financial reporting should be considered best practices to anyone doing this type of work. Holders of the Certified in Entity and Intangible Valuations (CEIV) credential will have a work file reviewed within the first year they receive the credential and then periodically after that. The new requirements are contained in the Mandatory Performance Framework (MPF), which is designed to make sure that the valuation expert adequately documents his or her work and thought processes.

Practice aid. A handy tool to use for compliance is a work file checklist of what the MPF requires for all the different aspects involved in fair value measurement. In past issues of *BVU*, we presented checklists for a number of valuation areas. Here, we give you a checklist for how to document your work on growth rates and the terminal value, and it is based on what is contained in the two MPF documents, which you can download from a special website set up for the CEIV credential (www.ceiv-credential.org).

Work File Checklist: Minimum MPF Requirements for Documenting Growth Rates and Terminal Value

<u>Growth Rates</u>

☑ The rationale, support, and reasonableness assessment for the selected growth rate(s) used in the analysis.

☑ The rationale for all inputs that comprise the terminal or long-term GR.

☑ When estimating the value of an entity, the rationale for selection of the terminal period when cash flows are capitalized into perpetuity. For example, if company management provides a five-year forecast, the valuation professional should not assume the period after the forecasted period should be the point where cash flows are capitalized into perpetuity without performing additional analysis.

☑ When estimating the value of an entity, the rationale for selection of the GR to be used for capitalization of cash flows into perpetuity. For example, if company management provides

Checklist continues on next page.

a five-year forecast, the valuation professional should not assume the terminal-period GR is appropriate after the forecasted period for capitalizing cash flow into perpetuity without performing additional analysis.

☑ Rationale for the use of other models (for example, the H-model, also referred to as the "fading growth" model) when growth at the end of the projection period is not expected to be sustainable.

Terminal Value Multiple Methods and Models

☑ The rationale for selecting the appropriate terminal value methods or model (can include one or more of the existing models, including the Gordon growth model, H-model (fading growth model), two-stage model, terminal exit multiples, key value driver formula, or other, such as salvage value or disposal costs).

☑ The rationale and support for each key assumption used in the terminal value method or model such as, as applicable:

- o The discount rate;
- o Terminal or perpetual growth rate;
- o Second-stage or high-growth growth rate for the H-model and two-stage model;
- o High growth stage duration or life for the H-model and two-stage model;
- o Return on invested capital (ROIC); and
- o Terminal market multiple (exit multiple).

☑ If more than one terminal value method or model is used, the rationale for the selected weighting assigned to each terminal value method or model and to reconcile the various indications of terminal values.

In future issues, we will provide other checklists that will go into specifics of the documentation requirements for other methods, inputs, and assets/liabilities.

(Source: This checklist is derived from the document "Application of the Mandatory Performance Framework for the CEIV." The information in this checklist has been summarized and adapted. See the actual document for additional explanation and requirements at www.ceiv-credential.org.)

CICBV Launches Proactive Practice Inspection Program

The Canadian Institute of Chartered Business Valuators (CICBV) has launched a practice inspection program that will subject work product done by members and registered students to a mandatory inspection. Any work product that is issued on or after Jan. 1, 2018, will be subject to the inspections, which are currently set to begin in 2019. Members are advised to inform clients that work done with reports issued after Jan. 1, 2018, will potentially be subject to these inspections. The clients and members will be required to provide inspectors with access to work product and files.

Unlike the United States and other regions that rely mostly on complaint-driven reactive investigation of work done by valuators, the CICBV is taking a proactive approach to enhance the confidence that the public and other regulatory bodies have in CBV work and help to maintain or improve the quality of services provided, as the association said in a statement announcing the program. One exception is the Certified in Entity and Intangibles Valuations (CEIV) credential from the AICPA, ASA, and RICS, which plans to implement a mandatory inspection program (the procedures are still being developed).

The CICBV began to consider mandatory inspection of work product back in 2016, based on the principle that it wanted to retain its independence and valuation as a self-regulated profession and be proactive in monitoring members.

How it works. The CICBV does not plan to regulate firms because only individuals are considered part of the CICBV and only those who sign off on the reports will be considered subject to the inspections. Work developed solely for internal use will not be subject to inspection. Each valuator or registered student must inform the CICBV annually if they've done (or taken responsibility for) any reports during the year in order to determine whether they're eligible for inspection. A valuator or registered student will not be subject to inspection more than one time in a four-year period. The CICBV does not plan to extensively inspect valuators annually, but the precise number of inspections to be completed will be determined based on the number of eligible valuators, coupled with the results of previous inspections.

When a valuator or registered student is selected for inspection, he or she will submit to the CICBV a list of all of the reports issued during the reporting period, including the date, type, and purpose of the report. The client will not be identified as part of this disclosure.

When an organization has an internal review process that encompasses many or all of the components of the CICBV review, the inspection committee will use that process to determine how extensive its own review needs to be. The discretion for that determination rests with the CICBV. In addition, the organization will strive to concurrently review people within the same organization in order to decrease the overall burden on that organization.

When a practitioner is selected for review, CICBV will typically review four reports, though that number could vary based on the results of previous reviews. Anyone who signs off on a report, including registered students, is considered to be potentially subject to inspection. This could include multiple signers on the same report.

It's important to note that it will always be the signers who are subject to inspection, even in circumstances where a partner of the firm signs the report for work product prepared by junior personnel. Also, any work product done under CICBV standards is subject to inspection under the program, even when other professional associations may also audit or inspect the work as well.

In comments to the CICBV during the exposure period, some members suggested that, when reports are subject to litigation, they should not be subjected to inspection by CICBV because the adversarial nature of the litigation is itself a form of review. CICBV disagreed, saying that the inspection program is a form of self-regulation and that the critique of a valuation report in the setting of litigation doesn't meet that objective.

Inspection will be focused primarily on whether the report complies with CICBV Practice Standards and Code of Ethics and whether the report is consistent with the nature of the engagement and is the type of deliverable associated with a competent valuator. The inspection will not involve attempting to second-guess the findings of the report, and the inspector will not attempt to determine whether or not he agrees with the findings of the report. The inspector will apply a reasonable standard to the assessment of the report and is not expected to apply a perfect standard.

Inspection process. As part of its final implementation of the inspection system, here are the steps that will occur during a typical review:

1. The CICBV selects the files and informs the practitioner.

2. The inspector visits the office to review the internal review practices of the group for whom the selected valuator is employed.

3. The inspector reviews the files and completes practice inspection checklists.

4. A draft of the inspector's report is created and discussed with the practitioner. The practitioner is able to comment on identified deficiencies for the final report.

5. The director of practice inspection for the CICBV issues a draft report to the practitioner for comments on any corrective actions.

6. The practitioner is able to provide comments and any disagreements with the findings outlined in the report.

7. The director of practice inspection amends the draft report as appropriate based on the feedback from the practitioner.

8. A final report is submitted. If there are ultimately no identified deficiencies, the inspection is closed and the practitioner notified.

9. When any deficiencies are minor or trivial in nature, the Practice Inspection Committee will close the inspection. Whether a deficiency is trivial or minor will rest with the judgment of the inspector.

10. Any deficiencies deemed to be significant or major could require a written corrective action plan from the practitioner or the implementation of corrective or remedial action to address the deficiencies. A further inspection may also be ordered.

Who will inspect. Valuators hired to serve as inspectors will be required to be certified business valuators (CBVs) with a minimum of five years of post-qualification practice experience. They will be required to adhere to confidentiality rules of the CICBV, a rule the association believes addresses some concerns with respect to confidentiality of the client information that is shared with the inspector during the process.

One proposal not adopted by the CICBV was that those CBVs hired to serve as inspectors be precluded from returning to private practice for up to five years. CICBV decided not to move forward with the provision because it believes the provision would increase the cost of hiring the CBVs, as well as make it more difficult to recruit. In addition, it would be a provision difficult to enforce. The raising of it as a concern suggests there is some unease about the CBV inspectors gaining access to confidential client data while working for CICBV, then returning with that knowledge to private practice, despite the confidentiality assurances laid out by the CICBV.

Work File Checklist for Documenting Valuation Multiples

The Mandatory Performance Framework (MPF) sets out requirements regarding how a valuation expert should adequately document his or her work and thought processes when engaged in a fair value for financial reporting assignment. It was specifically designed as part of the Certified in Entity and Intangibles Valuations (CEIV) credential now offered by the AICPA, ASA, and RICS. While CEIV holders are required to comply with the MPF, it should be considered best practices for anyone doing this type of work. We quote this paragraph from the MPF:

> **Valuation professionals without the CEIV credential.** As noted previously, the framework and the Application of the MPF were designed for use by all valuation professionals. Although only those valuation professionals who have the CEIV credential are required to adhere to the MPF documents, the Performance Requirements Work Stream believes that adhering to the MPF documents should be considered best practice by valuation professionals who do not have the CEIV credential and who perform valuation of a business, business interest, intangible asset, certain liabilities, and inventory used to support management assertions made in financial statements issued for financial reporting purposes.

Practice aid. A handy tool to use for compliance is a work file checklist of what the MPF requires for all the different aspects involved in fair value measurement. In past issues of *BVU*, we presented checklists for a number of valuation areas. Here, we give you a checklist for how to document your selection and adjustments of valuation multiples. This is based on what is contained in the two MPF documents, which you can download from a special website set up for the CEIV credential (www.ceiv-credential.org).

Checklist follows on next page.

Work File Checklist: Minimum MPF Requirements for Documenting the Selection and Adjustments of Valuation Multiples

☑ Prepare an exhibit of the market multiples of the guideline public companies and include the source of the data used. Also include the numerators and denominators used in each multiple and a discussion of any assumptions necessary for these calculations.

☑ Describe the process used to select a multiple based on a consideration of all the comparative analyses performed and the rationale for judgments along the way. This should include, but not be limited to, discussion of: (a) the decision regarding equity versus invested capital multiples; (b) the decision regarding the time frame of earnings or other metrics; (c) analysis of the comparative performance measures and how the analysis affected the selection of the multiples applied to the subject entity; (d) the comparative qualitative and quantitative analysis that affected the selection of the multiples applied to the subject entity; (e) the selection of the starting point of the multiples within the range; and (f) the rationale for adjustments, if any, to the starting point multiples to determine multiples applicable to the subject entity.

☑ Identify each significant accounting difference and adjustments made, if any, for better comparability.

☑ Document the calculation of the multiples of the entire company (if reporting units are being analyzed in a publicly traded company) and rationale for differences in the multiples used in valuing the subject entity.

☑ Show the calculation of multiples implied in a recent transaction and rationale for differences in the multiples used in valuing the subject entity.

Be aware that these are minimum requirements, so more information may be necessary. In future issues, we will provide other checklists that will go into specifics of the documentation requirements for other methods, inputs, and assets/liabilities.

(*Source*: This checklist is derived from the document, "Application of the Mandatory Performance Framework for the CEIV." The information in this checklist has been summarized and adapted. See the actual document for additional explanation and requirements at www.ceiv-credential.org).

Section IV.
Business Valuation Profession And Practice Management

30 Field-Tested Ideas to Bring in More BV Business

Classic face-to-face techniques continue to be the best methods to bring in valuation business, according to a BVR survey. Over 170 valuation firms, sole practitioners, CPA firms, and other entities with business valuation practices responded to the survey conducted during this past summer.

Prevalence of techniques. Three of the five most frequently cited marketing methods (see exhibit) all require the knack for personal selling. Electronic substitutes have become much more important but are not at the very top of the list. Social networking continues to be the fastest growing marketing method, used by 66% of respondents, almost double the percentage reported in 2010. Also, more practices are regularly updating their websites and adding free content than they did in 2010.

Name recognition programs (newsletters, public relations, websites, etc.) are used to support sales efforts in about half of the firms offering business valuation services. For the first time, the survey asked about marketing through the writing of articles in journals or industry publications. Over half (51%) say they use this technique, and, of those, 62% say this is a moderately to very effective marketing mechanism.

The survey reveals a big jump in the usage of the many directories available for valuation practitioners, expert witnesses, or other groups, with 43% of respondents using these directories (up from 20% in 2010). Some of this surge could be from an increased awareness that directories are generally free to members of the AICPA, ASA, and NACVA. Other directories mentioned include jurispro .com, experts.com, state bar association directories, and local business directories (e.g., Chamber of Commerce). While usage has increased, no one is thrilled by the results. Only 23% of those who use directories call the practice moderately successful, and no one says it's "very effective."

Most effective ways. Of course, usage is one thing and effectiveness is another. The big question is: "What really works?"

The most-used method—the face-to-face meeting with a prospect—is deemed "very effective" by 35% of those who use it. The same percentage feels its effectiveness is just a notch below that, which means that 70% say the technique goes beyond being just moderately effective. Other methods ranking high on the "very effective" list are public speaking, cross-marketing to existing clients, attending or sponsoring events with prospects, updating the website, writing for journals or industry publications, and the use of e-newsletters and blogs.

The gain in the usage of social networking sites has not been met with overly exciting results. It is "not effective" for 30% of those who use it, and only one individual says it is "very effective." A third of respondents who use it say it is "moderately effective" or slightly better. Part of the reason for this may be that firms are still finding their way with this technique and have yet to hit on the right formula.

Keep in mind that you should not dismiss a technique because many respondents do not praise it. Somewhere at some firm, somebody is using each of these techniques to bring in new business. In this spirit, we asked a separate question: What is the single most important initiative your BV practice carried out in 2015 to improve marketing or expand client development? The following list is not ranked in any particular order, and many of the ideas revolve around time-tested one-on-one contact. Hopefully, the following items will trigger one—or more—ideas for your firm:

1. Contact prospective clients proactively;
2. Focus on key referral sources and partner contacts;
3. Target market to attorneys;
4. Sponsor meet and greets with law firms;
5. Network with bankers;
6. Get to know the local SBA lender;
7. Sponsor events and conferences;
8. Attend industry conferences and network with peers;
9. Promote word of mouth from satisfied clients;
10. Cross-sell to clients of other areas of the firm;
11. Become a known expert in a niche area or industry;
12. Start doing some public speaking;
13. Increase community involvement;
14. Get involved with charity;
15. Teach;
16. Update your website;
17. Create a separate website for the business valuation practice;
18. Create a blog;

19. Revamp your logo;
20. Produce dual language brochures;
21. Send out email blasts on current developments;
22. Direct market to local legal referral sources;
23. Increase use of newsletter and related follow-up;
24. Maintain exceptional quality of work;
25. Deliver work on time;
26. Raise rates to attract bigger engagements;
27. Keep fees reasonable;
28. Hire more staff to allow more time for marketing;
29. Set specific goals for staff related to business development; and
30. Hire a firm to help with marketing.

The results reported here are from a larger survey designed to examine valuation firms in terms of performance, compensation, billing rates, marketing and practice development, and other elements. All of the responses are being analyzed, and a full report will be available soon. *BVU* will present more results in future issues.

What Marketing Techniques Do You Currently Use in Your BV Practice?

	2015	2010	2008
One-on-one meetings with prospective clients	89.4%	n/a	n/a
Public speaking	81.3%	55.6%	66.4%
Update to website	78.9%	65.4%	57.6%
Joining business associations/committees/boards	77.4%	60.0%	59.2%
Social networking sites (LinkedIn, Twitter, Facebook, etc.)	65.7%	35.0%	19.6%
Cross-marketing and meetings with existing clients	56.2%	43.9%	56.8%
Offering or attending seminars on BV where prospective clients are present	53.2%	55.1%	48.0%
Writing in journals or industry publications	51.4%	n/a	n/a
RFPs/"beauty contests"	46.8%	27.3%	20.8%
Regularly scheduled print or electronic newsletter or blog	46.2%	37.1%	36.8%
Listing in financial expert witness or other directories	43.1%	19.8%	14.1%
Public relations efforts in the media or elsewhere	42.9%	25.4%	32.0%
Emails to new prospect lists	41.5%	n/a	n/a
Paid or classified advertising	37.6%	31.2%	28.8%
Direct mail	28.7%	22.4%	22.8%
No marketing done	13.0%	n/a	n/a

Business Valuation Year in Review 2016

It was an eventful year for the business valuation profession in 2016, both from a U.S. and global perspective. Here is a wrap-up of some of the more notable developments, some of which set the stage for 2017 and beyond.

IRC 2704. Arguably the most talked about issue in 2016 was the issuance of the controversial proposed IRC Section 2704 regulations designed to curb estate valuation discounts for minority interests. The valuation community was shocked over the scope of the proposed rules, which would apply to family-owned operating businesses as well as asset-holding entities that are perceived to be pushing the envelope in terms of discounts. Appraisers were also stunned over how the regs essentially redefined long-accepted definitions of fair market value, marketability, and control.

A record number of speakers, including from the AICPA, ASA and NACVA, appeared at the IRS public hearing in Washington, D.C., to fight the regs. They all agreed that the rules are so broad and convoluted that they should be withdrawn permanently or, barring that, completely revised. At the time of this writing, the IRS has made no announcement on the fate of the proposed regs. Regardless of what happens, the matter demonstrates how the valuation profession can mobilize and speak with one compelling voice over issues of great concern. *BVU* applauds their efforts, which were also demonstrated in the collaboration over the CEIV credential.

CEIV. A groundbreaking development was the close collaboration of major valuation professional organizations (VPOs) to develop a new credential, Certified in Entity and Intangible Valuations™ (CEIV™), for professionals involved in fair value for financial reporting. For the first time, the AICPA, ASA, and RICS joined forces to bring more consistency to the profession and reduce the number of questions auditors raise about the valuations. A mandatory performance framework (MPF) has now been finalized, clearing the way for the new credential's launch. The MPF will require professionals to better document their assumptions, which will help make auditors more comfortable with valuation estimates, especially for intangibles. This will also ease the concerns of the SEC and PCAOB, which have been critical of the valuation profession in this regard. This issue has an article with more details on the new CEIV credential.

Methodology. The debate over the discount for lack of marketability (DLOM) heated up over the application (or misapplication) of a DLOM in New York statutory appraisal actions. An article, "NY's Unfair Application of Shareholder-Level Marketability Discounts," written by Gil Matthews and Michelle Patterson (both with Sutter Securities) (January 2016 *BVU*), triggered comments from readers who agree the problem lies with judges who lack training in valuation concepts and often build their value determinations on questionable or stale precedent. In the March issue, William C. Quackenbush (Advent Valuation Advisors), former chair of the ASA's business valuation committee, presented a follow-up article.

This also triggered a call for action for the profession to speak with one voice and eliminate the confusion over the use of discounts. One valuation expert offers up some nomenclature and—more importantly—a framework that he hopes will help in developing a common language that could be used in valuation reports (see the August 2016 *BVU*).

Speaking of DLOM, BVR conducted a survey on how practitioners quantify DLOM, which found that, while restricted stock studies and pre-IPO studies remain the most cited methodologies for quantifying a DLOM, their usage has declined a little. The results don't immediately signal any tidal shift in usage of methods, although we point out that the use of option price models has gained steam.

In the healthcare arena, a different approach to measuring the fair market value of physician compensation is designed to help ward off a crackdown by the government, which has been winning False Claims Act (FCA) lawsuits against a number of hospitals, reaping hundreds of millions of dollars in fines. The lawsuits have emerged out of the trend of hospitals acquiring medical practices, and the FMV of physician compensation is a key element of these cases. Instead of paying physicians the median compensation, hospitals could set fair market value compensation based on the resource-based relative value scale (RBRVS). This is a fee schedule that uses a complex formula to determine the payment due a physician for patient services and takes into account such factors as the resources used, practice expenses, malpractice expenses, geographic location, and others. Mark O. Dietrich explains this approach in the new edition of the *BVR/AHLA Guide to Healthcare Industry Finance and Valuation,* and it is also discussed in two articles, one in the April 2016 *BVU* and the other in the December 2016 *BVU.*

The July 2016 issue of *BVU* follows the continued interest in the implied private-company pricing line (IPCPL), a model designed to better estimate the cost of capital for small private companies (revenues below $150 million). The model was first introduced in 2012, and *BVU* ran a series of articles starting in 2013. The author of an article in the *Value Examiner* called into question certain aspects of the model, and the IPCPL developers responded. This kind of debate is healthy because, if the business valuation profession is to advance, it must be open to new ideas, techniques, and methodologies.

Data and publications. There was a significant expansion to private-company business transaction data in *Pratt's Stats,* which now has almost 26,000 acquired private companies plus up to 150 data points that include six valuation multiples and 13 financial ratios. BIZCOMPS, *Done Deals,* and the *IBA Market Database* also expanded their number of private-company transactions.

Pratt's Stats added 250 European transactions, including 132 deals from the United Kingdom and 38 deals from Germany (all converted into U.S. dollars). In 2016, the database rolled out a number of new features, including 45 additional data fields, including fields dedicated to purchase price allocation, franchise designation, and real estate asset value. There's also an enhanced ability to find more comps as transactions can now include up to three SIC or NAICS codes to reflect multiple lines of business. The search functionality was also improved, and you can now search by region, EBITDA, seller's discretionary earnings, and more.

Duff & Phelps released a fourth book in its line of cost of capital resources, the *2016 International Valuation Handbook - Industry Cost of Capital,* which provides cost of capital data and statistics from industries around the globe. The cornerstone book in this series, the *Valuation Handbook - Guide to Cost of Capital,* went through a number of refinements and additions for its 2016 edition, such as an expanded Chapter 12, which provides detailed answers to questions practitioners submitted. The series of four separate handbooks are all published annually with updated data and optional intrayear updates. (For a review of the 2016 edition, see the June *BVU*). Also in 2016, Duff & Phelps acquired the rights to the *SBBI Classic Yearbook* from Morningstar, which provides a history of the returns on the capital markets (i.e., "Stocks, Bonds, Bills, and Inflation") in the United States from 1926 to the present.

BVR added to its line of industry-specific special reports under the series title *What It's Worth.* New entries in the series are: hotels, breweries, wineries, auto dealerships, legal marijuana firms, and architecture/engineering firms.

Professor Aswath Damodaran (New York University Stern School of Business) issued his 2016 edition of "Equity Risk Premiums (ERP): Determinants, Estimation and Implications." It is 136 pages of data-rich material that gives a detailed picture of ERPs. He is a strong proponent of implied equity risk premiums, which are forward-looking estimates that are extracted by examining stock prices today and expected cash flows in the future.

We must mention that 2016 saw Shannon Pratt continue his long tradition of making significant contributions to the profession by co-writing several books. *Analyzing Complex Appraisals for Business Professionals,* 1st Edition (with John Lifflander), is focused on how to value businesses with considerable real assets. He also contributed to *A Consensus View—Q&A Guide to Financial Valuation,* 2016 edition (with James R. Hitchner and Jay Fishman). This book is in Q&A format with answers to over 150 of the most important business valuation questions these experts have been asked over the years. Both books are available from BVR.

Standards and guidance. The Appraisal Practices Board (APB) of The Appraisal Foundation adopted APB VFR Valuation Advisory No. 2: The Valuation of Customer-Related Assets. The 116-page document offers voluntary guidance on recognized valuation methods and techniques and "is not intended to be an authoritative valuation standard." Customer-related assets can include customer lists, order or production backlog, and contractual (and noncontractual) customer relationships.

A third exposure draft was issued of proposed changes for the 2018-19 edition of the *Uniform Standards of Professional Appraisal Practice.* Some of the issues under consideration deal with the definition of report and communication of assignment results. There's also a proposed revision of the definition of appraisal review, as well as splitting the existing Standard 3 into two standards.

The FASB issued three significant new accounting standards on revenue recognition, leasing, and impairment. The standard on revenue recognition is effective 2018 for calendar-year companies, with the other two kicking in shortly thereafter.

Regulatory. Aside from the Section 2704 matter, another major regulatory event occurred in 2016. In a long-awaited decision, the Department of Labor removed appraisals entirely—not just ESOP appraisals—from fiduciary treatment in its final rules designed to strengthen retirement security. The provision was part of extensive rules that require brokers and other advisers providing investment advice on retirement accounts to adhere to an ERISA-based fiduciary regimen. The proposed rule carved out just ESOP appraisals, but the final rules exempted all appraisals and fairness opinions.

In other news, the PCAOB issued a staff inspection brief that revealed that fair value measurements continued to be one of the key areas of inspection focus. The number of audit deficiencies regarding auditors' testing of fair value measurements associated with business combinations has increased. Plus, there have been frequent deficiencies in evaluating impairment analyses for goodwill and other long-lived assets.

In the healthcare arena, there are a few important developments worth keeping an eye on. One is accountable care organizations in the Medicare Shared Services Program. These groups do not seem to be achieving the savings that were anticipated, so this is an area to watch. Another issue is the merit-based incentive payment system, which will move a substantial amount of physician payments under the fee-for-service Medicare system to being merit-based. The Trump administration's "repeal and replace" stance on Obamacare is not expected to affect the move to payments based on quality. Another matter that came into the spotlight during 2016 was talk about the repeal of the Stark Law. But some experts believe that it's highly unlikely that the law will be repealed in its entirety because it generates a great deal of revenue for the government. There may be some changes to revenue-sharing rules between hospitals and physicians because the government wants them to work closer together and revenue sharing is the source of a lot of the Stark Law issues.

Legal. Page 235 has a rundown of the top valuation-related court cases from 2016. They include the Delaware Chancery decision in *Dell,* probably the most talked about statutory fair value decision of the year, which arose out of the 2013 management buyout led by the company's founder, Michael Dell. The court found that the deal price did not reflect fair value even though it recognized that the board and Dell himself made every effort to perform a proper sale. The court relied on a post-transaction DCF analysis for its fair value determination.

One case to keep an eye out for in 2017 is a pending Tax Court case in which an S corp valuation model is being used for the first time. The Van Vleet model (S corporation economic adjustment model) is being used in a pending U.S. Tax Court case (*Cecil et al. v. Commissioner of Internal Revenue*), which involves a gift of shares in a company that operates the famous Biltmore estate, which is now a tourist attraction. A much-debated issue in the valuation community is tax affecting the earnings of a pass-through entity (PTE), and there is no definitive answer. The tax-affecting issue has been argued in a number of Tax Court cases (most notably the *Gross* case). In all of these cases, the IRS and the Tax Court have refuted the notion that shareholder-level taxes affect a firm's value, so the valuation conclusions in these cases were based on earnings not being tax affected. The valuation community disagrees, so a number of models have been developed that are designed to reflect the impact of shareholder taxes on value.

In 2016, BVR updated a helpful tool for valuation experts involved in divorce engagements. It is a chart entitled "Charting Goodwill Jurisprudence," which gives you an at-a-glance look at a state's basic position toward enterprise and professional goodwill. You can find it in the Free Resources section of the BVR website (www.bvresources.com).

Global. The International Valuation Standards Council (IVSC) had a busy 2016 as it focused on the rollout of its 2017 standards (IVS 2017) and the implementation of the group's organizational and strategic plans for the next two years. IVS 2017 is set to be issued in early 2017, and the IVSC will push for worldwide adoption. At the Standards Board meeting, Sir David Tweedie said, bluntly, that "valuation is not a profession. If valuers wish to become a profession, and continue with self-regulation, then VPOs must adopt IVS and enforce compliance—no exceptions." IVSC and the World Association of Valuation Organisations (WAVO) strengthened their ties by signing a memorandum of cooperation (MOC) to jointly promote the importance of adopting the international valuation standards. Also, The Appraisal Foundation released a document titled "A Bridge From USPAP to IVS," which connects the two sets of standards to help make appraisals compliant with both sets of standards. This was a significant step toward establishing a set of globally accepted ethical and professional standards for valuation.

The IVSC also created a new Standards Review Board that will amend and approve international valuation standards. The new board will have two focused subject matter expertise boards reporting to it: a Tangible Assets Standards Board (covering real estate, plant and machinery, and personal property) and a Business Valuation Standards Board. The new boards will become operational once IVS 2017 is issued, and it is expected that the first meetings will take place in March 2017.

Work toward a global valuation credential moved forward as the International Institute of Business Valuers (iiBV) formed a special task force to consider the details of an international business valuation designation for member VPOs to offer to their constituents. The areas of focus include: (1)

expected competencies and curriculum of the international BV designation; (2) delivery mode, description of qualification, and qualification process; and (3) roles and responsibilities of the iiBV and the iiBV's member VPOs in the administration of the international BV designation. One of the recommendations is the creation of a designation to be known as the "IBV" (International Business Valuer) that would be appended to the qualified VPO's designation and administered by the VPO. The iiBV is developing an implementation plan for the global designation that is scheduled to launch this year.

In the area of global quality control, the International Association of Consultants, Valuators and Analysts (IACVA) and the World Association of Valuation Organizations (WAVO) issued a final version of global quality control standards for valuations. The standards put forth a peer review process similar to what's used in the accounting profession and that can also serve to head off government regulation in this area. The next step is for IACVA to develop an exposure draft on peer review procedures (see the article on page 246 for more details).

Of course, the Brexit vote was a big development in world news, and leading global valuation experts and finance professors chimed in on its impact on cost of capital. During a Duff & Phelps webinar, one message they all stressed is to maintain internal consistency between the elements of cost of capital and the current economic environment. Also, you need to consider that there may be a "new normal" in terms of interest rates, risk premiums, and growth. In the wake of Brexit, Duff & Phelps did not change its recommended U.S. ERP of 5.5%.

In 2016, NACVA launched the Global Association of Certified Valuators and Analysts (GACVA) to "open its doors to the international financial consulting community and those organizations and individuals interested in obtaining, holding, and supporting" the various valuation and financial forensics credentials the group provides. GACVA is an umbrella group for international chapters, which currently include Africa, Canada, Europe, the Middle East, and Taiwan.

Practice management. In a *BVWire* poll, practice management was the most cited concern for 2016. Troubling issues include competition, fee pressures, hiring, and succession planning. BVR also conducted its Firm Economics Survey, which examines BV firm performance, compensation, billing rates, marketing and practice development, and more. Some highlights:

- About two-thirds of business valuation firms say they expect to do more business than the previous year. Most of the revenue is coming from certain areas, the top area being tax, gifts, and estates, respondents say, which represents about one-third of total revenue on average.

- Almost nine out of 10 (86%) BV firms say they do litigation-related engagements. About a quarter of firms report that more than half of their business valuation revenue comes from such work. For the others, 22% say it makes up from 26% to 50% of their BV revenue and the rest (40%) say it represents up to 25% of their BV revenue.

- Traditional face-to-face techniques continue to be the best methods to bring in valuation business, such as one-on-one meetings with prospective clients, public speaking, and joining business organizations such as associations, committees, and boards.

Education. In 2016, BVR was proud to continue to support the Business Valuation Challenge, a college program created by Professor Herbert Kierulff of Seattle Pacific University. This marked the fifth year for the event, and it was hosted by the J. Mack Robinson College of Business and Department of Finance at Georgia State University (GSU). Teams from 18 colleges and universities participated in a "real world" competition during which teams of students value an actual company and present their results. BVR provides data, resources, and other materials for the Challenge, and GSU worked with the AICPA to coordinate industry mentors for each of the teams. The top teams in the 2016 Challenge were: GSU (Honors), GSU (Panthers), Mississippi College, the University of Tennessee, and Seattle Pacific University. BV firms interested in becoming involved and supporting this event can contact Dr. David Beard of GSU at dbeard@gsu.ed.

That's a look at some of what happened in 2016. We look forward to keeping you fully informed of important developments during 2017, which should prove to be an exciting year!

Business Valuation Industry in India Is Poised for Sustained Growth

By Bharat Kanodia, ASA, Veristrat Inc.
(San Francisco, Calif., U.S.A. and New Delhi, India)

Editor's note: This is the first in a series of articles Business Valuation Update *will publish in the coming months detailing the state of the business valuation industry in India. This article gives an overview of the current valuation market in India, including the provision of outsourced valuation services.*

The valuation industry in India is still in its infancy, but it is on the verge of growing rapidly.

Some of the demand drivers include International Financial Reporting Standards (IFRS) requirements that will boost fair value work, cross-border opportunities for valuation work related to 409a, private equity and hedge funds, and providing outsourcing services for U.S. firms (research, modeling, and full support). Also, new accounting standards soon to become effective will require publicly listed companies to disclose the value of brands they acquire.

A look back. Historically, tangible assets had to be valued for bank collaterals or financings and were mostly performed by either Indian Administrative Service (IAS) officers or other government officials or notary officers. Such officers performed valuations not because of their expertise in valuation but due to their credibility from being associated with a government entity or an authoritative organization.

Investment bankers, formerly known as merchant bankers, performed business or intangible valuations. They, too, were associated with government-owned banks or the Securities and Exchange Bureau of India (SEBI)—an SEC-equivalent agency for India. In a few cases, institutional companies such as Tata Consultancy Services (TCS) would perform them but were not considered in the same regard as the other government-based organizations.

Following India's economic liberalization in the 1990s, intended to expand the role of private and foreign investment, global financial institutions and Big Four accounting firms built large-scale operations in India. This ushered in the need for more sizable valuation projects. However, local chartered accounting firms perform tangible and intangible valuations that are required for small-to-midsize businesses.

Current picture. It is estimated that there are approximately 2,000 valuation professionals currently in India who are performing valuations on a full-time basis for domestic or global clients, though availability of talent is always a struggle. No formal university-based valuation education is currently offered, nor do U.S.-based valuation professional organizations (VPOs) offer courses in India. As a result, the primary methods currently available to engage valuation professionals in India is either to look for professionals working toward a Chartered Financial Analyst (CFA) designation or to attempt to spot talent that has the potential and intellectual ability to learn on the job.

Valuations currently performed by domestic firms in India are typically for tax, financing, estate, and accounting purposes. The valuations for global clients are centered mostly around financial reporting, equity and investment research or due diligence, transactions, tax, and transfer pricing. Economic liberalization in India did more than just lure foreign investment to perform offshore work. The exponential growth that India has seen in the last 15 to 20 years has caused the demand for domestic valuations to increase dramatically. Consequently, the firms performing such valuations have to increase their internal capabilities.

India's primary competitive advantage in the world of commerce is attributed to the lack of a language barrier with English-speaking countries. As such, it allows the Indian valuation industry to compete and offer its valuation capabilities toward increasing valuation demand worldwide.

The global valuations performed in India have only been done since 2006, after U.S. institutions introduced IFRS and stricter financial reporting standards. It is estimated that current distribution of valuations performed for domestic versus global clients is fairly equal. This equity of market share may continue, based on both the increased awareness of the availability of global valuation services being performed in India and the country's own GDP growth.

All the Big Four accounting firms have large operations in India. These operations are in many cities, and they conduct domestic and global valuations from their India operations. Their India employees are performing most of the U.S.-based valuation audit review work. Their employees are not only doing the basic valuations, but are also emerging as thought leaders in this arena. Other players having a team in India perform valuations include the majority of major or regional U.S. banks, large valuation firms, regional accounting firms, and other small-to-midsize valuation firms.

Outsourcing services. Most standard valuation components can now be performed in India, including, in some cases, partner-level reviews. The cost for valuation services U.S. firms perform in India on an outsourced basis is currently averaging about 50% of the cost of a valuation performed domestically on a long-term basis. The specific tasks performed vary based on the partnership agreement, risk management needs of the client, and qualifications of the audit team. The tasks now performed in India include:

- Data collection;
- Data review;
- Industry and economic research;
- Competitive and comparable analysis;
- Model population;
- Financial modeling;
- Math checks;
- Report writing;
- Reviewing valuation reports;
- Reviewing financial models;
- Reviewing and responding to audit questions; and
- Training.

Indian valuation outsourcing companies are being leveraged beyond transactional activities or basic modelling. More global companies are looking to Indian firms to provide high-value activities such complex financial modelling, responding to audit queries, and, in some cases, training of U.S.-based staff.

A U.S.-based valuation expert typically does the final valuation report sign-off for the majority of cases where a team based in India does the valuation. While certified valuation experts in India with CFA, ASA, CVA, and other designations are available to provide the final review and sign off, this talent remains scarce in the market. As a result, it's not efficient to try to offshore this component of the valuation.

I have been involved in India outsourcing since 2008, when the valuation industry there was virtually nonexistent. Since then, it has come a long way, and, with growth awareness and acceptance of a global workforce, the growth of this industry is limitless. It wouldn't be surprising to see industry growth at 20% to 25% over the next five to 10 years.

***Bharat Kanodia**, ASA, focuses on venture and private equity valuations with SaaS technology and has assisted with various valuation and audit firms in optimizing their U.S. operations. Bharat has worked with Ipreo, Veristrat, American Appraisal, and Silicon Valley Bank Analytics and has signed off on over 4,000 valuation opinions with $800 billion in assets.*

Seismic Shifts Underway in Business Valuation Practice in the U.K.

By Andrew Strickland,
Scrutton Bland, (United Kingdom)

More refined techniques are now sweeping away ideas and methodologies surrounding business valuation that have held sway for decades in the United Kingdom.

During a recent presentation I made to members of the forensic and valuations groups of the Institute of Chartered Accountants in England and Wales, I observed that the speed of change we are experiencing is remarkable in light of the fact that these static notions have been around for such a long time. Here is an overview of what's going on.

Credentials and standards. It is generally believed (often with little justification) that all qualified accountants should be sufficiently competent to undertake a valuation of a business undertaking. The competencies in evidence range from the specialist business appraisers working within the Big Four, together with other firms such as Duff & Phelps, FTI Consulting, and some specialist valuation boutiques at the top of the food chain. We then proceed by gradations, down to the lone sole practitioner with a hazy notion of business valuation based on some valuations undertaken for tax purposes long ago.

In the U.K., no separate, clearly defined body offers an appropriate credential in business valuation. Readers may be surprised that the Royal Institution of Chartered Surveyors (RICS) currently has very little footprint in the U.K. in the area of business valuation. RICS members will certainly undertake valuations in respect of trade-related properties, such as care homes for the elderly, certain hotels, gas stations, and similar. However, the current perception is that they remain firmly anchored to real estate, at least for now.

In this vacuum, some firms provide their own internal training and others put their valuation teams through the ASA's training program. Others use the CFA qualification as a suitable development tool.

As an example of a profile of a valuation expert in the U.K., let me say that I am a Chartered Accountant, which is broadly equivalent to a CPA in the U.S. I undertake business valuation work for various purposes including:

- Shareholder disputes;
- Divorce;
- Capital gains tax, inheritance tax, and tax on employment-related securities;
- Under the provisions of the constitution of corporates in respect of share transfers in an expert determination; and
- Advisory work in respect of corporate finance transactions, including leveraged management buyouts and trade sales.

I have also had some experience in the valuation of intangibles for the purposes of purchase price allocation on acquisitions.

I am also a director of the International Institute of Business Valuers (iiBV), and I chair its education committee. The CEIV credential being developed in the United States, in response to pressures from the SEC, is a matter of some consequence in parts of the U.K. business valuation topography. Whether this will give added impetus to RICS as one of the entities behind this initiative remains to be seen. Some consider the CEIV credential as the harbinger of increasing regulation and control of business valuation in the U.K., initially in valuation for financial reporting purposes and then extending into other areas.

This is a landscape that is undergoing significant change, as evidenced by the way that business valuation disputes are now being argued in the courts. The selection of a price earnings ratio from the public markets as the starting point for a business valuation has been long seen as a particularly blunt instrument. It is now being increasingly recognized that this has all of the sophistication of a flint hand axe. There is now far greater sophistication in the valuation tools that are used in practice, and those who are serious in their business valuation work recognize the importance of improved computational methods.

It seems likely that the publication of International Valuation Standards 2017 by the IVSC in January 2017 will lead to an increasing standardization of vocabulary, with bases, approaches, and methods being more precisely defined. I also consider that there will be a continuing improvement in standards of process, file creation, and reporting with respect to business valuation assignments.

Legal arena. The U.S. and the U.K. (together with Canada, Australia, and New Zealand) share the same medieval foundations for their legal systems, the ever-evolving and expanding systems of common law. In the U.K., common law is laced with a strong dose of pragmatism: The courts have a tendency to thirst for a proportionate answer in preference to a perfect answer.

The U.K. legal system has also identified that justice delayed can be justice denied. Some 20 years ago, the process of litigation started to show signs of collapsing under its own weight. There was the prospect of lawyers employing seemingly endless delaying tactics as a means of wearing down the other side; the standard tactical response to a claim was a counterclaim of significant size. The counterclaim may have had the flimsiest of foundations, but it served a purpose of obfuscation and delay. After months or years, as the court hearing approached, there would be last-minute attempts at settlement rather than trying to defend a threadbare case whose only virtue was that of being able to create delay.

The reforms to litigation procedures in the U.K. now mean that the parties are expected to seek mediation at an early stage, once the disagreement has been identified and the nature of the claim assessed. Although not obligatory, the parties are expected to mediate and to seek a compromise solution outside the court process. For many claims, the costs of litigation are such that the prospect of several days at trial forces compromise on the parties.

It has also long been a part of civil litigation in the U.K. that parties are meant to disclose all matters on which they are to rely in support of their position. There is virtually no prospect for a theatrical ambush in court if the information has been available to one of the parties before the court hearing takes place. The open disclosure of all important matters between the parties is therefore central to the litigation process.

No *Daubert* equivalent. As with the U.S., the common law concept of precedent can act as a brake on the development of current valuation ideas. However, there is not the same degree of rigor applied as seems to be present in the U.S. There is no direct equivalent to the *Daubert* challenge. The expert succeeds or fails according to his or her ability to impress the judge with the quality of the evidence and the way in which the expert deals with questions during cross-examination. A capable valuation expert should be able to demonstrate the quality of his or her opinions over those of the unschooled novice who is oblivious to current valuation thinking.

One of the impacts of the need for proportionality in contentious business valuation is that most business valuations for marital breakup purposes are undertaken on the basis of having a single expert who is jointly instructed.

Further evidence of the pragmatic approach the courts in the U.K. favor is a recognition that no point in any valuation computation is more precise than its least precise component. There have been cases in which the cost of capital has been computed with a degree of science (using the buildup method, for example), but this remains a relatively new development. There is also, in the U.K., at least for the present, a willingness to accept professional opinion, without the need necessarily for this to be supported by external authority.

Market approach dominates. For a very considerable number of years, the courts showed a robust resistance to the use of DCF techniques. They were suspicious that modest changes in assumption could have major impacts on value. However, this has changed over the last seven years, and now the DCF has been the main driver of the valuation conclusions in a small collection of cases.

The U.K. equivalent of the IRS, known as HM Revenue & Customs, also operates with a strong dose of pragmatism in respect of valuations for tax purposes. It will be seeking proportionality in respect to reaching agreements. It is also focused almost entirely on the markets approach, but there are often some rather strained attempts at linking the valuations of small private companies to the price earnings ratios or dividend yields of public companies. It is only in larger cases in which there will be a drill down in order to understand different capital structures and other factors that may differentiate the relevant company from the public guideline companies being used for comparison.

Sources of data. As for information used for the market approach, in the U.K., a mature stock market has several layers:

- The Financial Times Stock Exchange (FTSE) 100 is the largest 100 companies by market capitalization in the UK. These companies tend to have a very high international component to their earnings and make up the largest component of the total market capitalization.
- The FTSE 250 is the next 250 largest companies. These have a far greater domestic focus and are more likely to reflect the realities of the U.K. economy. The FTSE 100 and FTSE 250 are then aggregated to produce the FTSE 350 index. This is a relatively deep and liquid market.
- There is then the FTSE small cap, and, combined with the FTSE 350, this gives the FTSE All Share index.
- There is a secondary market known as the alternative investment market, or AIM. The average market capitalization of companies on this market is something like £50 million. The market prices of these companies need to be treated with some caution as they often reflect only thin trading volumes.
- There is a bond market in the U.K., and this is some six times as large as the equities markets.

As in the U.S., passive investment styles, through use of tracker exchange-traded funds and tracker open-ended investment companies, have been taking a rapidly increasing proportion of the markets in recent years.

There are various indices maintained that seek to provide information on pricing of transactions in private-company shares. The usefulness of these indices is limited by their lack of transparency because the underlying individual transactions are not disclosed.

As with other such information sources, the entities public companies take over will tend to have a disproportionate representation when compared with the actual population of private-company share transactions.

Conclusion. This is a very exciting time in the U.K. amid the massive shifting of the tectonic plates of the business valuation profession. And I do not see that pace of change slowing anytime soon.

Andrew Strickland, *for many years a corporate partner at Scrutton Bland, is now a consultant to the firm. He is a member of the valuation committee of the Institute of Chartered Accountants in England and Wales (ICAEW) and is on the board of the International Institute of Business Valuers.*

Time to Update the Guiding Principles to a Valuation Report

By Robert E. Kleeman Jr.,
OnPointe Financial Valuation Group LLC, (Englewood, Colo., USA)

In my 40 years in the business valuation profession, I have seen the typical valuation report go from three or four pages to 50 pages or more. The increasing complexity that has become inherent in the business valuation community has mandated a good part of this change.

The purpose of this article is to attempt to provide the preparers and users of these reports the knowledge to understand what is really being said in those pages. Many years ago, I provided CPE seminars on many business valuation subjects, including report writing. At that time, I indicated that the elements of a great valuation report could be summarized using the acronym TACO, which stood for:

Teach
Analyze
Communicate
Opine

Today, I find that the TACO concept must be taken to the next step, and I have developed the five "principles" (5 P's) of the report. I believe that, if the valuation expert keeps these principles in mind, it can be valuable in helping to ensure the overall quality and reliability of the report. For the individual reviewing and critiquing a report, these principles can help in the evaluation. With that in mind, let's review what I consider the five guiding principles to a successful valuation report.

1. Precision. (Definition: 1. The state or quality of being precise; exactness. 2. The ability of a measurement to be consistently reproduced.)

One of the first things I do when reviewing a business valuation report is to look at the opinion or conclusion of value. The more precise the conclusion is, the more concern I have as to the validity of the appraisal. I recently reviewed a report covering a 100% equity interest in a closely held company, and the appraiser determined the value of the company was $5,288,372.46. No appraiser today can operate with that degree of precision. In fact, if we look to the old standby, Revenue Ruling 59-60, we see that Sec. 3.01 states:

> A determination of fair market value, being a question of fact, will depend upon the circumstance in each case. No formula can be devised that will be generally applicable to the multitude of different valuation issues arising in estate and gift tax cases. Often, an appraiser will find wide difference of opinion as to the fair market value of a particular stock. In resolving such differences, he should maintain a reasonable attitude in recognition of the fact that valuation is not an exact science. A sound valuation will be based upon all the relevant facts, but the elements of common sense, informed judgment and reasonableness must enter into the process of weighing those facts and determining their aggregate significance.[1]

As appraisers, we must make subjective decisions regarding a myriad of items that go into the valuation conclusion. What is the specific company risk profile? What accounting adjustments must be made to the benefit stream to reflect "normalized" operations? What are the appropriate discounts for marketability and minority interests?

I would suggest that if competent business valuation professionals prepared two reports and the final opinions of value are within 10% of each other, they might well both be correct.

When we look at the real world, the public stock markets, we see various analysts following a specific stock, and we see a wide array of projected earnings and even pricing targets for the stock. Why does one analyst rate the stock as a buy, while another thinks that it is hold, and still another rates the security as a sell? The only precise value on a block of closely held stock is the actual cash that is ultimately paid in an arm's-length transaction, and we as appraisers cannot determine the ultimate payment.

2. Practicality (Definition: "The quality of being of practical use." "Of, relating to, governed by, or acquired through practice or action, rather than theory or speculation.")

What are the practical aspects of the report? Is it written in a manner to educate the reader, or is it filled with undefined technical terms and industry jargon? A well-written report helps the reader understand what the expert is trying to convey and why the appraiser should be believed.

Is the benefit stream based on historic information or is it based on future income projections? In short, is the most important part of the valuation, the measurement of future economic benefits, practical considering the facts surrounding the entity, the industry, and the economy? As Dr. Pratt would remind us: "The economic interest measure capitalized should represent *expected* future economic income."[2] If the report uses projected benefits, are they reasonable based on the historic information?

How was the capitalization rate achieved? What methodologies did the appraiser use? Are the conclusions of value well explained and documented in the report or were just conclusions without

1 Revenue Ruling 59-60, 1959-1 CB 237.

2 Shannon P. Pratt, *Valuing a Business, The Analysis and Appraisal of Closely Held Companies*, 5th ed., McGraw-Hill, 2008, page 247.

support provided? It always benefits the reader if the appraiser clearly defines the work done and, where practical, provides the calculations and exhibits to support the conclusions.

3. Plausibility (Definition: "Seemingly or apparently valid, likely or acceptable; credible; merit belief or acceptance.")

Every appraisal report must include assumptions the appraiser made. This is a natural part of the appraisal process. The question is: Are these assumptions plausible? Do we have an entity that has demonstrated mediocre earnings in the past years that is now showing projections with great improvement in future earnings? Or do we have just the opposite, an entity that has been very profitable but now is showing mediocre or no earnings? In real life, these situations can exist, the company, the industry, and/or the economy impacts any current value. Company fortunes can improve, or they can decline. A plausible report explains the impact of those outside variables to demonstrate the reasons for the apparent changes in economic results.

What sources did the appraiser use to get economic data? What about industry data? The data are readily available but can be expensive. But, without the data, how does the appraiser present a plausible discussion regarding the company's future considering the expectations of the industry and the economy? If the economy is expected to grow by 3% over the next five years, and the data indicate that the industry will grow at 3% over the same period, what data are presented to support an indication that the subject company will grow by 5% a year over the next five years? It might be true, but, without sufficient support, is it plausible?

What about the state/local economy? Unless the subject company operates in a national or global marketplace, the local economy will impact the company more than the national economy. As I write this, the Colorado economy is booming, while the Illinois economy is still in the doldrums. The local economy will impact the market the company operates in.

4. Proficiency (Definition: "Having or marked by an advanced degree of competence, as in an art, vocation, profession or branch of learning"; "a person who exhibits competence, an expert.")

Does the report adequately demonstrate the proficiency of the appraiser? I'm not suggesting that a first-time appraiser cannot produce a credible report, but what I am suggesting is that there should be adequate information in the report to allow the reader to determine the background and qualifications of the appraiser. Also, did more than one individual work on the report, and what are the qualifications of those individuals? It is not unusual to find out that the signer of the report had little or nothing to do with the production of the report.

Full-time vs. part-time practice. During my many years as a practitioner, I have consulted with many firms regarding the establishment and/or development of a business valuation niche as part of their CPA practice. In the 1980s and 1990s, I was of the belief that you could successfully operate a small-niche business valuation practice on a part-time basis. Today, I don't believe that is possible.

In 1998, Shannon Pratt published the "BV Body of Knowledge" as a study guide for the Accredited in Business Valuation (ABV) exam. Looking at that publication today, it is clear that the skill needed today to prepare a business valuation has greatly increased since 1998 when Pratt published that tome. Just as tax and audit have become much more detailed and specialized, so has business valuation. In my opinion, it is difficult enough to maintain a proficiency in business valuation today while practicing on a full-time basis, and I find it difficult to believe that a part-time practitioner in business valuation can maintain the skill set needed to complete a complex valuation assignment.

Let me be clear: Although I am a licensed CPA, I certainly am not capable of performing an audit on a company's financial statements. I performed my last audit engagement in 1974. The same with tax. I was a practicing tax professional until 1980 and was the partner in charge of our tax practice. I'm not sure I am qualified to perform a significant tax engagement today. I find that it is difficult enough to keep up with the advancements, as well as the controversies, in the business valuation arena. Business valuation is constantly evolving. Look at the issues of pass-through entities, the appropriate use of beta, and weighted average cost of capital, among others.

I always ask the age-old question: If I start having chest pains, do I want a part-time general practitioner or a full-time cardiologist to take care of me? I think the answer is obvious.

Does the appraisal report demonstrate the competency of the individual(s) that performed the engagement? Both the report and the underlying work papers must demonstrate the appraiser's competency to take on the engagement. Just because the appraiser hasn't performed 100-plus valuations or that he or she has never performed a valuation in this specific industry does not disqualify the appraiser. Valuation theory in a vacuum is useless, as is industry experience, if you don't know how to apply appropriate valuation techniques to the data. Many years ago, I had an opposing expert who was not a valuation expert but was an expert in the operations of the specific industry of the company being valued. The industry expert testified that he had performed more than 100 valuations using his methodology, so it had to be correct. Unfortunately, the judge stated that just because he had used the same methodology 100-plus times did not make the methodology believable and appropriate for the valuation. A practitioner with strong business valuation skills can obtain industry expertise from many sources to include industry research data, trade associations, as well as the client. Unfortunately, the opposite is not usually true.

The report should discuss in detail both the valuation techniques used in the engagement as well as the sources and details of the industry information that is pertinent to the specific engagement. It should also detail the qualifications of the individuals who worked on the engagement.

Certifications. I get a lot of mail regarding business valuation conferences, courses, and webinars. What has surprised me is how many of the presenters have 10 certifications or more behind their names. In one case, I counted 16 separate certifications (not counting the MBA and LLM) of an individual. How can one individual achieve and stay current with all those specialty designations? More important than the certifications is that the report needs to have clear language that allows the reader to judge the competency of the writer of the report.

5. Price (Definition: "the amount of money expected, required, or given in payment for something.")

Let me make it clear that I am not suggesting that the higher the price tag on the valuation report, the better the quality of the report is. Price alone does not make a quality report. I believe it is important for the user of the report to have some understanding of what it takes to perform a business valuation engagement. The cost of the report may indicate issues that need to be addressed.

I have had the privilege of talking to many business valuation professionals over the years, and some things are somewhat constant in the performance of a valuation:

- The typical USPAP-compliant valuation report requires between 70 and 80 hours of professional time, with more than 70% of that time performed by the BV professional, rather than the staff. If we do that math, how can an appraiser perform a USPAP-compliant report for $3,000 to $5,000? Is the professional actually working for less than $75.00 per hour? Or are corners being cut to save costs?

- What about all of the research costs? Industry reports can cost up to $1,000 per industry. Economic reports can cost several thousand dollars a year. That's fine if you are amortizing those costs over 40 or 50 reports a year, but what about only three to five reports a year?

- Can the appraiser adequately demonstrate the prior four P's in a three-to-five-page report?

- Is the report really an "Opinion of Value," or is it something less than that? USPAP, as well as several other professional organizations, allow the appraiser to perform a review report of another appraiser's valuation. However, those review reports are specifically *not* an opinion of value by the person performing the review report.

- What continuing education does the appraiser have in the business valuation practice? This is another cost that must amortized over the various reports the appraiser prepared.

Conclusions and recommendations. There should be no secrets in a business valuation report. When asked to review another appraiser's valuation report, the process always comes down to whether I can replicate the conclusions the appraiser arrived at using only the report provided. There may be points of disagreement, but, if there is sufficient information to allow me to replicate the conclusions, then they can be understood.

As you the reader are reviewing the report, you don't need to replicate the findings, but you do need to ask some basic questions:

- Is the report readable and can I easily understand what information is being conveyed in the report?
- Does the report inform me of the background and expertise of the appraiser?
- Is there appropriate substantiation for the data the appraiser is relying on? Is the economic and industry information reasonable and properly referenced?
- Are potentially contradictory issues discussed and reconciled in the report?
- Does the report demonstrate the very items referred to in Rev Rul. 59-60, i.e., relevant facts, elements of common sense, informed judgment, and reasonableness?

If the reader can say yes to the above questions, then the report is most likely to be of value to the user.

__Robert E. Kleeman Jr.,__ CPA/ABV, ASA, is managing director of OnPointe Financial Valuation Group LLC based in Englewood, Colo. Kleeman has more than 40 years' experience as a CPA and 35-plus years of experience in the valuation of business interests, including both publicly and closely held businesses and intangibles. Kleeman also has extensive experience as an expert witness and has provided testimony regarding business valuation and commercial damage issues.

Look Before You Leap Into Offshoring Some Valuation Components

By Bharat Kanodia, ASA, Veristrat Inc.
(San Francisco, Calif., USA, and New Delhi, India)

Editor's note: This is the second in a series of articles on the business valuation industry in India. The article on page 317 gives an overview of the current valuation market in India. This article goes into detail and also expands on the discussion of outsourced valuation services. Many valuation experts rule out this tactic, but, for those who consider it, here's what to think about.

When firms decide to offshore components of a valuation, they're often seeking the common benefits associated with offshoring: cost optimization, an ability to refocus on client expectations, and the ability to add capacity and capability under a more advantageous cost structure and a mechanism to enhance service quality. These reasons aren't mutually exclusive. Adding talent at a lower price is seen as a way to build service quality and resources to better meet client expectations. Offshoring offers the potential to improve both the top and bottom lines through alignment around these common goals.

However, successful offshoring is usually the result of building a sustainable, long-term business. Practices lose valuable time and resources when offshoring by not considering the long-term evolution of the business and how offshoring will impact it. Instead, they see offshoring as a quick fix or a way to remain competitive with other firms or cope with pricing pressures, without thinking of the impact on the business.

On page 317, we shared an overview of the current state of outsourcing of valuation in India. Here, we'll look at the components of the valuation most commonly outsourced, as well as how the valuation field is evolving in India as the experience and skill level increases.

Talent level, capabilities have increased. The traditional thought around outsourced valuation process was to carve out and send only portions of the valuation engagement to the offshore team. This was due to the fact that, five to 10 years ago, the talent for performing global or U.S.-based valuations in India was almost nonexistent. When companies were lucky to find good talent or groomed their own talent internally, the task of retention was daunting.

While the industry is still in its early stages in India, it has evolved to the point that finding talent has become easier. Retaining it, however, is still an uphill battle. Part of the reason for attrition of staff is that the capable individuals become bored with the tasks that are typically sent offshore. Most companies with an offshore team would only expect that group to perform the preliminary tasks of a valuation engagement. These tasks typically included industry research, economic research, data/model population, and comparable identification. These tasks will keep capable talent engaged only up to a certain point.

Once tasks are mastered over time and are the only ones being assigned, good talent tends to wander and seek bigger and better opportunities. What it is really seeking is better and more value-added tasks, which U.S.-based analysts traditionally did. The staff based in India is no different from the U.S. staff in that it's looking for ways to grow and build skills and seek new challenges.

Companies that looked toward offshoring as a long-term benefit and strategic tool understood that, to groom and retain strong offshore talent, they have to consider their offshore team as an extension of their U.S. team and not just as a means to perform elementary-level work for streamlined costs. As an extension of a U.S. team, an offshore team with the right talent mix can now perform almost all the components of a valuation that are expected from a U.S.-based team.

The core functions that can now be offshored to India with the right team can include audit review responses, training of U.S.-based staff, model development, financial analysis, and complex instruments modelling.

For more details on the tasks that can be done in India, please refer to my prior article on this topic, "Business Valuation Industry in India Is Poised for Sustained Growth," on page 317.

Types of firms now offshoring. Firms or individual practitioners can do offshoring to expand their team without taking on the liability or cost of hiring U.S.-based talent. Large and regional-sized banks, Big Four accounting firms, regional audit firms, and small-to-large valuation firms are all either offshoring teams to India or actively looking to do so. A company looking for a partner to explore offshoring in India has a wide variety of business types to look for when trying to find the right partner.

The growing variety of valuers operating in India is important because the most important aspect of selecting a partner is ensuring that your cultures and goals are aligned. Ideally, you would also want to work with a partner that has a strong foothold in valuation, not just someone who does any type of offshoring. This will help the partners get access to the best talent because they'll know it is a better opportunity and they would be able to groom that talent for long-term mutual benefit.

I have seen folks partner with large Indian firms that employ tens of thousands of people just because they are established and may have the right corporate structure or web presence. But bigger isn't always better—this approach tends to work well only if you, too, are a very large company and are only looking for a large offshore partner.

Other companies will contract with an individual or a group of individuals to serve as their offshore team. This, too, has its cons, as individual sentiments and circumstances will often start dictating the course of the offshore team, which, too, could also be detrimental to long-term partnership.

An ideal partner would be a firm, not an individual or a group of individuals, that has an extensive presence in the valuation space and is large enough to have appropriate corporate infrastructure and management already in place, without being bloated or top heavy with its own corporate policies and overhead for you to try to navigate, which can distract you from your own offshoring goals.

How engagements are priced. Three pricing structures are generally used in offshoring. They are listed chronologically in order in the exhibit and range from retail or wholesale, or from flexibility to upside potential.

The costs in the exhibit can vary depending on the size of the relationship and location of the offshoring partner. A partner in smaller Indian cities may be cheaper but would have restricted access to talent. However, an offshoring partner in larger cities such as Mumbai or New Delhi may cost 10% to 20% more but would have better access to talent. In general, it is safe to assume fully burdened costs can vary from $15 per hour to $50 per hour depending on the level of task or quality of talent.

Three Pricing Structures Used in Offshoring

Model	What It Is?	Assessment
Project-based	Fixed cost per project based on complexity. Team can flex depending on complexity and urgency.	+ Flexible option to account for variability - Less cost-effective if number of projects is higher - No dedicated resources leading to learning curve if projects sent over time
Leased employee	Monthly cost per employee. Offshore partner manages costs. Number of projects completed depends on individual capacity.	+ No hassle of cost management - Lack of transparency and upside
Cost plus	Salary plus overhead. Client manages costs. Number of projects completed depends on individual capacity.	+ Transparency achieved on key cost elements + Able to manage staff costs - Risk of cost increases transfers to customer - Offshoring partner provides initial training. Additional training client responsibility.

Three Big Mistakes Firms Make When Offshoring Valuations

Companies see offshoring of valuation work as a way to reduce costs, increase capacity, and better leverage talent, both in the United States and abroad. But the process hasn't always been smooth, and firms have made three key mistakes:

Overselling expectations internally. Even today, firms and practitioners have various reservations about offshoring. Some reservations are very valid, and some are based on perceptions. When someone in a company is trying to go against the grain and champion offshoring, he or she may face various pushbacks. This is normal, and it is to the firm's overall benefit to reconsider all aspects of their business before considering offshoring. However, when internal champions oversell offshoring and careful consideration doesn't happen, the result is often disappointment for internal partners because the promised benefits don't materialize. Instead of overselling, try offshoring as a concept first without allocating too many resources toward it. If it works for you, great. If not, it's not an expensive mistake.

Not finding the right partner. Offshoring is like life: Finding the right partner is critical to success. Your offshoring partner needs to have a strong foothold in valuation, so it can provide you with the best talent to serve your clients. It also cannot be too big or small. A company too small might not have the capabilities to drive success, while a company too large may have more layers to navigate than is reasonable for your company. A midsize company with the right infrastructure and strong management team should be a good place to start.

Not looking at offshoring as a strategic long-term tool. Don't offshore just to keep up with the Joneses. Try offshoring first as a pilot, and evaluate whether it works for your practice and team. But be open to full exploration and evaluation of offshoring, including both the positive and negative results.

In addition to the above, various small or individual valuation practitioners also partner on a revenue sharing model. Depending on the size of the relationship or the tasks that are involved, the revenue share spread is between 15% and 40%. As the relationship between two partners evolves and their interests align, partnerships become more seamless and the sharing of information is similar to sharing of information between different divisions of a company—in a good company. It is most important that the lines of communication are open between such partners, governance is streamlined, and decisions are transparent.

Offshoring is a very powerful strategic tool, which should be explored and evaluated for long-term gain of your practice. If you find the right partner—one that aligns with your interests—work with that partner transparently and set up an extension of your U.S.-based team with proper offshoring governance.

Bharat Kanodia, *ASA, focuses on venture and private equity valuations with SaaS technology and has assisted with various valuation and audit firms in optimizing their U.S. operations. Bharat has worked with Ipreo, Veristrat, American Appraisal, and Silicon Valley Bank Analytics and has signed off on over 4,000 valuation opinions with $800 billion in assets.*

12 Ways to Build a Program That Ensures Quality Fair Value Measurements

The valuation profession's response to criticism over the quality and consistency of fair value measurements for financial reporting has been to establish a Fair Value Quality Initiative. So far, as a result of this effort, we have the so-called Mandatory Performance Framework (MPF), a set of best practices, and a new designation known as the Certified in Entity and Intangible Valuation (CEIV). This is a new credential the AICPA, ASA, and RICS offer for professionals who do fair value work.

In addition to the steps that the profession is taking, individual valuation firms can take actions so that they are in lockstep with these efforts. Anthony Aaron is the chair of the performance requirements work stream of the Fair Value Quality Initiative. He spent most of his career at Ernst & Young and is now an adjunct professor in the Leventhal School of Accounting at the University of Southern California. Aaron provides a valuable list of elements designed to help create and maintain a process and a culture that promotes quality fair value measurements. While his focus is on fair value, many of the points he raises are just as applicable in other areas of a valuation practice.

1. Develop a 'quality charter.' A document can be created that describes all aspects of the valuation firm's quality program that everyone in the firm should adhere to, possibly through a formal "certification" of the document. This process creates a road map for quality-related processes and demonstrates a commitment to quality.

2. Create a 'tone from the top.' Without a commitment from a firm's leaders, the effort will be "doomed from the start," says Aaron. Not only must firm leaders commit to quality, but they also must communicate that commitment to their staff regularly. Third parties will also see this as a demonstration of a firm's commitment to quality.

3. Hire competent and ethical professionals. The hiring process should be designed to identify individuals who exhibit integrity and professional competence. This can be done by scrutinizing a candidate's education, training, experience, and demonstrated ethical behavior. This should be done regardless of whether the candidate is entry level or experienced.

4. Provide high quality training. Not only should training emphasize state-of-the-art valuation methods, but it should also promote ethical behavior.

5. Encourage professional accreditation. The valuation profession has several valuation professional organizations (VPOs) that confer accreditations and enforce a code of conduct and ethics. Members must also typically demonstrate continuing professional education to maintain or improve their level of competence.

6. Follow existing professional standards and guidance. Valuation firm employees must be required to adhere to existing standards of practice and guidance. This includes, but is not limited to, the MPF (FVQI), USPAP (The Appraisal Foundation), IVS (International Valuation Standards Council), ASA Business Valuation Standards (ASA), SSVS No. 1 (AICPA), and RICS Valuation-Professional Standards (RICS). Plus, there is ongoing guidance being issued on recognized methods and techniques specific to fair value measurement. These include practice aids from the AICPA and valuation advisories from The Appraisal Foundation.

7. Create a consistent process for engagement acceptance. Aaron advises valuation firms and professionals to create a standardized process for client and engagement acceptance. This process would include, but not be limited to: resolving any independence or conflict of interest issues, making sure prospective clients have integrity and are ethical, making sure the valuation firm or professional has the competence to perform the assignment, assuring that an appropriate engagement letter can be agreed upon (which memorializes the objective, scope, timing, and fees for the proposed engagement), and making sure that the fees to be charged are appropriate given the economics of the proposed engagement.

8. Develop a standardized work product. Standardized templates can be developed for such things as engagement agreements, reports (both comprehensive and abbreviated), spreadsheet analyses, documentary evidence, and so on. This not only helps ensure quality, but consistency as well.

9. Develop standardized work papers. Aaron says that this would typically be considered as part of the development of a standardized work product, but it now requires special emphasis in light of the recently published MPF. The MPF is very specific in describing the extent of documentary evidence you need in your work papers to withstand review by auditors, regulators, and others. Three important components of high-quality work papers are: (1) source documents (e.g., data from management or third parties); (2) analysis documents (e.g., spreadsheets); and (3) narratives (explanations as to "why" certain valuation methods were chosen and certain inputs were selected and "how" the valuation methods were applied).

10. Conduct internal 'independent' quality reviews. Use a "fresh set of eyes" to review each fair value measurement project. This should be someone who was not involved in the client assignment so that you can get an "independent" assessment of the inputs, methods chosen, conclusions, and all other aspects of the analysis.

11. Conduct ongoing quality process reviews. To test adherence to a firm's quality charter, periodic reviews of work product can be undertaken. This could also be tied into the annual performance review process for employees. A firm with multiple locations can establish a "roving team" for this quality control process.

12. Undertake other activities to promote quality and consistency. In addition to what's already on this list, Aaron says there are other activities to consider, such as "in-office" training. This can include "brown bag lunches," use of guest speakers, and regularly scheduled technical and quality teleconferences.

Aaron goes into a great deal more detail during a BVR webinar, Promoting Quality in Providing Fair Value Measurements for Financial Reporting, in which he offers 100 minutes of insights and recommendations on these steps as well as the FVQI and new CEIV credential. To access a recording, go to bvresources.com/pastevents.asp.

Willingness to Invest in Valuation Is a Key to M&A Success in Africa

Disagreements over the valuation of assets along with the transparency of the financial information available for review in the dealmaking process are often key factors in the ability to complete transactions in Africa. These factors are also important for the success of post-transaction integration, according to a new PwC survey[1] of financial analysts and corporate financiers.

The survey found that, across the continent, nearly 40% of deals fell apart because the parties could not agree on a valuation. There are a number of reasons for that, chief among them being valuation-related issues such as an inability to forecast how the assets will grow or respond to competitors, as well as the overall lack of reliability of multiples and comparable assets across the continent.

It isn't for lack of popularity. Competition for some assets is often a cause of inflated valuations, as investors press for increased presence in Africa, according to the report. One key factor cited in the survey as a trait of companies successfully able to close deals in Africa is the willingness to invest time and financial resources into the valuation process.

Valuation pays dividends after the transaction closes as well. One of the top reasons for completed deals is the transparency and quality of the targeted company's financial information, which is more likely to pass muster if the valuation resources aren't substantial.

Southern Africa. In the southern part of the continent, 64% of respondents say they favor the income approach to valuation, while 36% name the market approach as their preferred approach. The net income approach also has some popularity. Those who use the income approach as their primary approach almost universally say the income approach is the second choice.

Lack of data from publicly traded companies to use as a source for multiples data is a key reason for the popularity of the income approach. Within the income approach, respondents in Southern

1 "PwC Valuation Methodology Survey," 8th edition (www.pwc.co.za). The survey was completed from October 2016 to January 2017 and featured 87 complete and partial responses.

Africa prefer to use the capital asset pricing model (CAPM) to determine the cost of equity. Similar to previous surveys, most will apply a small stock premium.

The market risk premium is one area that has evolved from previous surveys, with a slightly wider range of 5.6% to 7.9% now in use. In 2012, the surveyed range was 4.7% to 6.6%.

West Africa. In West Africa, 58% of respondents to the survey favor the income approach, while 42% favor using the market approach as their primary method. Of those who favor the income approach, 91% say they use the market approach as their second choice.

Similar to the southern portion of the continent, the CAPM is the preferred way to determine the cost of equity. The market risk premium, on the other hand, has narrowed compared to previous surveys. The 2016 market risk premium spread was 6.4% to 8.9%, while, in 2012, it was 5% to 10%.

East Africa. As with the rest of the continent, the income approach is the widely favored approach, with 61% of respondents citing it as their primary approach to valuation. Of those, 79% say that the market approach is their backup approach.

The market risk premium range under the CAPM has expanded slightly from the results found in previous surveys. In 2016, the premium range was from 5% to 8.8%. By comparison, in 2012, it was from 5.2% to 8.2%.

Infrastructure investments. Africa's heavy need for infrastructure has led to more willingness to consider methods other than CAPM, which is used predominantly under the income approach, when it comes to valuation that involves infrastructure.

The primary alternatives include the market comparable approach and arbitrage pricing theory. Discounted cash flow is the overall approach favored by the majority of respondents with infrastructure investment.

What Makes a Business Valuation Firm an Attractive Acquisition Target?

By Nancy Fannon,
Marcum LLP (Portland, Maine, USA)

For the last several years, it seems as if everyone I talk to in our profession is trying to figure out a growth plan. Talk of growth is not new, of course—all of us have been trying to achieve it for years. In the early years, it came fairly easily: Valuation was effectively a brand new profession, with seemingly endless opportunities for those who jumped in the game ahead of the curve. Like any profession, we've evolved: The processes we use have grown in complexity, the data we rely on have gotten more extensive and reliable, and the courts have become exponentially more sophisticated, expecting the same of the experts who testify before them.

Many valuation analysts started their careers in large CPA firms. Understandably, these large CPA firms traditionally focused their energies on their bread and butter services: audit and tax. Valuation, with its almost "Wild West" feel and lack of recurring work, didn't quite fit into the repeat business model found in the compliance world of a traditional CPA firm. As a result, many of us left the large CPA environment to start our own firms, such that our profession is now largely comprised of small to midsized boutique valuation and litigation firms. For many of us, for much of our careers, this made great sense. Simply put, we don't operate like a CPA firm; rather, we are more akin to a law firm, with the nuances of discovery and record keeping attendant thereto. More importantly, lawyers engaging valuation and litigation analysts want to hire people they know are solely focused on the work they need done for their case—i.e., exactly the specialty, boutique firms we made ourselves into. The problem is that a small, boutique firm performing valuations and providing litigation support can only grow so much, due to lack of staff to handle large, sophisticated cases.

This leads us back to the discussion so many have been having over the last several years about growth: How do we achieve it? How do we provide meaningful and significant opportunities for our staff to grow their careers? For the partners at my firm, Meyers, Harrison & Pia LLC (MHP), the answer was to be acquired by the very type of firm we all "used to" work for—a large, national CPA firm: Marcum LLP.

We were not looking to be acquired; in fact, at the time Marcum approached us, we were (and still are) in the process of identifying and making moves to acquire other valuation practices. "Acquire or be acquired" was the path we seemed to be on. Based on many conversations I've had with my colleagues over the last few years, so are many of you.

So, what makes a valuation and litigation practice an attractive target? And just as importantly, what makes the buyer attractive to the valuation and litigation practice? Marcum wasn't the first firm to come courting us: we'd turned others down. So, what was it about this firm that was different?

Let's start with what made our firm attractive to a potential buyer. Marcum focused on five key attributes of MHP:

1. Our deep bench of experienced partners and staff;
2. Year after year of revenue growth and high profits;
3. Our well-established processes, procedures, and best practices;
4. The scalability of our work; and
5. The abundant cross-selling opportunities.

Each of these will be discussed briefly below:

- *Our deep bench of experienced partners and staff:* As we all know from our valuation experience, the creation of value requires depth of experience beyond what any one person can provide. MHP had four partners in its litigation practice, with a combined 100 years of experience in valuation and litigation support. Our staff of 15 professionals was solely dedicated to valuation and litigation support, allowing the team to fully develop the skills necessary to build a sophisticated practice.

- *Year after year of revenue growth and high profits:* When I merged my small firm, Fannon Valuation Group, into MHP in 2012, I was astounded at the metrics: highly billable up and down the organization, extraordinarily high realization across the board, and no debt. The firm was laser-focused on doing great (billable) work. Minimal downtime was spent on nonbillable activities—with the notable exception of continuing education and marketing, the latter of which is, after all, best achieved by doing great work.

- *Our well-established processes, procedures, and best practices:* As a firm solely devoted to valuation and litigation, MHP had established sophisticated valuation workbooks and templates, as well as a thorough quality control process. The complexities of valuation were regularly hashed through, establishing best practices and consistency of execution across the firm.

- *The scalability of our work:* For many years, each of the partners and senior staff focused on projects that small teams could perform. However, over time, we began to get larger and more complex projects, which required a greater number of staff for longer periods of time. Due to our relatively small size, we could only handle one or two of these projects a year. These projects tend to require significant amounts of junior staff time. Marcum saw the opportunity to leverage its staff of 1,500 professionals, allowing us to acquire more of these larger projects.

- *The abundant cross-selling opportunities:* Marcum believes its clients, contacts, and referral sources are hungry for valuation and litigation support services. Our merger allows us to cross-sell services across the breadth of the combined organization, leading to exponential growth opportunities for everyone.

But a deal is a two-way street. We had to be sure it was a good fit for MHP as well as for Marcum. Our considerations of whether or not to join with Marcum included many of the same factors Marcum considered, including Marcum's past financial success and stability and the future growth we believed we could achieve through scalability and cross-selling opportunities, as described above.

In addition to these shared concerns, two other issues were key to MHP's decision to sign on with Marcum, including:

1. Availability of career advancement opportunities for staff; and

2. Ability to operate autonomously.

As to each of these:

- *Availability of career advancement opportunities for staff:* A firm can only grow and promote staff if the growth of the firm allows it. MHP was doing this: Our revenues and profits had grown for many consecutive years, and we were actively seeking valuation firms to acquire in order to maintain our growth trend. However, Marcum presented an opportunity for *exponential* growth, far beyond what we believe we could have achieved on our own, as a small, boutique firm. In turn, this presents extraordinary career opportunities for our staff, "in at the ground floor" of what we intend to build into a significant national practice.

- *Ability to operate autonomously:* Marcum wanted to acquire us because we were already successful. Key to the partners was the ability to continue to operate under the direction of the superior leadership of Mark Harrison, under whom we had achieved that success. The MHP partner group all came from "Big Four" accounting firms ("Big Eight" for some of us!), and we well remember what didn't work and why we left. The ability to continue to operate as a successful valuation and litigation practice, branded and recognized as such by the marketplace we serve, was critical to us in order to continue our success. Marcum assured us that autonomy will continue.

Change always takes work and is at times uncomfortable, but both acquirer and acquiree are excited about the opportunities ahead of them. We continue to seek extraordinary valuation professionals and firms to add their expertise to our practice and grow with us (like you?!). Finally, we look forward to our staff having long and successful careers with Marcum.

Nancy Fannon *is partner-in-charge of the Litigation Support Services group at Marcum LLP, effective May 1, 2017. She can be contacted at nancy.fannon@marcumllp.com. Marcum LLP, headquartered in New York City, provides a full spectrum of traditional tax, accounting, and assurance services; advisory, valuation and litigation support; and an extensive range of specialty and niche industry practices. For more information, visit www.marcumllp.com.*

Update on DLOM, Fair Value, PTEs at NYSSCPA BV Confab

The 2017 conference season has started! BVR attended the annual business valuation conference of the New York State Society of CPAs (NYSSCPA) in New York City. As usual, it covered some of the profession's hottest topics. Committee chair Jeffrey Gibralter (Klein Liebman & Gresen LLC) opened the conference with kudos to conference co-chairs Mitchell H. Chosak (FSA LLC) and Jean J. Han (Baker Tilly Virchow Krause LLP) who put together an outstanding event. Here are some of the key takeaways.

BIZCOMPS analysis. Veteran valuator and business broker Toby Tatum discussed his methodology for using the BIZCOMPS database in the market approach. BIZCOMPS contains "Main Street" private-company transactions, and, unlike some other databases, the information on each transaction is limited, so you can't compare your subject company to specific transactions in the database. Because of this, you must regard the data in BIZCOMPS as samples or subsets or portions of all transactions, Tatum explained.

There is typically a large number of transactions for each SIC code, and the detail is limited, so this database is often best used under a "total market" theory. Generally, once you have chosen sample data based on your subject company, you then calculate statistical measures to analyze the data, such as median, mean, minimum, and maximum, and other measures for target financial metrics and multiples. Tatum points out, however, that you should always use a harmonic mean for any ratio with price in the numerator. This is consistent with the BIZCOMPS documentation, which says that, if these ratios are averaged using an arithmetic mean (a common error), high data points are given greater weights than low data points. The harmonic mean, on the other hand, gives equal weight to each data point.

In terms of the sample size, Tatum uses the magic number of 30 in terms of a minimum number of transactions to use in an analysis. For example, when doing a random selection of comps based on seller's discretionary earnings (SDE), sort the comps in ascending revenue order. Then select all of the first 20 comps with revenue less than the subject and all of the first 20 comps with revenue greater than the subject. That way, you have 40 comps all together.

Tatum often uses a more involved inferential statistical analysis when using BIZCOMPS data. He calls this the total market method (TMM), a term taken from the total market theory notion that applies to this database. Inferential statistical analysis is designed to help you make a decision when you don't have complete information. A complete discussion of his method is beyond the scope of this article, but his website (www.tobytatum.net) has more information on it.

As part of his analysis of the entire BIZCOMPS database, Tatum came up with some interesting findings, such as:

- There is "clearly a size effect" in the data, so you need to take company size into account;
- You do not need to adjust for differences due to geographical regions;
- Transactions from years ago are still valid, and no adjustments are needed for time differences; and
- All-cash deals are priced 10% lower than those with seller financing.

With regard to that last point, there is no universally accepted method for adjusting seller-financed transactions to their theoretical all-cash equivalent value. Tatum does this by adjusting the selling price-to-SDE ratio for each transaction by the average spread between the weighted harmonic mean value for all seller-financed transactions and the weighted harmonic mean value for all of the 100% cash at closing transactions in BIZCOMPS. He found that the weighted harmonic mean value of selling price to SDE for all seller-financed transactions is 2.21 and it is 2.00 for the all cash at closing transactions. Thus, it is reasonable to downwardly adjust the actual selling price for financed transactions by 10% to equate to an all-cash value.

Is valuation a profession? This was the title of the presentation by Mark Zyla (Acuitas Inc.), who focused on the recent developments in fair value measurements. Unlike accountants and lawyers, Zyla pointed out that valuation professionals do not have common education requirements, a single identification in the marketplace, a single set of standards, nor a disciplinary mechanism. For several years, the SEC has been speaking out as to the fragmentation of the valuation profession and that the profession would benefit from unified qualifications, standards, and oversight.

In response, a new valuation credential related to fair value for financial reporting has been developed under a joint effort of the AICPA, ASA, and RICS. These groups want to bring more consistency to the profession and reduce the number of questions auditors raise about the valuations. The new credential is Certified in Entity and Intangible Valuations™ (CEIV™), and it focuses on business entities and intangible assets.[1] Credential holders will be required to comply with a mandatory performance framework (MPF), which is designed to make sure that the valuation expert adequately documents his or her work and thought processes. This will unify valuation professionals with a common framework, standards, and body of knowledge. Also, there will be a proactive review process of all CEIV holders.

1 A special website has been set up at ceiv-credential.org that has more details on the credential and its requirements.

"The CEIV credential will ensure a transparent process that provides consistently accurate results that can be relied upon with confidence by clients, companies, regulators and the public," said Zyla, a noted authority on fair value[2] and one of the instructors in the AICPA's CEIV educational training program. Comments from the SEC so far are positive. "I would like to also acknowledge and encourage timeliness and quality in the ongoing important work to continually enhance valuation performance standards, credentialing, quality assurance, governance, and related matters," said Wesley Bricker, the SEC's chief accountant in a December 2016 speech.

Since the time of the conference, the CEIV exam has been finalized and a number of individuals have earned the new credential.

IVS development. Zyla also told attendees that, in the future, the valuation profession will have a more international focus. Along those lines, input is wanted to help set the agenda for the future development of the International Valuation Standards (IVS). The International Valuation Standards Council (IVSC), the global standard setter for valuation practice and the valuation profession, has opened an Agenda Consultation Paper on future revisions, which is available at www.ivsc.org. This is part of the IVSC's new efforts to continually evolve IVS instead of issuing completely revised standards every few years. IVS 2017[3] was recently finalized and becomes mandatory July 2017.

Zyla is chairman of the IVSC's new Standards Review Board and said that the board "distilled the main findings of our own gap analysis and collated the many valuable suggestions for revisions to IVS from stakeholders in previous consultations. We are looking forward to receiving views and recommendations on our IVS Agenda from practitioners, valuation professional organizations, academics, corporations and regulators, and working collaboratively with them to improve IVS." The comment period ends Aug. 15, 2017, and all comments will be posted on the IVSC's website.

DLOM deluge. There are close to 75 methods for estimating a discount for lack of marketability "with more arriving on a regular basis," said R. James Alerding (Alerding Consulting LLC) and Pasquale Rafanelli (Grassi & Co.) during their session. One new one they mentioned was an expansion of the *Mandelbaum* analysis they call "*Mandelbaum* on steroids." The *Mandelbaum* analysis has been used frequently since it emerged in a Tax Court case.[4] In that case, Judge David Laro cited nine specific factors for analysts to consider in developing a DLOM. The factors were identified as:

1. Company financial statement analysis;

2. Company dividend history and policy;

2 Among other publications and articles on fair value, he is the author of *Fair Value Measurements: Practical Guidance and Implementation*, 2nd edition (Wiley), available at www.bvresources.com/products/fair-value-measurements-practical-guidance-and-implementation-second-edition.

3 The standards are now available in print or PDF format, and they are a good resource for both U.S. and non-U.S. appraisers. Go to www.bvresources.com/products/international-valuation-standards-2017.

4 *Mandelbaum, et al.* v. *Commissioner*, T.C. Memo 1995-255.

3. The nature of the company, its history, its position in the industry, and its economic outlook;

4. The company management;

5. The amount of control in the transferred shares;

6. The restrictions on transferability;

7. The holding period for the stock;

8. The subject company's redemption policy; and

9. The costs associated with a public offering.

Of course, this list is not exhaustive, and the new approach expands this list from nine to 40 qualitative and quantitative factors arranged in several groups: factors that impact volatility, holding period, dividends and "other" (such as value of public versus private stock and owners with an adversarial relationship). You then assess all of these factors to adjust the starting DLOM up or down to get a concluded DLOM. Of course, a great deal of judgment must be used here. One concern is that, when you greatly expand the framework, you also increase the likelihood that some part of it will be challenged. The framework for this approach is included in the new *Discount for Lack of Marketability Guide* and Toolkit, of which Alerding was a co-developer (reviewed on page 389).

Alerding and Rafanelli covered what they consider the major DLOM methods, which they list as follows (with their comments):

- Pre-IPO studies: "Problems with the data";

- Restricted stock (benchmark) studies: "They're old, and some are not available";

- *Mandelbaum:* "Helpful to refine a DLOM, but there has to be an accurate starting DLOM";

- FMV Restricted Stock Study (Lance Hall), recently acquired by Stout and now called the Stout Restricted Stock Study: "An attempt to refine the traditional restricted stock studies method.";

- Mercer's quantitative marketability discount model (QMDM): "Good in combination with other methods"; and

- Option pricing theory: "Usually used in combination with other methods."

To give some perspective into who's using what, we note that last year BVR conducted a survey on the prevalence of DLOM methods. Restricted stock studies and pre-IPO studies remain the most cited methodologies for quantifying DLOM: 76% of respondents say they use restricted stock studies, and 43% say they use pre-IPO studies. A third (34%) of respondents use Partnership Profiles, and 18% of respondents cited the QMDM. As for the option models, 20% of respondents use the Finnerty model, Longstaff is at 13%, and Chaffee logged a 9% response.

In summary, Alerding and Rafanelli offered these observations and advice:

- No single method is acceptable on its own without the analysis and support of the appraiser;
- The appraiser should select the methods that are appropriate for the subject interest; and
- Some of the methods rely on databases that are subscription services.

PTE conundrum. Eric J. Barr (Marks Paneth) described his modified Delaware MRI method for valuing pass-through entities (PTEs), which adjusts for things such as entity-level PTE income taxes, income retained in the business, effective income tax rates of the owners, state income taxes, and other factors. If you go to his page on his firm's website (www.markspaneth.com), he has posted a number of his articles that go into the PTE valuation "conundrum."

Tax affecting the earnings of a PTE has been an issue of much debate in the valuation community, and there is no definitive answer. The tax-affecting issue has been argued in a number of Tax Court cases in which the IRS and the court have refuted the notion that shareholder-level taxes affect a firm's value, so the valuation conclusions in these cases were based on earnings not being tax affected. The valuation community disagrees, so a number of models were developed that are designed to reflect the impact of shareholder taxes on value. There is also research that demonstrates that a combination of clienteles (most notably, institutional investors, many of whom pay no tax) and tax deferral opportunities mute tax effects, so the existing models have likely overstated the magnitude of any adjustment that may be needed.[5]

Barr also mentioned that, for the first time, a case is pending in Tax Court[6] that may result in a change in the IRS's no-tax-affecting stance on valuing PTEs. Both the IRS and the taxpayer are using the Van Vleet model (S corporation economic adjustment model) in the case, which involves a gift of shares in the Biltmore Co., which operates the famous Biltmore estate, a Gilded Age mansion the Vanderbilts built that is now a tourist attraction.

GAAP woes. There's an average of 150 estimates in financial reports today as opposed to just 30 in 1995, observed Baruch Lev (New York University Stern School of Business), and some of these estimates are "sheer guesses" and "ludicrous." The move to fair value and complex accounting

5 See Nancy J. Fannon and Keith Sellers, *Taxes and Value: The Ongoing Research and Analysis Relating to the S Corporation Valuation Puzzle,* Business Valuation Resources, 2015 (available at www.bvresources.com/publications).

6 *Cecil et al. v. Commissioner of Internal Revenue.*

rules has resulted in a crazy quilt of historical accounting and fair value estimates that render traditional financial statements useless. Interestingly, he has a feeling why there has been a big move from managed funds to indexed funds. He believes that much of the poor performance of managed and hedge funds in recent years can be attributed to the deteriorating quality of the information they use. "My hunch is that the managers of managed funds found that their use of financial information is no longer relevant," he says.

A lot of the problem is due to intangibles. Most businesses today are rich in intangibles, but the accounting system completely misstates them, he says, so business valuations have to focus on non-GAAP data concerning the core strategic (mostly intangible) assets of the enterprise. What are these strategic assets? They are the ones that: (1) generate benefits; (2) are limited in supply; and (3) are difficult to imitate. These are the assets that create value, says Lev. He's not advocating for including the values of intangibles in the financial statements, just to recognize them.

In the recent book, *The End of Accounting*,[7] that Lev co-wrote with Feng Gu (SUNY Buffalo), the authors propose that companies issue a short document (can be one page), a "Strategic Resources and Consequences Report," designed to highlight "fundamental indicators" of value. Examples are: new-customer and churn rates (internet firms), accident severity/frequency and policy-renewal rates (car insurers), clinical trial results (pharmaceutical firms), and proven oil and gas reserves (energy companies). True, some companies realize the problems with financial information and try to overcome it by providing additional information—non-GAAP disclosures—particularly around the earnings calls. The only problem with this is that the practice is not uniform, says Lev. Some companies don't do it, and the ones that do may not do it all the time, so it's of very limited use to investors.

Some strategic assets, of course, are unique and difficult—if not impossible—to value, so essentially no published data are available. Instead of using "earnings" as a performance measure, Lev recommends a measure he calls "adjusted residual cash flows," calculated as follows:

- Start with reported "cash from operations";
- Add back expensed investments in strategic assets (customer acquisition costs, R&D, IT, brand creation, etc.—these are not regular expenses);
- Subtract three-to-five-year average of capital expenditure (to compensate for the addition of depreciation and amortization in cash from operations); and
- Subtract a charge for equity capital in use (this adjusts the measure for the different amounts of equity capital peer companies use).

Using this (or any other) non-GAAP measure may lead to skepticism because of the perception that they can be manipulated. But Lev points out that there already is "great skepticism" in GAAP

7 Baruch Lev and Feng Gu, *The End of Accounting*, Wiley, 2016 (available at www.bvresources.com/publications).

reports. How do you explain that 70% of all companies beat analysts' consensus without some manipulation going on? He does acknowledge, however, that there may be more skepticism with non-GAAP measures that are not standardized. He hopes that the recommendations he and his co-author present in their book are adopted and become standardized.

Estate planning valuation. Until the time of the conference, things were looking positive in Washington with respect to tax reform and the fate of estate and gift taxes. Then, the Russian matters took center stage and seemed to derail things, said attorney Ladidas Lumpkins (Prager Metis CPAs LLC). She outlined the valuation implications of existing tax reform proposals from a federal tax perspective:

- *Net operating losses.* A reduction in the corporate tax rate potential would diminish tax savings attributable to net operating losses (NOLs) and deferred tax assets;
- *Depreciation deductions.* Lower tax rates may produce diminished value for depreciable assets;
- *Capex expensing.* The impact related to depreciation deductions could be mitigated by immediate expensing of capital investments as proposed by the Tax Reform Tax Force; and
- *Choice of entity.* The reduction in the federal corporate tax rate may weaken the relative after-tax valuation advantage that investors in pass-through entities have enjoyed relative to investments in corporations that are subject to double taxation.

She and a colleague at Prager Metis, valuation and forensics expert Alfred Pruskowski, also talked about the Section 2704 proposed regulations that seek to curtail estate valuation discounts. The IRS wants to eliminate the technique of putting valuable property into entities such as family-owned partnerships or corporations just to reduce the value in the property to avoid estate and gift tax. To do this, the proposed regs address the treatment of some lapsing rights and restrictions on liquidation in determining the value of transferred interests in corporations and partnerships. Liquidation restrictions would be disregarded for valuation purposes. Bottom line: It appears that the proposed regulations eliminate almost all minority discounts for closely held entity interests, including operating businesses owned by a family. A record number of speakers descended on the IRS in Washington, D.C., in December 2016 to fight the controversial proposed regs, which were never finalized and got caught up in the change in administrations.

While these regs are in limbo, practitioners should take full advantage of existing estate valuation discounts, the speakers said. Pruskowski talked about the notable *Astleford* case from 2008, which allowed for two tiers of discounts (total of around 55%) that is of particular interest to business appraisers in valuing family limited partnerships and "layered" real estate holding entities. The case involved expert testimony from six experts (four for the taxpayer, two for the IRS), and, in the end, the Tax Court accepted a sizable combined discount for lack of marketability and control for a 50% general partnership interest. The court also allowed a fairly substantial discount for the "tiered" ownership interests inherent in the real estate limited partnership. Interestingly, the court considered the comparability data from sales of publicly traded REITs (real estate investment trusts) with data from sales of registered RELPs (real estate limited partnerships). While it declined to declare one dataset superior to the other, it does examine which set of sales transaction data applies more to the facts and circumstances of the various Astleford family interests. You can read an in-depth analysis of the case in a BVR free download.[8]

In the end, the Astleford estate saved around $12 million in taxes, according to Pruskowski, who says that these types of discounts will disappear if the proposed 2704 regulations go through as written. But these discounts still exist—at least for the foreseeable future—so take full advantage of the law, he advises. In gift tax and estate tax returns, you should disclose positions inconsistent with the proposed regs and have your work papers ready to show sufficient substantiation for the discounts.

The speakers also say to "stick to the status quo" for the foreseeable future in terms of issues such as estate tax freezes, intentionally defective grantor trusts (IDGTs) and to consider spousal limited access trusts (SLATs) and dynasty trusts (to preserve tax-free status forever). Also, individuals should avoid making any transfers that would incur gift tax. "The person who dies with the least amount of toys, wins!" as the saying goes, so strategies consistent with this notion are the order of the day, such as leaving assets to spouses (QTIPs) and giving assets away tax-free. Just make sure there is documentation of events and transactions that impact basis, they advise.

Succession planning. Attorney Neil Katz (Smith and Chwat Inc.) revealed an alarming statistic: 78% of small-business owners need to monetize their ownership in their firms to afford retirement, according to a recent CNBC survey. What's more, better succession planning is needed, as only 15% of firms are successful in transferring to the next generation—that's down from 30% 20 years ago.

One way to make for a more successful succession plan is for valuation experts to become part of the planning team as early as possible, says Katz. A planning horizon of five to seven years is typically needed for a business owner to maximize value. Of course, you may not always have the luxury of that time frame. If you have just two to three years, an "OK" plan can be done, but "forget it" if you have less than two years, he says.

One of the big functions a valuation expert performs early on is to give the business owner a reality check on value. Many owners feel that they represent "all of the value" of their firm. Others say they won't transfer their business at any price. Therefore, the role of the valuation expert is to help some owners separate emotion from reality, Katz observes.

Two other big issues often come up: (1) when there are kids in the business; and (2) when there are multiple owners. Typically, the owners/parents have one of two mindsets. Either they can't

8 The case is *Astleford v. Commissioner* (T.C. Memo 2008-128). An analysis is available at bvresources.com/freedownloads/Astleford.pdf.

see that the kids are ready to take over the business or they can't see that the kids are *not ready* to take over. It gets more complicated when some children are in the business and others are not. If the child who is not in the business is to become an owner, then how much say will he or she have in the running of the business and how will the co-ownership of the business affect the sibling relationship? If the child will not become an owner of the business, will he or she (and should he or she) benefit from the value of this business as a part of his or her parents' estate?

Katz pointed out that another notable difficulty is when the business is owned by multiple parties, related or unrelated. The co-owners may have different financial needs and goals and may have differing desires as to the succession of the business. While these differences may be able to be masked as long as the co-owners are alive and actively operating the business, once an event occurs that changes this relationship, if the plan is not fully discussed and documented, the business can suffer significant hardship created by conflict among the families.

Because you're dealing with family emotions, succession planning can be very problematic, even with the best-laid plans. Katz told the audience about one engagement in which an elaborate succession plan was worked out that met the goals of the family business owners and children, one of whom worked in the business and was poised to take over. That child was to be given the business, and the other child would get other family assets of equal value. Everything was set, and then the owners wanted to have a "family meeting" with everyone including the succession planning team. During the meeting, sibling rivalry from years ago was rekindled and the child who was never in the business suddenly wanted to be in it. The meeting turned into a free-for-all and ended with the kids storming out. The teary-eyed patriarch of the clan turned to Katz and said: "You broke up my family." He advises to watch out for those family meetings!

New York LLC law reform. Closing out the conference was a trio of speakers who talked about the need for the state of New York to reform its LLC statutes. CPA and valuation expert Edward F. Esposito and attorneys Peter A. Mahler (Farrell Fritz PC) and Bruce Rich (Carter Ledyard and Milburn LLC) said that the LLC is the entity of choice today and most states have upgraded their LLC statutes—except New York. They say changes are needed in New York to reflect changes in the tax code, innovations other states have adopted, and model legislation such as the Revised Uniform Limited Liability Company Act (currently enacted in 16 states and the District of Columbia).

Of particular interest to valuators is one of the "more obvious shortcomings" in New York's LLC law: the absence of a fair value buyout provision in judicial dissolution cases, such as the one found in New York's Business Corporation Law. Any such legislative change should also resolve the growing debate and lack of clarity concerning the marketability discount in New York fair value proceedings. The speakers also referred to a series of articles[9] in *Business Valuation Update* that call

9 See Gilbert E. Matthews and Michelle Patterson, "NY's Unfair Application of Shareholder-Level Marketability Discounts," *Business Valuation Update*, January 2016; William C Quackenbush, "DLOMs in N.Y. Statutory Fair Value Cases—A Follow-Up to Matthews," *Business Valuation Update*, March 2016; and Gilbert E. Matthews, "DLOMs in N.Y. Fair Value Cases: Private Company Discounts Are Not Caused by Lack of Marketability," *Business Valuation Update*, June 2016

attention to this matter and hope that the business valuation community could speak with one, clear voice on the issue.

With respect to DLOM, there seems to be no rhyme or reason to New York court decisions. The speakers mentioned a number of cases, including *AriZona Beverages,*[10] which was a partner buyout dispute and the largest fair value case in New York. One side argued for a zero DLOM because there had been several recent offers to buy the company, and the other side argued for a 35% DLOM. The court ruled that a 25% DLOM was appropriate but did not explain how it came up with that percentage. In the *Zelouf*[11] case, the court ruled that no DLOM should be applied because there was little likelihood that the controlling shareholder would sell the company in the near future. Mahler mentioned that he did a podcast[12] on DLOM in which he interviewed valuation expert Chris Mercer (Mercer Capital), who was one of the experts in the *AriZona* case.

BVU congratulates the NYSSCPA for an excellent and informative conference, and we look forward to attending next year!

10 *Ferolito v. AriZona Beverages USA LLC*, 2014 N.Y. Misc. LEXIS 4709 (Oct. 14, 2014). Available at bvresources.com/bvlaw.

11 *Zelouf International Corp. v. Zelouf*, 2014 N.Y. Misc. LEXIS 5595 (Dec. 22, 2014). Available at bvresources.com/bvlaw.

12 For a full listing of Mahler's podcasts, which focus on business divorce, go to soundcloud.com/businessdivorceroundtable.

Redefining the BV Profession at NACVA's Annual Conference

In today's so-called "connected" world, more people get their information electronically than ever before. That's great, but there's nothing like face-to-face interaction with your peers and BV thought leaders to help keep you informed about what's going on in the profession.

BVU was in Chicago at the annual conference of the National Association of Certified Valuators and Analysts (NACVA) June 7-10 where the theme was "Redefining Our Profession." Well over 500 attendees were on hand and were treated to all kinds of interesting and useful tips and advice from leading valuation practitioners. We attended sessions on all four days, and the most interest (in terms of an unscientific eyeballing of session headcount) was on topics such as cost of capital, DLOM, goodwill, intangibles, S corp valuation, buy-sell agreements, regression analysis, litigation engagements, the size premium, and complex family limited partnerships.

NACVA announced a number of initiatives to enhance the profession and benefit its members, such as a partnership with 20 universities to attract students to the business valuation profession. To help members move their practices into a long-term consulting role with clients, NACVA has an alliance with CoreValue, which offers training and support along these lines. Also, NACVA is now a "channel partner" with the Expert Witness Exchange, which matches up experts with attorneys. It has also set up a program in which members can offer their services to attorneys looking for an expert willing to do pro bono work.

At its conferences, NACVA does a particularly good job at arranging networking activities beyond the usual on-site receptions, lunches, and coffee breaks. Informal interactions with other professionals away from the conference venue can be just as valuable as sitting in a formal presentation. There were nightly "dine-arounds" where small groups go for dinner at local eateries and special events such as a dinner cruise and attending a Cubs game.

Two keynote addresses—one on cost of capital and the other on litigation issues—were well attended and provided some good takeaways. Here are some of them, and we'll have more in future issues of *BVU.*

Cost of capital. One of the keynotes was presented by Roger Grabowski (Duff & Phelps), who gave an update on recent research and controversies regarding cost of capital. He told a packed audience that we will see ongoing advances in estimating the cost of capital as researchers get a better grasp on how to price risk. Pure CAPM, where beta is the only measure of risk, is "baloney," he says.[1] He cites researchers such as Pablo Fernandez (University of Navarre), whose paper points to CAPM as an absurd model and is a "must read" for everyone, Grabowski advises, especially if you practice before the IRS (it uses CAPM).

We now have models with more factors, such as the Fama-French multiple factor models and modified CAPM, which adds a size premium. Grabowski pointed out that D&P's *Valuation Handbook*[2] contains some new methods for estimating beta and future editions of the handbook will have some new data designed to get a better understanding of beta.

In the meantime, he reminded attendees to avoid using a cost of equity estimate just because it was computed by a formula. Take a look at all of the companies in your list of comparables and graph each firm in terms of returns versus the market. One may move very differently, which can impact your beta. He gave the example of AOL, which reacts oppositely to the market (it goes down when the internet industry and the market go up). Therefore, if AOL is in your mix of comparables, the beta is too low.

Grabowski also mentioned that the question still arises as to whether the size effect is still applicable in estimating the cost of equity, especially after the early 1980s, when some commentators say it disappeared. The issue is addressed to some extent in the *Valuation Handbook*, but he pointed to more recent research that gives additional support for the size effect in the period since 1990. Data used in the *Risk Premium Report*[3] as published in the handbook have been reassembled to cover the period 1990 to 2016. BVR makes the resulting analysis available as a free download,[4] and it concludes that the data published in the handbook continues to be a valid basis for estimating the cost of equity capital.

Grabowski also mentioned that the *Risk Premium Report* will eventually include financial services companies, including banks. These entities have been excluded because they have different risk characteristics than other firms due to factors such as deposit insurance and debt levels. As co-author (with Shannon Pratt) of *Cost of Capital*,[5] he mentioned that the next edition will have more material, including additional work on the issue of the arithmetic versus the geometric average. He advised attendees to look at the Q&A section of the book and urged attendees to send in their questions, which help guide the development of future editions.

1 See Shannon P. Pratt and Roger J. Grabowski, *Cost of Capital: Applications and Examples*, 5th ed., 2014, Chapter 13, "Criticism of CAPM and Beta Versus Other Risk Measures." (www.bvresources.com)

2 Duff & Phelps, *Valuation Handbook - Guide to Cost of Capital* (www.bvresources.com/publications).

3 www.bvresources.com/products/valuation-handbook-risk-premium-toolkit.

4 *Duff & Phelps Update*, 1Q2017; sub.bvresources.com/Download.asp?DownloadID=936.

5 Ibid.

Courtroom trap. An interesting question was posed to a panel of judges during a keynote session moderated by Michael Kaplan (Kaplan Forensics). How do you handle it when a valuation uncovers tax fraud, such as skimming from a business? Of course, it gets on the record if you testify that you discovered such skimming and took it into account in your valuation. What is a judge's ethical responsibilities in terms of taking the valuation report and a transcript of testimony and turning it over to the proper authorities?

Judge Christopher Yates (Circuit Court; Kent County, Mich.) responded that, while, as a member of the bar, he has an obligation to report unethical behavior of attorneys, he has no similar obligation to report criminal behavior revealed by an expert witness. He said that in "rare" occasions when that has happened, he has referred the matter to the appropriate authorities.

If your valuation uncovers a criminal act, a public trial can expose the client and entangle you in the fallout, according to Judge Steven I. Platt (retired as a full-time circuit court judge in Maryland). The valuation expert can be called as a potential witness in subsequent actions against the wrongdoer, he said. The retaining counsel will be looking out for his or her client and not you as the expert, so you may have to hire your own attorney to defend yourself in this potential matter. When you stumble on a criminal act such as financial fraud, you need to inform the retaining counsel because it may be determined that arbitration is the better route to resolution. That way, the criminal activity is not propelled into a public forum but is kept private, eliminating the exposure.

BVU congratulates NACVA on a great event. Watch for more coverage in a future issue.

New Fair Value Regs and Credentials Highlight ASA Event

There was record attendance at the American Society of Appraisers' 12th Annual Fair Value Conference at the University of Southern California in Los Angeles. The reason for the large turnout is the growing importance of fair value for financial reporting and the recent efforts to improve the level of quality in this area of practice. A great deal of discussion related to the new credential for fair value for financial reporting, Certified in Entity and Intangible Valuations™ (CEIV™), and the related best practices known as the Mandatory Performance Framework (MPF). What's more, the AICPA announced another new credential for financial instrument valuation.

Co-organizer Ray Rath (Globalview Advisors), who is one of the first batch of professionals to be awarded the CEIV, greeted the audience and mentioned that there will be a live educational course for the CEIV credential in Houston October 4-6 (preceding the ASA's annual conference October 7-10). He also pointed out that experienced individuals without a valuation credential who are looking to earn the CEIV from the ASA do not have to take all of the valuation courses. They can take a "challenge exam" to earn the ASA's business valuation credential.

Before he addressed the crowd, co-organizer Tom Ryan, a professor in USC's Leventhal School of Accounting, told us that there are two fair value courses in each of the undergraduate and graduate programs in USC's accounting program. And that is "just the beginning," he said. Then, in his inimitable style, Ryan fired up the audience with a rousing welcome. He talked about the pressure on auditors to improve performance amid the ongoing deficiencies in fair value measurements being discovered by the Public Company Accounting Oversight Board (PCAOB). The pressure has been so significant that it led to the firing of several KPMG audit partners as well as a PCAOB employee over the leaking of inside information on PCAOB inspections.[1]

Be skeptical. George Wilfert of the PCAOB told the audience that, overall, the number of audit deficiencies have decreased. However, there is still a significant number of deficiencies regarding auditors' testing of fair value measurements associated with business combinations. A few years

1 www.complianceweek.com/blogs/accounting-auditing-update/kpmg-pcaob-dismiss-personnel-over-inspection-leak#.WV4wbLX3bYU.

ago, the number of deficiencies were skewed toward impairments, but that has now shifted to business combinations.

Wilfert mentioned that new proposed standards for auditors' use of specialists (including valuation professionals) were in the process of being released.[2] One of the matters the new rules seeks to reinforce is that of "professional skepticism," that is, do not simply corroborate the information you get from management or other third parties. You need to look at any negative evidence and address it, advises Wilfert.

Earlier this year, the PCAOB found that professional skepticism was lacking when a PwC auditor failed to adequately scrutinize accounts receivable, which may have led to an overvaluation of this asset. He "did not provide sufficient competent evidence to support the existence or valuation of accounts receivable," the agency said in a settled disciplinary order. The auditor (no longer with the firm) neither admitted nor denied the findings, and he was censured, fined $10,000, and barred for two years from associating with a registered public accounting firm.[3]

CEIV credential. The ASA has already begun to issue the CEIV credential (and so has the AICPA). Tony Aaron provided an update. Aaron is retired from Ernst & Young and is now an adjunct professor at the USC Leventhal School of Accounting and the chair of the performance requirements workstream group for the fair value quality initiative, which includes the development of the CEIV credential. This project is a collaborative one that involves a number of organizations, including the ASA, AICPA, and RICS. It is in response partly to regulators' concerns over the fragmented nature of the profession and the inconsistent quality of the work being performed in terms of fair value for financial reporting.

The education requirement for the credential involves a two-part course, one part on a body of knowledge and the second part on the MPF. There's also a two-part exam (60 questions in each part) covering both parts of the education. Someone in the audience commented that the questions in the first half of the exam (fair value body of knowledge) have been revised. This is not uncommon with exams of this type. The audience also had some concern that the body of knowledge training is too basic for experienced practitioners, so they should be exempt from that part of the training (but not the exam). Originally, individuals with a great deal of experience in fair value could skip the body of knowledge part of the education training (but would still take the same two-part exam). That was changed so that now everyone must take the same two-part education course regardless of experience.

The credentialing process will be subject to ongoing quality oversight and compliance with the MPF.[4] Anyone holding the CEIV credential can expect a compliance review within the first year of

2 Since his presentation, the proposal has been released and can be found at pcaobus.org/Rulemaking/Pages/docket-044-auditors-use-work-specialists.aspx. Comments are due Aug. 30, 2017.

3 pcaobus.org/Enforcement/Decisions/Documents/105-2017-007-Teles.pdf.

4 Available at www.ceiv-credential.org.

receiving their accreditation, Aaron says. He pointed out that these are not termed "peer reviews" and will not be done in response to complaints. Rather, they will be proactive, and there will be a required review of an engagement work file for each credential holder.

Representatives of the Big Four were on hand to comment on the CEIV and MPF: Mike Tully (KPMG), Austin Lee (Deloitte), Amanda Miller (Ernst & Young), and James Marshall (PwC). They all agreed that the fair value efforts are "on the right track," but they are taking a "wait-and-see" attitude on it in terms of credentialing their staff. Some individuals at their firms are getting it on their own at this point, they report.

One concern the auditors have is over the quality control process, which is still under development. The panel noted that each valuation professional organization (VPO) will handle the review process for the individuals to which they confer the credential. The panel also noted that this diverges from the other aspects of the program. That is, the AICPA, ASA, and RICS are all in lockstep in terms of education, training, and testing, but each VPO is responsible for its own review process. The panel wondered whether this would be perceived as a "fox watching the henhouse" situation.

An interesting question from the audience arose: If an auditor sees CEIV on a report, does that mean less review time and less cost? The panel agreed that the answer would be "yes, theoretically," but it remains to be seen whether that will actually be the result.

Another question: Will the efforts to improve fair value quality be extended beyond business entities and intangibles? What about financial instruments and tangible property such as M&E and real estate? The panel did not comment on anything formal in the works in that regard, but Tully noted that "anything done to raise quality in the profession is a good thing."

CVFI credential. While the auditor panel did not comment on fair value quality initiatives beyond those with respect to business entities and intangibles, a speaker added to the conference agenda at the last minute provided some information—at least with respect to financial instruments. Jeffrey High of the AICPA announced that the group is developing a new credential for professionals involved in valuing financial instruments. He noted that certain instruments, such as mortgage-backed securities, credit default swaps, complex bonds, and other derivatives, have been difficult to value and this has the potential to adversely impact markets and the global economy.

While we were aware that a second fair value credential was being considered,[5] this was the first formal announcement to our knowledge of such a credential. Full details were sketchy, and there was still some degree of mystery surrounding this matter. All of High's slides were marked "Confidential," and they were not distributed to the audience with the rest of the presentations. Requests we made for more information after the conference were not answered.

5 "New credentials coming up for fair value measurements," *BVWire*, June 3, 2015.

AICPA Unveils New CVFI Credential for Financial Instruments

The American Institute of CPAs will offer a new credential, Certified in Valuation of Financial Instruments (CVFI), which is expected to launch later this year. The AICPA is seeking comments on an exposure draft of guidance for CPAs and financial professionals on the valuation of financial instruments and their underlying components. Comments are due Sept. 27, 2017.

The exposure draft, the "Disclosure Framework for the Valuation of Financial Instruments and the Certified in Valuation of Financial Instruments ('CVFI') Credential," defines the level of documentation necessary for a professional working with securities and financial instruments to effectively demonstrate the valuation performed. There is a companion document, the "Application of the Disclosure Framework for the Valuation of Financial Instruments," which demonstrates how the framework would be applied for areas of valuation that are often either misapplied or insufficiently supported or documented in valuations for financial reporting.

The credential is for CPAs and non-CPAs and will involve about 30 hours of education in financial instruments. CFAs who are not versed in financial reporting or disclosures may also find this new designation of value. The CVFI will also be multinational in design and geared to global standards. Once finalized, CVFI credential holders will be required to comply with the framework and will be subject to a quality control process, which will be similar to the peer review process for accountants.

Unlike the CEIV credential, the CVFI designation is not being developed in collaboration with other valuation professional organizations (VPOs). When we asked why not, the AICPA issued this statement: "We recognized a critical market need and wanted to move forward with developing a credential to address that need. Our goal is for the CVFI to become a global credential that other valuation organizations are able to offer their members."

For more information, including links to the exposure draft and a sign-up form for future alerts, go to www.aicpa.org/Membership/Pages/financial-instruments-form.aspx.

The AICPA has since announced that its new credential is the Certified in Valuation of Financial Instruments (CVFI) and would launch later this year. Unlike the CEIV, it is not being developed in collaboration with any of the other VPOs. But it does have a similar look and feel: there is a "Disclosure Framework" that establishes parameters of documentation requirements and an "Application of the Disclosure Framework" that demonstrates how the framework will be applied. These are similar in function to the CEIV's Mandatory Performance Framework and Application of the Mandatory Performance Framework documents. Essentially, they serve as best practices for anyone doing work in these areas. See the sidebar for more information. There will also be a quality control process that will be similar to a peer review for accountants.

In addition to the discussions around the new fair value regs and credentials, the conference presented other interesting sessions that we hope will be the subject of future articles in *Business Valuation Update*. Here are some main points of interest.

Contingent consideration. Gary Raichart (Duff & Phelps) and Sorin Maruster (KPMG) were on The Appraisal Foundation task force that developed the Valuations in Financial Reporting (VFR) exposure draft, "Valuation of Contingent Consideration." It contains detailed discussions of the typical structures of contingent consideration, key valuation issues, valuation techniques deemed to represent best practice, methods for assessing the reasonableness of contingent consideration fair value estimates, and issues at subsequent measurement dates. The two speakers said that comment letters are being reviewed and a final version will come out soon. In terms of technical issues, they pointed out that, when valuing earnouts with a linear payoff structure, a scenario-based model should be used. If the payoff structure is nonlinear, use option pricing models, they advise.

Accounting update. It will be a "new world" under FASB's "Definition of Business" rules, which start to kick in next year, said Adam Smith (PricewaterhouseCoopers), who was formerly with the FASB. Under these new rules—the first ASU issued in 2017—you'll see more asset acquisitions in the future and fewer business combinations. Because of this, there will be two new areas of scrutiny. The first is a company's workforce value, which must be recognized in an asset acquisition. "We probably don't do a great job at valuing a workforce, so we may want to think about this," he said. The second area is noncompete agreements. Some view this as a separate transaction, while others view it as part of a business combination, he noted.

The new rules will not result in much of a difference in valuation work per se, he predicted, just in what gets measured and booked. Certain types of firms may see a lot more asset acquisitions instead of business combinations, such as technical and pharmaceutical companies. For example, a tech firm buying another for its workforce that may account for a large percentage of value may be now considered an asset acquisition.

Smith also mentioned the new lease accounting rules designed to more accurately reflect the financial picture of firms that lease assets. For example, a trucking company can show no trucks on the balance sheet if they are all leased. Of course, accounting changes of this sort generally would not impact the underlying economic value of a firm, but they do have impacts that valuation experts need to consider. For example, certain ratios will change when the new rules are implemented.

IVSC developments. The IVSC has made some impressive advances over the past year, releasing a final version of IVS 2017 in its efforts to harmonize valuation standards for the global economy. If you want to help guide the development of international valuation standards for financial instruments, the IVSC is taking applications, announced Kevin Prall, the IVSC's technical director for business valuation standards and also a senior manager at KPMG LLP. The IVSC is looking for members for its new Financial Instruments Board as well as supplemental members to its Standards Review Board. This board is part of the IVSC's new infrastructure within which focused subject matter expertise boards will continuously revise and improve IVS to help ensure that they add value and can be implemented by VPOs.

Prall asked for a show of hands of how many in the audience were aware of IVS, and about half said they were familiar with the international standards (which became mandatory July 2017). Of course, if your engagement involves non-U.S. entities, you need to be aware of IVS. But one attendee pointed out that he knows IVS because the Big Four consider it when reviewing a valuator's work, even if it doesn't involve an entity outside the U.S.

Prall also mentioned that the IVSC is looking for input on an Agenda Consultation Paper[6] on future revisions to IVS, which is part of the IVSC's new efforts to continually evolve IVS instead of issuing completely revised standards every few years. Your feedback is wanted by Aug. 15, 2017.

Prospective financial information. More attention needs to be paid to forecasts and projections, according to Dave Dufendach (Alvarez & Marsal). In the past, appraisers have often included language in their valuation reports stating that management projections have been accepted as provided without review—something auditors have expressed concern about. Appraisers should not simply accept the projections the client provides, plug them into a DCF, and then merely apply a discount rate.

One of his recommendations is for appraisers to become familiar with the MPF, which includes significant performance requirements related to PFI. The architects of the fair value quality initiative recognized the concern over PFI and included a section on professional skepticism in the MPF, which lays out that factors and common procedures to consider when preparing an assessment of a company's PFI. These include, but are not limited to: a comparison of prior forecasts to actual results, a comparison of PFI to industry expectations, checking PFI against other internally prepared financial information for consistency, a comparison of entity PFI to historical trends, an understanding of who prepares the PFI and how often is it prepared, and the performance of mathematical and logic checks. Dufendach also mentioned that the AICPA's "cheap stock" guide has some useful information on assessing PFI.

Valuation dilution. Dilution from future issuances of securities can have a big impact on the values of existing securities, but guidance is limited, says Amanda Miller (Ernst & Young). There are different types of dilution, which stem from the existing capital structure (preferred and common units), future financing rounds, management securities, and investor warrants. Modeling dilution is difficult, and the topic will be included in the future *AICPA Private Equity/Venture Capital Accounting and Valuation Guide.* Miller is co-chair of the task force for the guide. The first public release of a working draft is expected in May 2018.

Private capital markets. Dr. Craig Everett leads the Private Capital Markets Project at Pepperdine University (which is now part of the Peate Institute for Entrepreneurship, located on the Calabasas,

6 www.ivsc.org/files/file/view/id/859.

Calif., campus). Everett noted that, while the S&P 500 returns since 1950 are 8.7%, private-company owners think their cost of equity is between 8% and 10%. "There is clearly a problem here," he said.

The Pepperdine project is designed to understand the true cost of private capital across market types and the investment expectations of privately held business owners. The project represents the hard work of researchers in developing a private cost of capital method as a legitimate alternative to looking to the public markets. Their method is to ask private capital market players what returns they project. Everett announced that the 2017 edition of their research (based on a survey deployed in January 2017) is now available.[7]

The researchers divide the private capital markets into six segments aligned with the major institutional arms of the private investment world, each with different return, investment, and research characteristics: bank lending, asset-based lending, mezzanine, private equity, venture capital, and angel investors. The "money shot" in the report is a table that includes annualized gross financing costs (rate of return) for each major capital type and its segments. The data are summarized in the exhibit, but there is much more detail in the report, including first and third quartiles by different criteria, such as amount of financing, EBITDA levels, and financing stage.

Summary of Data From the Pepperdine Project

Type of Private Capital Funding	Pepperdine Median Rate of Return (Range)
Banks	4.0%-6.5%
Asset-based lenders	5.5%-14.0%
Mezzanine financers	10.0%-24.0%
Private equity groups	20.5%-27.5%
Venture capital investors	25.0%-35.0%
Angel investors	35.0%-60.0%

SEC update. Austin Lee (Deloitte) was a valuation specialist at the SEC for two years, and he mentioned that valuation is a continued theme in the regulatory enforcement at the agency. He pointed to the recent SEC enforcement action against the Pacific Investment Management Co. (PIMCO)[8] in which the SEC said the firm overstated the exchange-traded fund's value and provided "misleading" reasons for the fund's early success, which was premised on buying small pieces or "odd lots" of mortgaged-backed securities that sell at a discount to larger units. PIMCO paid $20 million to settle the charges without admitting or denying the findings of the investigation. Lee worked on the case while he was with the SEC.

7 Craig R. Everett, "2017 Private Capital Markets Report," 2017. Pepperdine University Graziadio School of Business and Management. digitalcommons.pepperdine.edu/gsbm_pcm_pcmr/10.

8 www.sec.gov/news/pressrelease/2016-252.html.

Lee also pointed out that the SEC is concerned that some banks are not looking closely enough at the FASB's new Current Expected Credit Loss (CECL) impairment standard for loans and loan losses that will become effective in 2019.[9] The new rule requires an expected-loss approach to accounting for credit losses that replaces the incurred-loss approach. Bank financial statements will have to show credit losses on loans and other financial instruments in a more timely fashion under the new standard, which has been called one of the most significant changes in the history of bank accounting.

It's impossible to cover all of the information presented at the conference, so we hope to provide follow-up articles in future issues. *Business Valuation Update* congratulates the ASA, Ray Rath, and Tom Ryan for an excellent conference, and we look forward to attending this event next year.

9 FASB Update 2016-13—Financial Instruments—Credit Losses (Topic 326): Measurement of Credit Losses on Financial Instruments (www.fasb.org).

News You Can Use From the NACVA Annual Conference

When we attend a conference, we hear a lot of things we already know—and we're sure you do also. But what we listen for are pieces of new information or advice that practitioners can use in their practice. We attended sessions on all four days of the annual conference of the National Association of Certified Valuators and Analysts (NACVA) in Chicago and picked up a lot of these nuggets, some of which we present below.[1] There was no shortage of great tips and information.

Read, read, read. When asked about overall updates in the profession, Marc Bello (Edelstein & Co. LLP) advised the audience to look at is what's being published and keep your library current. He mentioned the Shannon Pratt and Roger Grabowski book on cost of capital[2] and related books on that topic that their book has triggered. He also mentioned Jim Hitchner's new edition of his book.[3] One valuation expert in the audience told us he devotes two hours each day to reading in order to keep current, which is essential in this profession.

NACVA standards update. There have been no substantive changes to the latest NACVA standards, which had an effective date of June 1, 2017, said Carl Steffen (WSRP LLC), who has been the chair of NACVA's standards board. There were some minor changes (in grammar and syntax) but nothing material. He also announced the availability of an updated side-by-side analysis of the five sets of North American standards: NACVA, IBA, AICPA, ASA, and USPAP.[4] All of the standards are essentially addressing the same issues and do not conflict with each other, he says. A similar analysis is being prepared of the three sets of international standards (IVS, Canada, and RICS).

Transition to consultant. Valuation experts who want to move their practices into a long-term consulting role with clients may not know how to make that transition effectively. Some NACVA members have used a program from CoreValue that offers training and support along these lines. Michael Gregory (Michael Gregory Consulting LLC) is a former territory manager with the IRS

1 See page 354 for conference coverage related to cost of capital and an update on valuation standards.

2 Roger Grabowski and Shannon Pratt, *Cost of Capital: Applications and Examples PLUS Website,* 5th edition (Wiley). Available at www.bvresources.com/publications.

3 James Hitchner, *Financial Valuation: Applications and Models, + Website,* 4th edition (Wiley). Available at www.bvresources.com/publications.

4 The Business Valuation/Appraisal Standards Comparison Chart 2017 is available at sub.bvresources.com/defaulttextonly.asp?f=downloads.

who became a business valuer and subsequently transformed himself into a business consultant specializing in mediation. "I never would have thought this," he says, and advised the audience to "look outside yourself as to how to help others." To pinpoint potential clients, ask these questions: "Who comes to you?" "Who trusts you?" There's a definite opportunity if you can determine clients' needs and how to help them.

Don't stray from your expertise. Before accepting a litigation engagement, make sure it's in an area that you're comfortable with, advise Howard Zandman (Aprio LLP) and T.J. Liles-Tims (BVFF Partners LLC). Zandman conducted a full-day preconference litigation report writing workshop, and Liles-Tims ran a workshop on financial forensics. Don't think you can brush up on a specialized topic and expect to be ready to go on the stand. They also advise that you learn everything about the case. Zandman mentioned the website Pacer.gov to do background research and get case documents.

Don't cite case law. Other than cases such as *Mandelbaum*, do not cite case law in your valuation report, advises Michael Kaplan (Kaplan Forensics). One idea he offered is to get a memo from the attorney on the matter and attach it to your report.

Consider adverse regulatory rulings. If a supplier sends tainted food to a restaurant that gets in trouble for food poisoning, it can have an impact on valuation and damages. But, in today's world, the impact is heightened because word spreads much faster and wider than ever. When something bad happens to a company, it's all over the internet, says Chris Hamilton (Arxis Financial Inc.), who had a number of damages cases last year where adverse regulatory rulings were an issue. He advises that you consider this increased exposure as well as potential exposure due to increased transparency of regulatory actions. Check websites of government agencies (e.g., the Food and Drug Administration) for signs of trouble. A recent check of the FDA site reveals a famous supermarket chain being cited for undisclosed walnuts in chocolate chip cookies.

Check jurisdiction re: goodwill. Know the facts of the case and the law that applies to it, urges Alan Zipp (Alan Zipp, CPA PC). The U.S. Supreme Court has ruled that, while goodwill is an asset of the business, personal goodwill does not belong to the business. That's an important takeaway especially if you're dealing in a federal jurisdiction, he says. On the state level, different states treat personal goodwill differently, so make sure you understand how the jurisdiction you're working in treats it.[5] Also understand the standard of value in your state. Zipp recalled a case of his where the valuation expert on the opposing side did not use the standard of value the court uses in that state, so his opinion was rejected in favor of Zipp's opinion.

Consult with attorney re: grantor trusts. A session on intentionally defective grantor trusts by Eido Walny (Walny Legal Group LLC) made one thing clear: always contact an attorney if you want to have a discussion with a client over these mechanisms. Trusts can be extremely complex,

5 See Charting Goodwill Jurisprudence + Easy Reference Map, available at sub.bvresources.com/defaulttextonly.asp?f=downloads.

but you should be aware of the big issues that make them attractive for estate planning or M&A purposes. For example, assets can be sold into these trusts using only a fraction of the equity. Also, all of these trusts need valuation services—the audience liked that aspect of them.

Examine buy-sell agreements. The valuation provisions in a buy-sell agreement are too often just slapped together without thinking them through properly. For example, the agreement may use the term fair market value when it really means fair value, the date of the valuation may not be specified, or there's other vague language. Steven Egna (Valuation Resource Group LLC) advises that you take a look at clients' buy-sell agreements and make some suggestions for revisions if needed. After all, if a dispute or other event triggers the use of the provision, you as the valuator will be caught in the middle to sort it all out.

Get real in court. You need to inject reality and common sense into valuations for litigation purposes, according to Melissa Gragg (Bridge Valuation Partners LLC) and Peter Agrapides (Western Valuation Advisors) in a case law update session. Don't assume you can prevail by merely using the proper valuation theory and methodology—courts can ignore this if it doesn't make sense in real life. The speakers mentioned the "very interesting" *Neiman*[6] case in which tax affecting was rejected because the assets were being distributed and not being liquidated. While the valuation analysis was consistent with fair market value, it was against what was going on in reality.

Business Valuation Update congratulates NACVA on a great event!

6 *Nieman v. Nieman*, 2015 Ohio App. LEXIS 5021 (Dec. 14, 2015); available from *BVLaw* (www.bvresources.com/products/bvlaw).

Five Tips to Help BV Experts Succeed in Mediation

By Nancy Neal Yeend,
The End Strategy (Portland, Ore., USA)

Although the use of experts in mediation has increased over the years, there are still some challenges. There is resistance to using experts, and, even when included, they are underutilized. Fortunately, some best practices have emerged for experts to increase their inclusion in mediation, manage the process, and improve the chances for finding a resolution.

Simply put, mediation is a facilitated negotiation. Mediation is the disputing parties' last opportunity to control the outcome of the conflict. Mediation is not a complicated process, but, to succeed, there are critical factors to address: timing, mediator, players, and preparation. When these factors have been addressed, the probability of settlement is greatly enhanced.

1. Start it early. Settlement is far more likely when mediation is started very early in the litigation process. The reason: People are not as polarized when they first contemplate litigation. In addition, mediation started before extensive discovery not only saves money, but also means the parties are far more flexible.

Mediation is often overlooked as a way to settle a case early on because many attorneys still are under the mistaken impression that suggesting it is a sign of weakness. In actuality, the attorney who suggests mediation sooner rather than later is acting in his or her client's best interest. A number of years ago, many jurisdictions required counsel to discuss mediation with his or her client at the time litigation is contemplated. Experts can help encourage the attorney to consider whether the benefits of mediation outweigh the risks associated with trial.

2. Choose a mediator wisely. Selecting the case-appropriate mediator is critical. At a minimum, a mediator needs to have three qualifications: be trained in the mediation process, have mediated similar types of cases, and possess subject matter understanding. For civil cases, the national average for mediation courses is 40 hours of actual, hands-on instruction.

There are burned-out attorneys and retired judges who think that their past careers adequately prepare them to be mediators, and nothing could be further from the truth. Mediation is not at all like an administrative hearing, arbitration, or a trial. A decision-maker runs those forums. Mediation is also not the same as a settlement conference. In mediation, the parties are the decision-makers, as they retain control over the outcome. Settlement is up to the parties, and, ethically and by statute in many states, mediators are not permitted to coerce settlement or to give their opinion. A mediator may not become an advocate for any mediation participant or side.

Experts brought in earlier into the process can provide the attorney with additional benefits by helping select the case-appropriate mediator. This is especially useful when the expert has direct experience with the mediator in previous cases. The expert's insight can be of further value when planning the negotiation strategy. Understanding the mediator's style is invaluable knowledge for succeeding in mediation.

3. Know the players. Without knowing who all the players are, it is impossible to develop a viable negotiation strategy. Key to success of any mediation is to have all *decision-makers* present at the mediation. What is meant by the term *"decision-maker"*? Any person who can prevent the terms of a settlement from being fulfilled is a *decision-maker* and needs to be at the mediation. If a decision-maker is not present at the mediation, it is too easy for that missing person to say *"no"* to whatever everyone else thought was a solid settlement.

An additional concept to be discussed is *"full authority."* In some states, "full authority" means the policy limit or the last demand, whichever is less. Experts who have participated in mediations where these terms have not been clarified can help prevent these fundamental mistakes by discussing these principles with the attorney and getting clarification on these issues. A significant number of mediations fail because participants do not have full authority or all the decision-makers were not in attendance.

Experts can help identify who the key figures are, and they may have insight into whether a board of directors or some other entity needs to approve a settlement. Experts may also have observed the various decision-makers in other cases and may be able to provide insight into what types of information resonates with that person: written reports, charts and graphs, photos, etc.

4. Get the entire picture. Preparation for the mediation can be far more productive when the expert is brought into the process earlier and has all the information related to the first three factors. When experts are limited to only focusing on specific elements of the case, opportunities might be missed. Failure to prepare is the leading cause for failed mediations.

For example, the expert may be in an ideal position to educate the client about the facts that will help to prove or disprove the claim. The expert can translate technical terms and concepts, so that the client can understand and appreciate the strengths and weaknesses of the case. It goes without saying that the expert can also help educate the attorney as well as the parties on the other side of the mediation table. In addition, experts can be very helpful with developing the negotiation strategy because they have witnessed the other side's tactics in previous mediations.

Shannon Pratt on the Role of the BV Expert in Mediation

Experts can act as co-mediators as well as neutral experts, although the roles are significantly different. If acting as a co-mediator, the expert must comply with the ethical constraints of impartiality and neutrality and the goal of self—determination by the parties. The expert co-mediator can't give an opinion as to value but can provide information to assist the parties in making informative decisions and in formulating their own settlement.

When consulted as a neutral expert, the appraiser's role requires him or her to utilize his or her expertise to give an opinion that the parties can choose to either use or ignore. The recommendation by a mediator to employ the services of a neutral expert is far more common than the use by the mediator of an expert to co-mediate. Peter Adler, former president of the Society of Professionals in Dispute Resolution (SPIDR), noted that he has utilized the services of appraisers as both experts and co-mediators. In larger cases, where the parties themselves have independently employed two experts, it is also acceptable to ask the experts to select a third expert if the parties do not feel that they can rely upon either of the experts the other selected.

(Source: Shannon Pratt and Alina Niculita, *Valuing a Business*, 5th edition, McGraw-Hill, 2008; available at www.bvresources.com/products/valuing-a-business-the-analysis-and-appraisal-of-closely-held-companies-5th-ed)

5. Suggest options. The expert may be an extremely helpful resource when it comes to generating settlement options. Remember, mediation is a facilitated negotiation, and the person who goes in with the greatest number of options will always do much better than the person who only has one option—*"my way or the highway."* Experts can make suggestions as to what other people have done. This does not guarantee that this particular client will do it, but, statistically, people tend to accept options that they know other people have accepted. Having a suggestion come from the expert also helps make the option sound more neutral than if it came from the attorney, so the other side might be more likely to accept the idea or at least listen to the proposal. Perhaps the expert's suggestion will prompt the other side to not be outdone and come up with additional options. No one wants to appear to be unable to come up with ideas or to have the *"best"* ideas only come from the other side.

Including experts in mediation does a number of things that can help improve the prospect of a settlement. The expert not only brings his or her subject matter expertise, but also can provide numerous benefits that can help in resolving the case: assist with the selection of mediator, educate the client, translate complex terms or concepts, help design a negotiation strategy, focus the mediation preparation, and so much more. Involving the expert early in mediation often opens the door to further consulting!

***Nancy Neal Yeend** has mediated business-related matters for over 30 years, including trial and appellate-level cases. She has served as National Judicial College faculty for over 20 years. Yeend also serves as a coach on how to prepare for mediation. Her firm, The End Strategy (TES), is located in Portland, Ore. She can be reached at nancy@TESresults.com.*

How Do Your BV Firm's Billing Rates and Practices Stack Up?

Over 170 firms responded to BVR's survey last summer that forms the basis of *The BVR Business Valuation Firm Economics & Best Practices Guide,* 2017 edition. The wealth of data collected makes this survey the largest and most thorough analysis available of business valuation firms. Among many other aspects of BV firm operations, billing rates and practices were surveyed, and we present some of the results here.

Billing methods. Most firms bill on either fixed-fee or hourly billing—or both, as shown in Exhibit 1. Retainers are frequently used, and value-based billing is starting to make some slight inroads.

Exhibit 1. Which of the Following Billing Methods Do You Regularly Use for Business Valuation Engagements (Check All That You Use Regularly):	
Fixed or flat fees	88.4%
Hourly	86.6%
Retainer as a deposit against future fees	77.7%
Value based	29.5%
Percentage	10.7%
Other (percentage of transaction, "cost plus," etc.)	0.1%

The typical firm offers three standard billing approaches (the mean for the survey database is 3.0 billing formats per firm). Firms that use hourly billing generate 51% of their total billings from hourly arrangements. The range of responses for this question ran from 1% to 100% (firms that bill hourly exclusively), showing that the use of this billing practice varies widely within the BV profession. CPA firms are much more likely to use hourly billing rates than BV-only practices.

Hourly rates. While hourly billing is not the most common method of communicating fees to clients in the BV profession, it's used quite often, and these hourly rates are nearly always part of the project fee budgeting process, whether the client is aware of them or not.

The highest billing partner in the 2016 survey reports an hourly rate of $650. Eleven firms in the survey database now bill partners at rates over $450 per hour. Average billing rates for partners, senior analysts, junior analysts, and all "clerical" staff (including report writers, researchers, and designers) are reported in Exhibits 2 to 6. As you can see from the data, a number of interesting conclusions hopefully will be helpful to all firms when discussing pricing strategy for BV services.

Exhibit 2. Billing Rates—Partners

	Mean	Median	Range
All	$322	$323	$100-$650
BV firms	$328	$325	$100-$650
CPA firms	$309	$310	$50-$450
Large BV practices > $1M	$414	$410	$200-$650

Exhibit 3. Billing Rates—Senior Analysts

	Mean	Median	Range
All	$225	$225	$50-$400
BV firms	$232	$250	$50-$400
CPA firms	$218	$218	$120-$350
Large BV practices	$263	$260	$150-$400

Exhibit 4. Billing Rates—Junior Analysts

	Mean	Median	Range
All	$157	$150	$80-$275
BV firms	$162	$175	$80-$275
CPA firms	$148	$140	$80-$275
Large BV practices	$188	$200	$125-$250

Exhibit 5. Billing Rates—Researcher

	Mean	Median	Range
All	$101	$100	$35-$250
BV firms	$111	$100	$35-$250
CPA firms	$88	$85	$60-$160
Large BV practices	$131	$145	$35-$250

Exhibit 6. Billing Rates—Administrative/Clerical

	Mean	Median	Range
All	$77	$75	$35-$175
BV firms	$78	$75	$35-$175
CPA firms	$50	$125	$50-$125
Large BV practices	$94	$75	$50-$175

First, on average, BV firms tend to bill more than CPA firms at all levels (including researchers and administrative support, when billable). This is a reversal from the data in the last survey (2011). Not surprisingly, billing rates at firms that do litigation support services are higher, too.

Second, generally, the range and variation in billing rates are extremely high, leaving a lot of room for adjustment. There's no such thing as a "standard" hourly billing rate for a business valuation firm.

Third, larger firms (those with annual revenues greater than $1 million) tend to bill at significantly higher rates than smaller firms.

Rate increases. Three-fifths of the respondents to the 2016 survey increased their fees or rates in the last year—and they were significantly higher than in the past—as shown in Exhibit 7.

The mean increase for firms that raised their rates was 8.5%, and the median was 5.0% (the average rate increase in the 2011 survey was approximately 4%, by comparison). Including firms that did not raise fees in the last 12 months, the business valuation profession as a whole increased its rates 5.2% during the last year, a significant increase from 2.1% in the 2011 survey.

Exhibit 7. Did You Increase Your Fees or Rates in the Last 12 Months?			
	Percentage Increasing	Average Increase for Firms That Reported Increases	Median Increase for Firms That Reported Increases
2011	61.1%	3.9%	3.0%
2016	61.5%	8.5%	5.0%

Research cost recovery. The costs of DLOM, transaction, ERP, industry, and other research services are significant, and, for that reason, an increasing number of BV firms have begun charging a separate fee to recoup some of those client costs. The most typical amount charged by firms that do so is 5% on top of project fees. BV firms are more likely to charge for resources than CPA or other firms, as shown in Exhibit 8.

Exhibit 8. Does Your Firm Charge an Additional Fee for Business Valuation				
	All Firms	BV Firms	CPA Firms	Other Firms
2011 percentage answering "yes"	34.7%	39.6%	21.2%	35.1%
2016 percentage answering "yes"	42.9%	46.4%	39.1%	41.7%

Late fees. The practice of charging late fees for delinquent accounts is less widespread in the business valuation profession, as shown in Exhibit 9. CPA firms, borrowing from their tax and A&A practices, are more likely to charge late fees (or at least notify their clients that they might do so). Smaller firms are the least likely to assess these additional fees. Personal friendships with clients, along with less administrative support to administer billing practices, are likely reasons for this variance.

Exhibit 9. Do You Assess Late Fees for Delinquent Payments?				
	All Firms	CPA Firms	BV Firms	Other Firms
Yes	53.2%	58.7%	50.0%	45.4%

The most common late fee is 1.5% per month (or 18% annually)—47% of firms that charge late fees use this amount. The second most common is 1% per month (or 12% annually).

The full report, *The BVR Business Valuation Firm Economics & Best Practices Guide*, 2017 edition, reveals best practices in financial management, marketing, human resources and compensation, and professional and ownership standards. It is available at www.bvresources.com/products/the-bvr-business-valuation-firm-economics-best-practices-guide.

Ongoing Survey Reveals Need to Improve Report Writing

By Rod P. Burkert, CPA/ABV, CVA
Burkert Valuation Advisors, (USA and Canada)

Over the past four years, I have discovered a declining trend in the quality of valuation reports—and not just in the style of writing, but in the framework (i.e., professional standards) and content as well. As a long-time provider of a valuation report review service,[1] I have asked my report review clients about this. They tell me that when they actually get to writing the report, they are running out of time or budget or both—so the report gets short shrift.

You can argue that my judgment is based purely on subjective, anecdotal evidence, and I would have to agree with you. Therefore, this article not only discusses what I see as the current state of report writing, but it also presents objective evidence as to why the subject needs more attention.

Objective evidence. Between May 2013 and May 2017, I presented 16 report writing webinar series for the National Association of Certified Valuators and Analysts (NACVA). Each series was well attended and ran for six hours over three days. Day 1 covered The Report Road Map, Day 2 is devoted to professional standards, and Day 3 tackles errors and omissions.

On each day, we were required to have six poll questions for NASBA/CPE purposes, and I have tracked the results over four years for all 16 webinars. Out of the 18 poll questions I administer, I want to discuss—in three categories—13 of them, as I think they reveal some of the heights and plights of our collective report writing process and product.

I. The Demographics

1. How many years of BVFLS experience do you have?

(a) 0-3 years—19%
(b) 3-5 years—19%
(c) 5+ years—62%

---

1 Others who provide this service include Jim Hitchner (Financial Valuation Advisors Inc.) and Michael Gregory (Michael Gregory Consulting LLC).

As you can see, most of my webinar attendees have a fair amount of experience; almost two-thirds of them have five years of BVFLS experience or more, so report writing shouldn't be something they are struggling with at this stage of their career.

2. What is your practice/experience geared toward?

(a) Business valuation—83%
(b) Litigation support—17%

Most people are writing reports for the BV wheelhouse and can be expected to be writing detailed/ comprehensive reports regularly.

3. Generally, who do you write your reports for:

(a) An informed user/reader—56%
(b) An uninformed user/reader—44%

I define an informed user/reader as someone such as an IRS examiner and an uninformed user/ reader as someone such as a family law judge who has only seen a few business valuation cases in his or her courtroom. This is important because I believe whom we write for affects how we write, what we write, and how long the report needs to be.

II. The Process

4. Does your firm use report writing software?

(a) Yes—45%
(b) No—55%

I have nothing against report writing software if you invest the time to know how it works and customize it to your practice. (But I don't see that happening vis-à-vis my report review service.) My good colleague, Darrell Dorrell (FinancialForensics), wrote an excellent piece about report writing software in *Financial Valuation & Litigation Expert* (included in Resources).

5. Does your firm have a standard template to start each new report with?

(a) Yes—80%
(b) No—20%

This is good to see. A template allows every report to begin on common ground and reduces the errors that can occur when you start with the last report you prepared. Just a note of caution, however, that the more templates you have, the more you must update when changes need to be made. I have one template that I use to start every one of my valuation engagements regardless of the type of report, company, industry, or purpose.

6. Even if your firm does not have to comply with USPAP, does it voluntarily do so?

(a) Yes—48%
(b) No—48%

(c) I must comply with USPAP—4%

Appraisers who do or must prepare reports in compliance with USPAP have a slight numerical edge. And even though ABVs and CVAs are not required to do so, I think there is a higher standard of care perception when a report is prepared in compliance with USPAP. And the burden to comply with USPAP is not that difficult, so I don't understand why more people don't do so.

7. Do you prominently disclose all major valuation assumptions in one section of your report?

(a) Yes—82%
(b) No—18%

I don't think there is anything that can focus the attention of an appraiser more than seeing all of the major valuation assumptions he or she relied on in one place and make sure they are appropriately buttressed.

8. How does your firm deliver a final report?

(a) Print copy only—28%
(b) PDF copy only—11%
(c) Both print and PDF copies—61%

I have not delivered a print copy of a final report since Jan. 1, 2004. And, if you are not going to sit down with the client and use the report as a springboard to cross-sell consulting services, I don't see the point. A lot of time goes into a print copy, e.g., signatures, page counting, binding, etc., and I am uncertain what value it brings in today's digital workplace.

III. The Report

9. What areas of the report do you struggle to write the most?

(a) Company background—10%
(b) Economic overview/industry outlook—24%
(c) Valuation approaches—14%
(d) Discounts and premiums—42%
(e) Synthesis and conclusion—10%

On one hand, the large discounts and premiums percentage is not surprising. On the other hand, given all of the articles, books, and CPE sessions discussing this topic, people aren't getting it.

What this poll question does not capture is how often the appraiser makes the effort to relate sections such as the company background, economic overview, and industry outlook back to the subject company being valued. I see very little of this in the reports I review.

10. What term do you use when you express a conclusion of value (in noncalculation/nonlitigation reports)?

(a) Estimate—52%
(b) Opinion—48%

Our industry struggles when our professional standards cannot unify what we call our end result. And, of course, the nuance of the term "opinion" is not lost on me or other CPA/ABVers. But what about our clients or the attorneys representing our clients? They don't care as much about what term the standards say we must use as they do about using a term that sounds stronger and more confident about the end result.

11. Have you ever had one of your reports reviewed by a professional editor/proofreader?

(a) Yes—30%
(b) No—70%

If you paid five figures for a valuation report, wouldn't you expect it to be free of spelling errors, typos, and grammatical mistakes? And if you did catch some of these blemishes while reading the report, wouldn't you wonder about what you didn't find? As value pricing expert Ron Baker would say, people don't care about the labor pains—they want to see the baby. Our report is the baby, and all of our labor pains to birth it will be judged (fairly or not) on how the report reads. That 70% of us let something go out the door without proofreading is unprofessional. Here's a goal: start with your template report. At least then you know your starting document is the best it can be, spelling-, typo-, and grammarwise.

12. Is there someone in your firm qualified to review your reports?

(a) Yes—65%
(b) No—35%

While a proofreader will catch the writing errors, only someone with knowledge of valuation can grasp the actual content and gauge that there were no misapplications of valuation approaches, methods, procedures, or data. Again, if you paid five figures for a report, wouldn't you be dismayed to find out there was no quality control step?

13. After taking today's webinar, do you feel confident that your reports are in compliance with industry standards?

(a) Yes—87%
(b) No—13%

Resources You Can Use: Valuation Report Writing

Burkert, Rod, "Is Your Value an Estimate or an Opinion," *Business Valuation Update,* May 2012, pp. 9-10.

Burkert, Rod, "9 Ways to Improve Your Report Writing," *Business Valuation Update,* December 2010, pp. 1, 4-5.

Burkert, Rod, "Report Righter: The Company Backgrounder," *The Value Examiner,* July/August, 2011, pp. 44-45.

Burkert, Rod, "Report Righter: Use Highlights to Keep Your Report Flowing," *The Value Examiner,* May/June 2011, pp. 45-46.

Burkert, Rod, Report Writing: The Final Frontier in BV Productivity, 16th Annual Minnesota Society of Certified Public Accountants Business Valuation Conference, Nov. 2, 2016; Tennessee Society of Certified Public Accountants Southeastern Forensic & Valuation Services Conference, Oct. 28, 2015; and Financial Consulting Group University, May 5, 2015.

Burkert, Rod, "What Does Your Report Roadmap Look Like," *Business Valuation Update,* November 2011, pp. 40-41.

Burkert, Rod, Writing Reports for the Intended User, AICPA Forensic and Valuation Services Conference, Nov. 11, 2013.

Burkert, Rod, "You Say Potato …," *Business Valuation Update,* October 2011, p. 29.

Damodaran, Aswath, *Narrative and Numbers: The Value of Stories in Business,* 2017, Columbia University Press.

Davis, Jan, ed., *A BVR Special Report—How to Write Bulletproof Valuation Reports: Tips From the Experts,* Business Valuation Resources, 2015 (available at www.bvresources.com/products/how-to-write-bulletproof-valuation-reports-tips-from-the-experts).

Dorrell, Darrell, "Build or Buy? Is It Time for You to Take the Step?" *Financial Valuation & Litigation Expert,* August/September 2014.

Hitchner, James, Best Practices: Business Valuation Methods Report Writing, webinar by Valuation Products and Services LLC, Aug. 16, 2017 (archive available at www.valuationproducts.com/webinarspast.html).

Hood, L. Paul and Lee, Timothy R., Step Up Your Game: Effective Business Appraisal Reporting, webinar by Business Valuation Resources, Feb. 7, 2014 (archive available at sub.bvresources.com/trainingeventpast.asp?WebinarID=352).

Kleeman, Robert Jr., "Time to Update the Guiding Principles to a Valuation Report," *Business Valuation Update,* May 2017, pp. 9-12.

Sample Reports Library, Vols. 17-24, National Association of Certified Valuators and Analysts (available at www.nacva.com/store_category.asp?id=1&p=1).

"Seven Cases to Read Before Writing Your Next Valuation Report" (remarks of former IRS official Howard Lewis), *Business Valuation Update,* August 2014.

Trugman, Gary and Basson, Martin E., Preparing Reports for Litigation and the IRS, webinar by Business Valuation Resources, March 19, 2015 (archive available at sub.bvresources.com/trainingeventpast.asp?WebinarID=413).

Weiss, Stuart, "Anatomy of an Inflated Valuation Report," *Business Valuation Update,* October 2013.

Wood, David, "Report Righter: Connect the Dots," *The Value Examiner,* July/August 2010, p. 46.

Wood, David, "Report Righter: Fight Complexity," *The Value Examiner,* September/October 2009, pp. 36-38.

Wood, David, "Report Righter: Use Active Voice to Earn Trust," *The Value Examiner,* November/December 2009, pp. 30-31.

Given how much standards are beaten into us and how many checklists are floating around to help us, making sure we comply with standards would seem to be the easiest way to stay out of trouble. I think the possible 13% error rate is too high, but, when combined with Question 12, we can't wonder why one or more government agencies want to wade into our profession.

Back to the anecdotal side of things. In an interview with *BVWire News*, here is what former IRS territory manager and now valuation sole practitioner Michael Gregory said about reviewing reports and finding enough errors to typically generate *a four- to six-page paper* of significant comments: "What does this tell me?" he writes in his book, *Business Appraisals and the IRS*. "It tells me that you should have a third party conduct a real review of your work. It should be made a formal part of the work flow. The review should cover readability as well as technical competency, including math in spreadsheets."[2]

Final thoughts. Report writing is where our rubber meets the client's road—it's usually the last impression we leave. I also consider report writing to be the final frontier of BV productivity. My experience says we need to do more and do better to: (1) increase our effectiveness so that we are more confident in our conclusions of value; and (2) improve our efficiency so that we are more profitable on every engagement.

I believe most of us have a pretty good idea how our reports stack up in terms of where we're strong, where we're weak—and that can change from one report to the next. But, in general, we know. Which means we know what we have to work on. Still, people ask me how to improve the quality of their reports. The best ways to improve quality is to: (1) learn how to be a better writer; (2) have a proofreader review your report template for grammar, etc.; and (3) have a respected peer review your reports for content.

***Rod Burkert**, CPA/ABV, CVA is the founder of Burkert Valuation Advisors and a long-time instructor for NACVA's Consultants' Training Institute. Rod has built a mobile consulting practice by leveraging his professional network and social media, and, since March 2010, he has been traveling full-time throughout the United States and Canada in an RV with his wife and their dogs. See rodburkert.com/consulting to learn more about his report review service.*

2 "Former IRS Manager Gives Valuation Report Tip," *BVWire News*, Jan. 14, 2014 (www.bvresources.com).

ASA BV Committee Members Share Insights and Advice

The business valuation community is fortunate to have an impressive number of professionals who give a most precious asset—their time—to help enhance and guide the profession. They volunteer to serve on committees, teach courses, act as mentors, help organize conferences—do whatever they can to give back to the profession.

BVU had the pleasure of speaking with some of the dedicated individuals who serve as members of the Business Valuation Committee of the American Society of Appraisers (ASA). The incoming chair of the committee is Jeffrey Tarbell, who is a director in Houlihan Lokey's Financial Advisory Services business. We also spoke with vice chair Kenneth J. Pia, partner-in-charge of the Business Valuation Services group at Marcum LLP. Also giving their insights are Erin Hollis, the committee's treasurer, who is director of valuation at Marshall & Stevens Inc., and Ronald L. Seigneur of Seigneur Gustafson LLP, who serves as the committee's secretary.

BVU: *What is the role of the ASA BV Committee?*

Tarbell: The committee was formed in the early 1980s by a group of appraisers who shared a common interest in advancing the business valuation profession. Today, like then, the committee consists of industry leaders who volunteer their time toward two primary efforts: (1) the development and delivery of best-in-class business valuation education; and (2) the advancement of our profession through the establishment and endorsement of professional standards such as the ASA Business Valuation Standards, USPAP, and IVS.

BVU: *Do you have any specific goals for your tenure as committee chair?*

Tarbell: I have two primary goals for the next two years. The first goal relates to the Certified in Entity and Intangibles Valuation (CEIV) credential. Much has been accomplished to date, with the issuance of the Mandatory Performance Framework (MPF), Body of Knowledge, our own CEIV education course (BV 401), and the on-demand exam. However, work remains in order to develop a joint quality monitory program with our CEIV partners. The second goal pertains to our efforts to serve the large and growing international marketplace of business valuation professionals with high-quality and timely BV education.

BVU: *Ken, you're also on the ASA's subcommittee for business valuation education, whose work I assume dovetails with the BV committee?*

Pia: Yes, the goal is to make sure our curriculum material is as up-to-date as possible and includes all of the current hot topics in the profession, which is ever-evolving. Our educational offerings range from principles of valuation (POV) courses, which are more foundational in nature, to our webinars, which offer more higher-level technical material. All of this leads up to our Advanced Business Valuation Conference, this year in Houston, October 7-10, which covers the most relevant current technical material in the profession.

BVU: *You mentioned the new CEIV credential. More thoughts?*

Hollis: The ASA's commitment to the CEIV credential is for a universal standard of reporting and regulatory oversight.

Pia: Any time you can advance a subspecialty not only with education, but also with a credential is a good thing. People who prepare financial statements should be relying on people who are credentialed in the right areas. The MPF, I believe, is an overall best practice approach to fair value for financial reporting, and the more consistent business valuation professionals can become, then the better off the profession will be.

Seigneur: I am excited to see this credential coming to market as it has required a dedicated and collaborative effort by a large number of individuals representing their respective constituencies in a relatively short period. The CEIV appears to be fully responsive to the regulatory environment that will benefit from the competence and consistency in practice that the CEIV credential recognizes. The ASA has been a leader in the process, including the significant efforts to coordinate the new educational curriculum supporting the CEIV.

BVU: *In addition to the CEIV efforts, are there any other new ASA initiatives designed to enhance the profession?*

Tarbell: We always have a full plate of initiatives. One notable one is that the BV Standards Subcommittee has begun a project to review and update the ASA BV Standards and the Principles of Appraisal Practice and Code of Ethics. These documents are due for a refresh, and we have an outstanding group of folks looking at the issues.

BVU: *What do you see as the main challenges BV practitioners face today?*

Tarbell: Regulation is always an issue. We've taken some very big steps in the area of fair value for financial reporting through the establishment of the CEIV credential, but that's just one of many BV specialties. Regulatory threats persist in other areas as well, including employee stock ownership plan valuation and estate/gift tax valuation, to name a few.

Hollis: Major challenges include price and value dilution of valuation services based on those practitioners who are not credentialed and who do not adhere to a professional standard of care and ethics. Individuals who are not credentialed by a recognized valuation organization or educated in accepted valuation methodology saturate the marketplace with substandard work product and below-market price points and, in general, do a disservice to users of valuation services.

Seigneur: We are all being challenged ever more to become specialists within the specialty of business appraisal. Examples are ESOPs, family law, economic damages, financial forensics, compensation and the like. Keeping up with the evolving best practices and current technical resources in each niche area is a significant challenge that requires a constant commitment to life-long learning. I personally do a lot of expert witness work and see a tremendous opportunity for the next generation of technically competent younger appraisers and financial forensics folks to fill a growing void as the baby boomer generation continue to slow down and exit this aspect of our profession.

BVU: *Jeff, speaking of ESOPs, I see you're doing a session at the upcoming ASA Business Valuation Conference in Houston titled Issues Attracting Scrutiny of ESOP Valuation. Can you give us a few takeaways from your session?*

Tarbell: Between the [GreatBanc] Fiduciary Process Agreement and some recent federal court decisions, we now have a clear understanding of the DOL's hot button issues and the processes that it wants to see fiduciaries and their appraisers follow. I plan to discuss the valid and the not-so-valid issues addressed in these cases, and present solutions that I hope will help to keep appraisers and their fiduciary clients away from such trouble in the future.

BVU: Of course, this is a crucial time for the Houston area and BVR is happy to support this event.

Seigneur: We will be attending this conference in the middle of a special city that has a decade or more of rebuilding just ahead. Our firm has sponsored a family in need from Rockport, just to the south of Houston, and I would encourage others to find ways to help the area recover in some small way.

Hollis: The networking opportunities at events such as this are invaluable. I'm looking forward to seeing my fellow ASAs and mingling with the speakers in Houston.

Pia: This year's conference has a particularly strong slate of speakers and topics. Also, there's an emphasis on the practical aspects so that you will walk away from the sessions with something that you can put into practice right away.

BVU: *What advice would you give to individuals entering the profession?*

Seigneur: Seek out mentors and pay attention to what they can teach you. Be willing to make the shared sacrifice to better yourself. And by shared sacrifice I mean be willing to undertake activities on your own time to enhance your capabilities and knowledge. Write articles, give presentations, serve on volunteer committees and boards, and do so without an expectation of immediate compensation for doing so.

Hollis: I agree about a mentor. Having an excellent mentor is one of the best ways to learn the profession, and a good mentor will make you want to stick with the profession. Valuation is a unique blend of finance, economics, accounting, business, and law. The practice never gets stagnant.

Pia: You need a good solid education in valuation from college courses and through hands-on training at a firm. More colleges are adding valuation to their curriculum—I developed and teach a private company valuation course at Quinnipiac University in Connecticut. We also have a number of employees here at Marcum that we hired out of Texas Tech.

BVU: *Any other comments or remarks you'd like to make?*

Hollis: Do not underestimate the value of a credential, in both time or recognition. Not all credentials are equal. Something worth having is something to work hard for. You can never know enough, and someone will always know more than you. So do not shortchange yourself with mediocre education.

Pia: I'm very optimistic about the various committees now in place at the ASA. We are all very involved and committed to enhancing the ASA credential, which is evident by the progress made over the past five or six years.

Seigneur: Our annual gathering of some of the world's best minds in the areas we all work in is always rewarding and worthwhile. If you attend in Houston this year, make it a point to leave with at least three or four new friendships and lifelines you might be able to use and vice versa when back in the trenches.

Tarbell: The Business Valuation Committee is always eager to hear from ASA members who are looking for ways to get involved. If interested, please email me at. Other than that, I look forward to seeing everyone in Houston!

Action Ideas From the ASA Advanced BV Confab

When you attend a conference in person, you have the benefit of networking with practitioners inside and outside of the formal sessions. You can gather all kinds of interesting and useful tips and advice, which is exactly what we did at the recent Advanced Business Valuation Conference in Houston presented by the American Society of Appraisers (ASA). Here are a few of them, and we will have more in future issues.

Consider the CEIV credential. If you are involved in fair value for financial reporting, you should look into the Certified in Entity and Intangible Valuations (CEIV) credential offered by the ASA (as well as the AICPA and RICS). Bill Johnston (Empire Valuation Consultants), former head of the ASA BV committee, said that the new credential is designed to improve financial reporting valuations for U.S. publicly traded companies. Requirements for attaining the credential include experience, education, submitting to an ongoing engagement-level quality review process, and complying with a new Mandatory Performance Framework (MPF) to ensure confidence in the consistency and transparency in the credential holder's work.

The ASA, AICPA, and RICS are all officially approved to offer the CEIV credential, but getting it through the ASA offers several benefits, Johnston pointed out. The ASA is the only one of the three organizations that is solely focused on valuation and is a leader in financial reporting and fair value education. Also, the ASA is the only organization that offers a specialty designation for intangible assets.

During an awards ceremony at the conference, Johnston received the Jerry F. Larkin Award for outstanding volunteer service, particularly with the ASA's Rising Stars efforts and the new CEIV credentialing program.

Take a fresh look at your PFI procedures. At the ASA table, there were copies of the latest ASA Business Valuation Committee Special Topics (Paper #3): The Use of Management's Prospective Financial Information by a Valuation Analyst. It is available from the ASA as a free download, and you can find it in the ASA's *BV Review* for Spring 2017 (go to www.asa.org). A much higher level of professional skepticism is needed in this area because the perception is that too many valuation experts simply accept projections and forecasts they're given without applying enough scrutiny—or any scrutiny at all.

One attendee suggested doing a separate engagement letter for a forecast if it takes longer than what your basic engagement letter allows for. A common question is: What if you don't agree with the forecast management provides and management won't change it? It should be rejected until management works on it and makes it reasonable. Should you adjust the discount rate to reflect an unreasonable forecast? ASA training material says that is a "last resort," but it seems that many practitioners do it.

Look to customers when estimating goodwill. Bottom-up and top-down approaches to quantifying personal goodwill are gaining traction in marital dissolution cases, says Bob Morrison (Morrison Valuation & Forensic Services), who uses these approaches in Florida. An attendee in the audience mentioned that he estimates goodwill by examining how much the owner influences customer retention by analyzing the relationships. Morrison noted that, if you can get access to customer information in order to examine how much the owner influences customer retention, then that is a great way to analyze the relationships.

Ask key questions about compensation. To normalize compensation, you need to get certain information from management. Tax returns may not be reliable, says compensation expert Stephen Kirkland (Atlantic Executive Consulting). One thing to ask about is all related parties involved in the subject company—both humans and nonhumans (entities)—and get the responses in writing, he advises. Also, at the end of your data gathering, ask the question, "Is there anything else I need to know to normalize compensation?" That way, management can't come back with "you didn't ask," if you miss something. Kirkland says one company owner lost his license to practice but never disclosed it. He also advises that you put in the engagement letter that you will be delving into reasonable compensation—it's a sensitive topic, and some owners are surprised that it's part of the process.

Eliminate traces of advocacy. Being perceived as an advocate for your client is the No. 1 error in valuation reports in a litigation context, says Michael Paschall (Banister Financial). Other top errors include math mistakes, not doing a site visit, failure to support the rationale for discounts and weightings, an economy and industry section that is disproportionately larger than the company information section, and plagiarism.

Bulletproof your reports for court. Speaking of plagiarism, if you're in court, the opposition will catch you if you lift material from other sources, especially other valuation reports, says attorney David Aughtry (Chamberlain Hrdlicka), who has extensive experience with valuation disputes in court. "Canned gets you canned," he says. He also reports that 70% to 80% of valuation disputes boil down to a misapplication of the standard of value to the ownership interest.

Watch for these court cases. Outside the sessions, several attendees told us about a pending Tax Court case in Oregon that is a "clone" of the *Giustina* case, which involved the valuation of timberland. The pending case also involves a timber company, and the IRS is attempting to use the same methodology it used—and lost with—in *Giustina.* The IRS is attempting to value the underlying timberland as opposed to the going-concern value of the company. As in *Giustina,* the underlying assets are worth much more than the going concern, but there is no way a shareholder can sell his or her interest in the timberland to reap that higher value. Interestingly, the same IRS attorneys who were on the losing side in *Giustina* are also on this new case.

This same issue—of underlying asset value versus going-concern value—is one of the issues in the pending Tax Court case, *Cecil et al. v. Commissioner of Internal Revenue.* One of the attorneys for the taxpayer is Aughtry, who did a session at the conference and made some general comments on the case but could not discuss it in detail. But it's the same situation in that case: The land and property are worth much more than the operating company. The other matter of great interest in this case is the issue of tax affecting pass-through entities, which the IRS and Tax Courts have always rejected. In the *Cecil* case, the valuation experts for both the taxpayer and the IRS use tax affecting, although we understand the IRS backed away from this position in its closing arguments. Another case, the estate of Michael Jackson, also involves tax affecting, and the judge denied the IRS's motion to exclude the estate's expert's testimony concerning tax affecting. Depending on the outcomes of these cases, we could be having some very different conversations about tax affecting PTEs.

Use traditional ways to build your practice. During the networking breaks and while we were at the BVR booth, we asked attendees about the best ways they use to market their practices. You'd think that social networking would be high on the list of what's working well, but we were told that certain traditional methods are more effective, especially the face-to-face meeting with a prospect. Other methods that are proving to be effective include speaking at public events, cross-marketing to existing clients, sponsoring events prospects are likely to attend, and writing for practitioner journals or industry publications. Writing and speaking engagements are also a good way to position yourself as an authority on a specific aspect of valuation, which will help you compete in a profession where fee pressures are emerging.

We will have more coverage of the conference in future issues. *BVU* congratulates the conference planning committee for an excellent event: conference chair Bruce Johnson (Monroe, Park & Johnson Inc.), Rosanne Aumiller (Grant Thornton), Jaclyn Burket (SKY Valuation), Jay E. Fishman (Financial Research Associates), George Hawkins (Banister Financial Inc.), and Kevin Janke (Wipfli). Next year, the conference will be in Anaheim, Calif.

Section V.
Reviews Of Data Sources And New Books

Review: *Discount for Lack of Marketability Guide* and Toolkit

By Harold G. Martin Jr., Keiter (Richmond, Va., USA)

When valuing companies under the fair market value standard, many practitioners devote the majority of their report to explaining the valuation approach but then deduct a discount for lack of marketability (DLOM) that materially reduces value without providing adequate support. Such limited analysis of a DLOM is coming under increased scrutiny by the IRS as well as other users. The new *Discount for Lack of Marketability Guide* and the related Toolkit by Jim Hitchner, Jim Alerding, Josh Angell, and Kate Morris provides practitioners with the information and tools necessary to properly calculate and support a DLOM using both qualitative and quantitative methods.

The *DLOM Guide* is an excellent reference for both practitioners and users. It is a very detailed and well-documented text that includes a comprehensive discussion of the current theory, empirical studies, databases, and methods used to determine DLOMs.

The *DLOM Guide* presents the following qualitative, quantitative, and other types of methodologies used to determine DLOMs:

- *Qualitative methods:*
    - Legacy and more recent restricted stock studies;
    - Legacy pre-IPO benchmark studies;
    - *Mandelbaum* factors;
    - Acquisition method; and
    - *IRS DLOM Job Aid* factors.
- *Quantitative methods:*
    - FMV Opinions restricted stock database;

- Pluris restricted stock database;
- Valuation Advisors pre-IPO database; and
- Option pricing models, including Black-Scholes/Chaffe, Longstaff, and Finnerty.

- *Shareholder cash flow adjustment models:*
    - Quantitative marketability miscount model (QMDM);
    - NERA CAPM; and
    - Nonmarketable investment company evaluation method (NICE).
- *Other models:*
    - The bid-ask spread method; and
    - Long-term equity anticipation securities (LEAPS).

The authors discuss the relative merits of each of the empirical studies, databases, and methods. Discussion of relevant landmark Tax Court cases dealing with DLOMs is also included. Most importantly, the IRS's perspective on the various methods used to determine DLOMs as presented in the *IRS DLOM Job Aid* is discussed. Finally, case studies illustrating the application of the different methodologies are included.

The related Toolkit includes 10 Excel files providing a new and transparent restricted stock model, alternative option models, and QMDM. In addition, the Toolkit includes a detailed user manual discussing the use and application of the various methodologies. Finally, the Toolkit provides sample language discussing the methodologies for inclusion in a valuation report.

The primary model in the Toolkit is the Restricted Stock Study Quintile Calculator (RSQC), which permits estimation of a DLOM for a subject company by adjusting restricted stock discount data for differences in volatility, holding period, dividends, and other factors. The source of the restricted stock discount data is the *FMV Opinions Restricted Stock Study – Discount for Lack of Marketability Database* (FMV Database[1]), which must be separately purchased at www.bvresources.com. A representative example of the required inputs and the results the Toolkit produced using the RSQC model follows (see Exhibit 1).

The RSQC model matches the subject company to a quintile of restricted stocks from the FMV Database using criteria such as market value, revenues, profitability, etc. Sample output for the RSQC model using market value as the selected criteria is presented in Exhibit 2.

1 *Editor's note: Since the release of this article, the FMV Database has been renamed the* Stout Restricted Stock Study & DLOM Calculator. *For more information, please visit bvresources.com/stout.*

Exhibit 1. Restricted Stock Study Quintile Analysis: ABC Company Inc.

View Volatility Adjustment | View Holding Period Adjustment | View Dividend Adjustment | View Factor Adjustment | Unhide Detail | Hide Detail

Model Inputs	
Subject Company Fundamentals ($ in 000s)	**User Inputs**
Market Value of Equity (Marketable)	7,500.00
Total Revenues	20,000.00
Total Assets	5,000.00
Book Value of Equity	4,500.00
Market to Book Ratio	1.70
Net Profit Margin (After-Tax)	6.00%
Volatility	50%
Valuation Adjustments and Assumptions	
Select Type of Volatility Adjustment Model	Regression
Select Type of Holding Period Adjustment Model	Finnerty
Select Type of Dividend Yield Adjustment Model	None
Expected Holding Period (Years)	7.5
C Corp Equivalent Dividend Yield (%)	0.00%
What is your adjustment for other factors (%)?	10.00%
Apply registration rights adjustment?	Yes
Apply autocorrect option?	Yes
Select Weighting Method	FMV

Summary Output								
Quintile	**DLOM**	**Vol. Adj.**	**HP Adj.**	**Div Adj.**	**Fact. Adj.**	**Adj. DLOM**	**Weight**	
5th Quintile	25%	-6%	15%	na	10%	44%	2	View MV Quintile
3rd Quintile	14%	-4%	16%	na	10%	36%	1	View Rev Quintile
5th Quintile	28%	-8%	14%	na	10%	44%	3	View Asset Quintile
4th Quintile	26%	-6%	15%	na	10%	45%	2	View Equity Quintile
4th Quintile	14%	-3%	17%	na	10%	38%	1	View MTB Quintile
1st Quintile	11%	-1%	17%	na	10%	38%	1	View Margin Quintile
5th Quintile	10%	2%	17%	na	10%	39%	3	View Vol Quintile
Calculation of Median/Average/Wgt. Avg. DLOM								
Median	14%	-4%	16%	na	10%	39%		
Average	18%	-4%	16%	na	10%	41%		
Wgt Avg.	20%	-4%	16%	na	10%	41%		
Other Salient Statistics								
Minimum	10%	-8%	14%	na	10%	36%		
25th %Tile	13%	-6%	15%	na	10%	38%		
50th %Tile	14%	-4%	16%	na	10%	39%		
75th %Tile	26%	-2%	17%	na	10%	44%		
90th %Tile	27%	0%	17%	na	10%	44%		
Maximum	28%	2%	17%	na	10%	45%		
StDev	8%	3%	1%	na	0%	4%		
Coef of Var.	0.41	-0.95	0.07	na	0.00	0.09		

Exhibit 2. Market Value of Equity Quintiles Analysis

Table 1.0

Quintile	Count	Market Value of Equity Range ($000s) High	Median	Low	Median DLOM	Subject Company Value ($000s)	Indicated Discount	
1st Quintile	138	$8,430,007	$535,672	$298,615	11.2%	-	-	Not Selected
2nd Quintile	138	$296,985	$224,379	$166,248	12.2%	-	-	Not Selected
3rd Quintile	138	$166,154	$121,995	$88,761	19.8%	-	-	Not Selected
4th Quintile	138	$88,388	$62,106	$43,476	19.9%	-	-	Not Selected
5th Quintile	139	$42,802	$25,671	$2,832	25.0%	$7,500	25.0%	Selected Quintile

Table 2.0

Quintile	Count	Median Volatility	Average Holding Period (Yrs)	% of Companies Trading OTC or Other	% of Companies With Negative Profit	% of Companies with Dividends	% of Companies with Registration Rights	
1st Quintile	138	59.4%	1.08	38%	59%	25%	60%	Not Selected
2nd Quintile	138	69.1%	1.24	58%	63%	9%	41%	Not Selected
3rd Quintile	138	77.2%	1.26	57%	69%	8%	47%	Not Selected
4th Quintile	138	81.4%	1.30	64%	72%	2%	45%	Not Selected
5th Quintile	139	88.8%	1.33	75%	67%	4%	29%	Selected Quintile

The median DLOM of the selected quintile from the RSQC, the restricted stock study equivalent discount (RSED), serves as a baseline estimate of the subject company's DLOM. The RSED provides a preliminary estimate of the DLOM for the subject company given its illiquidity, volatility, holding period, dividends, and other criteria. The RSED may be further adjusted for differences between the subject company and the selected quintile for certain criteria using a regression analysis of the FMV Database, option pricing models, and/or a *Mandelbaum* factor analysis. Sample output of the RSQC model using alternative option models to estimate an adjustment for volatility is in Exhibit 3.

Exhibit 3. Sample Output of the RSQC Model Using Alternative Option Models

Required User Inputs	Ghaidarov	Finnerty	Regression	Chaffe	VFC Longstaff
Include Model in User-Selected Models	Yes	Yes	Yes	No	No
Selected Average, Median, or Wgt. Avg.	Wgt Avg				
Weight to Apply for Wgt. Average Calculation	1	1	1	0	0

Summary of Volatility Adjustment by Model					
Metric	Ghaidarov	Finnerty	Regression	Chaffe	VFC Longstaff
Market Value of Equity (Marketable)	-9%	-8%	-6%	-15%	-16%
Total Revenues	-5%	-4%	-4%	-8%	-10%
Total Assets	-14%	-11%	-8%	-21%	-22%
Book Value of Equity	-9%	-7%	-6%	-13%	-15%
Market to Book Ratio	-4%	-3%	-3%	-6%	-8%
Net Profit Margin (After-Tax)	-1%	-1%	-1%	-1%	-2%
Volatility	2%	2%	2%	4%	6%
	Not Selected	Not Selected	Selected Method	Not Selected	Not Selected

Summary		
Median	Average	User
-9%	-11%	-8%
-5%	-6%	-4%
-14%	-15%	-11%
-9%	-10%	-7%
-4%	-5%	-3%
-1%	-1%	-1%
2%	3%	2%
Not Selected	Not Selected	Not Selected

Models for Adjusting Volatility															
	Ghaidarov Option Model			Finnerty Option Model			Regression Model			Chaffe Option Model			VFC Longstaff Option Model		
Fundamental Metric	DLOM w/ Quint. Vol	DLOM w/ Subject Vol	Diff in DLOMs	DLOM w/ Quint. Vol	DLOM w/ Subject Vol	Diff in DLOMs	DLOM w/ Quint. Vol	DLOM w/ Subject Vol	Diff in DLOMs	DLOM w/ Quint. Vol	DLOM w/ Subject Vol	Diff in DLOMs	DLOM w/ Quint. Vol	DLOM w/ Subject Vol	Diff in DLOMs
Market Value of Equity (Marketable)	21%	12%	-9%	19%	11%	-8%	19%	13%	-6%	34%	20%	-15%	48%	32%	-16%
Total Revenues	16%	11%	-5%	15%	10%	-4%	17%	13%	-4%	26%	18%	-8%	40%	30%	-10%
Total Assets	26%	12%	-14%	22%	12%	-11%	21%	13%	-8%	41%	21%	-21%	55%	33%	-22%
Book Value of Equity	20%	11%	-9%	18%	11%	-7%	19%	13%	-6%	33%	19%	-13%	47%	32%	-15%
Market to Book Ratio	13%	10%	-4%	13%	9%	-3%	16%	13%	-3%	23%	16%	-6%	35%	28%	-8%
Net Profit Margin (After-Tax)	10%	9%	-1%	9%	9%	-1%	14%	13%	-1%	16%	15%	-1%	27%	26%	-2%
Volatility	7%	10%	2%	7%	9%	2%	11%	13%	2%	13%	16%	4%	22%	27%	6%

Exhibit 4. FMV Opinions Quintiles Analysis Adjusted DLOMs

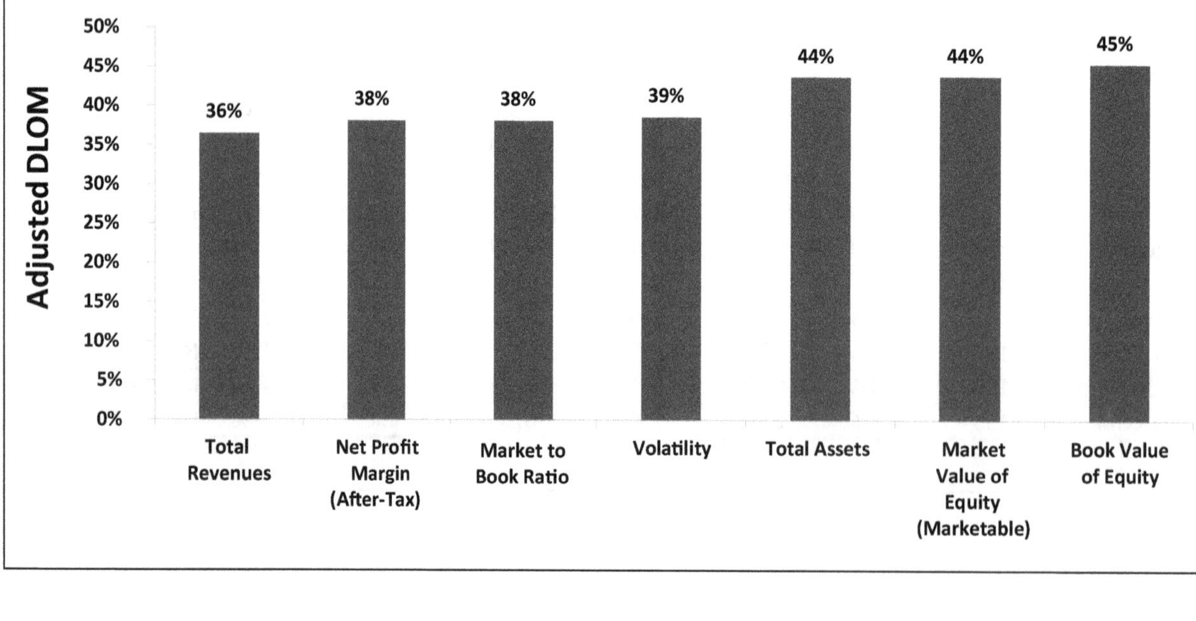

The adjustments the RSQC model calculated may then be used to adjust the RSED DLOM to a DLOM specific to the subject company. The RSQC model produces a graph presenting the adjusted DLOMs by subject company characteristic (see Exhibit 4).

Summary. I had the privilege of serving as a technical reviewer of the *DLOM Guide* and highly recommend this new resource for those practitioners who perform valuations for estate, gift, and income tax purposes, as well as for other purposes requiring the estimation of DLOMs.

Discount for Lack of Marketability Guide, James R. Hitchner, R. James Alerding, Joshua B. Angell, and Katherine E. Morris. Valuation Products and Services LLC, 2017. Available from Business Valuation Resources at www.bvresources.com/publications. Price is $199 for the 800-plus page guide, hard copy or PDF version, or $249 for both. Cost for *VPS DLOM Guide* and Toolkit, which includes both print and PDF versions along with downloadable, detailed Excel models, is $699.

Harold G. Martin Jr., *CPA/ABV/CFF, ASA, CFE, is the partner-in-charge of valuation and forensic services for Keiter, a certified public accounting and consulting firm located in Richmond, Va.*

Damodaran's New Book on the Power of Stories in Valuation

A good valuation should tell a story. This is so important that the highly respected Dr. Aswath Damodaran (New York University Stern School of Business) has devoted his new book to it. *Narrative and Numbers, The Value of Stories in Business,* is a must-read for valuation experts because it helps avoid the dangers of using numbers without any narrative when constructing valuations.

One danger of too much emphasis on numbers is that valuations become "plug-and-point exercises, tools to advance sales pitches or confirm pre-conceived values," he says. A valuation needs a marriage of narrative and numbers. "In a good valuation, the numbers are bound together by a coherent narrative, and storytelling is kept grounded with numbers," he says.

In fact, it is this combination of narrative and numbers that attracted Damodaran to valuation in the first place, he told *Business Valuation Update* in an interview. "I didn't want to become an accountant. It's too numbers-driven for me. I didn't want to be a strategist because it's too much storytelling. So in a sense, I wanted something that would help me expand the creative component of business—coming up with great valuation ideas with discipline. So that's what always attracted me to valuation, not the model-building, not the spreadsheets, not the number-crunching, and not the accounting."

He continues: "It's a fact that if you do a good valuation, it's like composing a tune, and the tune should actually sound good. So it forces you if you're a storyteller to be disciplined. And it forces you if you're a numbers person to think about the narrative. And to me that's an exciting place to be."

The book gives a fascinating look at how Damodaran combines narrative with numbers to evolve his valuations of firms such as Uber, Vale, Amazon, Ferrari, and others. To combine narrative with numbers, Damodaran advises a five-step process.

Step 1: Come up with a story line for the business. What is the firm's story? Company founders and managers will have their stories, but valuation experts need to develop their own, which may or may not be in sync with theirs. Damodaran's initial narrative for Uber was this: "Uber is an innovative car service company, with the untested potential to expand into other logistics businesses. It will expand the car service business (by attracting new users), while gaining a significant (though not dominant) market share and preserving its profitability." Someone else may come up with a narrative such as this: "Uber is a logistics company that will find a way to expand its profitable car service business model into the moving, car rental and electric car businesses."

Step 2: Test the narrative. See whether your story withstands several tests: history, experience, and common sense. Have any other companies lived the narrative you developed? What do they share in common? In terms of experience, have you valued any similar companies (or invested in any companies) and recall the problems you ran into in practice? To test for common sense, draw on first principles in economics and mathematics to evaluate your narrative's weakest links. For Uber, Damodaran justified his assumption of it gaining market share because the taxi and limo business was "a splintered, regulated and inefficient business that is ripe for disruption."

Step 3: Convert key parts of the narrative into drivers of value. This is a relatively simple step for valuation experts, who will look at the total market and boil it down to after-tax cash flow and then discount for time and risk. Along the way, key parts of the narrative will be connected to value. For example, a narrative that includes a storing competitive edge will convert to high market share and high operating margins.

Step 4: Connect the drivers of value to a valuation. Apply a valuation model such as the DCF to connect the drivers of value to value. Damodaran points out that the classic venture capital valuation takes a short cut by using expected earnings (or revenue) in a future period, an exit multiple (based on what others seem to be willing to pay today for similar companies) that converts that number into a future value, and a target return to discount that value back to the present (and adjust for risk).

Step 5: Keep the feedback loop open. You need to be able to admit that your initial valuation may need to be adjusted as events unfold. When he valued Uber, the comments Damodaran received from people in the venture capital and technology space gave him ideas that he incorporated into his DCF analysis.

Damodaran's goal with this book is to help a number cruncher build a narrative to back up his or her valuation—and help a storyteller convert a narrative into numbers. He has certainly accomplished that with this book.

Narrative and Numbers, The Value of Stories in Business, is available from BVR at www.bvresources.com/publications.

Book Review: *Financial Valuation: Applications and Models*, 4th Edition + Website

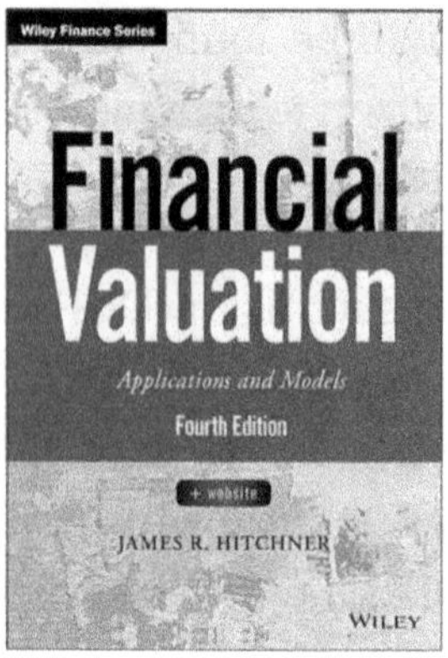

By Ronald L. Seigneur,
Seigneur Gustafson LLP (Lakewood, Colo., USA)

Editor's note: This is a review of Financial Valuation: Applications and Models (FVAM), *4th edition + Website, by James Hitchner. We note that there is also a companion book,* Financial Valuation Workbook: Step-by-Step Exercises and Tests to Help You Master Financial Valuation, *4th edition. The companion book is not reviewed here. Both of these books are available from BVR at www.bvresources .com/publications.*

It seems like just yesterday that my good friend and colleague, Jim Hitchner, invited me to be part of a diverse group of practitioners to take on the task of authoring the 1st edition of *FVAM,* first released in 2003. That was over 15 years ago, and I now have in hand my copy of the fully updated 4th edition of the book, which has so much new material there is now an ancillary website[1] (the "+ Website" reference in the book's title) supporting and extending the content of the book itself.

The book has 31 chapters. Arguably my favorite part of our book is Chapter 31, "Valuation Views and Controversial Issues: An Illustration." The chapter presents a sample report and identifies and discusses over 35 distinct elements business analysts often struggle with in practice. This approach not only provides guidance on how to address the controversies, but also does it in the context of how they might be articulated in a comprehensive report.

Chapter 30, "Special Industry Valuations," has been greatly expanded to provide tips and insights on a number of sectors, including oil and gas, restaurants, bars and nightclubs, and cable TV.

Rolling back to the front of the new 4th edition of *FVAM,* the book has the same familiar look as previous editions, including Val Tips throughout. Jim Hitchner, as not only the editor of *FVAM* but

1 The website is at www.wiley.com/go/FVAM4E.

the guiding light and cat herder, has made the treatise one of the most, if not the most, recognized publications in our profession. I must give a big shout out to Jim and Kate Morris, as well as Janet Kern and Karen Warner, for their significant commitment of time to this project. Three new chapters have been added on the international cost of capital (Chapter 7), reasonable compensation (Chapter 22), and healthcare compensation (Chapter 29). You will see numerous rewritten expanded chapters covering topics such as cost of capital/rates of return (Chapter 6), valuation discounts and premiums (Chapter 10), valuation of pass-through entities (Chapter 13), and business damages (Chapter 26).

This edition of the book has been updated and enhanced to embrace the most current thinking by a knowledgeable group of co-authors and the added efforts of Jim and Kate and their staff. Just as an example of the utility of the book, Chapter 27 provides concise summaries of difficult areas of valuation, such as valuing debt instruments, share-based compensation, real options, and early-stage technology companies.

The cost of capital chapter has evolved from the 1st edition to the new 4th edition. Chapter 6 provides, what I believe, is a thorough overview of the cost of capital challenges and the tools to construct and support cost of capital determinations. Starting with value drivers and key characteristics of cost of capital, to a solid discussion of each of the components within a buildup or CAPM model, to emerging and implied market returns and venture capital hurdle rates, this chapter is indicative of the depth found throughout *FVAM*. The chapter includes an addendum with an article titled "Twenty Ways to Calculate the Cost of Equity Capital: A Case Study," which is representative of the additional useful information provided throughout the book and on the supplementary website. Pages 1,225 to 1,228 list the 45 additional topics included at the *FVAM,* 4th edition, website, which effectively adds a few hundred pages of content to the combined work.

I, personally, am excited to have this book in my library and have been honored to be part of the collective effort. I highly recommend this book as a primary reference source for anyone involved in or relying on business appraisal and related services.

Ronald L. Seigneur, *CPA/ABV/CFF, ASA, CVA, CGMA, is managing partner of Seigneur Gustafson LLP in Lakewood, Colo. He can be reached at ron.seigneur@cpavalue.com or 303-980-1111.*

Section VI.
Data

Monthly Cost of Capital Data

Editor's note: The charts in this section display the cost of capital data for each month of 2017 that were originally published in the Business Valuation Update *newsletter. These charts are included to provide readers with a reference point for cost of capital data as of a particular valuation date. Because Duff & Phelps data are published once a year, we've included the most recent data as of December 2017 in Exhibit 3.*

Exhibit 1. 2017 Month-by-Month Cost of Capital

	Jan-17	Feb-17	Mar-17	Apr-17	May-17	Jun-17	Jul-17	Aug-17	Sep-17	Oct-17	Nov-17	Dec-17
30-Day Treasury Yield	0.44%	0.50%	0.46%	0.73%	0.67%	0.82%	0.96%	1.00%	0.96%	0.95%	1.06%	1.14%
5-Year Treasury Yield	1.93%	1.93%	1.99%	1.88%	1.84%	1.76%	1.93%	1.80%	1.73%	1.94%	2.01%	2.13%
20-Year Treasury Yield	2.79%	2.80%	2.81%	2.71%	2.71%	2.60%	2.65%	2.61%	2.51%	2.64%	2.63%	2.58%
Long-Term Inflation Estimate	2.30%	2.30%	2.30%	2.30%	2.30%	2.30%	2.32%	2.32%	2.32%	2.32%	2.32%	2.32%
Long-Term Rate of Growth GDP	2.20%	2.20%	2.20%	2.20%	2.20%	2.20%	2.20%	2.20%	2.20%	2.20%	2.20%	2.20%
Dow Jones 20-Bond Yield	3.25%	3.22%	3.17%	3.22%	3.07%	3.04%	2.94%	2.96%	2.95%	2.97%	3.08%	3.11%
Prime Lending Rate	3.75%	3.75%	3.75%	4.00%	4.00%	4.00%	4.25%	4.25%	4.25%	4.25%	4.25%	4.25%
Barron's Intermediate-Grade Bonds	4.79%	4.56%	4.35%	4.49%	4.33%	4.26%	4.22%	4.19%	4.09%	4.12%	4.07%	4.06%
Dow Jones Ind P/E Ratio on Current Earnings	21.4%	20.1%	20.9%	20.6%	20.3%	20.2%	20.5%	19.8%	19.7%	20.2%	20.8%	20.8%
Dow Jones Ind P/E Ratio on 2015 Operating Earnings Estimate*	19.5%	19.8%	19.8%	19.9%	18.1%	18.1%	18.8%	18.2%	18.2%	18.0%	19.9%	20.0%
Dow Jones Ind P/E Ratio on 2016 Operating Earnings Estimate**	16.9%	17.4%	17.6%	18.0%	16.4%	16.8%	17.3%	17.2%	17.0%	16.9%	17.9%	17.5%

* Changes from 2016 earnings to 2017 earnings in June 2017

** Changes from 2017 earnings to 2018 earnings in June 2018

Exhibit 2. Month-by-Month Cost of Capital Data Chart

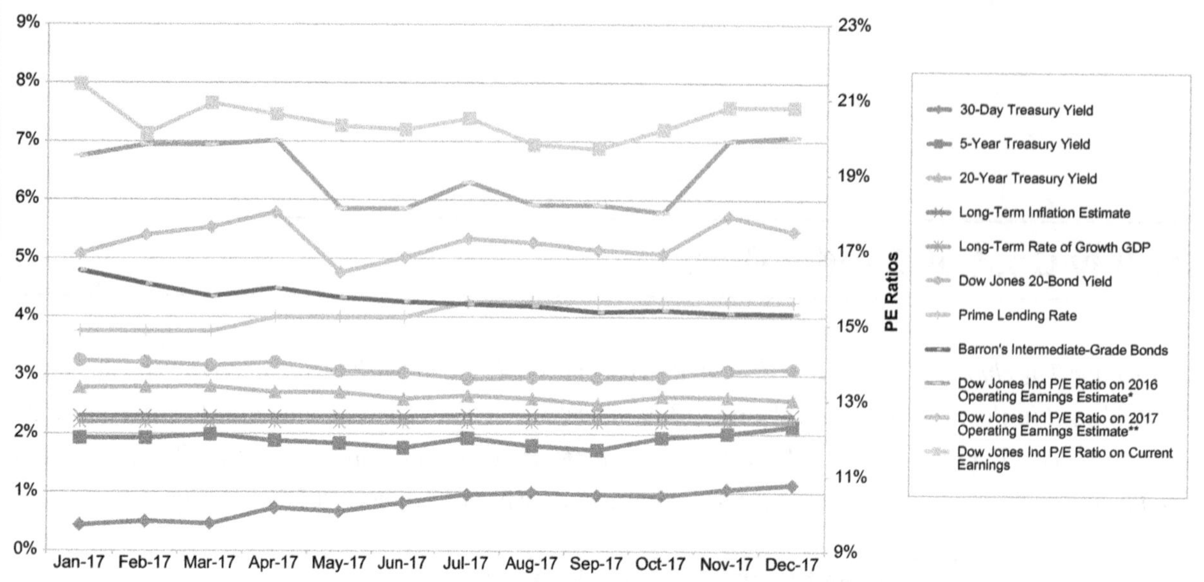

Exhibit 3. Duff & Phelps' 2017 Premiums Over Long-Term Risk-Free Rate[1]

Historical Equity Risk Premiums: Averages Since 1963 Data for Year Ending December 31, 2016.				
Measure Used for Size[2]	**Exhibit**	**1st**	**13th**	**25th**
5-Year Average EBITDA	A-6	4.8%	9.0%	12.5%
5-Year Average Net Income	A-3	4.4%	8.9%	13.0%
Sales	A-7	5.4%	9.2%	12.6%
Total Assets	A-5	4.6%	8.9%	12.8%

1 Source: *2017 Valuation Handbook – Guide to Cost of Capital* (A Exhibits) © Duff & Phelps, LLC. All rights reserved. Risk Premium Report cost of capital data include premiums where size is measured by eight size measures: market value of equity, market value of invested capital, book value of equity, five-year average net income, five-year average EBITDA, sales, total assets, and number of employees. Complete current and historical Risk Premium Report cost of capital data are available at bvresources.com/dp.

2 Each measure of size is organized by Duff & Phelps, LLC in 25 portfolio ranks, with portfolio 1 being the largest and portfolio 25 being the smallest. Smoothed average premiums are present here because they are considered a better indicator than the actual historical observation for most of the portfolio groups. Premiums may be adjusted for differences between historic market risk premiums and expected equity risk premiums as described in the *2017 Valuation Handbook – Guide to Cost of Capital*. NOTE: The new *2017 Valuation Handbook – Guide to Cost of Capital* includes two sets of valuation data: (i) Risk Premium Report data; and (ii) CRSP Decile Size Study (previously published in the Morningstar/Ibbotson *SBBI Valuation Yearbook*).

Bob Dohmeyer, ASA; Pete Butler, CFA, ASA; and Rod Burkert, CPA/ABV, CVA developed a model designed to be more reliable than the build-up method for estimating the cost of capital of a small privately held business. This model uses the authors' new implied private company pricing line 2.0 (IPCPL) and is indexed directly to the IPCPL cost of capital. The model allows adjustments for differences in systematic risk (i.e., beta), diversifiable and total risk (i.e., total beta), liquidity, and debt capacity. Exhibits 4 and 5 summarize the IPCPL Index over 2017.

Exhibit 4. BVR's Private-Company Cost of Capital Index Based on Four Company Revenue Sizes in $ Thousands

	Jan-17	Feb-17	Mar-17	Apr-17	May-17	Jun-17	Jul-17	Aug-17	Sep-17	Oct-17	Nov-17	Dec-17
1,000	19.0%	18.9%	18.7%	18.8%	18.7%	18.6%	18.3%	18.5%	18.4%	18.4%	18.3%	18.3%
5,000	17.3%	17.1%	16.9%	17.0%	16.8%	16.7%	16.6%	16.6%	16.5%	16.5%	16.4%	16.4%
10,000	15.5%	15.3%	15.1%	15.1%	15.0%	14.9%	14.9%	14.7%	14.6%	14.6%	14.6%	14.5%
15,000	14.6%	14.4%	14.1%	14.1%	14.0%	13.9%	14.0%	13.7%	13.6%	13.6%	13.6%	13.5%

Exhibit 5. BVR's Private-Company Cost of Capital Index Based on Four Company Revenue Sizes in $ Thousands

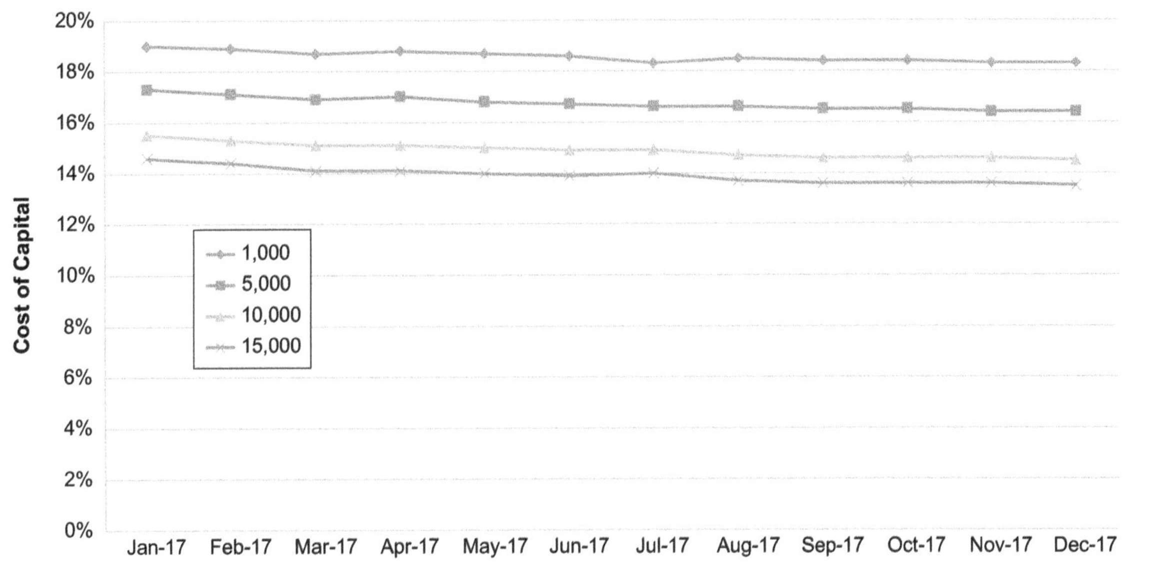

www.ingramcontent.com/pod-product-compliance
Lightning Source LLC
LaVergne TN
LVHW062119300926
849161LV00010B/2489
* 9 7 8 1 6 2 1 5 0 1 4 4 2 *